MISSISSIPPI
CONFLICT AND CHANGE

MISSISSIPPI

CONFLICT AND CHANGE
A New Edition

Revised and updated by
James W. Loewen and Byron D'Andra Orey
Edited by James W. Loewen and Charles Sallis

Written by James W. Loewen, Charles Sallis, Byron D'Andra Orey, Jeanne M. Middleton,
R. Bruce Adams, James A. Brown, Olivia Jones Love, Stephen C. Immer, and Maryellen Hains Clampit

University Press of Mississippi / Jackson

Publication of this book was made possible in part by support from the W.K. Kellogg Foundation.

The University Press of Mississippi is the scholarly publishing agency of
the Mississippi Institutions of Higher Learning: Alcorn State University,
Delta State University, Jackson State University, Mississippi State University,
Mississippi University for Women, Mississippi Valley State University,
University of Mississippi, and University of Southern Mississippi.

www.upress.state.ms.us

The University Press of Mississippi is a member of the Association of University Presses.

Any discriminatory or derogatory language or hate speech regarding race, ethnicity, religion, sex, gender, class, national origin, age, or disability that has been retained or appears in elided form is in no way an endorsement of the use of such language outside a scholarly context.

Maps by Ben Pease

Copyright © 2025 by James W. Loewen and Byron D'Andra Orey
All rights reserved
Manufactured in the United States of America
∞

Publisher: University Press of Mississippi, Jackson, USA
Authorised GPSR Safety Representative: Easy Access System Europe - Mustamäe tee 50, 10621 Tallinn, Estonia, gpsr.requests@easproject.com

Library of Congress Control Number: 2025938185

Hardback ISBN 978-1-4968-4523-8
Paperback ISBN 978-1-4968-5857-3
Epub single ISBN 978-1-4968-5858-0
Epub institutional ISBN 978-1-4968-5859-7
PDF single ISBN 978-1-4968-5860-3
PDF institutional ISBN 978-1-4968-5861-0

British Library Cataloging-in-Publication Data available

THIS BOOK IS DEDICATED TO THE ORIGINAL EDITORS AND AUTHORS OF *Mississippi, Conflict and Change*: James W. Loewen, Charles Sallis, Jeanne M. Middleton Hairston, R. Bruce Adams, James A. Brown, Olivia Jones Love, Stephen C. Immer, and Maryellen Hains Clampit. It is also dedicated to the memory of Boris E. Ricks, a devoted scholar and a lifelong friend, and to Kali Dior Orey, our future generation, in the hope that an honest account of Mississippi's history will empower and benefit her and others to come.
—BYRON D'ANDRA OREY

THIS REVISED EDITION IS DEDICATED TO ALL OF THE YOUTH AND YOUNG adults in Mississippi and across the United States who wish to critically explore Mississippi's history.
—JEANNE M. MIDDLETON HAIRSTON

CONTENTS

PREFACE AND ACKNOWLEDGMENTS ix
FOREWORD by James W. Loewen xiii
INTRODUCTION: Mississippi the Magnolia State xxiii
CHAPTER 1. The Uses of History 3
CHAPTER 2. The Land 13
CHAPTER 3. Indian Civilizations 24
CHAPTER 4. Explorers and Settlers: 1542–1763 59
CHAPTER 5. The United States Takes Control: 1763–1817 71
CHAPTER 6. The Frontier State: 1817–1840 82
CHAPTER 7. The Road to Conflict: 1830–1860 94
CHAPTER 8. Civil War: 1861–1865 115
CHAPTER 9. Reconstruction: 1865–1877 139
CHAPTER 10. Conservative Reaction: 1876–1890 176
CHAPTER 11. The Nadir of Race Relations 193
CHAPTER 12. Hard Times: 1910–1940 214
CHAPTER 13. Toward a New Politics: 1916–1954 232
CHAPTER 14. The Struggle for Racial Justice: 1954–1959 246
CHAPTER 15. Local People and Mississippi's Massive Resistance
    to Change: 1960–1967 261
CHAPTER 16. Desegregation and Cultural Changes: 1970–1980 304
CHAPTER 17. Barriers and Breakthroughs:
    Mississippi's Political Evolution through Reform and Resistance 317
CHAPTER 18. The Great Divide:
    Mississippi's Journey from Democrats to Republicans 335
CHAPTER 19. From Cotton to Casinos:
    Mississippi's Economic Shifts Through History 346
CHAPTER 20. Celebrating Achievements in Folklore, Art, Music,
    Literature, Journalism, and Sports 362
CHAPTER 21. Mississippi at the Crossroads:
    Moving in Two Directions at Once 400
INDEX 423

PREFACE AND ACKNOWLEDGMENTS

BYRON D'ANDRA OREY

AS A MIDDLE SCHOOL STUDENT, *MISSISSIPPI CONFLICT AND CHANGE* SERVED AS my Mississippi history textbook, profoundly shaping my understanding of the state's past. It provided context for the poverty I witnessed during visits to my grandmother in the Mississippi Delta. I vividly remember asking my mother why Black people had large plots of land but lived in small shotgun houses. Her response, "Honey, that's not their land," gained deeper meaning through this book's insights.

My personal connection with Jim Loewen, one of the authors, began in 1992 during my graduate studies when he mentored me in my work as a voting rights expert witness. In 2020, our paths crossed again as he invited me to collaborate on republishing *Mississippi, Conflict and Change*—an honor that carried significant responsibility. As I delved into the project, I gained a greater appreciation for the outstanding group of scholars behind the original work. Their collective expertise and dedication to uncovering Mississippi's complex history underscored the project's importance and the weight of my role.

The passing of Jim Loewen on August 19, 2021, added poignancy to this undertaking. His loss intensified the importance of preserving the original work's integrity while updating its content for contemporary readers. Our task evolved into a delicate balance of refreshing this seminal text while honoring the scholarship and vision of its authors.

When we embarked on this project, only three of the original contributors were still living. Sadly, I was unable to meet Charles Sallis before the book's completion; he passed away in the spring of 2024. However, I was fortunate to be able to provide a copy of the manuscript to Jean Middleton Hairston, another original contributor to the book, for her review.

This edition represents an effort to bridge past and present, maintaining the book's core insights while ensuring its continued relevance. It stands as a tribute to the original authors, aiming to carry forward their commitment to uncovering and confronting Mississippi's complex history.

The initial aim was straightforward: to republish *Mississippi, Conflict and Change* with minimal alterations, preserving its original essence. However, a reviewer's misinterpretation of our intent led to a suggestion for updating the book to maintain its relevance. This feedback prompted me to embark on a journey of refreshing, rather than rewriting, the text.

Jim's preference for concise history books, despite his respect for the comprehensive information in "glossy covers," guided our approach. We strived to strike a balance between providing substantive content and avoiding information overload, with a constant reminder to engage the reader without overwhelming them. We often had to resist the urge to include every fascinating detail, constantly being reminded of the book's primary purpose. This is, after all, a textbook designed for student learning, not an exhaustive historical treatise. It aims to provide a solid foundation rather than an all-encompassing chronicle of events.

While some language has been modernized for contemporary usage and cultural sensitivity, the core of the work remains intact. As a political scientist with a highly empirical background, tackling a history book presented unique challenges, requiring a balance of empirical rigor and the narrative nature of historical scholarship. Historical accounts often present conflicting numbers, making accuracy difficult. One source might report forty people present, while another claims two hundred. As Winthrop Jordan notes in *Tumult and Silence at Second Creek*, "*Numbers impose an exactitude that is inappropriate when applied to what are often very mushy 'facts.'*" Acknowledging this, some ranges in the text may be broad, reflecting these inconsistencies in historical records. This updated edition aims to honor the original spirit and scholarship while making it accessible to new generations. It serves as a bridge between past and present, continuing to illuminate Mississippi's complex history. The authors' vision and commitment to truth remain central, with Jim's passing only strengthening the resolve to ensure their contributions endure.

Revising this book demanded a keen awareness of how historical perspectives have evolved since 1974. The passage of time has significantly altered our understanding of key events. For example, when the original text was written, Freedom Summer was recent history, barely a decade old. Now, extensive scholarship has deepened our comprehension of its impact. Most notably is the research in the area of civil rights. Given this vast literature, this edition expands on events like the Emmett Till tragedy, reflecting current insights into its crucial role in catalyzing the 1960s civil rights movement. Such connections were less apparent in 1974, just two decades after Till's murder. This revision thus bridges the gap between past and present interpretations, offering a more nuanced view of these pivotal moments in history.

Updating the book from 1974 to 2024 presented significant challenges, requiring us to carefully select the most relevant topics to cover five decades of change. We relied on current research and consulted both academic experts and practitioners to guide our content decisions. Given my background in political science, many updates naturally focused on political developments. However, we made a conscious effort to maintain balance by addressing other crucial areas as well. This approach allowed us to preserve the book's core while incorporating modern perspectives and essential developments from the intervening years. One moment from the book's legacy stayed with me throughout this process. Judge Orma Smith once asked Jeanne Middleton what she had to say about including a graphic photo of a lynching. Her reply was simple, direct, and devastating: "Judge, Your Honor, sir, we believe that if a child is old enough to be lynched, he is old enough to learn about lynchings." That answer captures the spirit of this work and the necessity of teaching hard truths, even when they're uncomfortable.

In closing, we hope the reader remembers that this book was written as a textbook and, as a result, was not meant to provide an exhaustive history of Mississippi. This updated edition of *Mississippi, Conflict and Change* stands as a testament to the original authors' dedication, bridging the gap between their time and ours while preserving the essential truths they sought to reveal about Mississippi's history.

It is with deep respect and gratitude that I, on behalf of the original contributors, present this updated edition of *Mississippi, Conflict and Change.* May it continue to inform, challenge, and inspire its readers, just as it has done for decades.

This book owes its completion to the generous financial support of the W. K. Kellogg Foundation, for which I am profoundly thankful. University Press of Mississippi did an excellent job in sending the book to qualified scholars in the field for peer review and served as excellent editors. I also appreciate those who lent their expertise and support to this project. Thanks to Tom Head, Candace Love Jackson, Corey Miller, Brian Pugh, Ray Mikell, Mandi Bates, and Michael Morris for their editorial input. Corey Miller, Brian Pugh, Esmerelda Dickson, Kiyadh Burt, and Sondra Collins helped interpret economic data and policies. Rhonda Richmond, Charlie Braxton, and Andy Hardwick helped identify outstanding musicians. Michael Morris and Talamieka Brice advised on the history of lynchings. Joyce Lawson contributed to the state's historical timeline. Brittany Myburgh and Mark Geil helped identify leading artists. I owe a particular debt of gratitude to Jere Nash and Robert "Rob" Mickey, whose in-depth knowledge of the subject matter allowed me to make crucial edits and catch small errors that might have eluded a typical copyeditor.

Lastly, I thank Erin Shirley Orey for her patience and support, allowing me to use our kitchen table as an enlarged desk space. This seemingly small gesture was crucial in providing the space and focus needed to complete this project.

FOREWORD

*The Trials and Tribulations
of the Book You Hold in Your Hands*

JAMES W. LOEWEN

THIS BOOK HAD ITS ORIGIN IN AN "AHA!" MOMENT I EXPERIENCED IN A CLASS full of first-year college students way back in 1969.[1] The moment came on the first day of the second semester of my first year of full-time teaching, at Tougaloo College in Jackson, Mississippi. In addition to my sociology courses, I was assigned to teach a section of the Freshman Social Science Seminar (FSSS). The history department had designed this seminar to replace the old "Western Civ" course—History of Western Civilization—then required by most colleges in America. The FSSS introduced students to sociology, anthropology, political science, psychology, economics, and so on, in the context of African American history—appropriate enough, 99 percent of our students being African Americans.

African American history uses the same chronology as "regular" American history, of course, so the second semester not only began right after Christmas, but also right after the Civil War, with Reconstruction. I had a new group of students that first day in January, and I didn't want to do all the talking on the first day of class. So I asked my seminar, "What was Reconstruction? What images come to your mind about that era?"

The result was one of those life-changing "Aha!" experiences—or, more accurately, an "Oh, no!" experience. Sixteen of my seventeen students told me, "Reconstruction was that time, right after the Civil War, when Blacks took over the governing of the Southern states, including Mississippi, but they were too soon out of slavery, so they messed up, and reigned corruptly, and Whites had to take back control of the state governments."

I sat stunned. So many major misconceptions of fact glared from that statement that it was hard to know where to begin a rebuttal. African Americans *never* took over the Southern states. All Southern states had White governors and all but one had White legislative majorities throughout Reconstruction. Moreover, the Reconstruction governments did not "mess up." Mississippi in particular enjoyed a better government during Reconstruction than at any point later in the century. Across the South, governments during Reconstruction passed the best state constitutions the Southern states have ever had, including their current ones. They started public school systems for both races. Mississippi had never had a statewide system for Whites before the Civil War, only scattered schools in the larger towns, and of course it had been a felony to teach Blacks, even free Blacks, to read and write during slavery times. The Reconstruction governments tried out various other ideas, some of which proved quite popular. Therefore "Whites" did not take back control of the state governments. Rather, *some* Whites—Democrats, the party of overt White supremacy throughout the nineteenth century—ended this springtime of freedom before full democracy could blossom. Spearheaded by the Ku Klux Klan, they used terror and fraud to wrest control from the biracial Republican coalitions that had governed during Reconstruction.

How could my students believe such false history? I was determined to find out. I visited high schools, sat in on history classes, and read the textbooks students were assigned. Tougaloo was a good college. My students had learned what they had been taught. They had been attending all-Black high schools with all-Black teaching staffs—massive school desegregation would not take place in Mississippi until January 1970, a year later. In school after school, I saw Black teachers teaching Black students White-biased pseudo-history because they were just following the book—and the textbooks were written from a White-supremacist viewpoint.

The yearlong ninth-grade course "Mississippi History" was the worst offender. The one approved textbook, *Mississippi: Yesterday and Today* by John K. Bettersworth, said exactly what my students had learned. Other than "messing up" during Reconstruction, this book omitted African Americans whenever they did anything notable. Among its sixty images of people, for instance, just two included African Americans.[2]

This was the use of history as a weapon, and it was exactly what the all-White and all-segregationist Mississippi legislature had in mind in 1958, when it passed a law requiring Mississippi history in high school as well as fifth grade. This statute was part of a package of obstructionist measures designed to thwart *Brown v. Board of Education* and maintain "our Southern way of life," which every Mississippian knew meant segregation and White supremacy.

The legislators were right. The course *did* dispirit Black students. One high school student in Clarksdale, interviewed by the now-famous author Robert Coles, put it this way:

> I'm supposed to . . . pay attention to the teacher, when she tells us that "this is right, what the book says." If I speak up, they'll throw me out. If I keep quiet and repeat in class what the book says, I'll feel like a white man's n-----,

that's what. My mother says to remind myself what I really do know, and try to stay in school and on the teacher's good side, because you have to have a high school diploma, if you're going to get a good job later. But it's no joke, sitting there and holding in your temper. We leave the building and we say to each other that it's all a big lie, what they're trying to stuff down us. My mother agrees. My father agrees. They say the world is full of lies, and that's what you have to find out, when you're growing up. I asked them why they don't march into the high school and tell everyone that, but they tell me they'd be arrested, and I know they would. So, I guess you have to go along and keep your mouth shut.[3]

Bettersworth's book warped White students as well, toward White supremacy. Why should they agree that African Americans were equal human beings or should be allowed to vote in Mississippi—after all, they "messed up" last time, didn't they?

I knew John Bettersworth. In my junior year in college, I attended Mississippi State University, where he taught history. He knew better. Indeed, when he reviewed several books on Reconstruction in the *New York Times* Book Review, he made clear for that audience that he knew that the interracial Republican coalition that governed Mississippi during Reconstruction had done a good job under difficult circumstances.[4] But in his ninth-grade textbook, Bettersworth wrote what he knew the Mississippi State Textbook Purchasing Board wanted to read. He knew full well that historians did not (and still do not) review high school textbooks, so his professional reputation would not be sullied by this unprofessional conduct.[5]

Dr. Bettersworth could not have believed that his textbook was an innocent way to make a few thousand dollars without hurting anyone. At Mississippi State, he encountered the graduates of Mississippi high schools by the hundreds, and he knew how racist some of them could be—partly because they believed the BS (Bad Sociology) about African Americans in his textbook.

Perhaps as a passive form of resistance against their racist textbooks, many Mississippi teachers—White as well as Black—spent hours of class time making students memorize the names of the state's eighty-two counties, their county seats, and the date each was organized as a county. Or, perhaps more likely, they did this because it had been done to them. Regardless, these 250 twigs of information were useless and soon forgotten. Meanwhile, students learned nothing about the past from this book that would help them deal with the wrenching changes Mississippi was going through in the 1960s and '70s.

What must it do to my Black students, I wondered that January afternoon, to believe that the one time their group stood center-stage in the American past, they "messed up"? It couldn't be good for them. If it had happened, of course, that would be another matter. In that case, it would have to be faced: why did "we" screw up? What must we learn from it? But nothing of the sort had taken place. It was, again, Bad Sociology. I could fix *my* students, I knew. Indeed, the reading materials in the Freshman Social Science Seminar would give all Tougaloo students the information they needed to put their high school "education" in proper perspective. But what about the masses of students, Black and White, who didn't go to Tougaloo?

For more than a year, I tried to interest historians in Mississippi to write a more accurate high school textbook of state history. Finally, despairing of getting anyone else to do so, I put together a group of students and faculty from Tougaloo and also from Millsaps College, the nearby White school, got a grant, and we wrote it. The result, *Mississippi, Conflict and Change*, won the Lillian Smith Award for best Southern nonfiction the year it came out. Nevertheless, the Mississippi State Textbook Purchasing Board rejected it as unsuitable. In most subjects, the board selected three to five textbooks. In Mississippi history, they chose just one. Only two were available, which might be characterized "ours" and "theirs." By a two to five vote, the board rejected ours, accepting only theirs. Two Blacks and five Whites sat on the board. You can do the math.

Our book was not biased toward African Americans. Six of its eight authors were White, as were 80 percent of the historical characters who made it into our index. An index of 20 percent non-White looks pretty Black, however, to people who are used to textbooks wherein just 2 percent of the people referred to are non-White.

Mississippi, Conflict and Change also pioneered in its discussions of women. Back in 1974, many publications used courtesy titles for women but not men on second reference. Bettersworth, for example, introduced William Faulkner and then called him "Faulkner," but after introducing Eudora Welty, he thereafter called her "Miss Welty." It wasn't just Bettersworth, however. Nearly everybody wrote like that. Not until February 1, 2000, did the AP (Associated Press) change its practice and stop using courtesy titles for women. The difference might be minor, but it implies that women, unlike men, should be treated more politely, which in turn implies they are somehow weaker. It also led to the invention of "Ms.," since these second usages otherwise had to tell women's marital status ("*Miss*" Welty, not "Mrs."), while "Mr. Faulkner," even had it been used, does not tell whether he was married or not. Our vignette of Eudora Welty simply calls her "Welty."

Moreover, in contrast to the White supremacist fabrications offered in "their" book, our book showed how Mississippi's social structure shaped the lives of its citizens. So, after exhausting our administrative remedies, we—coeditor Charles Sallis and I, accompanied by three school systems that wanted to use our book— eventually sued the Textbook Board in federal court.

The case, *Loewen et al. v. Turnipseed, et al.*, came to trial in 1980, Judge Orma Smith presiding. Smith was an eighty-three-year-old White Mississippian who believed in the First Amendment—students' right to controversial information—and was bringing himself to believe in the Fourteenth Amendment—Blacks' right to equal treatment.[6]

For a week, we presented experts from around the state and around the nation who testified that by any reasonable criteria, including those put forth by the state itself, our book surpassed their book. Among other topics, they found *Mississippi, Conflict and Change* more accurate in its treatment of prehistory and archaeology, Native Americans, slavery, Reconstruction, Mississippi literature, the civil rights era, and the then-recent past, to 1974.

Then came the state's turn. The trial's dramatic moment came when the deputy attorney general of Mississippi asked John Turnipseed, one of the board members who had rejected our book, why he had done so. Turnipseed asked the court to turn to page 178, on which was a photograph of a lynching. "Now you know, some ninth-graders are pretty big," he noted, "especially Black male ninth-graders. And we worried, or at least *I* worried, that teachers—especially White lady teachers—would be unable to control their classes with material like this in the book."

As lynching photos go, ours was actually mild, if such an adjective can be applied to these horrific scenes. About two dozen White people posed for the camera behind the body of an African American man, silhouetted in a fire that was burning him. The victim's features could not be discerned, and no grisly details—such as Whites hacking off body parts as souvenirs—were shown or described. Nevertheless, our book was going to cause a race riot in the classroom.

We had pretested our book—along with Bettersworth's—in an overwhelmingly White classroom and an overwhelmingly Black classroom. Both had preferred ours by huge margins.[7] So we had material to counter this argument when our turn came for rebuttal. We never had to use it, however, because at that point Judge Smith took over the questioning.

"But that happened, didn't it?" he asked. "Didn't Mississippi have more lynchings than any other state?"

"Well, yes," Turnipseed admitted. "But that all happened so long ago. Why dwell on it now?"

"Well, it *is* a *history* book!" the judge retorted. And we nudged each other, realizing we were going to win this case. Eventually, in a decision the American Library Association ranks as one of its "Notable First Amendment Court Cases," the judge ordered Mississippi to adopt our book for the standard six-year period and supply it to any school system, public or private, that requested it, like any other adopted book.[8]

Turn to the lynching photo to which John Turnipseed objected. It gets across the key fact about a lynching: that it is a public murder, done with considerable support from the community. Often, as here, the mob posed for the camera. They showed no fear of being identified because they knew no White jury would convict them.

Figure F.1. Lynching of Omaha Black man. Library of Congress, Prints and Photographs Division, LC-USZ62-38919.

Was Turnipseed right? *Would* discussing lynchings cause "White lady teachers" to lose control of their classes? Even in 2020, no national textbook includes a photo like the one included in this book. *Should* we still avoid discussing lynchings? What is the purpose of history anyway? Should it be rosy?

Before leaving the topic of lynching, I must make two additional points. First, we dodged a bullet in cross-examination. Our "Mississippi lynching" photo was problematic. In the summer of 1971, I can recall searching through book after book in Tougaloo's Special Collections and file after file in the Mississippi Department of Archives and History, searching for a photo of a Mississippi lynching. I concluded that though Mississippi had lynched more people than any other state, it was (and remains) our poorest state, so cameras were scarce! Consequently, I was thrilled to find our lynching photo in famous sociologist Scott Nearing's *Black America* (1929). Nearing was still alive—indeed, he lived to be 100—and he was happy to give us permission to use the photo, but he no longer remembered where in Mississippi it was from. Nor did he have the negative; we had to copy the image from the book.

These days, with the internet, it's easy to ascertain that it's not from Mississippi after all, but from Omaha, Nebraska. If the Attorney General's office (or Bettersworth) had known, they would have made us look foolish. Recently, I have made use of our error to make a statement about Northern racism.[9] Two other lynching photos commonly used to illustrate "Southern lynchings" also come from the Midwest: from Duluth, Minnesota, and Marion, Indiana. Acts of violent racism have historically occurred all over the nation. In this era of Black Lives Matter (BLM), they continue to do so. Yet Hollywood and our popular culture typically locate severe racism in the Deep South.

The second point I need to make is to challenge you, the reader, to be a citizen and step up to the plate to organize your community, if you live in a town that ever had a lynching. The National Memorial for Peace and Justice in Montgomery, Alabama, created *two* historical markers for every lynching in their database. They display one. If you lead your community to "engage with and discuss past and present issues of racial justice," they will help you place the twin monument in your community. Remember, telling the truth about the past helps cause justice in the present. The conversations within your community sparked by this action will help race relations in the future.

Returning to the lawsuit, even though we won, most school districts in 1980 adopted Bettersworth's or one of two other books that appeared at adoption time. Nevertheless, our book won out in the end. As soon as it came out, it drew attention from the Center for Interracial Books for Children, a New York City organization briefly important in the 1970s. Robert Moore wrote an entire booklet comparing our book with Bettersworth's. Entitled *Two History Texts: A Study in Contrast*, Moore called Bettersworth's textbook "strikingly inferior" and ended his essay with this call: "With the publication of *Mississippi, Conflict and Change*, publishers and writers have an advanced model to emulate when they produce American history textbooks."[10] Judge Smith quoted Moore in his opinion: "By any reasonable criteria, including those used by the Mississippi review committee, *Mississippi, Conflict and Change* is not only eligible for adoption, but is far superior in format and content to all history textbooks we have seen."[11]

It took thirty years, but the cover article in the *Journal of Mississippi History* in April 2010 was a paean for our book. Entitled "The Three R's—Reading, 'Riting, and Race: The Evolution of Race in Mississippi History Textbooks," it reviewed most state history textbooks of the 1970s through the 1990s. Seven years later, Charles Eagles, professor of history at the University of Mississippi, published an entire book, *Civil Rights, Culture Wars: The Fight over a Mississippi Textbook*, on our little group, the book we produced (that you hold in your hand), and the lawsuit that resulted. Eagles discovered that our book was a model for the American Social History Project and its famous *Who Built America?* product. More importantly, with this legal precedent, he wrote, "Mississippi and other states would no longer dare to make students study books that presented a grossly distorted, White supremacist view of history." The Mississippi Historical Society suggested it was on board with this assessment by giving *Civil Rights, Culture Wars* its prize for the best book on Mississippi history in 2018.

Now you can read the book that caused this evolution.

Here are some things to look for. First, we do not simply tell students what to learn. Instead, *Mississippi, Conflict and Change* arms the reader with critical reading and thinking skills—historiography, for example—so they will not be defenseless. Indeed, readers are encouraged to do history themselves.

Our vignettes were also an innovation. We believed they help make history come alive, by giving readers enough detail that they might imagine how a given era or issue affected an actual person.

Notes

1. This introduction draws on James W. Loewen, *Teaching What Really Happened: How to Avoid the Tyranny of Textbooks and Get Students Excited about Doing History* (New York: Teachers College Press, 2018).

2. John K. Bettersworth, *Mississippi: Yesterday and Today* (Austin: Steck Vaughn, 1964). These were two "Old South" images: a drawing of a White mistress reading from the Bible to a group of slaves and a painting by a White artist showing cotton pickers. In addition, an illustration of boys on the deck of a steamboat may include a Black boy dancing a jig; since he is just 3/8″ tall, we cannot be sure. By 1974, Bettersworth had added head-and-shoulders portraits of two African Americans, political leader Charles Evers and opera star Leontyne Price.

3. Quoted by Robert Coles, "Much More Than a Textbook" (review of *Mississippi, Conflict and Change*), *Virginia Quarterly Review* 52:2 (1976): 316.

4. John Bettersworth, "After the War Was Won," *New York Times* Book Review, July 25, 1971.

5. And, for decades, his status remained high. Through 2020, the Mississippi Historical Society even awarded the John K. Bettersworth Award to "an outstanding teacher of middle or high school history in Mississippi." Finally, in the swell of anti-racism after the on-screen murder of George Floyd on May 25, 2020, aware that any competent high school teacher would have to denounce Bettersworth, the society took his name off their prize. Loewen, "How Two Historians Responded to Racism in Mississippi," *History News Network*, December 7, 2014, https://www.hnn.us/blog/153548.

6. Actually, nothing in our book was new to historians. It was controversial only in the context of Mississippi's educational climate of the time.

7. All thirty-two members of the Black class preferred our book in an anonymous poll. Among the thirty-one White students, twenty-nine preferred ours, one preferred Bettersworth, and one said "both."

8. *Loewen et al. v. Turnipseed, et al.*, 488 F. Supp. 1138 (North District of Mississippi, 1980).

9. Loewen, "My Lynching Photo Problem, and Ours," *History News Network*, August 3, 2017, https://www.hnn.us/blog/153970.

10. Robert B. Moore, *Two History Texts: A Study in Contrast (A Study Guide and Lesson Plan)* (New York: Council on Interracial Books for Children, 1974), 3, 12.

11. *Loewen et al. v. Turnipseed, et al.*, 488 F. Supp. 1138 (North District of Mississippi, 1980), 1149.

Recommended Readings

Charles Eagles, *Civil Rights: Culture Wars: The Fight over a Mississippi Textbook* (Chapel Hill: University of North Carolina Press, 2017).

Kristina Rizga, "How to Teach American History in a Divided Country," *Atlantic Monthly*, November 8, 2020, https://www.theatlantic.com/education/archive/2020/11/how-teach-american-history-divided-country/617034/. In this interview, Chuck Yarborough points out that students from across the state who attend the Mississippi School of Mathematics and Science in Columbus, where he teaches history, know little about Mississippi history, especially about the crucial eras of Reconstruction and civil rights.

Map 1. Mississippi

INTRODUCTION

MISSISSIPPI

The Magnolia State

Twentieth state to enter the Union, in 1817
State bird: Mockingbird
Area: 47,420 square miles
Population (2020): 2,940,057
State tree: Magnolia
State flower: Magnolia

THE NAME MISSISSIPPI MEANS, IN CHOCTAW, "FATHER OF WATERS." INDIAN civilizations built towering mounds of worship here many hundreds of years ago. Choctaw, Chickasaw, and other Native American societies built towns here and developed agriculture. Much later, Spanish, French, and British explorers maneuvered to take over the promising land.

Andrew Jackson gathered troops in Mississippi on his way to New Orleans and victory over the British in 1815. Jefferson Davis, president of the Confederate States of America, lived and died in Mississippi. The state has often been the focus of the civil rights struggle. In 1974, when *Mississippi, Conflict and Change* was first published, a growing number of new industries and government facilities stood as a sign of Mississippi's commitment to the future, the civil rights struggle continues but now includes gender and sexuality, labor, and women's reproductive rights.

Its people are diverse. Several thousand Choctaws live in East Mississippi. River towns and Delta communities are sprinkled with Lebanese, Greek, and Italian Americans. Black people whose ancestors came originally from West Africa make up 38 percent of the state's population. Whites of Western European ancestry constitute most of the rest. Mississippi also has a significant Chinese American population. Railroad companies brought Chinese and Chinese Americans to build railroads in the Delta. That accomplished, many remained and opened small businesses, leading to generations of Chinese American Mississippians throughout the state. Mississippi also has significant numbers of immigrants from India and Vietnam, and even larger numbers of Spanish-speaking men and women from Mexico and Central America. The increasing population of these immigrants in Mississippi led to one of the country's first Immigration and Customs Enforcement (ICE) raids on poultry processing plants in 2019. Notably, one of these raids targeted a plant where Hispanics had previously won lawsuits related to sexual harassment, racial discrimination, and national origin discrimination.

Mississippi has been the scene of many firsts: the first interstate railroad, the first 4-H Club, the first Black United States senator, the first state college for women, the nation's oldest tree farm, and the first state schools for the blind and deaf. In Columbus in April 1866, Memorial Day was first observed. The first cotton crop in the world produced entirely by machinery was harvested in Coahoma County. The first great championship boxing match in American history was fought in Mississippi in 1882, when John L. Sullivan defeated Paddy Ryan for the world heavyweight title. A pioneering surgeon, Dr. James Hardy, performed the world's first human lung transplant in 1963, and the world's first heart transplant (chimpanzee to human) in 1964, at the University of Mississippi Medical Center in Jackson.

In conclusion, Mississippi is a state of profound historical significance and cultural diversity, shaped by its Native American roots, European colonization, and pivotal roles in US history, including the Civil War and the civil rights movement. Its diverse population, comprising Native Americans, African Americans, and various immigrant communities, reflects a rich mosaic of cultures and traditions. Despite facing challenges, such as social struggles and immigration issues, Mississippi has been a pioneer in numerous fields, from agriculture and education to medicine and sports. The state's legacy of innovation and resilience continues to drive its progress, offering hope for a future that honors its complex past while embracing growth and inclusivity.

MISSISSIPPI
CONFLICT AND CHANGE

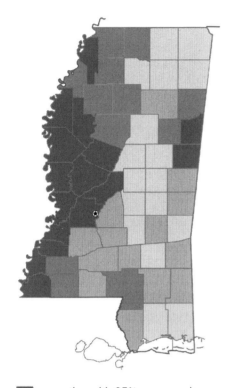
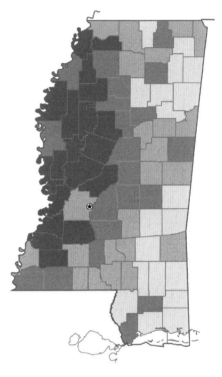

- counties with 85% or more slaves
- 50-84% slaves
- 31-49% slaves
- 30% or less slaves

- more than 74%
- 65-74%
- 58-64%
- 57% or less

Map 2. Enslaved Blacks

Map 3. Eastland Vote, 1954

CHAPTER 1

THE USES OF HISTORY

BEFORE YOU BEGIN ANY TEXTBOOK, BEFORE YOU START A NEW COURSE, YOU should ask yourself and perhaps your teacher, "Why am I doing this?"

To some extent, you may have no choice; certain courses are required for graduation. But there may be other reasons, good reasons, why the course is being taught and why you should take it.

The authors of *Mississippi, Conflict and Change* believe every student should know his or her own history, the history of their own state and people. In this chapter, before beginning the story of Mississippi's past, we will try to convince you that knowing your own history is an important undertaking and that it is worth your serious study.

"Why study history? The past is dead, isn't it? Everything in history happened so long ago. It cannot make much difference now." Many people believe such ideas. In fact, however, there are four important reasons to study the past.

THE PAST IS NOT DEAD

As William Faulkner, the famed novelist from Oxford, Mississippi, wrote, "The past is never dead. It's not even past." We live in the past as much as we live in the present. We were born in the past. We were formed by the past. To understand how we think, or what is going on around us in society, we must understand the happenings of the past.

Maps 2 and 3 reveal how historical patterns can persist through time. Senator James Eastland, a rigid segregationist, received support that mirrored patterns established a century earlier. His strongest backing came from the Mississippi Delta and other regions where plantation agriculture had once dominated—areas with historically high slave populations that remained bastions of racial segregation well into the twentieth century. This electoral pattern reflected the enduring legacy of slavery in shaping political allegiances, as White voters in these former slave-heavy districts continued to support politicians who upheld racial segregation and opposed civil rights reforms. Eastland's successful reelection thus demonstrated how the shadows of the past can influence present-day political landscapes, with the geographical distribution of his support eerily echoing the distribution of slavery from a bygone era.

> Sometimes the same vision of the future has been dreamed over and over: A large town will spring up here, full of manufactures of every kind . . .
> —*Aberdeen Independent*, April 30, 1853

> We believe Aberdeen will be in the best position of any city in North Mississippi to negotiate for any type of industry.
> —*Aberdeen Examiner*, January 17, 1963

At times, almost the same thoughts have been expressed, a century apart:

> Should the University of Mississippi be required to receive and admit applicants of the Negro race to the university classes, the members of the present Faculty would instantly tender their resignation.
> —John N. Waddel, Chancellor of the University of Mississippi ("Ole Miss"), September 28, 1870

> The University of Mississippi and other public schools will be closed if this can possibly be avoided, *but they will not be integrated!*
> —Ross Barnett, Governor of Mississippi, September 13, 1962

Even when an event seems to be new, even when people are doing something for the first time, their ideas about society were formed long ago. The actual causes of their feelings and their actions are deeply embedded in the past. Thus, in order to understand an event, whether it is an election, an effort to get new industry, a reaction to school desegregation, or whatever—we must start far back in history.

MODELS IN THE PAST

A second reason to study history is that the past contains models—actions and heroes and even villains—that we should think about. In every time period, some Mississippians of all races have acted with courage and dignity for the progress of their state and the good of its people. The leaders who established our public schools during Reconstruction, those individuals who wove great novels and songs from the materials of their daily lives, the founders of our junior college system, and those politicians who have developed into true statesmen—these are among the heroes of Mississippi history.

You will have to determine for yourself which persons and acts you admire and which you regret in each period. People in any time period decide what actions and people in the past they consider heroic. Thus, the list of history's heroes slowly changes. By studying the past, you can learn that some of the great figures of our state's history will no longer be labeled heroes by generations to come; others, now forgotten by history, will be redeemed and remembered for their courage and honor.

You have a special reason for studying the models in the past. You are members of a special group in Mississippi—the young. You have your own organizations and your own culture. But in a few years you will govern Mississippi. At that point, the actions that you take will be the actions that future generations of Mississippians, as yet unborn, will read about. In short, you will be the history makers.

There are always some persons who are swept along by the events but do not understand them. Others see what is happening and act to bring about progress. The choice of action is yours. Knowing your own history can help you make it.

BIOGRAPHIES

Throughout the book there are special sections, like this one, that talk about the lives of persons who made Mississippi history. As you read about each person, ask yourself these questions:

1. How would you describe the person's era or time period? What must we know about it in order to understand him or her?
2. Was he or she typical of this era? If not, how were they different from other Mississippians who lived when they did?
3. What were this person's failings? Their successes? To whom else could you compare them?
4. Are you interested enough in the person to do extra reading to find out more about him or her? After you finish the final biography, skim back over all of them and determine for yourself whom you admire, and why.

Write a biography like those in the book. As the subject, choose someone mentioned in the book but not fully discussed. Or, write a historical biography of someone in your community or a member of your own family.

CHAPTER 1.

ERRORS IN THE PAST

Historians supply us with a third reason to study history: "If you do not understand the mistakes of the past, you are condemned to repeat them." We can look into the past and see examples of policies that failed, golden opportunities that were not taken. Perhaps we can learn from past errors so that in the future we can make Mississippi a better society.

For example, compared with many other states, Mississippi once had a large and growing population. In 1920, only twenty-two states had larger populations than Mississippi. Since then, more people have moved out than have moved in, and Mississippi now stands thirtieth-fifth in population.

This sweeping change called for other changes in the state to encourage new kinds of employment and to cause new kinds of ideas to take hold. For a long time, however, new industries were not encouraged to come to Mississippi. Because they were interracial, professional football and basketball teams were kept out for a long time. In the 1960s, state officials refused to allow rock festivals in Mississippi. In 1970, educational consultants with the Mississippi Authority for Educational Television essentially banned Mississippian Jim Henson's *Sesame Street* because the interracial casting—of children—was deemed too controversial for the state's viewers.

In contemporary Mississippi, certain state leaders appear resistant to new perspectives of societal evolution, afraid of "outsiders." This mindset fails to recognize that a state unwelcoming to newcomers may also struggle to retain

Figure 1.1. Abandoned houses in Greenwood stand as mute evidence of the migration from Mississippi. Photographs in the Ben May Charitable Trust Collection of Mississippi Photographs in the Carol M. Highsmith Archive, Library of Congress, Prints and Photographs Division, LC-DIG-highsm-37348.

its current population. The exodus of recent college graduates immediately after completing their studies is a telling indicator of this issue. By not embracing change and diversity, these leaders may inadvertently contribute to a brain drain that hinders the state's growth and potential. This phenomenon underscores the need for a more open and progressive approach to governance and community building in Mississippi.

Despite its many natural and cultural attractions, Mississippi has faced challenges in attracting and retaining both its own residents and outsiders due to its reputation, which has been shaped by past policies and mistakes. The state's beauty, with its medium-sized cities, lush forests, and clean air, offers the potential for a unique blend of rural and urban living. However, historical policies and past errors have given Mississippi a negative image, leading to an exodus of college-educated individuals and limiting its ability to attract new residents.

To transform Mississippi into a thriving and attractive destination, it is essential to learn from the mistakes of the past and develop policies that promote economic and social progress. By addressing the state's historical challenges and creating a more inclusive and forward-looking environment, Mississippi can build a brighter future that attracts and retains its own young people and draws in new residents who can contribute to its growth and development.

THE PAST IS POWER

The fourth reason for studying history is this: If you do not know your own history, you will be ignorant and helpless before someone who does claim to know it. They can tell you what happened to cause you and your society to be the way that they are, and they can therefore tell you what needs to be done now to bring about change. They may be wrong or biased, but if you do not know the true story, you will never find this out and you might believe them. Thus, they will be able to control you.

A person's understanding of history, or of what happened in the past, depends upon his or her ideology. An individual's ideology, as we will use the word, means his or her picture of how society operates. Every person has a slightly different ideology, and this may not correspond to what is happening in society. Often a person's ideology is what he or she *wants* to believe about society or what they are *told* to believe, rather than what is true.

A person's ideology is often influenced by their interpretation of history, and this can be illustrated by the example of the "myth of Reconstruction" in Mississippi. This myth, which portrays the post–Civil War period as a time of corrupt governance, excessive power for Black citizens, and heightened racial tensions, has been widely accepted by many Mississippians in the past and may still be held by some today.

Figure 1.2. Sunset in Mississippi.

However, historical evidence suggests that Mississippi was actually led by a diverse group of competent leaders, both White and Black, during Reconstruction. Despite this, the myth of Reconstruction has persisted, demonstrating the power of ideology to shape historical narratives and influence people's beliefs.

This example illustrates how ideology can shape our understanding of history and how historical narratives can be influenced by biases and preconceptions. It highlights the importance of examining historical events critically and based on evidence, rather than accepting myths and ideologies without question.

Nevertheless, the myth of Reconstruction still lives, particularly in Mississippi politics. If those who believe it are White, they often conclude that Blacks are not qualified to hold public office despite the examples of successful Black leadership on all levels of government. If they are Black, they may conclude that Whites will never support or accept Black candidates in Mississippi.

It is easy to see how such an ideology can lead Whites to try to keep Black voters and political leaders away from the polls and out of office. It can also lead Blacks to remain politically passive. Thus, we can see how an ideology helps prevent change.

Other myths about Mississippi's past live on in the minds of many people. These myths include "the noble savage," "the Old South," "slave loyalty," "White supremacy," and "New South Progress." As you read this book and do other research, you can discover the truth about these myths, truths that many Mississippians still do not know.

It is clear, then, that our view of the past affects our understanding of the present. It works the other way around, too. The way we view the present—our picture of how society works today—can bias our picture of how society worked in the past. We view the past through the lens of the present. That is why every generation seems to have a different view of its past.

History is power. The people on top of society, those who determine its policies, know this. Therefore, they influence the way history itself is written. Poor people do not write history books. The materials historians use are also not often written by the poor. The writers of history and of historical materials are usually members of the upper and middle classes of society, and thus are their friends.

HISTORICAL MATERIALS

To learn the history of Mississippi, you need much more than this textbook. To prove or disprove something we have written, you need historical materials. These materials are all around you. Find the oldest person in your family, or in your

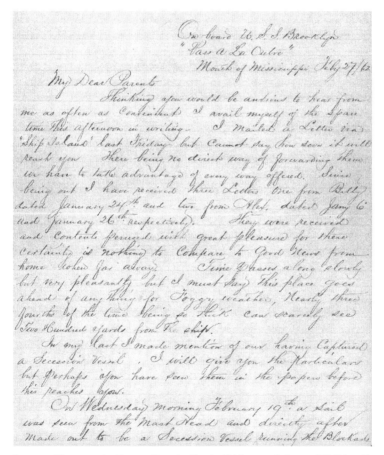

Figure 1.3. The materials of history. From the Charles H. Morrison Collection (COLL/5376) at the Archives Branch, Marine Corps History Division, https://www.flickr.com/photos/usmcarchives/, licensed under CC BY 2.0 https://creativecommons.org/licenses/by/2.0/.

neighborhood or community, and ask them about the past years. Look in your attic, garage, or in your family's bible or scrapbook. Visit your community library and find out if it has a "local history" room or a clipping file. Go to the courthouse in your county and check for files, records, and old county newspapers. If you can, visit some of the places where history was made. Colleges, universities, and the Department of Archives and History in Jackson can also aid you. Even some folk songs or novels may help you learn history.

Therefore, to some extent, historians may not tell what actually happened. They tell what they *think* happened. Since they themselves are well thought of, they may write history in such a way that their own status can be explained and defended.

In a passage in his famous novel *1984*, George Orwell discussed historical bias. He wrote: "who controls the past controls the future. Who controls the present controls the past."

In order to understand why Mississippi is as it is, you have to understand the past. And you have to do it for yourself. Do not let other people, including the authors of this book, tell you the answers. Figure them out for yourself.

HOW TO USE THIS BOOK

In this book, we will not present you with a simple set of dates and names. To ask when the Civil War was fought is to ask a dull question. The answer is easy: 1861–1865. However, the interesting and important questions deal with historical issues: Why was the Civil War fought at all? Why were enslaved Blacks used in the South but not very much in the North? Or to take another example, why does Mississippi have so little air pollution? These are the kinds of issues we will ask you to think about.

So, begin. Read this book. Think about it. Ask your teacher for more information about the main issues. Develop questions. Ask your parents and other people in the community what they think about the questions as you develop them. Find historical materials. Discover for yourself the history of your state. In the process, you may discover a great deal about who you really are and what Mississippi is. You may even be able to figure out where you and Mississippi are going in the future.

QUESTIONS TO ASK OF HISTORICAL SOURCES

You cannot accept what you read simply because it is written down. As we have pointed out, an author's ideology influences what he or she writes. At the same time, any author, whatever their background, or ideology, may write the truth. Therefore, you must sift through their words, separating truth from falsehood. These questions can help:

1. When and where did the author live?
2. For what purpose did he or she write? What audience did they have in mind?
3. What was the author's social class?
4. What was their race? Sex? Age? Sexual orientation? Religion?
5. What were their basic assumptions about Black people? About White people? About American Indians or others?
6. What was their ideology?
7. Do they cite facts to support their conclusions?
8. Does what they say about Mississippi seem to be true from your own experience?
9. How do their conclusions compare with those of other authors you have read? Is he or she biased?
10. Is what he or she is talking about relevant to your life and to present-day society?

Recommended Readings

Bradley G. Bond, ed., *Mississippi: A Documentary History* (Jackson: University Press of Mississippi, 2005).

Westley F. Busbee Jr., *Mississippi: A History*, 2nd ed. (Malden, MA: John Wiley & Sons, 2015.

Mississippi Museum of Art, *Picturing Mississippi, 1817–2017: Land of Plenty, Pain, and Promise* (Jackson: University Press of Mississippi, 2017).

Mississippi Department of Archives and History, *Telling Our Stories: Museum of Mississippi History and Mississippi Civil Rights Museum* (Jackson: University Press of Mississippi, 2017).

Dennis J. Mitchell, *A New History of Mississippi* (Jackson: University Press of Mississippi, 2014).

Ted Ownby, Charles Reagan Wilson, Ann J. Abadie, Odie Lindsey, and James G. Thomas, Jr., eds., *The Mississippi Encyclopedia* (Jackson: University Press of Mississippi, 2019).

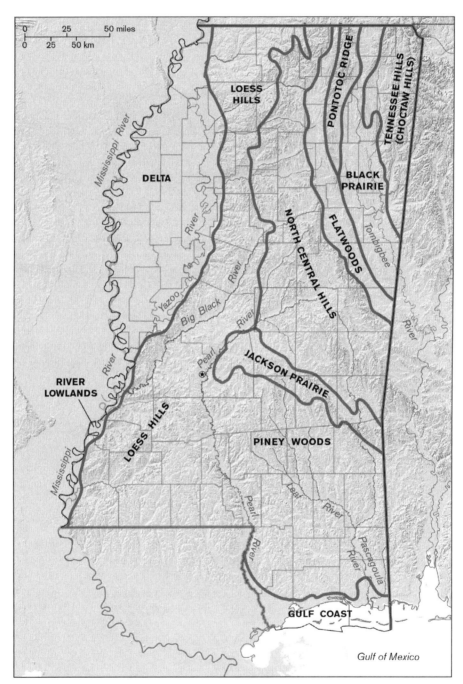

Map 4. Land Areas of Mississippi

CHAPTER 2

THE LAND

BEFORE HUMAN SETTLEMENT, MISSISSIPPI WAS A LAND OF DIVERSE GEOGRAPHY and ecology, spanning nearly 400 miles from the Gulf of Mexico to its northern borders. This land was not uniform, but rather consisted of a range of environments, including sandy coastal areas and dense delta swamps. Map 4 provides a visual representation of this variety, illustrating the different geographical features and ecosystems that make up the state.

From the sandy shores of the Gulf Coast to the lush vegetation of the Delta region, Mississippi's landscape is characterized by a rich diversity of natural habitats. This variety has played a significant role in shaping the state's history, influencing everything from the development of its economy and culture to its unique ecological challenges and opportunities.

Over the centuries, men built on lands, cleared it, and changed it; as they did, they put their names on it and labeled it. But the land also changed the people who lived upon it. Different kinds of soil, different topographies (slopes, hills, plains, streams, and so on), differences in forests and grasses, all led to differences in the ways men worked, different social structures, and differences even in the ways people thought and in the accents of their speech.

Therefore, the history of Mississippi must begin with the interrelation of the land and its people.

THE DELTA

The Delta was Mississippi's last frontier. Before the 1850s, most of the area was swamp and covered in thick forest. There were no towns except for a few river settlements. The interior was wilderness. Enslaved Blacks and Irish labor gangs built a system of levees to halt the annual floods, but during the Civil War it fell into disrepair.

During this period, the Delta region underwent significant changes, as swamps and wetlands were drained to create farmland, and a system of large plantations was established. This development was driven by a growing demand

CHAPTER 2.

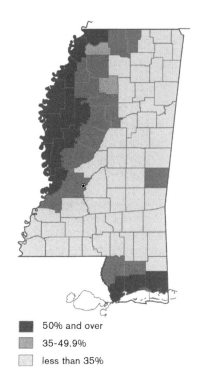

Map 5. Prohibition Vote, 1934

■ 50% and over
▨ 35-49.9%
□ less than 35%

for cotton and other agricultural products, as well as by technological advancements that made it possible to cultivate land that had previously been unsuitable for farming. The success of the Delta's cotton industry led to the accumulation of wealth and power by a small group of landowners, who became known as the "Delta aristocracy."

Exploring the state's history reveals that the most significant division in Mississippi politics existed between the Delta region and "the hills," the label for the counties in the eastern part of the state with less arable land. This division has played a pivotal role in the state's history, dating back to a time even before the Civil War. The division was caused by the development of two very different kinds of societies. In the Delta, a few White plantation owners controlled the labor of tens of thousands of Black farm workers and became quite wealthy. In the hills, farm families, mainly White, worked their own land, usually making just enough to support themselves. Cotton crops could be grown over and over again in the fertile Delta. However, hill soil was quickly worn out by cotton, so that farmers had to switch to other crops for a living.

Because it was rich, and because in most of the state's history Black people were prevented from voting, the aristocracy controlled politics in Delta counties. Over and over, the same lawyers and planters would be reelected to the Mississippi legislature. They were able to build up seniority and power, and they dominated state government in Mississippi for many decades. This domination only increased the hostility between the hills and the Delta. Refer to map 5 to understand how this split, first based on differences in the land itself, came even to influence ideas about alcohol and politics.

Since the United States entered World War II in 1941, the Delta's influence in the state has declined. Its population shrank steadily as people moved north. For years, Delta leaders did not welcome industry. As labor-saving machines appeared and farm jobs decreased, other opportunities were not made available. Only in the 1970s did industry really begin to come to the Delta, including suppliers for automotive parts and, with the legalization of gambling in the 1990s, a thriving casino industry in Vicksburg, Greenville, and Tunica. Despite this, the outmigration of its people continued.

THE RIVER LOWLANDS AND THE NATCHEZ DISTRICT

Just south of the Delta and still along the Mississippi River lies the first part of the state settled and farmed by Europeans and Africans. Once called the Natchez District, this area is made up of the River Lowlands and the southern part of the loess-and-loam-covered hills. It extends from Vicksburg to the Louisiana border.

The rich soil of its bottom lands and loess-covered hills was well suited to plantation farming at first. Based on cotton, a Natchez aristocracy arose during

Figure 2.1. Dunleith, a Natchez mansion. Photographs in the Carol M. Highsmith Archive, Library of Congress, Prints and Photographs Division LC-HS503-1867.

the early 1800s. As was to happen in the Delta, White planters brought in Black farm workers, but in this earlier era the Blacks were enslaved. Planters built up huge fortunes and constructed great mansions, some of which still stand.

Three disasters in the early years of the twentieth century combined to make cotton farming less profitable. First, the soil itself had been worn out by repeated cotton crops. Next came the boll weevil, which hit Southwest Mississippi first in its march northeastward in the 1910s. Meanwhile, repeated floods covered the river lowlands.

These three factors ended cotton farming as a source of wealth and power in the Natchez District. While Natchez attracted industry and tourists, the rest of the Old Natchez District did not find a substitute for cotton. Gradually, the rural counties of the southwest lost population, which led the mayors of the district to aggressively campaign for new industries, such as factories, auto parts suppliers, and gaming.

THE LOESS HILLS

The strip of hills covered by loess and loam continues from below Natchez north to the border with Tennessee. Its western edge forms the border of the Delta and is called the Loess Bluffs. In general, the western half of the strip has better soil than the eastern half. In some areas, the land rolls gently and can be plowed for crops. In other places, such as near Vicksburg and Yazoo City, it is eroded into sharp hills, which are too steep even for pastures. The best land in this section lies in the flat bottoms of river and creek valleys.

Before the Civil War, much of this land, like that of the Old Natchez District, was organized as cotton plantations. Mansions and courthouses, built by enslaved Blacks, sprang up from Holly Springs in the north to Brookhaven in the south. But the soil, unlike the deep flat earth of the Delta, was quickly worn out by cotton. Even after the Civil War, planters and sharecroppers continued to try to grow cotton on it, but erosion was the major result. Many of the old plantations were broken up into smaller farms, abandoned to nature, or redeveloped.

Below Jackson, farmers switched to tomatoes and other vegetables. Throughout the Loess Hills, farmers began to raise cattle, hogs, and dairy cows. Map 6 shows the distribution of pastures throughout Mississippi during the 1970s: on it, the outline of the Loess Hills can be traced almost without error.

From the Loess Hills two legacies emerged from the plantation days: a relatively large Black population, and leftover feelings of segregation in some members of the White population. Perhaps tied in with these feelings is the fact that some Loess Hills counties have never made much economic progress. Dating back to the 1970s, Jackson, Canton, Grenada, and some other towns attracted light manufacturing, mostly of wood-based products. But overall, the rest of the area did not

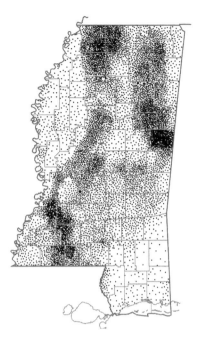

Map 6. Pastureland, 1949

prosper. In recent years, however, several new industries have moved in, including Nissan in Canton and Continental Tires in Clinton. There is evidence that if these counties can pull together, they can develop economically and culturally.

THE NORTH CENTRAL HILLS

A broad belt of narrow ridges and valleys, the North Central Hills were primarily settled by small farmers. They tried to grow cotton without much success, for the land, especially on the hillsides and hilltops, was simply too poor. Later they shifted to corn, livestock, and dairy cows with somewhat greater success, but now they have moved to the towns of the region and to industry.

In the early 1900s, North Central Hills farmers felt powerless compared with the rich planters and city businessmen. They became a source of support for White politicians who appealed to anti-Black prejudice.

By the latter third of the century, the hill counties tried to industrialize. Except for the industrial center of Meridian, they had moderate success. Community leaders emphasized the availability of cheap labor and offered tax breaks under the Balance Agriculture with Industry Program (BAWI) program. Consequently, they attracted slow-growing industries that offered low wages, such as shoe companies and shirt manufacturers. These factory jobs allowed workers to survive, if that, and support families, but they did not make their children wish to stay. Like then, what remains needed in Mississippi is industry that uses skilled labor and pays high wages.

THE FLATWOODS

The narrow belt of Flatwoods in Northeast Mississippi is made up of broad, rolling hills and flat-bottomed valleys. The soil is fertile, but it is not well drained. Therefore, most of the Flatwoods belt, as its name implies, remains forested. There are no major towns in this belt; most of the people who do live here drive to work in the towns to the east or west.

THE PONTOTOC RIDGE

The Pontotoc Ridge curves down from the Tennessee line in Tippah County. Its soil is rather good, but the land is cut by streams and valleys. A string of towns and villages, including Ripley, New Albany, and Houston, is located on the Ridge.

Along with the Black Prairie towns and those of the Tennessee Hills to the east, Pontotoc Ridge towns once led Mississippi in educational progress. School systems introduced many new techniques, including individual instruction, ungraded classes, team teaching, and televised teaching. These towns and the communities to the east made good use of an extensive junior college system. This educational progress was matched by economic growth. Pontotoc Ridge towns developed industries that drew rural workers from the Flatwoods to the west.

THE BLACK PRAIRIE

The Black Prairie, also known as the Tombigbee Prairie, is an extension of the Alabama Black Belt, which was so named because of its fertile Black, loamy soil. The Black Belt was settled long ago by White planters and large numbers of enslaved Blacks, so today "Black Belt" also refers to Black people.

Map 7 shows a concentration of Black farmers during the 1950s exactly corresponding to the lines marking off the Black Prairie and the Pontotoc Ridge.

During the first half of the nineteenth century, Aberdeen and Cotton Gin Port in Monroe County became thriving towns. Cotton, shipped down the Tombigbee River to market, was the main export. Though cotton is still grown, many farmers outside the Delta, turned to dairy herds and beef cattle. In map 6 you can trace the outline of the Black Prairie, compared with the less fertile hills on either side.

The Tennessee Valley Authority (TVA), a federal government project started during the Great Depression of the 1930s, continues to supply much electricity to Northeast Mississippi. Its inexpensive power helped attract new industry, but its overall influence has probably been more important than its electricity. Because of the TVA, many farmers were brought in closer touch with the outside world.

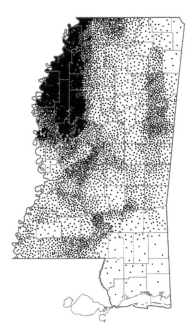
Map 7. Black Farm Population, 1950

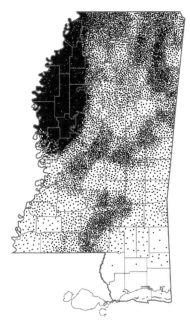
Map 8. Cotton Production, 1949

Figure 2.2. New Deal programs in Mississippi.

Attitudes and ideas began to change, and once-isolated communities developed close ties with urban centers.

As a result of their alertness and their community participation, Black Prairie and Pontotoc Ridge towns attracted new industries. To some extent these were slow-growing, low-wage industries such as clothing manufacturing.

CHAPTER 2.

THE TENNESSEE HILLS

The Tennessee Hills, located in the northeastern corner of Mississippi, are an extension of the rolling hills of Middle Tennessee. This region is characterized by gentle, rolling terrain, with many hills composed of sand and gravel. The valleys in this area are home to thick, sandy soils that are not well suited for agriculture.

The Tennessee Hills are considered part of the Appalachian region, a cultural and geographical area that extends from southern New York to northern Mississippi. This region is known for its unique culture, history, and natural beauty, and the Tennessee Hills offer visitors a chance to experience the Appalachian landscape and culture in Mississippi.

Despite their sandy soils and limited agricultural potential, the Tennessee Hills are an important part of Mississippi's natural and cultural heritage. The region offers a diverse range of outdoor recreational opportunities, from hiking and camping to fishing and boating, and it provides a window into the state's connection to the larger Appalachian region.

The independent farmers of this area established no plantations and rarely enslaved Blacks. At the same time, they had no sympathy for slaveholders, and when the Civil War came, some of them fought for the Union cause. In 1980, these counties had very few Black residents. By 2020, the Black population in various towns ranged from 7.9 percent to 46.5 percent. In fact, two of Mississippi's six sundown towns—towns that excluded non-Whites from living there—were located in this northeast corner (sundown towns were much commoner in northern and western states). After beginning with poor soil, inadequate transportation, and no great natural resources, residents of the Tennessee Hills have done a good job of industrializing.

THE JACKSON PRAIRIE

Sometimes called the Central Prairie, the Jackson Prairie is a narrow belt of lowlands with low, broad hills. Its underlying soil is a blue-gray clay that expands greatly when wet and shrinks when dry. Therefore, some buildings and highways tilt, crack, and even slide downhill with the changing seasons.

During the 1970s, the Jackson Prairie was good farmland. Farmers raised hogs, dairy and beef cattle, chickens, corn, and other crops. The Jackson Prairie tends to vote with the Piney Woods and North Central Hills electorate.

THE PINEY WOODS

The Piney Woods is a large land area but has a small population. The soil is sandy and poor, too poor in most places for farmers to make a good living from cotton or any other crop.

Historically, the Piney Woods was settled by a few hardy pioneers, who made a living through the combination of lumbering, small farms, and commerce. These independent families came to Mississippi with little money and could not afford to buy the richer lands of the prairies or the Delta. Land in the Piney Woods was cheap.

When Indian cessions opened up to the northern half of Mississippi, many Piney Woods families left to seek better farmland in the north. Most of those who were left could not afford enslaved Blacks and might not have purchased them if they could. As a result, the population of Piney Woods, especially in the southern half, is mostly White.

In past years, the Piney Woods had only one natural resource: trees. In the early 1900s, much of the lumber was stripped from the soil, leaving some areas desolate. Faulkner wrote of the destruction: "This land, said old hunter. No wonder the ruined woods I used to know don't cry for retribution. The very people who destroyed them will accomplish their revenge." Advancements in agriculture and agronomy led to more careful, scientific lumber practices.

Stone County once raised most of Mississippi's sheep. Some of Mississippi's most industrialized cities and towns also were in the Piney Woods. Laurel, Hattiesburg, and the cluster of Summit-Magnolia-McComb developed diversified

Figure 2.3. Men unloading logs at a sawmill in Lumberton. Courtesy of the Archives and Records Services Division, Mississippi Department of Archives and History.

economies. Other Piney Woods residents commuted to work in the urban complex on the Gulf Coast.

Deep-lying oil fields were discovered in the Piney Woods. By 2020, the oil and gas industry in Mississippi was under pressure from renewable energy (especially solar and wind) and cheap natural gas for hydraulic fracturing ("fracking"), a controversial method for extracting oil and gas trapped in sedimentary rock.

THE GULF COAST

The sandy lowland along the Gulf of Mexico was the first part of Mississippi to be explored and settled by the French and Spanish. They built no large farming communities, however, because the sandy soil and poor drainage were not suited to crops or livestock. The French heritage still lives in the names of some of the people and in the Louisiana accents in speech and cooking. Other immigrants, including Lebanese, Yugoslavs, and Italians, have also settled here, as well as Africans and Northern Europeans.

Partly because of the diversity of its population, the coast was once more tolerant in its politics and folkways than other areas of the state. Alcohol and gambling were permitted, officially or unofficially. Gulf Coast convention hotels admitted integrated groups in the 1950s, when the rest of the state was still rigidly segregated.

Figure 2.4. Recreation on the Gulf Coast of Mississippi. Courtesy of the Archives and Records Services Division, Mississippi Department of Archives and History.

A VARIED STATE

The maps in this book indicate Mississippi's great variety. The Delta basin is unlike the Gulf Coast, which is itself very different from the Piney Woods, the Prairies, or the Pontotoc Ridge further inland. Different products are manufactured in different areas, and different crops and livestock are raised.

Recommended Readings

David T. Dockery III and David E. Thompson, *The Geology of Mississippi* (Jackson: University Press of Mississippi, 2016). A comprehensive guide to the geological features and history of Mississippi.

James E. Fickle, *Mississippi Forests and Forestry* (Jackson: University Press of Mississippi, 2001). A detailed exploration of Mississippi's forest ecosystems and the history of forestry in the state.

Ken Murphy, *Mississippi: Photographs* (self-published, 2007). A beautiful collection of images capturing the diverse landscapes and unique charm of Mississippi.

Ted Ownby, Charles Reagan Wilson, Ann J. Abadie, Odie Lindsey, and James G. Thomas, Jr., eds., *The Mississippi Encyclopedia* (Jackson: University Press of Mississippi, 2019). An extensive reference work covering the history, culture, and people of Mississippi.

Deanne Love Stephens, *The Mississippi Gulf Coast Seafood Industry: A People's History* (Jackson: University Press of Mississippi, 2021). An insightful look into the history and culture of the seafood industry along Mississippi's Gulf Coast.

CHAPTER 3

INDIAN CIVILIZATIONS

THE FIRST PEOPLE WHO SETTLED ON THE LAND OF MISSISSIPPI LEFT VERY LITtle trace of themselves. They had no written language, as far as we know, and they left no written history. Who were they? How did they work, live, and play?

Their history has two parts. The first is the story of Native American life and development before Europeans and Africans came to Mississippi. For a long time, we did not know much about these early civilizations because they were considered "prehistoric": they did not leave the kinds of materials that historians usually use in writing history. It is important to note that some early explorers, Christopher Columbus included, destroyed cultural and Indigenous artifacts to craft a narrative that Indigenous peoples had no discernable culture or history. Thus, for information about them, we have long depended on archaeology, the scientific study of a civilization by its physical remains. Archaeologists use mounds, arrowheads, pottery, tools, bones, and other clues, along with their knowledge of other cultures and their imagination, to build a picture of a past civilization. Now, however—as reflected in the readings recommended at the end of this chapter—historians increasingly draw on a much wider range of Native American sources in ways that challenge our current understandings.

The coming of Europeans brought about drastic changes in the old civilizations and destroyed them. This destruction forms the second part of their history. Most of the information for this part comes from White Europeans and Americans, who did not understand what they saw. Europeans held strong ideas about what was "right" in religion, social structure, and government, and looked down on cultures that differed from theirs. This attitude of judging another culture by one's own standards is a kind of bias. Most European writing about Native Americans reflected a European bias.

ORIGINS

Many archaeologists believe that the first people in the Americas came from Northern Asia 40,000 or more years ago. These first Americans moved across

Figure 3.1. An archaic Indian food-gathering camp. A woman prepares food near a small fire while another carries firewood. Meat strips slowly roast over the fire. Stored food fills the rear of the temporary shelter. A few men barter with a distant visitor. From *Prehistoric Indians at Maramec Spring Park* by Richard A. Marshall. Courtesy of the James Foundation.

from Siberia to Alaska. They reached present-day Mississippi at least 10,000 years ago.

From what we can guess by studying spearheads, bones, and other remains, the first people to reach Mississippi were hunters. They were nomads and they followed large animals they killed for food and clothing.

Later, the early Mississippi Indians gathered mussels, oysters, berries, and wild plants for food. Rabbits, turkeys, bear, deer, buffalo, and fish provided meat. The men did the hunting, traveling into the woods in search of game. Once they had killed an animal, they marked their trail and returned to camp. The women then went to the kill, skinned the animal, and carried it to the village. No part of the animal was wasted. They ate the meat immediately or dried it to eat in the winter. The women used the brains to cure the skins for making clothes, and the men made bowstrings out of the tendons and intestines.

These Native Americans lived in huts made of poles and branches. Their tools included knives, spears, baskets, nets, fishing gear, stone axes, and whistles. They traded with Native Americans near Lake Michigan for tools and ornaments made of copper.

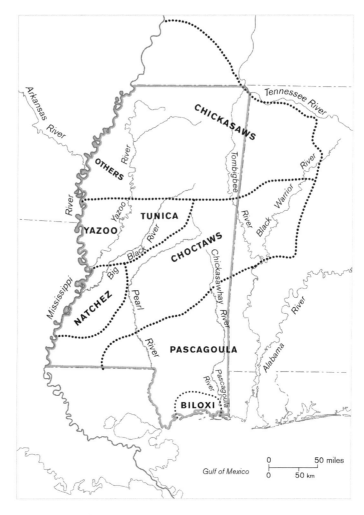

Map 9. Indians in Mississippi

THE WOODLAND ERA, 1800 BC–AD 1000

Perhaps, from a new migration of people or ideas from Mexico, the idea of agriculture took hold. Corn had been bred in Mexico from wild plants; Indians from Mississippi were growing it by 1500 BC. Other early crops included squash, beans, tobacco, and plants that some people consider weeds, such as sunflowers and pigweed.

Gradually, the population increased. Now that they had to tend and harvest their crops, people were no longer nomadic. The growing of corn provided a stable food supply. Now larger groups of people could live together. They built large villages in the large rich river bottoms. They buried their dead in large cone-shaped earth mounds. They made and decorated bowls and other articles of pottery.

ARCHAEOLOGY AND HISTORY

Imagine you are an archaeologist in AD 3000 investigating the ruins of an ancient country, the United States. You are examining the ruins of your hometown and your house. What kinds of things might be preserved? What would not? What do you think an archaeological team might conclude about our civilization and your family from examining the remains? Could they tell if you were poor or rich? Could they tell how many people were in your family? What did they eat? What did they do? Could they tell what the kitchen was used for? How could they prove it? And what about the strange ceremonial room, with mirrors and water basins, used in rituals? What would they conclude from the remains of the nearest downtown area?

THE MISSISSIPPI ERA, AD 800–1700

Meanwhile, in the distant forests of Mexico and Guatemala, a highly developed culture was emerging. A thousand or more years ago, perhaps by boat across the Gulf of Mexico or overland through Texas, came people with word of these new ideas. In Mexico, people worshipped the sun. Their society was tightly organized; the same persons ruled the government and the religion. They built huge plazas and pyramids, and their large cities were supported by farmers growing more than fifty different crops.

Figure 3.2. The Winterville Mounds, near Greenville. Courtesy of the Archives and Records Services Division, Mississippi Department of Archives and History.

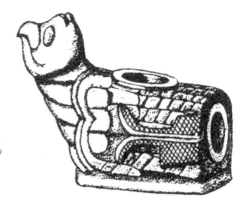

Figure 3.3. A pipe from Emerald Mound, near Natchez. From *Archeology of Eastern United States*, edited by James B. Griffin. Reprinted by permission of University of Chicago Press.

Most of these ideas took hold in what is now Mississippi, though their development was less complete. Mississippian Natives built large flat-topped pyramid mounds; on top were wooden temples and homes for priest-rulers. Farmers planted many new crops, and hundreds of villages were built. Pottery and painting were highly developed. People believed strongly in a life after death, and priest-rulers were buried with great ceremonies.

TRADE ROUTES AND CULTURAL CHANGE

In every time period, Mississippi Natives were not isolated. Mississippi is located at the crossroads of several main trade routes. At times, trade up and down the Mississippi River has been important. In other periods, people from Alabama and Mississippi have traded westward with groups living in Arkansas and Oklahoma. The Tombigbee and Tennessee rivers to the east have also been a highway for trade. When people live near such crossroads, they can pick up ideas from distant societies and use them in their own culture. Tools, art objects, and ideas reached and influenced Mississippi from as far away as Wisconsin and Ohio to the north and Mexico and Guatemala to the south.

FROM PREHISTORY TO HISTORY

After the Spanish explorer De Soto came through Mississippi in 1540, several members of his expedition wrote accounts of the trip. These journals, later supplemented by the writings of early French and British explorers, are the first historical materials describing the Indians.

When the Europeans first arrived, three major Native groups were living in Mississippi: Choctaws, Chickasaws, and Natchez. Smaller tribes included the Tunicas and Ofos, while on the coast lived the Biloxis and the Pascagoulas. The

Choctaws were the most numerous, totaling nearly 20,000. There were about 8,000 Chickasaws, and the Natchez and their allies numbered perhaps 6,000. The Natchez lived in nine villages along St. Catherine's Creek near the present city of Natchez. The more numerous Choctaws and Chickasaws scattered their towns over a wider area.

ORIGIN OF THE CHOCTAWS AND CHICKASAWS

According to a myth shared by the Choctaw and Chickasaw tribes, the two groups were once a single people living in the western regions of what is now the United States. Led by two brothers named Chacta and Chicksa, the people decided to embark on a journey to find a new home. They carried with them a sacred pole that would guide their travels.

Each night, they would plant the pole in the ground, and in the morning, they would continue their journey in the direction that the pole leaned. They followed the pole eastward until they reached the Mississippi River and crossed into what is now Winston County in Mississippi.

During a heavy rainstorm, the group paused, and the band that would become the Chickasaws crossed a creek and moved away from the main group. The next morning, still in the rain, the Chickasaws continued their journey, while the Choctaws found that the pole stood upright, indicating that their journey was over. In this way, the single group of people split into two distinct tribes, the Choctaws and the Chickasaws.

AGRICULTURE

All three groups, but particularly the Natchez and Choctaws, were accomplished farmers. Although they continued to hunt and gather food, they relied mainly on crops—corn, melons, pumpkins, beans, tobacco, and others. They cleared patches of land along stream bottoms near their villages by killing the trees and removing the underbrush, and they planted seeds between the stumps. They used hoes made of curved sticks and buffalo shoulder bones to keep out weeds.

Because their populations were small and their agriculture was efficient, the three nations did not have to farm all of the usable land around them. And because they had no iron plows or horses to pull them, they could not farm the tough soil of the prairies. Therefore, they cleared only a small part of the land, using the rest for hunting, gathering, and recreation.

The clearing and planting were done by groups of people working together. The Native Americans had beliefs different from ours about how land is owned and who owns it. They felt that the land was like the air or the sun, provided for the benefit of all people. A man or woman had a right to use the land, but not to own it. Tribes held land in common, with definite boundaries between their territory and their neighbors.'

TOWNS AND HOUSES

Houses were either round or rectangular. To build them, men set poles in the ground and tied them together at the top. Then they lashed smaller poles or lengths of cane to the poles. Small branches and grass mats filled the gaps, and plaster made of clay and grass covered the walls. A narrow door provided the only opening.

The houses were loosely grouped into villages or towns. Among the Chickasaws, each town had a log fort, ceremonial grounds, a council house, and a ball field. Choctaw towns were similar. Natchez towns were connected by paths to their Great Village, which had a central plaza. Low mounds, on which the Natchez built temples and homes for their leaders, surrounded the plaza.

DIFFERENCES AMONG THE TRIBES

Some people have made the mistake of thinking that Native Americans were (or remain) all alike. There was even an ignorant old saying, "See one Indian, see 'em all." This saying is completely false.

As the myth of their origin tells, the Choctaws and the Chickasaws were closely related. They spoke almost the same language and had similar types of government and social structure. The Natchez, however, were very different from the two larger groups. Although we cannot be sure, the Choctaws and Chickasaws seem somewhat like the Woodland Indians. The Mississippi era apparently made only a moderate difference in their cultures. However, the Natchez were perhaps the direct descendants of the builders of the great temple mounds in the Mississippian period, a time of advanced mound-building cultures in the southeastern United States. Natchez civilization kept the idea of a tightly organized society, and religion was very important to them.

NATCHEZ RELIGION

According to Natchez myth, their religious beliefs came from a man who was a messenger from the sun. The man had looked down on earth and observed that people who could not even control themselves were trying to govern other

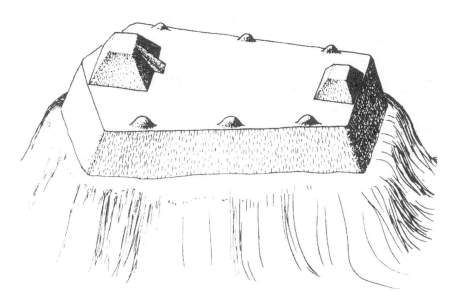

Figure 3.4. Emerald Mound, in Southwest Mississippi, was built in the Mississippi Era, but was still used by the Natchez much later. From *Archeology of Eastern United States* edited by James B. Griffin. Reprinted by permission of University of Chicago Press.

people. The messenger told the Natchez that to govern others they must first learn how to guide themselves. To live in peace and to please the Supreme Spirit, they had to observe a few simple rules: kill no one except in self-defense; do not take another man's wife; do not steal, lie, or get drunk; do not be greedy, but give freely, especially food to hungry people.

The Natchez believed in the Supreme Spirit who dwelled within the Supreme Fire, the sun. They also believed in many minor spirits. Their temple was built on a mound, and inside it two men kept a fire burning continuously to honor the sun.

The Natchez believed strongly in life after death. When a great leader of the tribe died, relatives, servants, or others might volunteer to be put to death in the funeral ceremonies, believing that such a death would win them eternal life. It also raised the status of their relatives back on Earth.

Here, it is important to make a distinction between what Europeans saw and what they think they saw when it comes to Native American belief systems. When colonists described a ceremonial practice they witnessed, we can usually accept what they said. The Natchez had a colorful ceremonial component to their lives. In their writings, colonists like Le Page Du Pratz, Dumont de Montigney, and several missionaries wrote descriptions of these events and often went on to interpret what they saw, sometimes in terms of their own Christian beliefs.

CHICKASAW AND CHOCTAW RELIGION

Natchez life was dominated by religion. Life among the other two main tribes was not. The Choctaws and Chickasaws held many features of their religions in common. The Choctaws believed in a Great Spirit and in minor spirits, but religion did not influence their lives as much as it did among the Chickasaws.

The Chickasaws believed in an all-powerful force, Ababinili, made up of the Four Beloved Things Above: Sun, Clouds, Clear Sky, and He That Lives in the Clear Sky. This force made all men out of dust. Its agents, or minor gods, did things for the earth and for the people on the earth. Since the Chickasaws felt the sun was the part of the Ababinili closest to them, they burned fires in each village to represent the sun.

The Chickasaws believed that people still lived after their death, and that Ababinili let some live in happiness in the sky while others lived in pain and suffering. Burial practices help determine the fate of a person after death.

NATCHEZ SOCIAL STRUCTURE

Religion affected the social structure of the Native American societies, especially among the Natchez. The Natchez were divided into two main castes, Commoners and Nobility. Within the Nobility were three further divisions: Suns, Nobles, and Honored Persons.

The ruling class, the highest rank of the Nobility, was the Sun Class. People from this class ruled each village, and the Great Sun ruled the entire tribe.

Figure 3.5. The way the Sun was carried expressed the respect the people had for him. Library of Congress Rare Book and Special Collections Division. LC-USZ62-115625.

Tradition said that the Great Sun watched over the Natchez people as an actual representative of the sun among them. Since he led not only the government but also the religion as well, he was very powerful and could do almost anything he chose.

However, the people did not submit to him without questions. An elected council of advisers helped him make decisions, and they had a great deal of influence. The Suns who headed each town also held much power and could sometimes oppose the Great Sun.

Mississippi's Indigenous nations maintained sophisticated social structures. In the Natchez system, Nobles and Honored Persons formed the second and third ranks of society, serving as war chiefs and advisers to the Great Sun. The Natchez, Choctaws, and Chickasaws all employed moiety systems—dual social organizations where one group held seniority. These moieties regulated social life, particularly marriage practices, with nations like the Natchez establishing specific rules about whether marriage partners could come from within or outside one's moiety.

Another unique characteristic of the Natchez social system involved marriage. Unlike many other systems in the world, in which persons of high status marry others of high status while the poor marry the poor, among the Natchez each member of the higher castes had to marry a Commoner. Thus, through marriage, the children of a Commoner could rise to a higher position.

CHOCTAW AND CHICKASAW SOCIAL STRUCTURE

Though the Choctaws and Chickasaws were closely related, they differed in important ways. The Choctaws had many more people than the Chickasaws and were more settled. The Chickasaws were much more warlike, at least after the British came, and the men of the tribe concentrated on hunting and fighting. Although they also farmed, the Chickasaws traveled and traded all the way east to the Atlantic Ocean and west to the Great Plains. The social structure of the Choctaws and Chickasaws was far less rigid than that of the Natchez. There were no castes. Each tribe was divided into several different clans, or *iksas*. Men could not marry within their own clan, but had to look to another clan for a wife.

Very little is known about the culture and social structure of the early Choctaws because their culture did not strike European eyes as very odd. Their funeral customs were very different from those of European burials, so European observers wrote about them. Otherwise, we have very little historical material about the Choctaws in early times. We do know they were good farmers. They produced a surplus of corn, which they traded to nearby Indians for animal skins and other products. And they were capable fighters when defending their homeland. They also produced the oldest field game in America, stickball.

Figure 3.6. The famous Choctaw stickball game, from which the modern game lacrosse developed. George Catlin, *Ball-play of the Choctaw—Ball Up*, 1846–1850, oil on canvas, Smithsonian American Art Museum. Gift of Mrs. Joseph Harrison Jr., 1985.66.428A.

GOVERNMENT

Government among the Choctaws and Chickasaws was freer and more democratic than among the Natchez. In fact, some writers claim that the government of the tribes was almost ideal: it was strong enough to make decisions for the tribes yet allowed a great deal of freedom. There were very few rules and almost no control from a central government. Each village elected two chiefs: one called the *minko*, who ran the government, and another who led the village in war. The military leader was clearly under the control of the civilian leader. Paid advisers, called *tishu minkos*, consulted with the minkos.

A national council met at least once a year to decide matters of a national interest, such as entering a war, making peace, or agreeing on trade with another tribe. The meetings were open and speeches were given by the elected leaders and assistants. Then the floor was open for discussion, and any adult man could speak. No one interrupted a speaker but waited until he had finished.

Perhaps because they had such a small population, the Chickasaws had a single major chief for the whole tribe. The Choctaws divided their territory into three districts, each headed by a minko.

WOMEN IN NATIVE AMERICAN SOCIETIES

In Indian societies, particularly among the Choctaws and Chickasaws, women held positions of honor and respect. These cultures, like many others, exhibited clear distinctions between gender roles, which were reflected in clothing, aspirations, and occupations. The division of labor was well defined: men, for instance, were responsible for venturing into swamps to harvest cane, while women utilized their skills to weave this cane into intricate baskets.

Women did most of the work. They tended the livestock, and with help from their husbands and children they planted, tended, and harvested the crops. They carried the water, and got the firewood. And they raised the children, especially the girls.

The men built the houses and did the heavy clearing of new land. They also made war, hunted, and made certain wood and stone tools. Talking with their children, they passed on tribal culture and history. Usually, only men were elected in politics, although women had some influence.

Among the Natchez, men usually had more influence in politics and society than did the wives. But women could be major leaders, even Suns. Natchez society was very unusual in that the social position of the mother, not of the father, influenced the status of their children. And when the Great Sun died, not his own son but the son of his closest female relative became the new elder.

Matrilineal kinship formed the foundation of social organization among Mississippi's Indigenous nations. This system determined not only family membership but also broader social affiliations including iksas, clans, and moieties through maternal lineage. The system's influence extended to leadership, with high-ranking women sometimes serving as chiefs.

European colonists, coming from patrilineal societies, often misinterpreted these social structures. However, some Europeans, particularly English traders, strategically used this system by marrying high-ranking Indigenous women to gain tribal membership and trading advantages. These cross-cultural marriages produced children who navigated both worlds, sometimes adopting their European fathers' names when beneficial. The matrilineal system gradually eroded under increasing European colonial influence in the Southeast.

WHITES ARRIVE

When European explorers made their first main contact with the Indians, the three major Mississippi nations had stable cultures, social structures, and governments that met their needs. Within fifty years, European technology, religion, politics, diseases, and wars had caused major changes in these cultures. Within one more century, the Indian civilizations were almost destroyed.

English traders reached the Chickasaws by 1691. Within ten years the French had reached the Natchez. The Europeans offered the Natives guns, ammunition, metal knives, axes, cooking equipment, beads, thread, and alcoholic drinks. Most importantly, they sold pigs, cows, and horses to the Indians; these animals had been unknown in North America before the Europeans came.

In return, the Natives sold honey, corn, and other foods, furs, salt, herbs, and slaves. Later, they grew livestock and cotton for export. They also ran inns on the Natchez Trace and other routes. And as time went on, the Indians took over European methods of house-building and European clothing. Europeans, meanwhile, learned Indian methods of agriculture and warfare.

The trade items made a tremendous difference to the Natives because the new tools were better than their old ones. Metal knives, axes, and hoes cut better and lasted longer than the old wood, bone, and stone tools. Of course, tribes with guns had a tremendous advantage over tribes without them.

NATIVE AMERICANS AND SLAVERY

Before Europeans and Africans came to America, Indian nations in Mississippi held slaves. When they took captives from other people in war, they enslaved them. The women of the tribe were especially grateful for this, as they needed help in their many jobs. The enslaved people could be adopted by a family, could marry within the tribe, and thus, could become regular citizens. Importantly, in stark contrast to the later enslavement of Africans (and some Native Americans), slavery among Native American societies was rarely a status that was inherited by the next generations.

When the British met the Chickasaws in Northeast Mississippi, they were willing to trade goods and money for the Chickasaws' slaves. They encouraged the Chickasaws to attack other tribes in order to capture more slaves. The Chickasaws virtually wiped out the smaller Delta tribes, and they delivered the Native Americans from the Gulf Coast to the British for sale at the slave auction in Charleston, South Carolina.

Figure 3.7. Susan Denson, a Choctaw artist, weaving a basket. Courtesy of the Archives and Records Services Division, Mississippi Department of Archives and History.

Soon the English and French were bringing Africans in chains to America, usually via European colonies in the Caribbean. Chickasaws and Choctaws, especially those from families who had intermarried with Whites, bought them. Missionaries used enslaved Africans of the Chickasaws as interpreters, because they could speak both Chickasaw and English. Enslaved Africans also cleared land, built roads and bridges, and helped with the daily work in the homes and fields.

By 1861, the Chickasaws in Oklahoma were a slaveholding nation, and most of them and many Choctaws sided with the Confederacy in the Civil War. After the war, however, the enslaved Africans were emancipated and eventually adopted into the tribes.

THE NATCHEZ AND THE FRENCH

The Natchez were the first of the three nations to deal with the Europeans at close range. The French settled near their towns on St. Catherine's Creek. Where the city of Natchez now stands, the French had a fort built, Fort Rosalie, and a small community grew up around it.

At first, relations were good. But in 1729, a new French commander, the Sieur de Chépart, was appointed. He wanted to get more land for the French plantations, but all nearby land was unavailable except for the Natchez town of White Apple. Chépart ordered the Natchez to turn it over to him.

THE NATCHEZ WAR

Rather than turning White Apple over, the Natchez began to plot the destruction of the French. They planned a joint attack with the Choctaws and Chickasaws. The plan called for the Natchez to attack Fort Rosalie on the same day the Choctaws turned on New Orleans. They planned to approach the French under the guise of trade and peaceful relations.

When the time came, the Choctaws stayed on the side of the French. The Chickasaws secretly helped the Natchez, but they did not attack the French themselves. Only the Natchez fought against the French. The Natchez won, killing 229 French people, including Chépart. The Natchez almost completely destroyed a place called Fort Rosalie and captured about 300 prisoners. After that, the French decided not to rebuild the Natchez settlement, and it stayed mostly empty for nearly fifty years.

French leaders sent several forces of French and Choctaws against the Natchez. The Choctaws supplied around 700 warriors, which greatly outnumbered the Natchez forces. In January 1730, they rescued most of the prisoners the Natchez had taken at Fort Rosalie. Almost a year later, the Natchez leader surrendered.

Some tribesmen managed to escape by fleeing to the Chickasaws or crossing the Mississippi River. The French sold the rest into slavery in the West Indies. The Natchez civilization, probably the most unusual in the entire Southeast, was at an end.

INDIAN-EUROPEAN ALLIANCES

The Choctaws and Chickasaws did not remain at peace for long. Economic relations between them and the European powers led to political alliances. Between 1690 and 1763, France and Great Britain fought several wars for control of North America. In Mississippi, the European powers used the Native Americans to do much of their fighting for them.

British and French traders would give goods only to those Native Americans friendly to their side. To prove their loyalty to the European country with which they traded, they, at times, had to attack the Europeans and Native Americans on the other side.

British traders quickly established a relationship with the Chickasaws. They provided goods at reasonable prices and did not send missionaries to try and convert the Native Americans to Christianity. French traders even tried to make an alliance with the Chickasaws, but their trade goods did not equal those sold by the British and their prices were higher. The French did become friendly with the Choctaws.

THE CHICKASAW WARS

Beginning in 1720, the Chickasaws raided French shipping on the Mississippi River. These raids were so successful that they often cut off New Orleans from French settlements in St. Louis and the North.

Bienville used a divide-and-conquer strategy in 1723, pushing the Choctaws to attack the Chickasaws. He feared that if these two powerful tribes united, especially with English support, they could threaten French control. By turning these tribes against each other, Bienville worked to protect French interests.

In a letter to the Company of the West, Bienville cynically noted that having the two tribes fight each other would weaken them both without costing French lives. To incentivize the Choctaws, Bienville offered them gifts in exchange for Chickasaw scalps.

The conflict ended with the Choctaws defeating the Chickasaws, who appealed for peace in 1724. Bienville's ruthless manipulation had paid off in the short term by reducing the power of two potentially dangerous adversaries to French colonial rule.

In 1733, the French replaced Chépart with Bienville, who demanded that the Chickasaws turn over to him all the Natchez who had fled to them for protection after the Natchez War. The Chickasaws refused. In 1736, Bienville planned a two-pronged attack on the Chickasaws. One strategy of French and Choctaws was to attack from the north and from the south. But the French timing was faulty, and the northern force attacked first. The Chickasaws defeated them easily and confiscated guns and powder. Then, the Chickasaws retreated into their fortified town of Ackia, present-day Tupelo. Bienville attacked Ackia from the south, but the Chickasaws who had arranged strongly built houses to protect each other, quickly pinned down the enemy. Realizing they could not attack Ackia without cannons, Bienville's forces retreated.

In 1740, Bienville prepared to move against the Chickasaws again. The Chickasaws, fearing his huge force, agreed to sign a peace treaty and promised to stop interfering with French water traffic. However, peace did not truly come to the Mississippi Valley until the British took over French territories in 1763.

Following these conflicts, most of the Natchez refugees who had sought shelter with the Chickasaws decided to leave by the 1740s. They migrated to South Carolina, possibly alongside some Chickasaw people who also chose to relocate there. The most significant remaining group of Natchez settled in various villages dispersed across Alabama.

MISSISSIPPI INDIANS IN THE AMERICAN REVOLUTION

Between 1763 and 1776, the Chickasaws and Choctaws finally made peace with each other; the Choctaw tribes to the north that had fought the Chickasaws during the French period left them alone. When the American Revolutionary War broke out, the Chickasaws fought again.

Because of their long friendship with the British, the Chickasaws remained friendly to them and fought against the new American nation. The Chickasaws became the main British line of defense in the Old Southwest. They guarded the area along the Mississippi River up to the Ohio River.

In 1780, the American General George Rogers Clark captured the area north of the Ohio River (the Old Northwest). Clark then built a fort south of the Ohio in Chickasaw country. Led by James Colbert, the Chickasaws besieged the fort and forced the Whites to retreat. This Chickasaw victory stopped the American advance into the Old Southwest.

The Spanish joined in the war against the British, and in 1781, they captured the last British posts guarding British West Florida. Many British subjects fled to Chickasaw land for safety. The Chickasaws, meanwhile, again began raiding the river traffic as they had done in the French wars fifty years before. They were successful and almost closed the river to Spanish shipping between St. Louis and New Orleans.

The Choctaws managed to remain neutral during the Revolutionary War, although they sent a message of friendship to the new American government. They also supplied scouts who served with the American army under George Washington, Anthony Wayne, and other generals.

When the Revolutionary War ended, Britain was no longer a power in the Old Southwest. The Choctaws and Chickasaws did not know which to support, the Spanish or the new United States. But along with many other southern tribes, they sent representatives to Hopewell, making peace with the United States and exchanging the new nation land in northern Alabama for a trading post.

WHITE PRESSURE AGAINST THE INDIANS

Gradually, from the settlements along the Mississippi River, the Gulf Coast, and the Tombigbee River near the coast, more and more White settlers and enslaved Africans moved north. Other pioneers trickled into Chickasaw and Choctaw land over the Appalachian Mountains to the east. Many Native Americans came to feel that the Whites were threatening their identity and independence. They knew that other Native American tribes on the Atlantic Coast had been destroyed or pushed off of their homelands, and they wanted to avoid such fate.

DO WE GO TO WAR AGAINST THE UNITED STATES?

In 1811, the Shawnee chief Tecumseh journeyed through the Old Southwest, urging all of the Native American tribes to join his plan to unite and drive out the Whites. After he addressed a joint council meeting of the Choctaws and Chickasaws, Pushmataha, a Choctaw chief, rose to answer.

The following selections come from two speeches. Try to imagine the atmosphere at the meeting after Tecumseh finished. If you had been in the audience, what would you have done? Survey this chapter to see the results of Pushmataha's choice of friendship with the United States.

Tecumseh: "The Whites are already nearly a match for us all united, and too strong for any one tribe alone to resist. Unless we support one another with our united forces, unless every tribe combines to stop the ambition and greed of the Whites, they will soon conquer us one by one, and we will be driven away from our native country and scattered as autumn leaves before the wind. . . .

"Before the Whites came among us, we enjoyed the happiness of unlimited freedom, and we knew neither riches, nor poverty, nor oppression. How is it now? Wants and oppressions are our lot. Are we not controlled in everything, and dare we move without their permission? Are we not being stripped day by day of the little that remains of our ancient liberty? Do they not even now kick and strike us as they do their Black-faces? How long will it be before they will tie us to a post and whip us, and make us work for them in their cornfields as they do the Blacks? Shall we wait for that moment, or shall we die fighting before we submit to such shame?"

Pushmataha's reply: "I appear before you, my warriors and my people, not to throw in my plea against the charges of Tecumseh, but to prevent your making of a rash and dangerous decision. Nor do I stand up before you tonight to contradict the many facts alleged against the American people, or to raise my voice against them in useless charges. The question before us now is not what wrongs they have to our race, but what steps are best for us to take a deal with them. . . .

"The war, which you are now considering against the Americans, is a clear breach of justice, yes, a fearful mark on your honor and on that of your fathers. If you examine the question carefully that this war will mean nothing but destruction to our entire race. It is a war against a people whose territories are now far greater than our own. They are far better provided with all necessary tools of war, with men, guns, horses, wealth, far beyond that of all races combined. . . . Let us not fool ourselves with the hope that this war, if begun, it will soon be over, even if we destroy all the Whites within our lands and lay waste to their homes and fields. Far from it. It will be but the beginning of a war that will end in the total destruction of our race."

NATIVE AMERICANS IN THE WAR OF 1812

Under the influence of Pushmataha, the Choctaws and Chickasaws decided not to join Tecumseh. Tecumseh persuaded some Creek Indians in Alabama and Georgia to attack the settlers to the west. The War of 1812—despite its name, a more than three-year-long war between the United States and Britain—was called the Creek War in the Mississippi Territory. It began with the Creek assault on the Fort Mims settlement in August 1813.

This attack angered the White settlers against all Indians. However, Pushmataha offered to help defeat the Creeks by leading a force of Choctaw warriors against them. Throughout December 1813 and January 1814, 700 Choctaws fought with the Americans and won two decisive victories over the Creeks on the Black Warrior River. With the Creeks defeated, the Choctaws returned to their homes. Eight months later, one thousand warriors under Pushmataha helped General Andrew Jackson defeat the British at New Orleans. This victory made Jackson a household name in the new American nation.

THREATS AGAINST NATIVE AMERICAN CULTURE

In addition to the outside threats to their way of life represented by the American settlers and armies, the Native Americans faced a threat from within. Their traditional culture was being influenced by new forces. The new tools and other trade goods had been changing the ways they worked, cooked, and dressed. One of the lasting effects of the European entry was the intermarriage of French and British men with Choctaw and Chickasaw women.

The children of these marriages became influential because they could read and write and communicate with the Europeans and the new Americans, whereas most full-blooded Native Americans had to use interpreters. When the United States began to demand more and more of their lands, the power of the mixed families increased. By the 1820s, some of these families, such as the Colberts among the Chickasaws and the Folsoms and LeFlores among the Choctaws, controlled much of Native American politics.

INFLUENCE OF MISSIONARIES

Christian missionaries, which included the Catholic priests of the French and the Protestant ministers of the Americans, had a great impact on the traditional Choctaw and Chickasaw cultures. These men, influenced by their biblical teachings, taught the Native Americans that they would experience eternal damnation if they died without accepting Christ.

Their efforts, along with other European influences, gradually undermined many Native Americans' faith in their own beliefs and religion. The French used their missionaries as spies among the Choctaws to keep informed of any developments that might threaten French settlements. The Chickasaws avoided this by not allowing French priests to enter their land.

Missionaries also provided services. They helped tribal leaders combat the destructive whiskey trade. They taught Native Americans to read and write and to use modern farming methods. Aware that United States commissioners cheated Natives out of their land by bribing leaders with money and whiskey, missionaries also tried to make sure treaty negotiations were fair. Some, such as Cyrus Kingsbury, spoke out so strongly against these unfair practices that the commissioners kept him away while talks were going on.

THE TOWER OF BABEL

An example of the influence of Christian missionaries is the following story, which was developed by the Choctaws after the coming of Europeans. It shows a mixture of Choctaw culture and the Jewish and later Christian belief in the origin of languages. Compare it with the story of the Tower of Babel in the Bible (Genesis 11:1-9).

Many generations ago, Aba, the good spirit above, created many men, all Choctaw, who spoke the language of the Choctaw and understood one another. These men came from the bosom of the earth, being formed of yellow clay, and no men had ever lived before them. One day they all came together and, looking upward, wondered what the clouds and the blue space above might be. They continued to wonder and talk among themselves, and at last they determined to try to reach the sky. So they brought many rocks and began building a mound that was to touch the heavens. That night, however, the wind blew strong from above and the rocks fell from the mound. . . .

The men were not killed, but when daylight came and they made their way from beneath the rocks and began to speak to one another, they were astounded. They spoke various languages and could not understand each other. Some continued to speak the original language of the Choctaws, and from these sprung the Choctaw tribe. The others, who could no longer understand this language, began to fight among themselves. Finally, they separated. . . . This explains why there are so many tribes throughout the world at the present time.

THE ROAD TO REMOVAL

The Choctaw and Chickasaw tribes had a long history of alliance with the United States, having supported the American cause in the War of 1812. They had formal treaty agreements with the US government that guaranteed their sovereignty and rights to their land. Many tribal leaders believed that their loyalty and assistance to the United States would ensure the protection of their lands.

However, despite these treaty provisions, the years following 1785 marked a period of erosion of Native American sovereignty and land rights. The US government refused to recognize their treaty obligations, and increasingly sought to acquire Native American lands east of the Mississippi River. After 1820, it began to insist on the relocation of all Native American tribes to territories west of the river.

This policy of forced relocation, known as the Indian Removal, was a devastating blow to the Choctaw and Chickasaw tribes, as well as to many other Native American communities. It resulted in the loss of ancestral lands, the disruption of traditional ways of life, thousands of deaths, and widespread suffering and hardship for the affected tribes.

AMERICAN RESENTMENT

Americans resented the fact that relatively few Native Americans controlled much more land than they ever used for farming. White Mississippians were accustomed to the idea that one person owned a definite piece of land and could not understand the Native Americans' idea of the entire tribe owning all the land together. Whites, then, considered the land almost vacant, unowned, and unused. They neither cared, recognized, nor understood that land to the Choctaws and Chickasaws was more than just a farm. It was their homeland, the resting place of their ancestors, and the center of their religion. Ultimately, numerous Americans were motivated by the opportunity to acquire a portion of the new land, sell it for a profit, and thereby achieve wealth.

In addition to their desire for land, Whites had another reason for wanting to remove Native Americans. The territory was not under the control of Mississippi. State laws did not reach into the Choctaw and Chickasaw lands, even though the lands were inside the state boundaries. Runaway enslaved Africans, also called maroons, and White criminals could hide in Native American lands and be safe from Mississippi law. Sometimes they intermarried with the Indigenous peoples or formed new communities.

Many Whites felt that Indians were an inferior race of people, people who could never be "civilized." They viewed the Indians as something in the way, like tree stumps, to be cleared out before the land could be settled. These Whites saw nothing wrong with forcing the Indians to move from their homelands to a strange new country they had never seen.

Not all White Mississippians agreed. Some of them supported the Native Americans' right to stay on their homeland and in Mississippi.

UNITED STATES PRESSURE

Under President Thomas Jefferson's leadership, a strategy was implemented to acquire land from the Choctaws and Chickasaws through the signing of treaties, which are formal agreements between the US government and a native tribe. Jefferson's primary objective was to safeguard the United States from foreign influences. His approach involved granting land ownership to men who would cultivate and hunt on the land while also serving as militia to protect the nation. This was in contrast to the alternative of arming the Native Americans. Through the signing of Fort Adams, the Native Americans ceded their land to the United States. In 1802, the Choctaws relinquished their territory, and a sizable portion of the Mississippi territory was included in the deal, without receiving any compensation in return. This marked the beginning of the US government's acquisition of Native American lands during Jefferson's administration, setting the stage for future land cessions and the eventual forced relocation of Native American tribes.

The United States did everything it could to weaken the capacity of the Choctaws and Chickasaws to resist removal. Trading posts within the Indigenous communities were used to tie the Native Americans to the government. United States agents encouraged Native Americans to run up large bills at the stores, and before long, they owed thousands of dollars. Then, government agents forced the leaders to meet with them and give up land to pay the debt. They did this twice to the Choctaws, in 1803 and 1805.

In 1805, Choctaw chiefs and head warriors met with US government officials for treaty negotiations characterized by feasts and the use of liquor—a common practice in treaty dealings at the time. The resulting Treaty of Mount Dexter ceded approximately 4.1 million acres of land in southern Mississippi to the US government for $50,500. According to James Barnett in his book *Mississippi's American Indians*, $46,000 of the payment went to Panton, Leslie and Company, a firm representing the Choctaws, to settle debts owed to merchants and traders. Interpreter John Pitchlynn received $2,500, and $2,000 was designated to "protect the Choctaw from settlers." This pattern of selective distribution often benefited individuals and specific interests rather than the broader Choctaw population.

In addition, the United States used bribery, threats, and blackmail to force Native Americans to give up their land. With almost every treaty, the United States agreed to pay a tribe several thousand dollars each year, as part payment for the land. Tribes used their annual payments to support their schools and other tribal expenses. The government would then stop payment for some minor excuse, leaving the tribe very short of money. American agents would agree to resume the payments only if the Native Americans gave up more land.

The American commissioners also told wonderful stories of how good the Western land was and how happy the Indians would be there. But when Andrew Jackson and General Thomas Hinds tried this argument on the Choctaws in 1819, Pushmataha coldly replied, "I am well acquainted with what the country contemplated for us. I have often had my feet sorely bruised there by the roughness of its surface."

Similarly, Levi Colbert led a party of Chickasaw leaders in 1826 to look at the western land the Americans wanted the Chickasaws to settle on. He reported: "They have represented it as a country suited to the convenience of the Indians and one in which all the wants and necessaries of life could easily be secured. But this we doubt. The country we now live in is one that pleases us."

From 1800 on, knowing that they could not defeat the United States in war, the Choctaws and Chickasaws tried to adopt some of the institutions of the Whites. The Choctaws felt that if they lived like Whites, with similar laws and government, then perhaps the American leaders would respect the Choctaw nation. Choctaws set up schools, became Christians, built churches, and formed a constitutional government. However, the great changes the Indians had to make in their cultures caused divisions among their people and leaders; to advance their own interests, the United States encouraged these divisions.

PUSHMATAHA, WARRIOR AND STATESMAN

Figure 3.8. Pushmataha in his general's uniform. Charles Bird King, PUSH-MA-TA-HA. CHACTAN WARRIOR, from History of the Indian Tribes of North America, ca. 1837–1844, hand-colored lithograph on paper, Smithsonian American Art Museum, Museum purchase, 1985.66.153,311.

Pushmataha, one of the greatest chiefs of the Choctaws, was born about 1764. As a boy he was quiet, but his constant hard work brought him success as a hunter. Often Choctaw hunting parties crossed the Mississippi to hunt bear and deer on the western side. During one of these trips, Caddo Indians attacked, and Pushmataha was separated from the other Choctaw hunters. He pushed on to the south, finally coming to the Spanish settlements on the Red River.

He stayed with the Spanish for several years, working as a guide and scout and exploring much of Oklahoma and Northern Texas. When he returned to the Choctaws around 1800, he organized and led several war parties against the Caddoes and Osages, until, in 1805, they made peace.

By this time, Pushmataha was a respected leader and could speak four languages: Choctaw, Spanish, French, and English. He was chosen chief of a tribe district and became a leader in dealings with the United States. He fought with United States troops against the Creeks and later, the British. As an award for his leadership, the federal government made him a brigadier general.

After the War of 1812, Pushmataha continued his allegiance to the United States while he tried to get a fair treaty. At Doak's Stand in 1820, his knowledge of the

West served the Choctaws well. Andrew Jackson planned to give the Choctaws land in what is now Southern Oklahoma. The western boundary was to run south from the headwaters of the Canadian River to the Red. Pushmataha pointed out that such a line would never reach the Red River but would go off into Mexico. The line was changed.

On Christmas Eve 1824, after leading a delegation of Choctaw leaders to Washington DC, to settle further land disputes, Pushmataha died. He was buried there with full military honors. His name is the name of a county in Southern Oklahoma, where many of his people still live.

THE POLITICS OF REMOVAL

By the 1820s, the lands of the Choctaws and Chickasaws were entirely surrounded by White-owned territory. But the real push to remove the Native Americans of Mississippi came not from Mississippi at all, but from Georgia.

In Georgia, the Cherokees had been completing a remarkable acculturation. Within only one generation, they had developed a written alphabet, published a newspaper, and changed their form of government into a republic modeled after the United States. But Georgia's leaders became alarmed when the Cherokees put forth their own constitution. They realized that the Cherokees were successfully dealing with the new American culture and seemed to be in Georgia to stay. White Georgians greedily coveted Cherokee lands.

Therefore, in 1827, Georgia passed a law that extended state rule over the Cherokee nation. No longer would tribal courts and leaders be respected. Instead, disputes must be settled in the White man's courts. At the same time, Cherokees were prohibited by Georgia law from appearing in court.

The Cherokees protested this unjust system all the way to the United States Supreme Court, but without success. The citizens of the United States, especially those in the Old Southwest, wanted the Native Americans pushed out.

In 1828, Andrew Jackson was elected as president. In spite of his close association with the Native Americans in war and peace, Jackson agreed with the idea of removing them from their lands. Congress passed the Indian Removal Act in 1830.

THE CHOCTAWS ARE THE TARGET

Because the Choctaws lived farthest west of the southern tribes, because they had already done some hunting and settling in the western lands, and because there was some internal dissent within their tribe, the Choctaws were selected as the first target for removal. Once the Choctaws left, Jackson felt the Cherokees and others would follow their example.

The final blow to Choctaw resistance to removal came in 1829 and 1830, when the Mississippi legislature passed laws extending state authority over Choctaw and Chickasaw lands. These laws criminalized tribal officers performing their duties and declared that land rights guaranteed by treaties with the United States were no longer valid in Mississippi. Furthermore, the legislature enacted a law to abolish the tribes, imposing fines and imprisonment on anyone identifying as a "chief, mingo, or head-man." Mississippi thus set a precedent for other states to follow in the forced removal of Native Americans. These acts signaled the end for Native Americans' way of life in Mississippi. As soon as they passed, the trickle of White settlers into Choctaw and Chickasaw lands became a flood. Trespassers moved onto the land in violation of existing treaties. Government agents did nothing to protect the Native Americans.

During the spring of 1830, removal was the main topic of conversation in Mississippi. Some Mississippians pointed out that the Native Americans were becoming better and better farmers, were educating themselves, and were even getting college degrees. Since they showed such signs of acculturation, argued these persons, they should be allowed to stay. However, the majority of White leaders were eager to open Indigenous lands to cotton plantations regardless of the practices of Native peoples.

The Treaty of Doak's Stand, signed between the Choctaws and the United States in 1820, resulted in the Choctaws giving up half of their remaining land in Mississippi in return for an equal amount of what is now Oklahoma. This treaty did not demand that Choctaws leave Mississippi, but the commissioners had urged them to go west. Very few did.

THE LAST DANCE AT DANCING RABBIT CREEK: THE END OF CHOCTAW INDEPENDENCE

In 1830, US officials orchestrated a calculated scene at Dancing Rabbit Creek, creating a carnival-like atmosphere with food, alcohol, and roaming gamblers while deliberately excluding missionaries who might strengthen Choctaw resistance. The negotiations revealed how White supremacy created different opportunities for mixed-blood and full-blood Choctaws.

Mixed-blood leaders, more familiar with White customs and often holding elevated social status due to their partial European ancestry, secured better terms through hard bargaining than other southern tribes would receive. However, when removal became inevitable, these leaders primarily protected their own interests, accepting bribes of land and money to ensure their families could remain in Mississippi while others were forced westward.

The final treaty, signed by 126 full-blood and forty-four mixed-blood Natives, required the Choctaws to surrender their Mississippi lands for Oklahoma

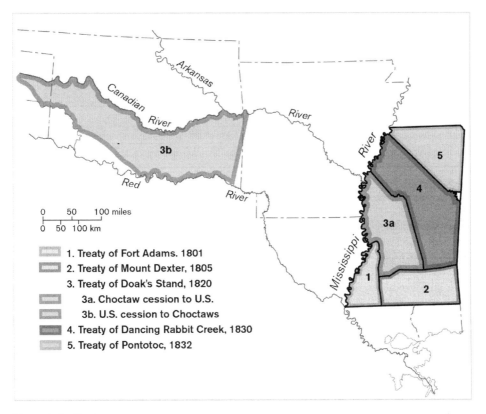

Map 10. Indian Cessions

territory. While Article 14 technically allowed individuals to stay as private landowners, this provision primarily benefited mixed-blood leaders. Most full-blood Choctaws who remained behind became nomads or sharecroppers, eventually merging into communities of free Blacks and poor Whites—a stark testament to how White supremacy shaped even internal tribal divisions.

To appease some chiefs and lower-ranked individuals after seizing their land, Articles 15 through 19 of the treaty granted land and other benefits. For instance, Article 15 awarded LeFlore, Nitakechi, and Mushulatubbee each a 2,560-acre reservation in Mississippi to keep or sell. Additionally, LeFlore and Nitakechi received annuities of $250 as long as they held office.

GREENWOOD LEFLORE, BIRACIAL: HALF NATIVE AMERICAN AND HALF WHITE

Greenwood LeFlore, son of Louis LeFleur, a French Canadian trader, and Rebecca Cravat, a French Choctaw woman, was born in 1800. Shortly after his birth, his father opened a trading post on LeFleur's Bluff, near what is now downtown Jackson.

LeFlore spent his early years at the trading post. When he was twelve, family friend Major John Donley took him to Nashville, Tennessee, to attend school. During his six years there, Leflore fell in love with and then married Donley's daughter. He returned to Mississippi in 1818 and became an American citizen.

Figure 3.9. Greenwood LeFlore. Courtesy of the Archives and Records Services Division, Mississippi Department of Archives and History.

LeFlore's influence as a tribal leader began to grow, and he became a leader of the faction of younger tribal members who opposed any more land cessions to the United States. However, he believed that the Choctaw way of life was coming to an end, and in the 1820s, he pushed for increased acculturation with White American practices. He became chief of one of the Choctaw districts, but lost his office in 1830. He then drafted a removal treaty in secret conference with the United States commissioners and persuaded the Choctaws to accept it. However, Andrew Jackson realized that the LeFlore treaty would cost the United States more than $50 million, far more than he wanted to pay. On his advice, the Senate rejected the treaty. Jackson demanded that the Choctaw leaders gather at Dancing Rabbit Creek to sign a treaty that would forcibly remove the tribe from their ancestral lands. LeFlore did succeed in adding Article 14, which allowed a few Choctaw families to remain in the state; many Choctaws accused him of selling out his people to the United States.

His accusers based their attacks on the fact that LeFlore received 2,500 acres of Delta land from the commissioners, becoming a wealthy planter as a result. He did not go with his people to Oklahoma, but became part of Mississippi's White society. He owned 15,000 acres of Mississippi land, 60,000 acres in Texas, more than 400 enslaved Blacks, a store, a sawmill, and a steamboat.

Figure 3.10. Malmaison, LeFlore's mansion near Greenwood, was evidence of his wealth and power. Library of Congress Prints and Photographs Division, HABS MISS,8-CARL.V,1.

LeFlore served in the Mississippi Senate from 1840 to 1844 before retiring to his plantation. In 1861, he firmly opposed secession, remaining loyal to the United States until his death in 1865. Leflore County and its county seat, Greenwood, Mississippi, are named for him.

MANY CHOCTAWS TRY TO REMAIN IN MISSISSIPPI

Under Article 14, to stay in Mississippi and obtain land, a Choctaw had to register with Colonel William Ward (a United States agent) within six months. Ward had argued for removal, and he tried to make sure that few Choctaws registered for land within the time limit. He refused to see many people, and in some cases, he simply would not let them sign up when he did see them. Often, he was drunk and could not be found. Thus, in this additional way, many Native Americans were cheated of their lands.

Several years later, Congress investigated Ward and concluded that Ward had not been fit for his job and that the Choctaws were cheated.

THE TRAIL OF TEARS

The actual removal of the Choctaws began in 1831. The War Department was responsible for overseeing the process, but it mishandled the task completely. Supplies were placed in Arkansas weeks before the Native Americans reached them; by then, the commodities had rotted. In October, one group of several thousand Choctaws reached Vicksburg to order the necessary steamboats. By the time boats could be found, winter had come.

According to Angie Debo, the winter of 1831 brought "one of the worst blizzards in the history of that region." Officials had allowed Choctaw families to take almost nothing with them, claiming that transportation facilities were limited. Blankets, tents, food, and other supplies were supposed to be furnished by the War Department along the way. However, when 2,500 Choctaws were left by the steamboats at Arkansas Post, Arkansas, only sixty tents were made available for them. Most of the Native Americans were forced to huddle together in the open through the bitter storm.

The War Department was better organized for the next wave of migrants a year later. But as these Indians reached Memphis, they were hit by a cholera epidemic that was sweeping the lower Mississippi Valley. Heavy rains then turned Arkansas roads into swamps, and many Choctaws died of exposure. Some seemed not even to care; they felt a hopeless grief when they abandoned their ancient homeland and the bones of their beloved dead.

Figure 3.11. This was the first time the United States "removed" an entire people. It would not be the last. *Family Removal.* Jerome Tiger. Courtesy of the National Museum of the American Indian, Smithsonian Institution, 23/6112.

REMOVAL OF THE CHICKASAWS

The end for Chickasaw society in Mississippi came quickly. As soon as the Treaty of Dancing Rabbit Creek was completed, the United States began to pressure the Chickasaws to give up their land, now the only Native American territory in Mississippi. The Treaty of Pontotoc in 1832 ensured Chickasaw removal. In it, the Chickasaws gave up the last of their Mississippi land for part of the new Choctaw lands in the West.

However, Chickasaw leaders, headed by Levi Colbert, had managed to secure a clause in an earlier treaty that held that the Chickasaws had to inspect and approve the Western land on which they were to settle. Because of this clause, Chickasaw leaders were able to delay departure until 1837, when they began their forced march to Oklahoma.

MISSISSIPPI NATIVES IN OKLAHOMA

The western part of the new land was very dry, so the Choctaws lived mostly in the eastern third of the territory. The Chickasaws joined them, farther west. For a time, the two tribes lived together under one government; later the Chickasaws were given a separate grant of land within the original Choctaw lands. The United States then placed other tribes on these lands, whittling away at the territory that had once been given to the Choctaws.

When the Choctaws first arrived, they were tired, sick, and nearly starved. Nevertheless, they began to build new institutions. In 1842, the Choctaws set up a formal school system. In 1848, the Chickasaws wrote a constitution. When the Civil War began in 1861, most Choctaws and Chickasaws, having long ties with the South, sided with the Confederacy. Also, the Confederates promised to make them a state. They took part in battles in both Indian Territory and Arkansas. After the war, they go through a Reconstruction period like the Confederate states.

In 1884, the Choctaws passed a law requiring school attendance. Many Choctaws went on to college, and at this time, the Choctaws were better educated than most White or Black settlers in the West.

White American settlers continued streaming into Choctaw and Chickasaw lands, however. Native American leaders tried to convince Congress to grant statehood to Indian Territory, but they did not succeed. Gradually, non-Indians began to outnumber Native Americans even in Indian Territory. In 1897, tribal ownership of the Choctaw and Chickasaw lands, once given to the Native Americans "forever," was ended by the Atoka Agreement. This agreement provided for land allotments to individual families; no longer could the tribes hold land as a nation. The tribal governments lost most of their power for many decades.

Finally, in 1907, Indian Territory became part of the new state of Oklahoma. Choctaw schools were destroyed by the United States, which took them over in 1899, deemphasizing tribal culture and higher education but stressing job training.

NATIVE AMERICANS IN MISSISSIPPI AFTER REMOVAL

Although they had lost their land by 1837, Native Americans did not disappear from Mississippi history. Thousands of Choctaws and some Chickasaws remained in the state. Some Choctaws believed they owned their land legally under Article 14 of the Dancing Rabbit Creek Treaty. Other Choctaws and Chickasaws simply refused to leave their homes.

Between 1844 and 1854, an additional several thousand Indigenous people departed from Mississippi. White raiders burned their homes, tore down their fences, and physically assaulted them. Native Americans had almost no rights in court, so they finally had to leave. Most of those who stayed did not own property, so they had to live on the poorest land as far from Whites as possible. Some of them intermarried with Whites or Blacks and gradually lost their identity as Choctaw or Chickasaw. However, the majority stayed in Choctaw communities, living apart from Blacks and Whites, and retained their language.

THE FINAL CHOCTAW REMOVAL

After the Civil War, the Mississippi Choctaws worked as landless farmworkers for White landowners, did odd jobs, helped cut the forests of the Piney Woods, and hunted and fished for food. When they entered towns, they were kept separate from Whites. A few counties in eastern Mississippi maintained one-room schools for Choctaw children, but no schooling beyond about the third grade was provided.

Efforts to erase Native American identity soon intensified with the establishment of boarding schools designed to force assimilation. Richard Henry Pratt, the architect of this movement, introduced the infamous slogan, "Kill the Indian, save the man." His mission was to strip Native American children of their culture by uprooting them from their communities and immersing them in American customs and values. Forcing cultural erasure was seen as a means to eliminate the Native American identity entirely.

After the land-allotment program began in Indian Territory, United States officials tried again to remove the Mississippi Choctaws. In 1903, they persuaded about 1,500 of the more than 2,500 Choctaws to go west. Some of the schools for Choctaw children in Mississippi were closed.

In 1918, the US Bureau of Indian Affairs opened a Mississippi agency. Between 1920 and 1944, the federal government bought land and established a small reservation for the Mississippi Choctaws. This reservation consists of seven scattered pieces of land, most of which is unsuitable for farming. It totals about twenty-seven square miles in East Mississippi.

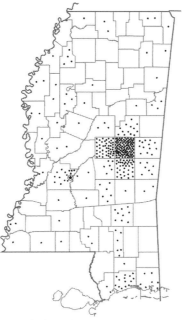

· each dot = 10 persons   Map 11. Choctaws, 1970

HOPES FOR THE FUTURE

Some improvements were made between the Choctaws and the Bureau of Indian Affairs. In 1945, the tribal government was reestablished under "The Mississippi Band of Choctaw Indians." Later the civil rights struggle, aimed at reducing racial injustices endured by Blacks, helped the Choctaws as well. Federal programs were established under the Office of Economic Opportunity (OEO) and other agencies. Mississippi Choctaws increasingly enrolled in college programs and pursued vocational training opportunities. Under the new self-determination policies of the federal government, Phillip Martin, their chief from 1977 to 2007, helped recruit a company that made wiring harnesses for cars. The company performed so well that they expanded it after only three years. The region's economy received its greatest stimulus, though, from the establishment of casinos alongside a resort featuring a cutting-edge golf course and water park.

As casino dividends and other financial opportunities have prompted increased interest in claiming Choctaw heritage, many people with mixed ancestral backgrounds have sought tribal membership. However, the Mississippi Band of Choctaws maintains the nation's strictest tribal membership requirement—a 50 percent Choctaw blood quantum. This stringent requirement carries a dark irony: it employs the same blood quantum concept that US officials once hoped would eventually eliminate tribal membership through intermarriage and assimilation.

Figure 3.12. Choctaw Central High School students examine options for their class rings. Photo by Ariel Cobbert.

After the passage of the Indian Self-Determination and Education Assistance Act of 1975, the Choctaws became eligible for federal grants to address widespread poverty. The tribe successfully petitioned to replace federal administrators with members of the Choctaw Nation to oversee these grants. The passage of two crucial pieces of legislation by Congress in 1978—the Indian Health Care Improvement Act and the Indian Child Welfare Act—helped address health disparities in Native American communities.

The Mississippi Band of Choctaw Indians marked several historic achievements. In 2011, they elected their first female Chief, Phyliss J. Anderson, who led the tribe until 2019. The following year, Carolyn Crawford broke new ground by becoming the first Native American woman to serve in the Mississippi House of Representatives. Adding to these accomplishments, the tribe's girl's basketball program has built an impressive dynasty, securing eight championship titles.

The Choctaw people of Mississippi have managed to preserve their language and elements of their traditional culture, despite the many injustices they have endured. Unlike many other Eastern Indigenous groups, the Mississippi Choctaws still reside on a portion of their ancestral lands, which has helped them maintain a stronger connection to their heritage and traditions.

EMMETT YORK, TRIBAL CHAIRMAN

Much of the Choctaws' struggle after World War II and much of their progress can be seen in the life of Emmett York. He was born in the Choctaw community of Standing Pine in 1903, during the final Choctaw removal. His father had gone to Oklahoma the year before to get his land allotment, leaving his family in Mississippi. For several years, he commuted back and forth, but he ultimately lost the allotment because he failed to live on it continuously. However, he was able to buy 100 acres in Leake County, and, unlike many Choctaws who had to work as sharecroppers (landless farmworkers), he became a small farmer on his own land.

In 1918, when the Bureau of Indian Affairs opened its Choctaw Agency in Mississippi, several Choctaw children were sent to school in Oklahoma. Emmett was among them. He was then fifteen years old, and his only schooling had been a few months of "mission school." In about seven years, he graduated from high school and migrated to Nebraska to work.

He returned to Mississippi as a carpenter, working for the Bureau of Indian Affairs. Later, he followed his mother and brother into tribal office, serving on the tribal council for twenty-two years. He helped found Choctaw Central High School in 1964, after years of delay. Now, Mississippi's Choctaw students no longer had to go to Oklahoma for high school. At about the same time, York helped reestablish a tribal court system, which had been lacking in Mississippi since 1829.

York realized that Native Americans had to unite to solve their problems, and he helped establish the United Southeastern Tribes, an organization of Cherokees, Choctaws, Miccosukees, and Seminoles. He served as its chairman until his death in 1971.

RESPECTING HISTORY: MISSISSIPPI'S REPATRIATION OF NATIVE AMERICAN REMAINS

In 2024, the Mississippi Department of Archives and History (MDAH) repatriated (returned the remains of) ninety-five Native American ancestors and 1,500 burial objects to the Chickasaw Nation from sites in northern Mississippi. MDAH followed the Native American Graves Protection and Repatriation Act to ensure these sacred remains were properly returned with respect.

Recommended Readings

James F. Barnett Jr., *The Natchez Indians: A History to 1735* (Jackson: University Press of Mississippi, 2016).

James F. Barnett Jr., *Mississippi's American Indians* (Jackson: University Press of Mississippi, 2012).

Ned Blackhawk, *The Rediscovery of America: Native Peoples and the Unmaking of US History* (New Haven, CT: Yale University Press, 2023).

Kathleen DuVal, *Native Nations: A Millennium in North America* (New York: Random House, 2024).

Jesse O. McKee and Jon A. Schlenker, *The Choctaws: Cultural Evolution of a Native American Tribe* (Jackson: University Press of Mississippi, 2008).

Tom Mould, "Chahta Siyah Okih" in *Ethnic Heritage in Mississippi*, edited by Shana Walton and Barbara Carpenter. (Jackson: University Press of Mississippi, 2012).

Evan Peacock, *Mississippi Archaeology Q & A* (Jackson: University Press of Mississippi, 2005).

Claudio Saunt, *Unworthy Republic: The Dispossession of Native Americans and the Road to Indian Territory* (New York: W. W. Norton, 2020).

Samuel J. Wells and Roseanna Tubby, eds., *After Removal: The Choctaw in Mississippi* (Jackson: University Press of Mississippi, 2004).

CHAPTER 4

EXPLORERS AND SETTLERS

1542–1763

IMAGINE A GROUP OF WEARY MEN STANDING ON THE BANKS OF A MIGHTY RIVER in May 1542, exhausted from conflicts with Indigenous peoples and months of traversing unknown territory. Many of the men wear makeshift skirts of grass or animal skin, as their clothing has worn away during their journey. Their swords are dull, and their remaining armor is rusty. At the forefront of this group stands their leader, Hernando de Soto, a Spanish adventurer.

What drove these men to endure nearly four years of struggle and hardship in this unfamiliar land, so far from their homes? The answer lies in the ambitions of European nations to explore America in search of riches and resources to send back to their home countries, and in the desire to secure glory through adventure and through spreading their Christian faith.

This chapter will describe the international rivalries that developed during this era, the role of French exploration and settlement in the region, and the eventual end of French control of Mississippi. We will explore the motivations and challenges faced by the various groups who sought to claim and shape this land and consider the lasting impacts of their actions on the history of Mississippi and the United States as a whole.

SPANISH EXPLORATION

When Christopher Columbus arrived in the Americas in 1492, a frenzied race began among the major European powers to claim land in this newly discovered territory. Portugal, Spain, France, England, and Holland all vied for control of territories in the Americas, using islands in the Caribbean as bases for their exploration and conquest.

Spanish explorers and conquerors such as Hernán Cortés, Francisco Pizarro, and Hernando de Soto led expeditions to various parts of the Americas, conquering lands and peoples in their pursuit of riches and glory. Cortés captured Mexico, Pizarro took Peru, and De Soto ventured north from Mexico into what is now the southwestern United States.

These explorers were motivated by a range of factors, including a thirst for adventure, the desire for wealth and fame, and the opportunity to claim land and resources for their respective countries. The European monarchs who sponsored these expeditions were equally motivated by the prospect of filling their treasuries with the wealth of the New World. In exchange for their service, explorers were often promised control of large territories and a share of any riches they discovered.

This era of exploration and conquest had profound and lasting impacts on the Americas, shaping the course of history and setting the stage for the development of modern nations and societies.

DE SOTO EXPLORES PRESENT-DAY FLORIDA

Hernando de Soto had already won wealth and fame with Pizarro in Peru, but he wanted more. He led 800 men and women from Cuba to Florida, landing at Tampa Bay in 1539.

Spanish interest in Florida had begun almost twenty-five years before, when Ponce de Leon tried to explore it in 1513. Six years later, another expedition sailed along the northern shore of the Gulf of Mexico. The Spaniards still dreamed of mythical "Cities of Gold" somewhere in the interior.

De Soto's expedition wrote an amazing story of cruelty and courage. According to Paul Jacobs and Saul Landau: "For three years, everywhere they went, they raped, robbed, and killed the Indians, including even those who befriended them. Indian hospitality to Whites was repaid with the wholesale slaughter of men, women, and children. The Spaniards burned unsuspecting villages in which they had slept, taking the village chiefs as hostages and the village children as slaves."[1] In 1540, a major battle took place. De Soto encountered the Choctaw-speaking people around Mabila, in western Alabama. In a fierce battle, the Spaniards conquered Mabila and burned it. But in the fire, they lost most of their own supplies.

Now, De Soto had to post guards to keep his Spaniards, enslaved Africans, and Native American captives from slipping away to live with Indigenous tribes. He crossed into Mississippi near present-day Columbus and camped for the winter among a group of Chickasaw villages near Pontotoc. The Spanish built huts for themselves and pens for their horses and pigs.

But when they prepared to leave in March 1541, De Soto demanded 200 Chickasaws to carry supplies for the expedition. The Chickasaws had had enough. On a dark night, they slipped into the Spanish camp with hot coals in clay pots. The

Spanish awoke in panic as their wooden huts turned into flaming death traps. They rushed out with no weapons to meet the attackers.

De Soto and a few of his men frantically saddled their horses and charged the Chickasaws, giving the rest of the Spaniards time to organize a defense. Therefore, the Chickasaws did not wipe them out, but the Spanish lost forty men and almost all their supplies.

Now desperate, the Spanish pushed west, through the swamps and forests of the Delta. In May 1541, they reached the Mississippi River, crossed over, and wandered through Arkansas. Finally, after trying to reach Mexico overland, they returned to Mississippi in 1542. Hernando De Soto died and was buried in the river.

As the Spanish floated down the Mississippi, the Natchez, then probably the most powerful of the Mississippi Indians, attacked them from canoes. But the Natchez did not pursue beyond their own lands. Finally, the Spanish reached the Gulf of Mexico, moved west, and reached Spanish settlements. When they arrived in September 1543, they had lost nearly half the expedition.

DE SOTO AND MISSISSIPPI HISTORY

What difference would it have made if DeSoto had never come to Mississippi? Read to the end of this chapter for evidence to support your answer. Should the book have given DeSoto as much space as it did?

FRENCH EXPLORATION

When De Soto's expedition floated down the Mississippi, Europeans passed out of Mississippi's life for almost 100 years. An occasional Spanish explorer or English trader wandered through, but the main exploration was taking place elsewhere. The three great powers each had other colonies to develop: England, the original thirteen colonies; France, Canada; and Spain, Mexico. They had little time to explore the lower Mississippi Valley. Not until the mid-1600s did Mississippi, again, become important to Europe.

The first French explorers were a priest, Father Pierre Marquette, and his guide, a trader named Louis Joliet. In 1673, they led a group of French and Native Americans south to find the mouth of the Mississippi River, but turned back when they reached the Arkansas River.

In 1682, La Salle explored the Mississippi River all the way down to its mouth and claimed the entire Mississippi Valley for France. He named all the land drained by the Mississippi River "Louisiana" in honor of his king, Louis XIV.

La Salle returned in 1864, but he missed the mouth of the Mississippi River and landed on the Texas coast. There, his men revolted and murdered him.

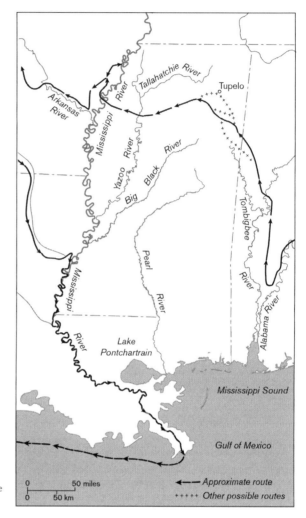

Map 12. De Soto's Route through Mississippi

THE RACE FOR SETTLEMENT

At the end of the 1600s, England, France, and Spain wanted to settle the Mississippi Valley. France sought to control the land because it was rich in furs that could be sent to Europe. It also wanted to prevent the English colonies along the Atlantic Coast from expanding past the Appalachian Mountains.

England desired the valley because they hoped it would serve as a wedge between the Spanish colonies in Florida and Mexico. Also, some of the original English colonies had charters granting them the land as far west as the Pacific Ocean. If they could settle and control this land, it would become part of the English empire.

Spain wanted the Mississippi Valley to link its colonies in Florida and Mexico and to control the trade with the interior. All three nations felt they had plausible claims to the land, but they had to enforce their claims to make them valid. The

Spanish already had a base at the best harbor on the Gulf Coast, Pensacola Bay, and did not try to settle along the Mississippi River. England and France did.

THE FRENCH SETTLE THE COAST

Pierre Le Moyne d'Iberville led the French expedition. He and his younger brother, Jean Baptiste Le Moyne de Bienville, came from a family of explorers and soldiers. Iberville previously helped settle Canada and handled ships in several victorious battles against the English. Bienville came with him in 1699 as a midshipman and remained.

The French settled first on Cat Island off the Gulf Coast. They moved to the mainland when they found out that the Indigenous people of Biloxi were friendly. They built their first base, Fort Maurepas, near Ocean Springs.

NEW FRENCH SETTLEMENTS

In 1702, war broke out in Europe. The French ordered Iberville to move the Maurepas community to the Mobile River, nearer their Spanish allies at Pensacola, in case English raiders came. To replace Fort Maurepas, the French built a post at Biloxi, which became their base for exploring the interior. Bienville did much of the exploring because his brother Iberville had many duties as head of

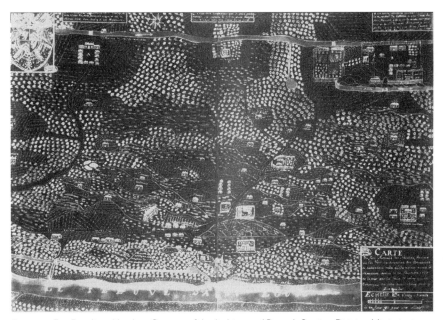

Figure 4.1. Fort Rosalie at Natchez. Courtesy of the Archives and Records Services Division, Mississippi Department of Archives and History.

the colony. Bienville was able to deal peacefully with the Indians and established trading posts and forts among them. In 1716, after some conflict, he convinced the Natchez to build Fort Rosalie for the French on the Natchez Bluffs. It quickly grew into the largest French post, because it offered relief from the insects, poor soil, and damp climate of the coast.

INDIAN RELATIONS

The European explorers and settlers relied on Indigenous peoples for food, supplies, and labor. In some cases, such as with the French and the Natchez tribe, the Europeans settled directly among the Indigenous populations. However, despite this dependence, the Europeans often did not make sufficient efforts to live peacefully with their neighbors.

The attitudes of the Europeans toward the Indigenous peoples were shaped by a sense of superiority, based on their technological advancements and their belief in their own cultural and racial superiority. This led the Europeans to look down on both the Indigenous peoples and the African peoples they encountered, assuming that they were inferior in all respects.

This attitude of superiority and the resulting mistreatment of Indigenous peoples and Africans contributed to growing tensions and conflicts between the different groups. The Europeans' lack of respect for the cultures and ways of life of the Indigenous peoples, as well as their exploitation of their labor and resources, created resentment and resistance among the native populations. These tensions would continue to play out over the course of American history, shaping the relationships between different racial and ethnic groups in complex and often negative ways.

Religion also played an important part in these feelings. Europeans believed they had a mission to spread Christianity to all the world. The Europeans considered the differences between themselves and the Indigenous people as inferiorities and thus regarded their spirituality or worship practices as wrong.

COLONIAL CHARTERS

In keeping with their ideas about operating colonies, the French did not want to spend much money on Louisiana. Rather than investing in long-term development, the French kings were primarily interested in extracting wealth from the colony as quickly as possible and sending it back to France. To do so, they offered charters to private businessmen and wealthy nobles, who were attracted by the prospect of earning great wealth. The holder paid all the expenses. In return for the charter, the government received a share of the profits.

To minimize expenses, the directors regularly reduced the amount of supplies allocated to the settlers. Nevertheless, the colonies were costly. In 1712, Antoine Crozat received a charter to operate Louisiana for fifteen years. At that time, he was one of the richest men in France. After five years, he abandoned the charter, having poured most of his fortune into Louisiana and receiving no return. The colony was still largely unexplored, and the settlers had not yet turned to agriculture. There were only a few hundred French individuals in Louisiana, too few to make it profitable.

THE MISSISSIPPI COMPANY

John Law, a Scottish adventurer who served as treasurer to Louis XIV, tried next. He organized the Mississippi Company to settle and develop Louisiana, and sold stock to investors in France. His high-pressure advertising campaign promised great profit to investors and quick riches to the settlers. He encouraged farmers to move to Louisiana because he realized that only by building up the population and growing crops could the colony prosper.

His plan collapsed in 1720 when the investors discovered that most of his promises were false and that they were losing money. When they tried to sell their stock, the "Mississippi Bubble" burst. Law fled France, a ruined man.

In spite of this financial failure, the Mississippi Company controlled Louisiana for about ten more years. From Louisiana's standpoint, Law's administration

Figure 4.2. Old Spanish Fort in Pascagoula, built under Law's administration, is neither Spanish nor a fort. Courtesy of the Archives and Records Services Division, Mississippi Department of Archives and History.

Figure 4.3. This "Veue de Camp de la Concession de Monseigneur Law" shows the colony at Biloxi in its early years. Courtesy of the Archives and Records Services Division, Mississippi Department of Archives and History.

succeeded. Recognizing the value of agriculture, Law brought thousands of White settlers into Louisiana and began importing large numbers of enslaved Africans from the French West Indies and Africa. This increase in population stabilized the colony and ensured its survival.

LIFE IN MISSISSIPPI UNDER THE FRENCH

The early French colonists were trying to establish agricultural settlements in a new land under new and different conditions. Their job was hard, and it was made harder still by their own leadership. Administration was divided between a royal governor, in charge of military and Indian relations, and an intendant, in charge of finance and justice. Often the two quarreled. The settlers themselves had little say in their own government; decisions were made by the appointed officials or in France. Moreover, many officials used their jobs in the colony to get rich and return to France to live. Since they had no real commitment to the new land, corruption was common. The settlers had to cope with shortages and delays in their food and supplies.

The French found that their European crops did not grow well in the new climate and soil, and they turned to Indian crops. Unlike the natives, however, they did not practice a balanced agriculture. Back in Europe, tobacco had become popular, and many colonists in Mississippi grew it and nothing else, not even food crops.

The tobacco was then sold in France to bring money to the charter-holders, but it did not feed the settlers in Mississippi. Despite propaganda campaigns to convince French peasants to cross the ocean, word of the colony's problems reached France. Since most colonists were brought in as indentured servants—workers who signed a contract to work for a landowner for a set number of years in exchange for transportation to the New World—they had little hope of becoming rich. Therefore, few came. As a result, colonial leaders brought over prisoners, prostitutes, orphans, and even inmates of an insane asylum.

Women came to Mississippi from the very beginning. Law arranged with orphanages to send "casket girls," with their belongings packed in small trunks called *casquettes*. They quickly married bachelors in the Louisiana colony. Their life was much harder than it had been in France, however, and at one point, to protest their living conditions, women staged a rebellion.

Conditions were very different in Britain's colonies in North America. Their families were encouraged to settle, with some voice in their own government and some chance of owning their own land. In the Louisiana colony, settlement was not particularly encouraged as an end in itself; rather, its purpose was to advance French imperial goals. These differences in who came, how many, and for what reasons help explain why France later lost out to Britain as a colonial power in North America.

SLAVERY UNDER THE FRENCH

Along with the increase in the White population, the number of enslaved Blacks increased greatly from the 1720s. At first the French had enslaved Indigenous peoples, but they escaped easily. Thus, the French turned to Africans.

The Native Americans were able to escape because they were in their own homeland and accustomed to living in the woods and living off the land. After they escaped, they could quickly rejoin their families. The Africans, however, were in a strange land, separated from their families and their way of life. If they did escape, they could not blend in with the Indigenous population, for their skin color and their language marked them as different. Therefore, the Europeans could recapture Africans more easily.

Of course, enslaved Blacks were also expensive. Most colonists had to buy them on credit, and slave traders charged high interest rates. Moreover, many died on the long voyage from Africa to New Orleans. Some of those who arrived alive had diseases from the voyage and either could not be sold or died before reaching the plantations.

Almost from the beginning, Blacks worked as mechanics, carpenters, blacksmiths and field hands. In severe emergencies, the French armed enslaved Blacks and used them as combat troops. As early as 1736, Bienville militarized a company of armed slaves led by free Blacks in his campaign against the Chickasaws.

However, the possibility of slave uprisings bothered the French. This fear increased during the Indian wars, especially when the Natchez tried to persuade the enslaved Blacks in Fort Rosalie to join them by offering them freedom. In 1724, Bienville wrote the first "Black Code," a list of laws defining how Blacks should act and how Whites could treat them. Bienville's was the first of many "Black Codes" in Mississippi. Under its provisions, masters were required to give religious training, specifically Catholicism. Slave owners were to provide for slaves who were disabled by illness or disease. But enslaved individuals could not own property or testify in court, and if they struck Whites so as to produce a bruise, they were to be put to death.

CAUSES OF SLAVERY

Enslaved individuals were not a cheap labor force. White men could live and work in the tropics, so there was no biological reason to import Africans. Why, then, did the French enslave Africans and force them to work on plantations in the West Indies and Mississippi? Why did the South become dependent on slavery, while other sections of the country, such as New York and New England, did not?

To answer these questions, consider the background of the settlers in both places.

Colonists who settled in New England and New York came from England, Holland, and France. Most were farmers, unskilled laborers, or merchants; a small share were members of smaller sects of Christianity who sought to escape religious persecution. Once they arrived, those from England controlled most of the affairs of their colony, selecting officials and making laws.

Mississippi, on the other hand, was controlled, at first, by nobles and wealthy businessmen in France who did not work with their hands. Later, wealthy planters, who again avoided manual labor, controlled the colony. The poor and working-class people who came to Mississippi had almost no voice in the government of the colony.

COLONIAL WARS

Between 1689 and 1763, Britain and France fought repeatedly in Europe and in colonial outposts across the globe, including North America. The previous chapter has told how they and the Spanish involved Native Americans in these contests. Throughout this period, the Chickasaws opposed the French. Thus, the Chickasaws provided the westernmost limit of British influence from the Atlantic colonies to the east.

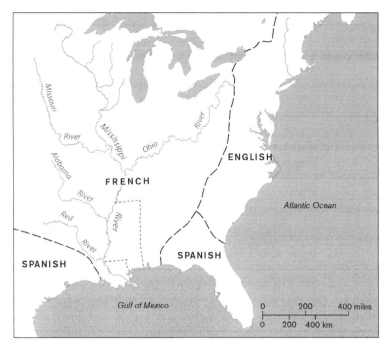

Map 13. Colonial Powers, 1754

The Choctaws usually fought alongside the French, although for a while some allied with the British. The Natchez were first friendly to the French, then rose against them; the French destroyed bands of Natchez warriors in 1731.

Spain remained in the picture, holding most of Florida and Mexico. Occasionally, the Spanish governed additional land, including parts of Mississippi, as a result of treaties with the other powers.

CLIMAX OF BRITISH-FRENCH RIVALRY

Outright war between Britain and France in North America began in 1754 and lasted until 1763. Among British colonists, it was called the French and Indian War, while in Europe it was known as the Seven Years' War. Britain won a decisive victory in the battle to control North America.

The fate of Louisiana depended on the outcome of this war. By 1762, the French knew they had been defeated. In a secret treaty that year, the French repaid their ally, Spain, for its aid by granting Spain New Orleans and all of Louisiana west of the Mississippi River. When the Seven Years' War ended in 1763, Britain received all of Louisiana east of the river from France and Florida from Spain. As the British flag went up in Natchez and Pensacola, French Mississippi came to an end. Under the British, then the Spanish, and then the United States, great changes were to come.

Note

1. Paul Jacobs and Saul Landau, *To Serve the Devil*, vol. 1: *Natives and Slaves* (New York: Vintage Books, 1971), 15.

Recommended Readings

François Furstenberg, *When the United States Spoke French: Five Refugees Who Shaped a Nation* (New York: Penguin, 2015).

Christian Pinnen and Charles Weeks, *Colonial Mississippi: A Borrowed Land* (Jackson: University Press of Mississippi, 2021).

CHAPTER 5

THE UNITED STATES TAKES CONTROL

1763–1817

BRITAIN RULED PRESENT-DAY MISSISSIPPI FOR SIXTEEN YEARS, FROM 1763 TO 1779, calling it West Florida. During these years, the most important development for Mississippi was the increasing growth and restlessness of the Atlantic colonies. They finally revolted against Britain in the American Revolutionary War (1775–1783), which established the United States.

During that war, Spain seized the opportunity to conquer West Florida. For the next sixteen years Spain sought to control the territory, encouraging Europeans to settle in it. The Spanish attempted to convince the Chickasaws and Choctaws to join them in resisting the power of the United States. The Spanish then sent a Creek army to attack Chickasaw territory, but it was quickly defeated. The

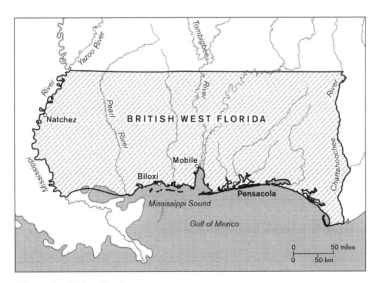

Map 14. British West Florida

influence of the United States grew greater and greater. In 1795, Spain ceded the land to the United States, giving up actual possession in 1798.

The United States organized the new land as Mississippi Territory. During the next fifteen years, more land was added until the territory grew to include the present-day states of Mississippi and Alabama. Much of this land was still occupied and claimed by the Choctaws and Chickasaws, but as chapter 3 shows, they were increasingly pressed by White settlers (many bringing enslaved Blacks) moving west. As the population of the territory grew, its people began thinking of statehood.

BRITISH SETTLEMENT

The first result of the Treaty of 1763 was that many French-speaking settlers of Mississippi moved west of the river to escape British rule. Their place was taken by new settlers from the British colonies, who brought with them new behaviors and ideas.

The British moved in gradually. The first arrivals were soldiers, who occupied Mobile and Pensacola and rebuilt Fort Rosalie at Natchez, renaming it Fort Panmure.

By 1768, stories of the fertile new land in British West Florida, had excited the adventurous, land-hungry settlers of the older British colonies. When the British government chose to offer free land to veterans of the French and Indian War, the number of settlers steadily increased.

Natchez, almost abandoned since the Natchez attack in 1729, quickly became the center of West Florida because the River Lowlands and Loess Hills around it supplied the best land for settlement. Also, the Mississippi River provided easy

Map 15. Old Natchez District

and cheap transportation. To the east and north, transportation was difficult, and West Florida grew slowly. By the 1770s, only three settled areas existed in the colony: the land along the Tombigbee River above Mobile; Pensacola, the capital; and the area around Natchez.

WEST FLORIDA IN THE REVOLUTIONARY WAR

During the 1770s, it gradually became clearer that the American colonies would split with Britain. In the face of increasing revolutionary pressure, many colonists loyal to England ("Tories") left their old homes for areas they hoped were safer. These people wanted to stay out of the approaching war. West Florida became a haven for them, especially after 1775.

SPAIN ENTERS THE WAR

Natchez remained generally peaceful, except for an unsuccessful raid in 1778 led by an American named James Willing. In May 1779, however, Spain entered the war against Britain. The British were preoccupied with their battles against the Americans on the Atlantic Coast. The Spanish commander took advantage of the situation. He struck quickly, capturing Natchez in September, Mobile in 1780, and Pensacola in 1781.

While the Spanish were busy with Pensacola, Natchez rebelled against Spanish control. The locals managed to trick the Spanish soldiers at Fort Panmure into surrendering. After that, they prepared to defend themselves against a Spanish army that was coming north from New Orleans. They based their hopes on the ability of Pensacola to hold out and to send them aid. When news came of its fall, the Natchez revolt quickly collapsed.

THE TREATY OF PARIS, 1783

At the end of the Revolutionary War, the British signed treaties with Spain and with the United States. The British treaty with the United States fixed the southern boundary of United States territory at the 31-degree line, or thirty-first parallel, where the boundary between Mississippi and Louisiana is today. The treaty also gave Americans access to the Mississippi River so they could ship their goods to market.

However, the British-Spanish treaty granted Spain continued control over West Florida. The Spanish argued that since they had conquered West Florida during the war, Britain had no right to give the land away in a peace treaty. Spain

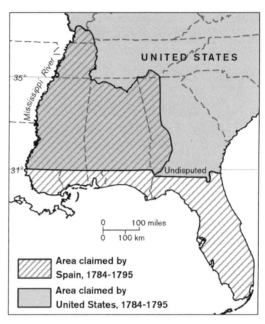

Map 16. Disputed Territory, 1783–1795

claimed the land, and since her military forces occupied the forts, the United States could do little. Spain also claimed control of the Mississippi River and promptly closed it to American shipping.

SPAIN AND THE SOUTHWEST

The United States comprised the original thirteen colonies, now reconfigured as states, along with the Old New Hampshire Territory and the Old Southwest, a region that Spain also partially claimed. The new nation was dominated by Easterners, who were preoccupied with the problems of setting up a national government and thirteen state governments. Settlers in the west desperately needed the river. Since no roads ran to the east, farmers had to ship their goods on the Mississippi.

The Spanish knew how important the river was to the Western settlers. They knew, too, that these Westerners were not committed to remaining in the Union, and they attempted to lure them to become friendly toward Spain. To encourage American settlement in Spanish West Florida, they made it easy to get land grants. Although the Catholic Spanish did not allow Protestants to practice their religion in Spain, they relaxed this rule in Natchez. Finally, they entered into a conspiracy with General James Wilkinson, a US Army officer and a successful Kentucky businessman. Wilkinson was supposed to persuade western settlers to leave the Union and choose Spanish control.

However, most Westerners never seriously considered rebellion. In addition, the new United States government began to take an interest in western problems. It appointed Westerners to office, took a stand in favor of opening the Mississippi River, and sent American troops to resist Indian raids.

THE SPANISH YIELD TO AMERICAN CLAIMS

The Spanish commanders were aware of their vulnerability and understood that a strong attack by the Americans would likely be successful. Therefore, in 1795, Spain and the United States signed the Treaty of San Lorenzo. Spain agreed to give up her claims to land above the thirty-first parallel and to allow Americans to use the Mississippi River. However, the matter of the river remained unresolved until 1803, when the United States purchased Louisiana, including New Orleans, from France.

CONGRESS CREATES A MISSISSIPPI TERRITORY

The Spanish delayed their actual withdrawal for three years. In 1798, a joint team of surveyors drew the new boundary. William Dunbar, a Mississippian, surveyed for the Spanish, while Andrew Ellicott represented the United States. Finally, the United States took over; now the land became Mississippi territory, but its boundaries were not those of the present-day state. The territory was a thin rectangle extending from the Mississippi River east to Georgia. After the United States gained control of Mississippi, racial discrimination became more systematic and severe than it had been under Spanish rule. People of mixed racial heritage, who had sometimes enjoyed greater freedoms than dark-skinned Black people under Spanish rule, found themselves classified as "Black" under the new laws and social customs imposed by the United States. Meanwhile, slavery and plantation agriculture continued to grow in Southwest Mississippi.

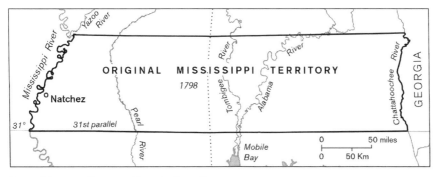

Map 17. Mississippi Territory as Organized in 1798

SIR WILLIAM DUNBAR, MISSISSIPPI SCIENTIST

William Dunbar was born in Scotland in 1750, the fourth son of a Scottish nobleman. He graduated from King's College in Aberdeen, where he studied astronomy and math. Because he was the fourth son, there was almost no chance for him to inherit his father's estate, so he sailed for America when he reached twenty-one. His ambition in America was to make money and live well. Following an unsuccessful attempt near Baton Rouge, Dunbar relocated to Mississippi in 1792 and established himself as a prominent planter.

Dunbar was also the most brilliant scientist in the new territory. He studied astronomy, biology, the weather, and almost everything else he could investigate. He developed a press for making cotton into square bales, which were easier to ship than the old sacks had been. He processed cottonseed oil and recognized its usefulness almost a century before it was used commercially. Among his other investigations, he kept records of the temperature, rainfall, and barometric pressure, and the rise and fall of the Mississippi River.

Andrew Ellicott, the American surveyor, introduced him to then-president Thomas Jefferson (1801–1809). Dunbar's brilliance impressed President Jefferson; in 1804, he asked Dunbar to explore part of the Louisiana Purchase. Congress did not fully fund the expedition, and Dunbar could explore only as far as Hot Springs, Arkansas.

Near the end of his life, Dunbar served as a judge in the Mississippi Territory and as a member of the territorial legislature. He spent his last years on his plantation conducting experiments and died in 1810.

ORGANIZATION OF MISSISSIPPI TERRITORY

Winthrop Sargent, appointed by President John Adams (1797–1801), became the first governor of the new territory. Originally from Massachusetts, he was a Federalist, a member of the same party as Adams. His task was challenging, as he had to establish a completely new government from scratch. He immediately organized a court system and militia, and divided the territory into districts with justices of the peace, sheriffs, and other National Guard officers. Natchez served as the territorial capital. However, in 1802, the government relocated six miles east to Washington. Despite this, Natchez continued to be the primary commercial hub and the main town in the territory. By 1808, it had grown to a population of 3,000, boasting two printing shops and two newspapers.

Figure 5.1. John J. Audubon painted this view of Natchez in 1822. Courtesy of the Archives and Records Services Division, Mississippi Department of Archives and History.

OPPOSITION TO SARGENT

Resistance to Governor Sargent's rigid leadership style rapidly increased, particularly among settlers who opposed the Federalist Party. Colonel Anthony Hutchins and Cato West headed the opposition and complained to the United States House of Representatives. At the same time, elections took place for a general assembly, which was set to share legislative responsibilities in governing the territory alongside Sargent. Sargent's opponents dominated the assembly and tried to limit his power.

In the presidential election of 1800, Sargent's party lost. Thomas Jefferson, the new president (1801–1809), replaced Sargent with William C. C. Claiborne, a member of his own Democratic-Republican party.

DISPUTED LAND CLAIMS

Claiborne arrived in May 1801 and was immediately confronted with numerous land claim disputes. These issues largely stemmed from the rapid changes in ownership that Mississippi had experienced in the thirty years prior to becoming a United States territory. France, Britain, Spain, and the state of Georgia had all sold land in Mississippi, making it challenging to determine the rightful ownership of each parcel of land.

Georgia claimed the land under her original colonial charter, which extended all the way to the Pacific Ocean. In addition, it enacted legislation to form Bourbon County, covering the area from Georgia's boundary to the Mississippi River.

In 1795, Georgia granted land to three groups of speculators within this territory. They sold some of the land before the act authorizing the grants were replaced.

All these conflicting claims, involving years of dispute, had to be decided. In April 1802, Georgia finally gave up its claim to land in Mississippi Territory for a payment of $1,250,000. Under this agreement, the territory was to become one state. As for the other titles, federal courts eventually decided that those claimants living on the land as of March 3, 1803, would be favored over others contesting their title.

THE NATCHEZ TRACE

More problems also faced the young territory. Roads were terrible. In 1801, the United States negotiated with the Choctaws and Chickasaws for the right to build a road across their land. This road, the Natchez Trace, was really only a narrowly cleared path from Natchez to Nashville, Tennessee. For much of its length the Trace followed Native American trails and pathways. The Trace proved increasingly important to the growing territory, as it provided the best way for travelers to move north. Boatmen could float down the Mississippi to New Orleans or Natchez and then walk back to Tennessee, instead of fighting their way back upstream and against the current on the Mississippi River.

Figure 5.2. Mount Locust, old inn on the Natchez Trace, still stands. Photographs in the Ben May Charitable Trust Collection of Mississippi Photographs in the Carol M. Highsmith Archive, Library of Congress, Prints and Photographs Division. LC-DIG-highsm-42683.

ROBBERS ON THE TRACE

Because it was so well traveled, the Natchez Trace quickly became the hunting ground of bands of criminals. One of the most famous of these robber bands was the Mason-Harpe gang, which consisted of Samuel Mason, his son John, Wiley Harpe, and several others. They hid in the swamps near what is now Vicksburg and raided travelers on the Trace. Governor Claiborne offered a $2,000 reward for their capture.

According to one legend, when Harpe heard of the reward, he left the gang and went to Kentucky. Two other members waited until Samuel Mason was asleep, then killed him and cut off his head. When they brought his head forth to claim the reward, a man in the crowd recognized their horses as belonging to men who had robbed his group earlier and killed one of his partners. The two men were captured, tried, convicted, and hanged.

THE UNITED STATES TAKES THE COAST

As more American settlers entered the territory, Mississippi became the center of another dispute between the United States and Spain. The purchase of Louisiana from France had opened the Mississippi River to American shipping. However,

Map 18. Mississippi Territory

since the coast was still in Spanish hands, settlers along the Pearl, Pascagoula, and Tombigbee rivers were still cut off from the Gulf. Overland transportation west to the Mississippi was slow and expensive.

Some settlers living near the Spanish lands were violently pro-American, especially the Kemper brothers—Reuben, Nathan, and Samuel. They campaigned so much against the Spanish control of the Gulf Coast that in August 1805, a group of Spanish citizens came across the border to kidnap them. After one attempt in which they got the wrong man, they returned, found all the Kempers at home, and captured them. On the way to Baton Rouge, the Spanish capital, the Kempers escaped by calling out to a group of American citizens to assist them.

The Kempers' plotting came to a head in September 1810. One hundred Americans attacked and captured the Spanish fort at Baton Rouge. In October, under the presidency of Madison (1809–1817), American forces were instructed to seize control of the remaining part of Spanish West Florida, stretching from the Pearl to the Perdido rivers. They accomplished this, except for Mobile, which stayed under Spanish control until the War of 1812.

THE AARON BURR CONSPIRACY

During the years of dispute with Spain, rumors spread throughout the United States that Aaron Burr, Vice President of the United States (1801–1805), was conspiring with General Wilkinson to separate part of the western territory from the United States to form his own country. The Spanish feared he would encourage some of the western territories to secede. In January 1807, Burr and his group halted along the Mississippi River, across from Natchez, where he surrendered. On February 2, Burr was tried for treason before a Mississippi territorial court. When Attorney-General George Poindexter declared that there was not enough evidence to hold him, the charges were dropped.

However, a federal judge ruled that Burr should remain in custody. Burr managed to escape the following night, but by the end of February, he reappeared in Mobile. He was soon recaptured and transported to Richmond, Virginia, to face trial for treason. He was eventually acquitted of the charges.

THE WAR OF 1812 AND THE CREEK WAR

When war broke out again between the United States and Britain, Mississippians played an important role. In August 1812, General Ferdinand L. Claiborne mobilized the Mississippi militia for defense of the territory. The Creek attack on Fort Mims in August 1813, the following year, spread terror through the territory. The Choctaws and Chickasaws offered their services to Claiborne, and he eagerly accepted. The Mississippi forces moved north from their forts while General Andrew Jackson, commanding an army of Tennessee volunteers, moved south.

After the incident at Fort Mims, American forces attacked the Creek town of Tallussahatchie in November, killing all its inhabitants, including women and children. The next month, troops under Brigadier General Claiborne targeted the Creeks' central stronghold, destroying their "Holy City," a key site of their military and religious activities. Documents captured in that battle showed that the Creeks had received support from the Spanish in Pensacola. Claiborne advised the War Department: "Seize Pensacola and you disarm the Indians. It is the real heart of the Creek Confederacy."

In March 1814, Jackson captured the Creek stronghold of Horseshoe Bend. This battle broke the Creek resistance, and they asked for peace.

THE BATTLES OF PENSACOLA AND NEW ORLEANS

Next, Jackson captured Pensacola from the Spanish. Meanwhile, the British had taken Ship Island, off the Mississippi coast, and prepared to move against New Orleans. Jackson rushed to its defense. His men, supported by Choctaw warriors, overwhelmingly defeated the British on January 8, 1815. This battle, fought after the treaty ending the war had already been signed in Europe, sent Jackson's popularity soaring and ultimately propelled him to his election as president in 1828.

After the war concluded in 1815, residents of Mississippi began to return home, and the state's population increased. The 1810 census recorded a total of 40,400 people, including both free individuals and enslaved Blacks. By 1816, this number had risen to 75,500, encompassing free Whites, free people of color, and enslaved individuals. With this sudden growth, the prospect of statehood appeared increasingly timely and appropriate.

Recommended Readings

Robert Haynes, *The Mississippi Territory and the Southwest Frontier, 1795–1817* (Lexington: University Press of Kentucky, 2010).

Adam Rothman, *Slave Country: American Expansion and the Origins of the Deep South* (Cambridge, MA: Harvard University Press, 2005).

CHAPTER 6

THE FRONTIER STATE

1817–1840

IN 1817, A PORTION OF THE MISSISSIPPI TERRITORY WAS ADMITTED AS MISSISsippi, the twentieth state in the Union. Only the lower third of the state had been settled by Whites and Blacks. However, only the land close to rivers was being farmed. The Old Natchez District, with 8 percent of the state's land area, comprised 60 percent of its total population and 75 percent of its enslaved Africans.

Frontier Mississippians faced the tasks of establishing towns and schools, building roads, and combating frontier violence. In 1830, the Choctaws were forced to begin moving west. Settlers rushed into the new lands and resented the control of state politics by the Natchez planters.

By 1832, quarrels among different sections of the state prompted the creation of a more democratic constitution. In 1836, new counties were formed in Native American lands. By the following year, the expulsion of the state's Chickasaws began. All of Mississippi was now open to settlement, and in 1837, the stage was set for the full development of a cotton economy based on plantation slavery.

GROWING SECTIONALISM

Most large plantations in the late 1700s were located near the Mississippi River, where crops could easily be shipped to market. By 1800, the state's wealthiest men lived in the Natchez District. For years, these men dominated territorial government.

As new settlers moved into the eastern, backwoods part of the territory, Mobile and Huntsville (in present-day Alabama) grew. Restless and dissatisfied with Natchez's domination, these frontiersmen felt the law would better serve their interests if they had more say in it. On two occasions, in 1803 and 1809, the settlements along the Tombigbee River, north of Mobile, requested that Congress split the expansive territory. Both times, Congress denied these petitions.

TOWARD STATEHOOD

Under the terms of the Georgia settlement of 1802, Mississippi was eligible for statehood once it reached a population of "60,000 free inhabitants," or earlier if Congress deemed it appropriate. By 1816, Congress started considering it timely. At that point, there were nineteen states in the Union, with nine slave states and ten free states. Admitting Mississippi as a slave state would restore the balance of power between slave and free states. But, before Congress could pass the enabling act for statehood, a problem arose: Should the territory be divided? George Poindexter, territorial representative for Mississippi, argued strongly to keep the territory united. Natchez leaders, at first, opposed the division of the territory. Yet, as the population in the eastern river valleys grew, Natchez realized it could not dominate the entire territory. In December 1816, Congress decided in favor of two states.

Backwoodsmen in the eastern half were pleased, because now they would be out from under control of the Natchez aristocracy. Leaders of other Southern states were also pleased, because they were getting a sister slave state now (Mississippi) and the promise of another (Alabama) in the near future; these states would help them prevent Congress from passing laws that could harm slavery.

Congress split the Mississippi Territory along the current boundary between Mississippi and Alabama. The western half promptly began the process of transitioning to statehood. This emerging state comprised of 25,000 White residents, 23,000 enslaved Blacks, a small number of free Black people, and Native Americans.

CONSTITUTIONAL CONVENTION OF 1817

On July 1, 1817, just four months after Mississippi was granted statehood by Congress and President James Madison, a group of delegates was chosen to draft a state constitution. The convention convened in a Methodist church located in Washington, Mississippi, just a short distance from Natchez.

Delegates from the "river" counties dominated the convention; thirty-two of forty-seven hailed from the Old Natchez District. David Holmes from Adams County, who had served as the last governor of the Mississippi Territory, presided over the convention and was poised to become the state's first governor. Every governor between 1817 and the next state constitution in 1832 served as a delegate in the 1817 convention. Thus, the convention constituted a powerful "in-group" of political leaders. For the next fifteen years, the Natchez area continued to dominate state politics.

THE 1817 CONSTITUTION

The constitution drawn up by this convention was the least democratic of any state constitution ratified by a state admitted after the War of 1812. To vote in Mississippi, citizens were required to be White, male, taxpaying property-owners over the age of twenty-one, who had lived in the state for at least one year. Requirements for officeholders were even more stringent. To be a state senator, for example, a citizen had to be at least twenty-six years old and own at least 300 acres of land (or land worth at least $1,000). To serve as governor, a man had to be at least thirty, a resident of Mississippi for at least five years, and the owner of at least 600 acres of land (or land worth at least $2,000.

FRONTIER VIOLENCE IN THE NEW STATE

Early settlers in Mississippi, venturing eastward from the river in small groups, had little impact on the vast and untamed wilderness. Bears were still a common sight, and violence was prevalent, with force often being the only law. Joseph Baldwin described the allure of Mississippi's frontier, noting its record of criminal deeds, including chilling murders, grand bank heists, and widespread exploitation of Indigenous peoples and theft of their lands. This dark history is an indelible part of the state's past. In the early days of statehood, laws were passed to curb the violence that accompanied frontier life. In the early 1820s, Governor George Poindexter devised the Poindexter Code. Many of its laws were as harsh as the crimes they legislated against. Even minor crimes could be punished by death.

Later, Governor Gerard Brandon labeled Mississippi's criminal laws the "Bloody Code." In 1836, the legislature set aside state funds to build a penitentiary where criminals would be rehabilitated and then allowed to rejoin society. Ten years later, with the penitentiary complete, the state began revising its criminal code.

GEORGE POINDEXTER, 1779–1855

George Poindexter was one of Mississippi's most important early leaders. As Mississippi politician and historian John F. H. Claiborne wrote, "The history of his career is, in fact, the history of the Territory and the State, so closely was he connected with everything that occurred."[1]

Poindexter was born in Virginia. At twenty-three, he migrated to Natchez and began to practice law. Two years later he was appointed attorney-general of Mississippi Territory. He cleared the Natchez Trace of the organized robber bands that had terrorized it. From this beginning, he went on to carve out a distinguished career as a judge, territorial representative to Congress, governor, and United States senator. At the Constitutional Convention of 1817, he almost singlehandedly shaped Mississippi's first constitution.

His life was filled with hard times. In 1822, he lost his second wife, his son, and his second race for Congress. Despair, bitterness, and illness followed. For a time, he could not walk, but by 1830 he was well enough to serve in the United States Senate. He served four years as president pro tempore of the Senate. Then, in 1836, he lost his seat to Robert Walker. Disgruntled, Poindexter moved to Kentucky with his third wife. He later came back and practiced law in Jackson, where he died in 1855, an embittered old man.

Claiborne called Poindexter "the ablest man who ever lived in the State." But he was not a "popular" man.[2] Ironically, this man who shaped so much of early Mississippi history has been almost completely forgotten.

TRANSPORTATION

Mississippi had few good roads before 1860. Since river counties dominated the government, towns in the eastern backwoods were seldom connected even by dirt roads. As late as 1854, it took forty hours to travel from Oxford to Jackson.

In 1812 the steamboat *New Orleans* first came to Natchez from Pittsburgh. Three years later, the *Enterprise* steamed up from New Orleans. Now goods could come upriver as well as down. Flat-bottomed steamboats were designed

Figure 6.1. Steamboat loaded with cotton. Detroit Publishing Company photograph collection, Library of Congress Prints and Photographs Division, LC-D4-500913.

to float in shallow water; soon they provided regular service on the Pearl, Yazoo, Tombigbee, and smaller rivers.

In the 1830s Mississippi built railroads. Enslaved Blacks worked for eight years to build the West Feliciana Railroad. It connected Woodville, Mississippi, and St. Francisville, Louisiana, and was the first interstate railroad in America. It carried cotton to river ports to be shipped to market.

THE GROWTH OF TOWNS

With increasing interior settlement, many frontiersmen thought the state capital should be more centrally located. The state legislature appointed a commission to find the most suitable place. The commission finally decided upon Le Fleur's Bluff on the Pearl River.

To honor Andrew Jackson, the capital city took his name. Before the city was built, a plan was designed to make it as convenient and as impressive as possible. Smith Park and the Old Capital Green still remain as evidence of the original plan.

Enslaved Blacks began to build the brick State Capitol in 1822. In that year, the state legislature met for the first time in Jackson in a plain frame building. The new town grew slowly at first because it was not on a major road. Mississippi encouraged settlers to come to Jackson by offering them cheap land. To get this land, a man had only to promise to build "a neat log or frame house, not less than 30 feet in length," by November 1831.

Figure 6.2. The first capitol in Jackson. Courtesy of the Archives and Records Services Division, Mississippi Department of Archives and History.

The Treaty of Dancing Rabbit Creek in 1830 opened much of north Mississippi to settlers. The removal of the Chickasaws seven years later opened the rest. The great land boom was underway.

Towns throughout the state grew as settlers came to Mississippi to settle its newly opened land. In 1830, Robert Walker celebrated the boom: "Already the feet of thousands press upon the borders of this new purchase to pitch their tents in the wilderness. . . . Kentucky's coming, Tennessee coming, Alabama's coming, and they're all coming to join the joyous crowd of Mississippians." In 1833, seventeen "Choctaw Cession" counties were organized, and three years later thirteen counties were set up in the former Chickasaw lands. From 1830 to 1840, Mississippi's population grew enormously, from about 137,000 to 376,000 (including enslaved Blacks).

"THE WIZARD OF MISSISSIPPI"

As with any emerging state, Mississippi's initial leadership primarily consisted of individuals who were new to the area. Entrepreneurs, legal professionals, and investors were among those who migrated to Mississippi in its early days. One such man was Robert Walker, who moved to Natchez from Pennsylvania in 1826. Walker went into law and invested in plantations and slaves. Then, in 1836, he defeated George Poindexter for the United States Senate. "A mere whiffet of a man," he weighed less than 100 pounds. His health was bad and his voice wheezy, but he was full of energy and knowledge.

Walker was always a Jacksonian Democrat. He played a large role in the United States' annexation of Texas. In 1844, he helped nominate James K. Polk for president; in return, President Polk (1845–1849) appointed him Secretary of the Treasury. Walker was the first Mississippian to serve in a president's cabinet. During his administration of the treasury he financed the Mexican War without scandal, earning the nickname "the Wizard of Mississippi." He believed in the expansion of the United States, and after Mexico's defeat he sought to annex the entire country.

In 1857 he faced his toughest job. President James Buchanan (1857–1861) appointed him governor of Kansas Territory. Although Walker was from Mississippi and had been a slaveholder, he was determined to have fair voting in Kansas's referendum on whether the territory (and soon state) would allow slavery. When he learned that pro-slavery forces had stuffed two ballot boxes, he threw out the votes.

Reaction was swift. Southern leaders called him a traitor. Buchanan, a Pennsylvanian who safeguarded the interests of slaveholders, withdrew his support for Walker. Walker then resigned. He now knew that the argument between North and South had split the Democratic Party and threatened the Union. In 1860 he supported Stephen A. Douglas for president, but when Lincoln won he stayed with the Union. His work in Europe during the Civil War helped break down Confederate credit, defeat the South, and end the war.

He is the prime example of someone who began his journey in the early days of Mississippi's frontier and rose to achieve a notable career on the national stage. He died in Washington in 1869.

SECTIONALISM AGAIN

Very different social structures were emerging in different parts of Mississippi. As late as 1830, the plantation system had triumphed only in the Old Natchez District. To the east lay the Piney Woods, with a social structure very different from the river counties. The soil was poor, and settlers worked as herdsmen, lumbermen, and small farmers.

To the north and east, the Loess Hills were being settled and plantations were being built. Finally, separated by 100 miles of Choctaw land, there were counties of rich land—Monroe and Lowndes on the Alabama border.

POLITICS AND SECTIONALISM

As Mississippi grew, it faced a number of challenges. One of these challenges was the inadequate road system in newly developed areas. This made it difficult for people and goods to move around, hindering economic development and growth.

Another challenge was financial instability, caused in part by too few banks. Despite periods of prosperity, Mississippi struggled with economic uncertainty and volatility. This made it difficult for businesses and individuals to plan for the future and invest in long-term growth. The power of the river counties was threatened by the new eastern counties, which tried to be seated in the state legislature. There were quarrels and bitter feelings. The Old Natchez planters and merchants were members of the Whig Party; most of the new Mississippians followed President Andrew Jackson and were members of the Democratic Party.

President Jackson (1829–1837) represented a growing political movement in the United States. His supporters wanted greater participation by the "common man" in politics. They also wanted free public schools. Jackson carried Mississippi by huge margins in 1824 (when he lost), as well as 1828 and 1832 (when he won his two terms in office).

South Carolina passed a nullification ordinance against Congress's Tariff of 1832—meaning it claimed that it did not need to honor any act of Congress it considered unconstitutional. South Carolina was throughout its history known as the most rabidly pro-slavery state, and its slaveholders opposed a tariff that would make Northern goods more expensive to purchase. Some Mississippi

Democrats also supported nullification, but others stood by President Jackson in his standoff with South Carolina over the enforcement of federal law. The Mississippi legislature took no action. A "nullifier" faction developed in Mississippi and joined hands with the Whigs. The two groups had little in common other than their dislike of President Jackson. In several elections, the Whig-Nullifier combination was able to beat the Jacksonian Democrats.

PRESSURES TO AMEND THE CONSTITUTION

The Constitution of 1817 was quickly becoming outdated. Many Mississippians favored a more democratic approach to state government. They wanted to abolish property qualifications for the right to vote or hold office. They also wanted to limit the terms of officeholders, revise the court system so it could better service the expanding territory, and provide seats in the state legislature for new counties.

Finally, Gerard Brandon, Mississippi's first native-born governor, persuaded the legislature to ask the people whether they wanted a new constitution. In August 1831, the public voted "yes." In December, the legislature called for a constitutional convention. Delegates were elected and met in Jackson on September 10, 1832.

A MORE DEMOCRATIC CONSTITUTION

Provisions of the 1832 Constitution were ahead of their time. Under the new constitution, all public officials were to be elected rather than appointed. Property qualifications for voting and office holding were abolished. "Every free White male person of the age of twenty-one years or upwards" who was a citizen of the country and a resident of the state could vote. No longer could people be jailed for debt after they had paid as much as they were able.

TWO MEN SPEAK OUT ABOUT THE 1832 CONSTITUTION

"The 1832 Constitution is an additional stride towards the establishment of pure and democratic constitutions which cannot but excite in every American citizen feelings of both hope and fear."

"I do not think I err materially when I assert that in this state we have too much democracy."

From your understanding of Mississippi at this time, try to determine what region of the state each speaker represents.

EDUCATIONAL DEVELOPMENTS

Before 1868, Mississippi had no formal system of education. Wealthy planters hired tutors for their children and sent their sons abroad or to the North to continue their education, but refused to tax their own massive wealth (held mostly in enslaved Blacks) to finance a school system. There were some public schools during the administration of Governor David Holmes (1817–1820), but most schools were private academies run by ministers.

In 1811, Jefferson College opened in Washington, Mississippi. In 1818, Elizabeth Female Academy, one of the first institutions in the United States to confer degrees on women, was founded in Washington. In 1826, Hampstead Academy, now Mississippi College, opened in Clinton. Today, Mississippi College remains the state's oldest institution of higher education.

Early financial support for public schools came from the federal government through the sale or leasing of public land granted to Mississippi. Franklin Academy, founded in 1821 in Columbus, was perhaps the first school in the state to get such funds.

UNIVERSITY OF MISSISSIPPI

Public higher education in Mississippi began in 1840, when the state legislature allocated funds from the sale of federal lands to establish a state university. After a four-year search, Oxford was selected as the site for the university, and the local community donated a large tract of land. In 1848, the University of Mississippi opened its doors with a faculty of four and an initial enrollment of eighty students. This institution would eventually become known as the University of Mississippi, commonly referred to as "Ole Miss." The nickname "Ole Miss" has its roots in the antebellum South, where enslaved people used the term to address the mistress of the plantation. Today, the university has taken significant steps to distance itself from its Confederate past. It has removed statues, retired its former mascot, Colonel Reb, stopped playing "Dixie" at sports events, and banned Confederate flags from its games. Additionally, it relocated a Confederate statue from the front of the campus to the Confederate cemetery at the back, symbolizing a broader effort to move away from its historical ties to the Confederacy. Each of these actions represents a meaningful step toward creating a more inclusive and forward-looking institution.

Figure 6.3. Historic Provine Chapel at Mississippi College. Historic American Buildings Survey, Library of Congress Prints and Photographs Division, HABS MISS,25-CLINT,1A-.

A PUSH FOR PUBLIC SCHOOLS

In 1844, Governor Albert Gallatin Brown played a key role in significantly promoting public education. He had attended two of Mississippi's finest schools, Jefferson College and Mississippi College. In his successful campaign for governor, Brown pushed for public education for Whites, arguing that the education of a people ensures the safety of its government.

Governor Brown's ideas did not get serious results until 1846, when the state legislature levied a special school tax. However, voters in each area had to accept the tax before it went into effect. In most places the vote failed. Wealthier families continued to send their children to private schools, and only the poor attended the public schools. In rural farming communities with challenging road conditions, it was often difficult to assemble enough students to establish a school. The majority of public schools offered only elementary-level education.

THE SWING TO COTTON

When the United States took control of the Natchez region, tobacco and indigo, previously the major crops, were being replaced by cotton. At times, beef, pork, and corn had also been raised in Mississippi. Then, in 1795, a man from Georgia who had examined Eli Whitney's cotton gin met Daniel Clark, a Natchez planter.

The Georgian described Whitney's gin to Clark, who took a crude sketch of the invention to his enslaved master-mechanic, Barclay. In a short time, Barclay designed and built Mississippi's first cotton gin. Soon the invention was in widespread production in the territory.

Cotton soon became America's leading export. Mississippi produced 20,000 bales of cotton in 1821; nine years later that total had increased to 100,000 bales. In 1839, Mississippi produced 387,000 bales, the largest crop in the nation.

THE PLANTATION ECONOMY

The expansion of the cotton economy caused many Mississippians to think that one had only to grow cotton to get rich. Land and enslaved Blacks became an urgent desire. Joseph Holt Ingraham observed in 1835: "As soon as the young lawyer acquires sufficient funds to purchase a few hundred acres of the rich alluvial lands, and a few slaves, he quits his profession at once, and turns cotton planter."

"You have to spend money to make money," and cotton plantations required a large investment. When Mississippi first started opening up new areas for people to live, one could easily get land there. Later on, as more people wanted the best land, it became necessary to make a significant initial payment to acquire it. Enslaved Blacks were also expensive. Planters would borrow money or secure items on credit. Many planters mortgaged their crops several years in advance and hoped for a good year with large profits to pay back their debts.

THE PANIC OF 1837

In the 1830s, Mississippi's prosperity and the new land open for settlement encouraged planters to overextend themselves. To service the expanding state and its explosive demand for credit, the number of banks in Mississippi increased from five in 1836 to twenty-four two years later. These banks issued far more paper money than they could back with gold or silver.

In 1836, President Andrew Jackson reversed the "easy money" policies of his administration and issued the Specie Circular. This order required gold or silver for the purchase of government lands. Planters and farmers who had bought land had only paper money. When their land payments came due, they had no gold or silver and simply could not pay. Many of the new banks closed, and thousands of settlers were ruined.

Many farmers packed up their clothes, evaded their creditors, and moved west. Texas had recently separated from Mexico, and it appeared to be the new "land of opportunity." "G.T.T." (Gone to Texas) signs on doorways were familiar sights throughout the Old Southwest.

PROBLEMS ON THE HORIZON

Other threatening clouds were gathering. Within the state, the Loess Hills and Prairies were rapidly being exhausted by repeated cotton crops. In 1857, an experienced geologist wrote that "Mississippi is a new state. It dates its existence only from 1818; and notwithstanding all its fertility, a large part of the state is already exhausted; the state is full of old deserted fields." It seemed as if cotton plantations would provide wealth for only one generation.

Meanwhile, a growing number of Northerners and some Southerners believed that the institution of slavery could not be morally justified. Their attacks on slavery and its defense by slaveholders gradually grew in intensity. Finally, the issue of slavery came to dominate the last decades before the Civil War.

Notes

1. John F. H. Claiborne, *Mississippi as a Province, Territory, and State*, vol. 1 (Jackson: Power & Barksdale, 1880), 360.

2. Claiborne, 429–30.

Recommended Readings

Charles C. Bolton, *Poor Whites of the Antebellum South: Tenants and Laborers in Central North Carolina and Northeast Mississippi* (Durham, NC: Duke University Press, 2004).

Mike Bunn and Clay Williams, *Old Southwest to Old South: Mississippi, 1798–1840* (Jackson: University Press of Mississippi, 2023).

James C. Cobb, *The Most Southern Place on Earth: The Mississippi Delta and the Roots of Regional Identity* (New York: Oxford University Press, 1992).

Nadine Cohodas, *The Band Played Dixie: Race and the Liberal Conscience at Ole Miss* (New York: Free Press, 1997).

John Hebron Moore, *The Emergence of the Cotton Kingdom in the Old Southwest: Mississippi, 1770–1860* (Baton Rouge: Louisiana State University Press, 1988).

Adam Rothman, *Slave Country: American Expansion and the Origins of the Deep South* (Cambridge, MA: Harvard University Press, 2005).

CHAPTER 7

THE ROAD TO CONFLICT

1830–1860

THE DECADES BEFORE THE CIVIL WAR WERE TROUBLED TIMES FOR MISSISSIPPI and the South. National events seemed to threaten the South's power in the Union. Northern abolitionists, Black and White, increased their attacks on slavery, and White Mississippians reacted by defending slavery more and more. During the 1840s and 1850s, arguments over the expansion of slavery divided the nation. John Brown's 1859 raid on the federal armory at Harpers Ferry, an attempt to incite a slave revolt, along with Abraham Lincoln's election as president in 1860, brought the sectional tensions in the United States to a breaking point. These events led to the secession of several Southern states, and then the decision of the Union to resist secession, setting the stage for the Civil War.

Meanwhile, everyday life revolved mainly around "King Cotton." Most Whites worked on small farms or in small towns; most Blacks were enslaved on large plantations. Under the slavery system, social distinctions were clear-cut. At one end of the scale were the wealthy planters; next came merchants, independent farmers, poor Whites, the few remaining Native Americans, free Blacks, town slaves, house slaves, and—at the bottom of the scale—the field slaves. Enslaved Blacks maintained what dignity and family life they could within such a system; so did poor Whites. Political and social events were dominated by the planter elite, an elite that eventually would lead the state into secession and war.

WHERE WAS SLAVERY MOST WIDESPREAD?

Planters who were wealthy enough to hold large numbers of enslaved Blacks usually were also able to acquire the rich lands of the River Lowlands and the Loess Hills. Small farmers, who were in the majority, had to settle for the poorer soil.

Most Whites held no slaves at all. Of those who were slaveholders, the majority held only a few. Planters who owned thirty or more people constituted about 5 percent of the White population. Thus, the stereotype of an Old South filled with

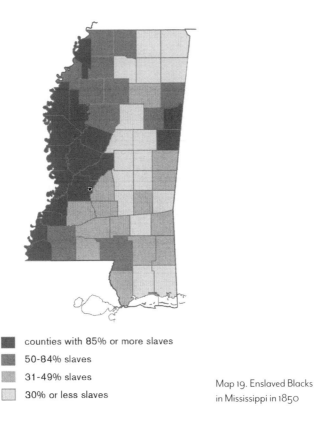

- ■ counties with 85% or more slaves
- ■ 50-84% slaves
- ▦ 31-49% slaves
- ☐ 30% or less slaves

Map 19. Enslaved Blacks in Mississippi in 1850

huge, gracious plantations on which White families relaxed with tall drinks and beautiful music is not true. It was true that the planters dominated state politics, but they were only a small portion of White Mississippi.

At the same time, living and working on big plantation farms where slavery was practiced was what most Black people experienced. Although some worked on smaller farms owned by independent farmers, most were part of bigger groups. The numbers on plantations usually ranged from ten to five hundred people.

THREE KINDS OF ENSLAVED BLACKS

In Mississippi, there were three different classes of people in bondage: town slaves, house slaves, and field slaves. Only a small percentage of the slave population lived in towns. Because town life was more varied than life on the farm, enslaved Blacks had the opportunity to develop more skills. They worked as mechanics, wagoners, domestic servants, blacksmiths, carpenters, and builders. In large towns like Natchez and Jackson, enslaved Blacks worked in factories and mills. Some Blacks helped build the transportation system. In the 1830s, Blacks were often bought to build railroads. They also maintained steamboats and worked as firemen and dockhands.

Figure 7.1. Quarters for town slaves still stand in Natchez and have been refurbished as a bed and breakfast. Historic American Buildings Survey, Library of Congress Prints and Photographs Division, HABS MISS,1-NATCH.V,10-.

Figure 7.2. Picking cotton on a large plantation. From *Mississippi-Fahrten* [*Travels on the Lower Mississippi, 1879–1880*] by Ernst von Hesse-Wartegg.

House slaves, who worked as cooks, seamstresses, maids, nurses, gardeners, and coachmen, were more likely to be mulattoes or biracial. Many enslaved women were coerced or forced into sexual relationships with White men, resulting in biracial offspring. Their living conditions were considered better than those of field slaves. Enslaved Blacks working in households typically ate the same food as their masters, accompanied White families on travels, sometimes emulated their manners, and were occasionally taught to read and write, despite its illegality. Consequently, class distinctions emerged between house slaves and field slaves.

For men and women who toiled in the fields, the year centered around the cotton crop. Field slaves worked from sunrise to sunset. Before dawn broke, a bell echoed through the quarters, waking the slaves for the day's work. At daylight, they began working in the fields, stopping only at midday to eat lunch and rest. Those too old or too sick to work did light jobs and took care of the young enslaved children. Children helped the house servants or worked alongside their parents in the fields.

During the off-season, enslaved Blacks took the crop to market, repaired fences, and cleared new ground. Their owners often hired them out as craftsmen, railroad workers, and woodcutters.

THE "ART" OF THE OVERSEER

On many plantations, enslaved Blacks worked under the supervision of White overseers and Black drivers, who were given authority by the slave masters. The overseer had a great deal of power, especially on plantations of absentee landlords. He sent the enslaved Blacks to the fields, watched their labor, inspected their quarters, and kept the records.

Since the job of the overseer depended on the amount of cotton he produced for his employer, his primary concern was to make the enslaved Blacks work hard. It was his responsibility to keep them in good condition so they could work. Many overseers resorted to violence. Joe Clinton, an enslaved African born in Panola County, commented that his master was a "good, kind man," but his overseer, Marcus Brown, "was terrible, cruel, and mean and would beat n-----s up every chance he git."

Black drivers were sometimes used as foremen to supervise field work. Frederick Law Olmsted, a Northern traveler, described a field with thirty or forty enslaved Blacks tilling the field under a driver. The driver walked among his fellow slaves, wielding a whip, occasionally letting it fall on one of the workers, continually shouting to them, "Shove your hoe, there. Shove your hoe!" Some drivers acted more as go-betweens, helping the master get his cotton produced, but also helping the field hands.

DO TERMS MAKE A DIFFERENCE?

This book gives far more attention to enslaved persons and their points of view than any other Mississippi history book. However, we often called them "slaves." Around 2010, some tour guides questioned this term: "When people are referred to as slaves, it is dehumanizing," said one. "Enslaved persons" became preferred.

What do you think?

We agree and changed some of our uses of "slaves."

A further controversy arose about "freedom seekers," preferred by some as "fugitive slaves." Here we don't agree. Of course, fugitives *did* seek freedom, but they also *were* fugitives under the law of the time, so we retain that term. But maybe, by 2030, our usage will look hopelessly out of date.

CRUEL TREATMENT

If a slaveholder or overseer believed that an enslaved Black person had committed a wrongdoing, they often administered severe punishment, typically in the form of a beating or lashes from a whip. One enslaved Black man recalled a whipping that he witnessed:

> I saw Old Master get mad at Truman, and he buckled him down across a barrel and whipped him till he cut the blood out of him, and then he rubbed salt and pepper in the raw places. It looked like Truman would die, it hurt so bad.

This harsh treatment had other aims. It required them to be submissive, it made them fear White men, and it attempted to make them feel that Whites were "naturally" superior to Blacks.

Laws existed against deliberately killing or crippling enslaved Blacks; nevertheless, slaveholders could punish them in any manner they desired. Enslaved Blacks were rarely killed, however; they were too valuable. In 1845, a good field slave was valued at $700. Today, that would be roughly equivalent to $58,000. By 1850, the price had increased to $1,000, which in today's terms would be around $83,000. The price continued to rise, reaching $1,800 in 1860. These figures underscore the escalating value of an enslaved field worker during this time, indicative of the growing demand for slave labor in the United States in the years leading up to the Civil War.

LIVING CONDITIONS OF THE ENSLAVED BLACKS

The planter provided food, housing, and clothing. The enslaved Black's diet had little variety. One writer noted that "bacon, corn-bread, and coffee invariably appeared at every meal." A peck of meal and about three pounds of meat (usually pork) were supplied weekly to each slave family. Enslaved Blacks usually ate dinner in the fields, either carried with them in a bucket or delivered to the fields at noon. The slave "quarters" usually consisted of crude huts with dirt floors. A visitor to a plantation in North Mississippi noted that: "[T]he Negro cabins were small, dilapidated, and dingy; the walls were not chinked, and there were no windows. There were spaces of several inches between the logs, through which there was clear vision. Everything within the cabins was colored black by smoke." Overcrowding was the rule. On the plantation of George T. McGehee of Wilkinson County, there were eleven houses for seventy-three enslaved Blacks. On the other hand, E. J. McGehee furnished twenty houses for his forty-five enslaved Blacks.

FAMILY LIFE

Some slaveholders allowed their enslaved Blacks to live in fairly stable families. Others did not. The owners had final authority over the slave family, and the enslaved father had no legal rights regarding his wife and children. At times, families would be broken up and the members sold separately to different buyers—sometimes in different states. However, young children, especially, were not usually separated from their mother. Thus the woman had to play the main role in holding the family together.

Many enslaved children were not allowed to have a carefree childhood. A former slave in Calhoun County was eleven years old when the Civil War began. She described her childhood up to that time:

> They didn't give us nothing much to eat. There was a trough out in the yard where they poured in mush and milk and us children and the dogs would all crowd 'round it and eat together. We children had homemade wooden paddles to eat with, and we sure had to be in a hurry about it because the dogs would get it all if we didn't. . . . The overseer sent us to the field every morning by 4:00 o'clock and we stayed till after dark. By the time cotton was weighed up and supper cooked and eaten, it was [often] midnight.

CHAPTER 7.

RESISTANCE

Considering the conditions of the enslaved, it is not surprising that very few were content. Many found ways to express their anger. They might protest through careless work, theft, or deliberate destruction of the master's property. When slaves stole, the enslavers concluded that all Blacks were thieves. They failed to see that stealing was a subtle form of resistance. Some enslaved Blacks also protested their long work hours with no pay by pretending to be ill, and Whites concluded Blacks were lazy—a highly ironic conclusion for Whites to reach given that they forced other humans to perform tasks they themselves refused to do.

Some enslaved Blacks ran away. Most of them either returned or were captured. Slaveholders and sheriffs hired Whites as "patrollers"; they could seize any Blacks found away from his plantation without a pass. Few enslaved Blacks escaped from Mississippi as compared with states like Virginia.

Sometimes resistance was overt and violent. A former slave told of an old woman who became angry when she was reprimanded by an overseer. She took her hoe and "chopped this man to a bloody death." The Coffeeville *Intelligence* reported that some enslaved workers banded together and took over a barn for two days to protest the overseer's whipping of a fellow slave.

Usually, enslaved Blacks were more secretive in their method of resistance. They often sang in the fields, and their masters thought that their spirited songs meant they were happy. But some of these songs were codes, and the Whites could not understand their real meaning.

Blacks used the church as another means of resisting their enslavement. Church meetings were among the few occasions when many Black people could get together without alarming Whites. Consequently, a church service could disguise a political discussion or the sharing of sensitive information, even when Whites were present. Again, codes and double meanings deceived the enemy. In the midst of the horrifying conditions of slavery, religion provided a glimmer of hope and a sense of comfort.

RESTRICTIONS ON ENSLAVED BLACKS

The White population had deep-rooted fears of mass rebellion. In 1835, rumors near Jackson caused a complete mobilization of the White community to meet the real or imaginary threat. Henry Foote, later to be governor of Mississippi, described the scene: "In the town of Clinton, in Hinds County, where I then resided, the panic awakened was so great that night after night, the [White] women and children of the place were assembled at a central position, where they remained till daylight, while the male citizens moved in armed squads over the settlement, in order to meet the earliest approach of the incendiary forces, who were expected confidently to come to our midst from the direction of Madison County."

From 1826 to 1860, at least four slave uprisings were attempted in Mississippi, though none was successful. Whites responded with tighter controls. Some of the most common restrictions were:

1. Enslaved Blacks were not permitted to learn to read or write. White persons who taught them were punished.
2. Enslaved Blacks must have a pass to leave the plantation.
3. Enslaved Blacks could have no social contact with free Blacks or with other Whites who worked on the plantation.
4. Enslaved Blacks could not defend themselves against Whites and could not testify against them in court.
5. Enslaved Blacks could not be legally married.

FREE BLACKS

According to the 1830 census, there were only 519 free Blacks in Mississippi. Their position was insecure. Whites worried especially about them and felt they might influence other enslaved Blacks to try to win their freedom. Therefore, free Blacks were not really free, but were increasingly restricted.

Free Blacks could not act as ministers or work under printers. They could be arrested at any time unless they carried with them a certificate of freedom. They were severely punished for any act or word of aggression toward Whites. They could not buy or sell whiskey or own firearms or grocery stores. Free Blacks could never testify in court against Whites; if found guilty of minor offenses, they were whipped as slaves would have been.

THE BARBER OF NATCHEZ

William Johnson, a free Black in Natchez, was an exceptional man. The son of a Black woman and a White man, Johnson regularly did business with Whites and became quite wealthy. He owned over 1,000 acres of land and eight enslaved Blacks and operated three barber shops. In 1851, Johnson was murdered by a White man. His murderer was never convicted because the only witnesses—Blacks—could not testify in court against a White.

CHAPTER 7.

BETWEEN TWO WORLDS: FROM MISSISSIPPI TO AFRICA

The Mississippi Colonization Society, founded by White enslavers, aligned with the broader American colonization movement in advocating for the "repatriation" (meaning returning to one's homeland) of formerly enslaved people to Africa. Many enslavers, citing Christian principles, supported this effort by linking emancipation to emigration, while others wanted to get rid of the "threat" of free Blacks in Mississippi. Isaac Ross, who owned Prospect Hill Plantation near Port Gibson, Mississippi, made an unusual provision in his 1836 will. After his daughter Margaret Reed's death, his plantation would be sold to fund his enslaved workers' voluntary emigration to Liberia—a destination chosen because Mississippi's 1822 Slave Code prohibited manumission within the state.

When Margaret died, the Ross family challenged the will, arguing the emigration would violate the Slave Code. However, in *Ross v. Vertner* (1840), the state Supreme Court ruled that the law did not apply to emancipation outside Mississippi. The will's provisions were finally fulfilled when 272 formerly enslaved people from Prospect Hill sailed to Liberia. There they established a settlement named after their Mississippi home, Prospect Hill.

WOMAN'S PLACE

The rights of White women in the Old South were also limited. Especially in the upper class, girls were taught to be gentle, graceful, and submissive. A Mississippi wife, after criticizing her husband, had second thoughts: "I have no right to say a word; he earns the money. I make nothing and have no right to anything but to receive thankfully what is given me." According to the myth of Southern White womanhood, upper-class women lived a life of ease. A visitor to a plantation near Yazoo City in 1858 reported: "Besides reading and the light work of the needle, our ladies gave their time to various pleasures—visiting and receiving visits, music, vocal and instrumental, the dance, cards, and tete-a-tete." But this situation was the exception, not the rule. Most Mississippi White women married early (usually in their teens), had many children, and stayed home to work. Historian Anne Firor Scott writes: "Fine ladies thought nothing of supervising hog butchering on the first cold days in fall, or of drying fruits and vegetables for the winter. They made their own yeast, lard, and soap, set their own hens, and were expected to be able to make with equal skill a rough dress for a slave or a ball gown for themselves."[1]

The wife of a small farmer had to work still harder, for she did more things with her hands. She worked alongside her husband and children in fields, in addition to doing the housework.

Figure 7.3. This statue in front of the Capitol shows the influence of the myth of White womanhood. Courtesy of the Archives and Records Services Division, Mississippi Department of Archives and History.

White men made fun of the *idea* of women voting or speaking in public. The women's rights movement did not get far in prewar Mississippi. Nevertheless, important gains were made. In 1831, Mississippi College granted degrees to two women and became perhaps the first coeducational college in America to do so. Eight years later, Mississippi became the first state to give women the right to own property separately from their husbands. This law came from a case involving Betsy Love, a Chickasaw woman who had married John Allen, a White man. His creditors sued to get her property in order to pay off his debts. The Mississippi Supreme Court ruled that since they had married under Chickasaw law, and Chickasaw law recognized the property rights of women, Mrs. Allen did not have to pay. The legislature then enacted this principle into Mississippi law.

By 1860 women were becoming discontented with their assigned role in Southern society. But the big change would come with war, defeat, and Reconstruction. Never again would the place of Southern White women be the same.

PLANTER LIFESTYLE

Numerous plantations were basic farms where slaves were continuously working to clear the land and expand the fields. Even by 1860, much of northern Mississippi had been settled for less than twenty years. Frontier conditions still existed; even wealthy planters lived in log houses.

At the top of the scale of plantations, however, stood impressive estates with hundreds of acres, large mansions, and fifty to 500 slaves. These estates were practically worlds within themselves. Although such plantations were rare, they were the dream of most smaller planters and farmers. After the Civil War, these large plantations became the stereotyped image of the Old South in novels and later in movies.

Today, reminders of this heritage exist in the antebellum mansions in Natchez, Holly Springs, and many other cities and towns. With high columns in front, woodwork and glass from Philadelphia and New York, and furniture and draperies from France and England, these homes remain truly impressive.

LIFESTYLE OF THE AVERAGE WHITE MISSISSIPPIAN

Most White people worked hard and had neither time nor money for the leisurely activities of the very rich. More and more slaveholders hired out their skilled enslaved Black workers. This meant White workers had to compete with cheap labor and could not earn a decent living. The small farmer usually had only his children to help him. Those farmers who enslaved a person or two worked alongside them in the fields. In *A History of the Old South*, Clement Eaton describes the "plain people" who held no or few slaves:

> Most of them lived in log houses of the type called "dog-run cabins," consisting of two rooms united under the same roof but with an open space or "breezeway" between them. The boys and girls slept in the loft under the roof. The furniture was largely handmade; gourds were used for dipping drinking water from the wooden pail.
>
> Everyone worked. According to Monroe Billington: "[H]ousehold activities centered around the huge stone or brick fireplace, where the hardworking yeoman's wife cooked a monotonous diet of pork and cornbread, sweetened by sorghum molasses. The family washing was done outside the home, clothes being boiled in a huge Black pot over an open fire. In addition to cooking, washing and mending, the fanner's wife also raised chickens, tended the family vegetable garden, and even helped in the fields at harvest time. Children were required to do a multitude of household and barnyard chores, including hauling drinking and washing water from a nearby well, spring, or creek."

SLAVERY SEEN AS A "NECESSARY EVIL"

When Mississippi was a colony and a territory, many White Mississippians had felt uneasy about slavery. "Slavery can only be defended perhaps on the principle of expediency," William Dunbar had declared in 1802. "Slavery is condemned by reason and laws of nature," reasoned the Mississippi Supreme Court in 1818. In the same year, George Poindexter, then in Congress, said, "It would be a blessing, could we get rid of the slaves; but the wisest and best men among us have not been able to devise a plan for doing it."

Ten years later, Governor Gerard Brandon pointed out to the Mississippi legislature that poor Whites were also victims of the system, because the rich did not have to depend on them for services. And so the gap between classes widened. As late as 1831, Sergeant S. Prentiss, a Whig lawyer, told his brother: "That slavery is a great evil, there can be no doubt—and it is an unfortunate circumstance that it was ever introduced into this, or any other country. At present, however, it is a necessary evil."

WHITES VIEW SLAVERY AS A "POSITIVE GOOD"

Just five years later, Prentiss introduced the following resolution to the legislature: "Resolved, That the people of the state of Mississippi look upon the institution of domestic slavery, as it exists among them, not as a curse, but a blessing, as the legitimate condition of the African race . . . and we will allow no present change, or hope of future alteration in this matter." In just a few years, White Mississippi had done an about-face. Good cotton prices and the opening of the Native American lands had increased the demand for enslaved Blacks. By 1840, there were more Blacks than Whites in the state. In the 1850s, despite eroding soil, Mississippi agriculture had one of its greatest booms in history. The number of enslaved Blacks in the state increased by another 40 percent. By 1860, Mississippi produced almost one-fourth of the nation's entire cotton crop. Planters had no plans to do away with a system that was making them rich.

Figure 7.4. A renovated dogtrot cabin, with "thru hallway" enclosed, is still a solid home. Courtesy of the Archives and Records Services Division, Mississippi Department of Archives and History.

ABOLITIONISM

Some Whites and many free Blacks had condemned slavery as morally wrong before America became a nation. By the end of the Revolutionary War, most Northern states had freed enslaved individuals. In the early 1800s, some Southern Whites became active abolitionists. By 1827, 106 of the 130 antislavery societies in the nation were in the South.[2]

In 1829, David Walker, a free Black man from North Carolina, issued his *Appeal*, a call to the enslaved to throw off the chains of bondage. In 1831, William Lloyd Garrison in Boston began his crusade against slavery with a weekly journal, *The Liberator*. In the 1840s, the antislavery Liberty Party and then the Free Soil Party entered candidates in local and national elections. Daniel Webster stated: "The subject of slavery has not only attracted attention as a question of politics, but it has struck a far deeper chord. It has stirred up the religious feeling of the country; it has taken hold on the conscience of man." As abolitionism grew, the South became more and more defensive. Suspected abolitionists in Mississippi were kept under observation. Mississippi postmasters seized and destroyed antislavery literature in order to try to keep abolitionist ideas out of the state. In 1836, the Mississippi legislature condemned abolitionism.

THWARTED FREEDOM:
THE LIVINGSTON CONSPIRACY AND ITS AFTERMATH

While the Mississippi Colonization Society advocated for returning formerly enslaved people to Africa, a more direct challenge to slavery emerged in 1835 in Livingston, located in Madison County. A group of White abolitionists allegedly conspired with enslaved people to organize an insurrection against local enslavers. When the plot was discovered, the response was swift and brutal. The enslavers established a committee to investigate and punish those involved. The planned date of the uprising—July 4, symbolically chosen as America's Independence Day—instead became a day of terror. The committee ordered the hanging of several enslaved Black people accused of participating in the plot, followed by the execution of two White conspirators. The violence continued in the days that followed, as the committee's investigations led to more arrests, beatings, and executions. Through torture and coerced confessions, they expanded their net of suspects, resulting in additional deaths of both enslaved people and accused White collaborators. This bloodbath in Livingston demonstrated how Mississippi enslavers would resort to extreme violence to suppress both Black resistance and White abolition efforts, even as they publicly supported more "moderate" approaches like colonization.

THE RIGHTS OF WHITES

When plantation owners felt threatened by ideas of abolitionism and slave revolt, they reacted by taking away the civil rights of Whites. The rights to read whatever one wanted to read, to speak out even if one's statements were unpopular, and even to think unpopular thoughts were threatened. This reaction to White Mississippians who "get out of line" has been a theme in much of Mississippi's past. Defending a racist society meant weakening the state's democracy even further.

RELIGION IS USED TO JUSTIFY SLAVERY

While condemning abolition, White Southerners also created an ideology justifying slavery. They tried to free themselves from the guilt of enslaving their fellow men by telling themselves that enslaved Blacks were not really people at all. Blacks, they said, were inferior, a "lower order" of people, almost like animals. Slavery, according to the slaveholders, was really a blessing for Black people rather than a curse.

In these years, the South was a stronghold of Protestantism. Most White Mississippians were either Methodists or Baptists, with a sprinkling of Presbyterians and Episcopalians. And support for slavery was sought in religion. The Bible "proved," ministers said, that it was "God's will" that Black people be servants. Furthermore, churchgoers claimed slavery brought the benefits of Christianity to "savage, heathen" Blacks.

As time went by, the churches in America began to fall apart over the issue of slavery. In 1838, the Presbyterians split into northern and southern branches. The Methodists and Baptists followed in 1845.

THE DEFENSE OF SLAVERY GROWS STRONGER

Many voices were raised in praise of slavery. It became "unpatriotic" in the South to question the morality of the institution. Undoubtedly, many people who were unsure of their views about slavery were either convinced by these arguments or else kept their mouths shut.

In the eastern half of the state were independent small farmers who did not own Blacks. They did not always agree with the slaveholders' defense of slavery. Sectional disputes, which had begun while Mississippi was a territory, continued to influence state politics.

THE NATIONAL BALANCE OF POWER

Just as there was sectionalism within Mississippi, there were feelings of sectionalism in the nation. Since the North had a larger population, it controlled the House of Representatives. White Southerners had felt a need for a balance of power in the Senate for many years. This need was a consideration when Mississippi obtained statehood in 1817.

In 1820, the Missouri Compromise kept the balance of power in the Senate by admitting Missouri as a slave state and Maine as a free state. Its most significant provision kept slavery out of the northern part of the Louisiana Purchase. The extension of slavery into new lands annexed by the United States remained an important issue for years to come. Many Southerners felt the South would become a political minority in the nation if slavery was limited in the territories.

As time passed, Southerners and Northerners argued over other things: the federal funding of roads and canals, national banks, the tariff, and the power of the national government. The South was against most of these. Underlying most of the issues was the persistent criticism of slavery. When the South realized it was being outvoted, it began to use "states' rights" as a defense. States' rights was the ideology the balance of power between the federal government and the states should be maintained in favor of the states. The defense of slavery was usually dressed up in this ideology. In many cases, however, slaveholders displayed their true interests when they demanded a much stronger national government if it meant safeguarding slavery. For instance, Southern lawmakers successfully prevailed upon the US Navy to help the country seek out new potential territory in the Caribbean and Central America. These lawmakers engineered the passage of the Fugitive Slave Act of 1850, which gave the federal government substantial new powers that violated the "rights" of Northern states not to assist the return of escaped slaves.

MISSISSIPPI, TEXAS, AND MEXICO

In 1844, Albert G. Brown was elected governor of Mississippi. Democrat James K. Polk, a Tennessee slaveholder, was elected president. The national Democratic Party platform emphasized "Manifest Destiny." Many Americans believed that it was the United States' destiny to extend from the Atlantic to the Pacific.

After Texas won its independence from Mexico in 1836, it asked for admission to the United States. Abolitionists, however, were not in favor of annexing the Republic of Texas. They feared it might be divided into several slave states, upsetting the balance of power. Most Southerners hoped that Texas would enter the Union. After bitter argument, Texas became a state in 1845.

One year later, a border dispute between the United States and Mexico flared into war. Mississippi slaveholders hoped the United States would win more territory, from which new slave states could be carved. When President Polk asked the state for one regiment of troops to fight in Texas, Mississippi sent two. Jefferson Davis served as an officer and developed a new "V-formation" battle line. John A. Quitman served in the battles of Monterrey and Mexico City. He became military governor of Mexico City and later governor of Mississippi.

At the end of the war, the United States took land from Mexico extending to the Pacific Ocean. Southerners received the space they had desired, although most of it was unfit for plantations. But the new land only increased the tension between North and South over the expansion of slavery.

SLAVERY IN THE WEST

The showdown came in 1850, not over slavery itself, but over its extension into the new territories. The North asked that slavery be prohibited from any new state. Southerners wanted slavery spread to all new states.

When gold was discovered in California in 1848, the rush was on. In one year, there were enough settlers on the West Coast to apply for statehood. Most of them wanted California to enter the Union as a free state.

THE COMPROMISE OF 1850

Congress worked out the Compromise of 1850, a final attempt to please both North and South. It allowed California to enter as a free state. This upset the free/slave balance in the Senate. It set the boundaries of Texas where they are today, and paid Texas $10,000,000 to give up its claim to New Mexico. All new territories in the West were to decide for themselves whether they would be free or slave. The slave trade in the District of Columbia, but not slavery itself, was ended. A severe fugitive slave law was passed that provided for the return of runaway slaves even if they escaped to free states.

Some Southerners, often called "Fire-eaters," had become so passionate in their defense of slavery that they could accept no compromise. They had developed an ideology that said that slavery was good, and they sincerely believed it. Slavery, they believed, was protected by the Constitution. Legislation regarding slavery was a matter for the states, not Congress. Congress, they argued, had no right to abolish the slave trade in the nation's capital.

SLAVERY AND THE LAW

Imagine that you are living in Cairo, Illinois, in 1851. A fugitive slave, escaped from his owner in Mississippi, has made his way north along the river. He knocks on your door, asking for food and help. Would you help him? Remember that according to the law, you must turn him into the police, who would return him to his enslaver. Should you obey this law? Should all laws be obeyed, no matter what they say?

MISSISSIPPI CONSIDERS SECESSION

In 1834, Mississippians at a Democratic convention had declared: "A constitutional right to secession from the Union, on the part of a single state, is utterly unsanctioned by the Constitution, which was framed to establish, not to destroy, the Union." Yet fifteen years later, a state convention declared itself in favor of secession as a "last resort."

The people of the state were divided. Some favored remaining in the Union. Others agreed with former Governor Brown, now a United States congressman, who said in Jackson, "So help me God, I am for resistance to the Union and my advice to you is . . . pray to God and keep your powder dry."

Governor John A. Quitman asked the legislature to call a convention of slave states to meet in Nashville, Tennessee, in June 1850, to plan a course of action. Fire-eaters wanted the South to secede, but they were outvoted. Most White Southerners wanted to stay in the Union.

THE DEMOCRATS SPLIT

Jefferson Davis and Henry Foote, both Democrats, represented Mississippi in the Senate in 1850. They disagreed on states' rights. Davis felt the federal government had no right to force states to change their policies. To him, the United States was a confederation of independent states that had agreed to form a national government.

Foote, on the other hand, was a Unionist. He believed that Mississippi was a creation of the United States and should remain part of the Union. All of Mississippi's congressmen except Foote opposed the Compromise of 1850. The Fire-eaters, including Davis and Governor John A. Quitman, criticized Foote's position and demanded his resignation. Foote did resign, but he did so in order to bring the question to the people. He returned to Mississippi and ran for governor in 1851 against Quitman.

THE 1851 RACE FOR GOVERNOR

It was a hot summer. "Mississippi was in a blaze from east to west, and from north to south." The contest for governor in 1851 reflected the split in the Democratic Party. Those who favored secession were known as States' Rights Democrats. Their candidate was Quitman. Those who opposed secession were called Unionist Democrats; they supported Foote.

Fearing defeat, Quitman withdrew from the race, and the States' Rights Democrats nominated Jefferson Davis in his place. Davis resigned his Senate seat to return to Mississippi to campaign. Foote won, but by only 999 votes. Mississippi would remain in the Union for the present. However, as time passed, the states' rights movement gained strength.

HENRY S. FOOTE, UNIONIST

Born in Virginia in 1804, Henry S. Foote attended Washington College. In 1827 he moved to Vicksburg, where he began his career in politics and earned a reputation for being the worst shot in the Southwest. An outstanding speaker, Foote was able to "move, thrill, and enthuse vast multitudes of people as could no other orator of his day."

In the 1851 gubernatorial race, he announced that "he stood where Jackson stood, in '31 and '33, with the whole Democratic party, in opposing nullification and secession." For the next ten years he fought to preserve the Union. In 1854, when it became clear that the Fire-eaters would control Mississippi, he went to California to continue his battle for a Union undivided. Four years later he returned to Mississippi and urged his fellow Democrats to unite in support of Stephen A. Douglas in the 1860 presidential election. He felt that Douglas was the last hope for the United States to remain united. But his efforts were in vain.

During the emotional period after John Brown's raid on Harpers Ferry, when mob violence often ruled, Henry Foote was a champion of human rights. He was the prosecuting attorney of a White man named Hardwick who killed a Black man by lashing him to death. Foote claimed Hardwick "would certainly have been hanged if the victim of his atrocity had been a White man," but he was acquitted. Disappointed, Foote wrote, "When will men learn that perfect justice and humanity constitute the wisest policy of the fortunate and the powerful of this world?"

With the outbreak of the Civil War a year later, Foote could no longer choose both the South and the Union. He finally decided to support the South. In 1861, he represented Tennessee in the Confederate House of Representatives.

When the war was over, he became a voice of optimism. The South, he believed, "will, indeed, be far better off in time to come without slavery than with it." Although he believed that gradual emancipation would have been better than the program adopted, he was in favor of the Thirteenth, Fourteenth, and Fifteenth Amendments to the Constitution. He died shortly after the end of Reconstruction, in 1880.

NATIONAL TENSIONS GROW

The Compromise of 1850 had not solved the issue of slavery and its westward expansion. In 1852, Harriet Beecher Stowe published *Uncle Tom's Cabin*, one of the most effective pieces of antislavery literature ever written. Her story of heartbreak due to slavery sold more than 300,000 copies in its first year.

In 1854, Congress passed the Kansas-Nebraska Act, organizing the territories of Kansas and Nebraska. Since both territories were above the Missouri Compromise line, slavery had been prohibited there. The author of the bill, Stephen A. Douglas of Illinois, suggested that residents of the territories could decide for themselves if they wanted slavery. His proposal was called popular sovereignty. The White South liked the idea, and slaveholders moved into Kansas. But so did free Northerners. A miniature civil war broke out in the territory.

By 1854 the Whig Party was dead, destroyed by arguments over slavery, the Compromise of 1850, and the Kansas-Nebraska Act. Southern Whigs abandoned the party and went over to the Southern wing of the Democratic Party. A new party, with its power in the North and West, was formed. It was called the Republican Party and had as its central objective the prevention of the spread of slavery into the territories. Many Republicans wanted to abolish slavery altogether. Although the Republican candidate for president in 1856, John C. Fremont, was not elected, Southerners became alarmed at the idea of a Republican president in the White House.

Meanwhile, the Supreme Court, dominated by slaveholding Southerners, muddied the national waters. In its 1857 *Dred Scott* decision, the Court ruled that Blacks could never be citizens and therefore could not sue in court. The Court also said that slaveholders could take their property, including enslaved Blacks, into the territories. The *Dred Scott* decision pleased the South because now all the territories were open to slavery. Many Northerners were outraged because the Court had nullified the Compromise of 1850.

However, the South knew that the new territories in the West would eventually ask to enter the Union as free states. Slaveholders hoped that the federal government would protect slavery in these western lands, even if the people there objected. The North opposed this notion.

HARPERS FERRY

On October 16, 1859, abolitionist John Brown led an "army" of thirteen White and five Black men to take a mountain fortress in Virginia. He planned to set up a base from which he could make raids to free enslaved Blacks nearby. The raid, which lasted only thirty-six hours, ended in failure. Brown, along with his men who survived the raid, was captured. He was later hanged for treason.

The news spread rapidly. A Vicksburg paper announced that Harpers Ferry had been seized and that the town was now "in possession of 600 to 700 Whites and Blacks." The incoming Fire-eater governor, John J. Pettus, told Mississippi in December 1859, "The scene at Harpers Ferry is not the end, but in my opinion only the beginning of the end of the conflict." He warned Mississippians to prepare for battle.

MISSISSIPPI IS ALARMED

In pre–Civil War Mississippi, newspapers stoked White fears by constantly reporting on alleged slave resistance and abolitionist threats. When real violence occurred, like an overseer's killing in Sunflower County or an enslaver's death reported in the *Natchez Daily Courier*, papers like the *Jackson Mississippian* often blamed White abolitionists for inciting unrest.

This paranoia sparked widespread violence. Northern visitors suspected of abolitionist sympathies faced brutal treatment—in Lexington, vigilantes tarred and feathered an Ohio abolitionist until he fled, while another man spent 103 days on a chain gang for supporting racial equality. The Second Creek incident near Natchez in 1861 proved the deadliest, when enslavers formed a "vigilance committee" claiming to fear a slave uprising coordinated with Union forces. Their campaign of terror led to the execution of three dozen enslaved people within weeks, with deaths reportedly reaching 200 over two years.

Lafayette County responded with harsh new laws: strict patrols in slave quarters, a 10:00 p.m. curfew, mandatory written permission to leave plantations, and restrictions on entering towns at night or Sundays. Free Black residents faced even harsher treatment—in December 1859, the Mississippi Legislature demanded their expulsion from the state by July 1860, institutionalizing the campaign to crush any resistance to White supremacy.

THE PRESIDENTIAL ELECTION OF 1860

Fears of White Mississippians were at their peak as the presidential election approached. The Republican Party chose Abraham Lincoln of Illinois as their candidate. He ran on a platform restricting enslaved Blacks to the slave states. The Democratic Party met in Charleston, South Carolina. Slaveholders wanted a platform plank declaring that neither Congress nor the territories themselves could abolish slavery or restrict the right to enslave people in the western lands. Northern Democrats wanted popular sovereignty for the territories. When it became clear that the convention would not vote for the Southern position, the delegates from eight Southern states walked out.

Both wings of the Democratic Party then met independently in Baltimore. The national party nominated Douglas as its candidate. The Southerners chose John C. Breckinridge of Kentucky. Meanwhile a new party, the Constitutional Union Party, nominated John Bell of Tennessee. Its platform emphasized national solidarity and opposed secession.

With the Democrats split, Republicans felt certain of victory. Some Southerners threatened to secede from the Union if Lincoln won. When the votes were counted, the Republican ticket had swept the North and West, winning the election. Douglas carried only Missouri. Bell won most of the border states; Breckinridge carried the Deep South, Delaware, and Maryland.

All eyes were now on the South. In 1851 it had not seceded. This time, Southerners had promised to do so. Would they keep their promise?

Notes

1. Anne Firor Scott, *The Southern Lady: From Pedestal to Politics, 1830–1930* (Chicago: University of Chicago Press, 1970), 31.

2. Gordon E. Finnie, "The Antislavery Movement in the Upper South Before 1840," *Journal of Southern History* 35, no. 3 (August 1969): 319–42.

Recommended Readings

S. Charles Bolton, *Fugitivism: Escaping Slavery in the Lower Mississippi Valley, 1820–1860* (Fayetteville: University of Arkansas Press, 2019).

Walter Johnson, *River of Dark Dreams: Slavery and Empire in the Cotton Kingdom* (Cambridge, MA: Harvard University Press, 2013).

Winthrop D. Jordan, *Tumult and Silence at Second Creek: an Inquiry into a Civil War Slave Conspiracy*, rev. ed. (Baton Rouge: Louisiana State University Press, 1996).

Anthony E. Kaye, *Joining Places: Slave Neighborhoods in the Old South* (Chapel Hill: University of North Carolina Press, 2007).

David J. Libby, *Slavery and Frontier Mississippi, 1720–1835* (Jackson: University Press of Mississippi, 2004).

Randy J. Sparks, *Religion in Mississippi* (Jackson: University Press of Mississippi, 2001).

CHAPTER 8

CIVIL WAR

1861–1865

"MISSISSIPPI IS OUT!" CRIED THE *OXFORD INTELLIGENCER* ON JANUARY 9, 1861. "We stop the press, at 8 P.M., to announce that a dispatch has just been received from Jackson, announcing Mississippi has formally seceded from the Union. Oxford is brilliantly lighted, bells are ringing, and guns are being fired. Three cheers for our gallant State."

In 1850, when South Carolina discussed the possibility of secession, Mississippi did not support the idea. However, a decade later, Mississippi joined South Carolina in leaving the Union. One by one, the other Deep South states joined them.

Many Mississippians rejoiced in the news. Scattered groups around the state, however, opposed secession and did not support the new Southern movement. Meanwhile, enslaved Blacks waited to see how the action would affect them.

For some Mississippians, the only question was whether there would be war. Within a few months, the answer came with stunning force as the nation entered the most destructive conflict in its history. And it was in Mississippi, with the fall of Vicksburg, that the turning point of the war came.

THE SECESSION CONVENTION

When the news of Lincoln's election reached Mississippi, Governor John J. Pettus asked the legislature to authorize a state convention to consider secession. The legislature passed an act calling for the election of delegates in December 1860. The convention met on January 7, 1861.

Those who favored immediate secession—mainly the old "Fire-eaters"—entered candidates in every county. Their opposition was divided and caught off guard. "Cooperationists" wanted to secede only after neighboring states had seceded. "Unionists" wanted to stay in the Union and work out differences within it. When the convention opened, the Fire-eaters were in control.

The secession motion, sponsored by L. Q. C. Lamar, came up for a vote on January 9. J. S. Yerger tried to amend the motion to seek a "final adjustment of all difficulties . . . by securing further Constitutional guarantees within the present Union," but he failed. James L. Alcorn tried to secure an amendment that would keep Mississippi in the Union until Alabama, Georgia, Florida, and Louisiana had seceded, but that also failed. The people who didn't want to secede right away tried to get a vote from everyone on it, but the Fire-eaters, a group who strongly supported secession, stopped that from happening.

Finally, the motion to secede came to a vote. Of the ninety-nine delegates voting, eighty-four were for secession, fifteen against. The Ordinance of Secession declared that Mississippi and its citizens had no more obligations of loyalty to the United States. It said that the state "resumed its rights as a free, sovereign, and independent" commonwealth and removed the provision in the Mississippi Constitution requiring an oath of allegiance to the United States.

OPPOSITION TO SECESSION

Because the convention refused to submit the issue to the people, we cannot be sure which sections of the state would have supported the action and which would have split or remained loyal to the Union. It is clear, though, that Mississippi Whites were not solidly behind secession.

Generally, opposition to immediate secession centered in the River Lowlands and the Tennessee Hills. Many small farmers in the Piney Woods also opposed secession, but their representatives in the convention did not.

Opinion also divided along economic or class lines. The very rich and the very poor did not want to fight, the rich because they could gain nothing through war, and the poor because they did not want to die to protect rich men's property. This division increased as the war dragged on, for poor Whites did most of the fighting.

SUPPORT FOR SECESSION

If the convention had allowed Mississippians to vote on secession, however, they would probably have favored it. Most of the people felt that separation could be achieved peacefully, that there would be no war if Mississippi left the Union. Others said that even if war came, it would be a short one.

Many White Southerners had grown up in a romantic militaristic tradition which emphasized preserving "honor" at all times. They saw Northern attacks on slavery as attacks upon their honor, and they felt any measures were justified to defend that honor. Then, too, the years before the convention had seen the rise of "Southern nationalism." Fire-eaters had praised the South as a proud and strong section, and the idea that it might lose in a contest of arms with the North was unthinkable. Some also felt they would be better soldiers than Northerners because their way of life dealt more with the outdoors and guns.

MISSISSIPPI JOINS THE CONFEDERACY

Jefferson Davis, however, held no such illusion. He foresaw a long and bloody war. Twelve days after the Secession Convention passed the Ordinance of Secession, Davis resigned from the United States Senate. He closed his farewell to his colleagues with these words: "If in the pride of power, if in contempt of reason and reliance of force, you say we shall not go, but shall remain as subjects to you, then Gentlemen of the North, a war is to be inaugurated the like of which men have not seen." The Confederacy was formed in February 1861, with Jefferson Davis as its president. In late March, Mississippi ratified the Constitution of the Confederate States of America.

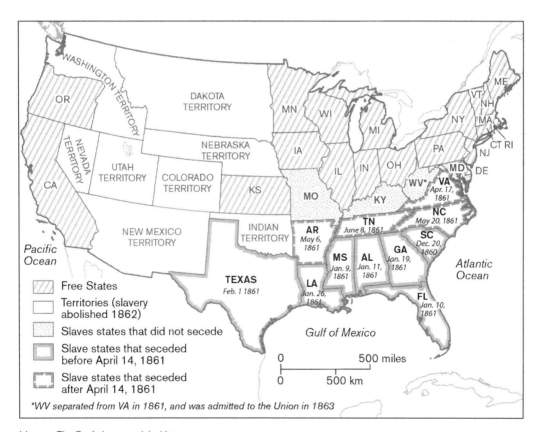

Map 20. The Confederacy and the Union

SOLE PRESIDENT OF THE CONFEDERACY

Jefferson Davis was born in Kentucky and grew up in Woodville, Mississippi. He graduated from the United States Military Academy at West Point and then served seven years on frontier posts in the Midwest. In 1835 he resigned from the army, married, and joined his older brother Joseph as a planter in Warren County. Within three months, however, his bride died of malaria and Davis himself became seriously ill.

In 1845 he won election to Congress and married Varina Howell. In the Mexican War the next year, Davis commanded the First Mississippi Regiment in the Battle of Buena Vista. He returned home a wounded hero and was appointed to the United States Senate by Governor Albert G. Brown. There, he opposed the Compromise of 1850, which, among other provisions, admitted California as a free state, because he wanted the federal government to ensure the extension of slavery to the newly acquired Western territories from Mexico.

In 1853, President Pierce chose Jefferson Davis to be secretary of war, a job he handled with energy and efficiency. Davis then moved back to the Senate. He believed in the right to secede from the Union, but in 1861 he argued against secession, knowing it would mean war.

His days as president of the Confederacy were not happy. As the war went against the South, as the casualties piled up, and as the Union blockade took hold, Davis faced bitter criticism.

When the end came, Davis tried to escape but was captured and put in jail. He thought he would be executed, but in December 1868, he was discharged. In the late 1870s, Jefferson Davis settled at Beauvoir, a large estate near Biloxi. There, he wrote his memoir, *The Rise and Fall of the Confederate Government*, which included a defense of his career.

In his final years he found himself no longer the target of criticism. Now he had become the hero of the "Lost Cause." He was not blamed for losing the war, but was praised as a martyr who had suffered with dignity. In his last public speech in 1888, the eighty-year-old Davis told his audience: "The past is dead; let it bury its dead, its hopes, and its aspirations; before you lies the future—

Figure 8.1. Jefferson Davis. Library of Congress Prints and Photographs Division, LC-USZ62-92005.

a future full of golden promise, a future of expanding national glory, before which all the world shall stand amazed. Let me beseech you to lay aside all bitter sectional feelings, and to take your places in the ranks of those who will bring about a reunited country." In the mind of Jefferson Davis, the Civil War had finally ended.

THE WAR BEGINS

The Civil War began on April 12, 1861, when Confederates began firing upon Union forces inside Fort Sumter, South Carolina. Three months earlier, however, Mississippians had taken over Fort Massachusetts on Ship Island off the Gulf Coast.

On April 19, President Lincoln ordered a blockade of the seceding states, including the Mississippi Gulf Coast. Late in the year, Union forces occupied Ship Island. Gradually the Union blockade became more and more effective.

THE STATE PREPARES FOR WAR

Although Mississippi had declared its independence, the state in reality was not very independent. Agriculture and the slave system on which it rested formed the base of its wealth and power. Secession, however, hurt agriculture. Mississippi planters depended upon outside agencies for financing, transporting, and selling their cotton. War cut off these connections, leaving the state's economy almost helpless.

Mississippi also had to depend upon outside sources for nearly all manufactured goods. The state had almost no industries capable of producing the tools of war. Most of the few it did have were destroyed or captured within the first two years, as Union forces swept over the western part of the state.

The Confederate government did not ask for any men until the fall of 1861, but Mississippians volunteered. Governor Pettus did not have uniforms, weapons, ammunition, or food for the troops. There were times when the training wasn't very good and the rules weren't strictly followed. Many of the elected officers knew little about fighting and leading military units. The leaders of Mississippi desperately needed time to organize. But time they did not have. The strategic importance of the state was too great.

THE IMPORTANCE OF MISSISSIPPI

Mississippi was crucial to the Confederacy for two main reasons. First, its loss would cut the Confederate States in two. Second, the state controlled Mississippi River traffic. Northern generals quickly made plans to regain control of the river.

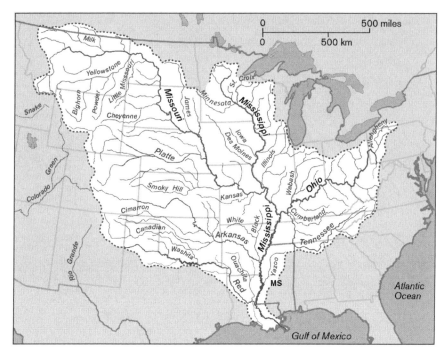

Map 21. Mississippi River Valley

In February 1862, Ulysses S. Grant, who was in charge of some Union troops, took control of Forts Henry and Donelson, posing a threat to the Confederate defenses located along the Mississippi River.

BLOODY SHILOH

In the East, Robert E. Lee and Stonewall Jackson won victory after victory. But in Mississippi, the war did not go well for the Confederacy.

The next objective of the advancing Union armies was the strategic railroad junction of Corinth. Confederate General Albert Sidney Johnston gathered 40,000 men there to stop Grant's advance.

The Union forces moved along the Tennessee River to Pittsburgh Landing, near Shiloh Church in Tennessee, a mere twenty miles from Corinth. There Grant camped to wait for reinforcements.

But on April 3, 1862, Johnston's army marched north from Corinth. Three days later, Johnston launched his main offensive against Grant. In the fierce fighting in the afternoon, Johnston was killed. Night fell with the Union lines pushed back but still intact and with both armies exhausted.

That evening the reinforcements Grant had been expecting arrived. Throwing these fresh troops into the line, Grant launched a dawn attack against the

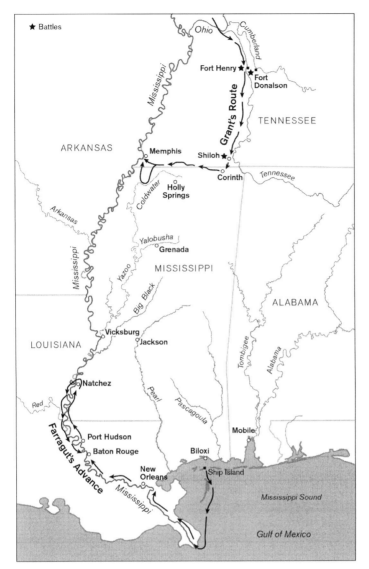

Map 22. Western Campaigns, 1862

still-exhausted Confederate force. The Rebel troops fought well, but late in the afternoon they fell back to Corinth.

By the end of May, 125,000 Union soldiers faced the 52,000 defenders of Corinth, and Southern leaders knew it was merely a matter of time before Corinth fell. To save their army, the Confederates pulled out of Corinth on May 30, 1862, without a fight.

The Battle of Shiloh had brought the war to the northern border of Mississippi. Although neither side could claim a decisive victory, in the long run the South had suffered the greater loss. Albert Johnston was dead, and the Union armies had not been stopped. Grant continued on the road to Vicksburg.

THE WAR IN NORTH MISSISSIPPI

Grant decided to repeat the formula successful in Tennessee by moving down parallel to the Mississippi River but some miles away from it. This would cut off the defenders of Vicksburg and make the fort useless.

In November 1862, he began an overland invasion of Mississippi. He established a huge base at Holly Springs and continued south as far as Water Valley. Meanwhile, General Sherman moved down the river toward Vicksburg.

However, two bold attacks by Confederate cavalry convinced Grant to give up his plan. Nathan Bedford Forrest entered West Tennessee, disrupted telegraph connections between Corinth and Memphis, and attacked Union supply lines.

Earl Van Dorn, a Mississippian, moved north from Grenada, aiming for the huge Union base at Holly Springs. The Union commander panicked and surrendered the base to what he thought was a huge force. Van Dorn destroyed it and escaped.

ATTEMPTS AT VICKSBURG

Grant then tried one idea after another to crack Vicksburg. In the spring of 1863, he tried to send a force down the Coldwater River to the Yazoo River to sneak up on Vicksburg from the rear. However, the rivers were too narrow, and Confederate raiders threatened the gunboats. At the same time, Grant attempted to completely bypass Vicksburg by constructing a canal that would redirect the Mississippi River through a narrow area of land in Louisiana. This too failed.

GRANT GETS BELOW VICKSBURG

Grant finally decided that the boldest course was the only one that would work. He marched his army below Vicksburg on the Louisiana side. He then ordered Admiral David D. Porter to run the guns at Vicksburg at point-blank range with his ironclads and transport barges. On the night of April 16, Porter swept past the batteries with nine ships and a fleet of barges.

With both the army and navy positioned below Vicksburg, the situation appeared to be almost impossible. His men had made it and the ships had come through with little damage, but Grant was cut off from his supplies. The confederates still held Port Hudson, cutting off help from the south. Supplies from the north would have to come past seven miles of enemy guns or be carried over thirty-seven miles of terrible roads. General Sherman wrote his wife: "I tremble for the result. I look upon the whole thing as one of the most hazardous and desperate moves of this or any other war."

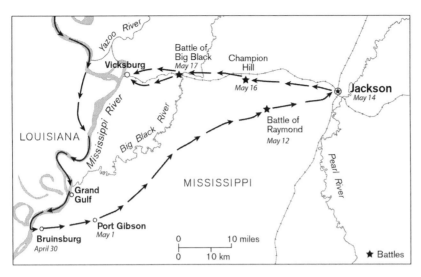

Map 23. The Road to Vicksburg

What neither Sherman nor the Confederates knew was that Grant was abandoning every rule about supply lines and relying on one fact—the richness of the Mississippi land in the early summer. Once below Vicksburg, Grant set up one of the most successful deceptions of the war. He sent Colonel Benjamin H. Grierson on a cavalry raid down from Tennessee through Eastern Mississippi. He also sent Sherman on a short raid north of Vicksburg into the Delta. As a result of these raids, John C. Pemberton, commander of the Confederate forces in Mississippi, never guessed Grant's true purpose until far too late.

THE ROAD TO JACKSON

Using Porter's navy, Grant crossed the Mississippi at Bruinsburg on April 30. His campaign strategy during the next month would be considered one of the greatest in the history of war. Its success established Grant's reputation as a general and led to his later assignment as commander of the Union forces. The end result was significant; Vicksburg's capture and the Union winning at Gettysburg on the same day changed the course of the war.

There were two keys to Grant's success. First, his brilliant tactics always gave him greater numbers than the enemy in each battle, even though the Confederates often had more troops in the general area. In turn, these tactical maneuvers depended upon precise knowledge of the land and of the location of the enemy. This information was provided by formerly enslaved Black individuals who were supportive of Grant as the Union forces advanced northeast from Bruinsburg. Since Pemberton had sent his cavalry north after Grierson, his Confederate forces operated in the dark. Pemberton never knew exactly where Grant was.

Figure 8.2. Porter's fleet sweeps past Vicksburg. Library of Congress Prints and Photographs Division, LC-USZ62-30.

With Black Mississippians guiding them, Union forces took Port Gibson, Grand Gulf, and Raymond. At 5:00 a.m. on May 14, 1863, aware that the primary Confederate force was located west of Clinton and too distant to pose a threat, Grant proceeded to advance toward Jackson.

THE FALL OF JACKSON

A cannon barrage met the Union forces. As Sherman's troops moved into position, according to an observer,

> an old Negro ran up to the men waving his hat and yelling at the top of his voice, "I'se come to tell you-all that the Rebels is left the city, clear done gone. You just go on and you will take the city. . . . "
>
> The Negro offered to guide them and the men agreed to follow. Sure enough he led them right into the unsupported and unguarded rear of the southern artillerymen. Full of joy, the Union soldiers surged ahead, moving through backyards and over fences. They quickly overtook the Confederates, capturing six guns and 52 prisoners. Sherman could now walk into Jackson.

The defenders, under General Joseph Johnston, had fled to Canton. Grant next turned west, defeated Pemberton at Champion's Hill, and forced him to fall back into Vicksburg. On May 18, 1863, the siege of Vicksburg began.

Figure 8.3. Living quarters for Union troops during the siege of Vicksburg. Library of Congress Prints and Photographs Division, LC-USZ62-11875.

THE SIEGE OF VICKSBURG

As both sides settled into their trenches, a routine developed. The men in the trenches kept firing at each other, and the Union army twice tried to breach the defenses with mines. Gradually, Union trenches pushed nearer to the Confederate lines.

Between the lines, soldiers did not spend all their time fighting. They often declared unofficial truces to smoke or share food. These pauses in combat led to hundreds of men from both sides meeting between the lines, discussing the weather, their sweethearts, and the mistakes of their officers. Such fraternization moments offered a brief interlude from the harsh realities of war and highlighted the shared humanity of soldiers on both sides, despite the conflict that divided them.

LIFE WITHIN THE TOWN

During the siege of Vicksburg, the city's residents and defenders found themselves in a critical situation. Essential supplies such as food, water, and medical aid were running low. The constant bombardment from Grant's forces and Porter's fleet forced them to take drastic measures for survival. They had to retreat into basements and caves to shield themselves from the ongoing attacks. Despite the hardships, the inhabitants managed to survive. They resorted to consuming their

Figure 8.4. Cave used for shelter in Vicksburg. Courtesy of the Archives and Records Services Division, Mississippi Department of Archives and History.

own mules, which one defender described as "rough-textured and darker than beef, yet surprisingly tasty, sweet, and succulent." They even continued to publish a newspaper until the very end.

SURRENDER: JULY 4, 1863

As June was coming to a close, the earth displaced by soldiers digging rifle trenches on both sides of the line began to overlap. Pemberton knew that Grant could take Vicksburg at any time with a single charge. He surrendered on July 4. Five days later the Confederate forces at Port Hudson surrendered, opening the Mississippi all the way to New Orleans. President Lincoln could now say, "The father of waters rolls unvexed to the sea."

In victory, Grant was generous. A Confederate officer told of the surrender: "When the Federals first appeared . . . no word of exultation was uttered to irritate the feelings of the prisoners. On the contrary, every sentinel who came upon post brought haversacks filled with provisions, which he would give to some famished Southerner, with the remark, 'Here, Reb, I know you are starved nearly to death.'"

FINAL BATTLES IN MISSISSIPPI

With the end of the Vicksburg campaign, the most important fighting of the war ended for Mississippi. But Joseph Johnston still roamed in the rear. Grant ordered

Sherman to drive Johnston as far away as possible, and Sherman moved east. He captured Jackson on July 17 and burned the city so completely that people called it "Chimneyville."

Sherman raided Meridian in February 1864, and destroyed many stores there, but he did not try to occupy it. After returning to Vicksburg, he was transferred to Tennessee, where he launched his famous "march through Georgia."

Figure 8.5. A Union gun crew fires on Vicksburg. Library of Congress Prints and Photographs Division, LC-USZC4-1754.

Figure 8.6. An interpretation of Jackson, burned. Library of Congress Prints and Photographs Division, LC-USZ62-13205.

In June 1864, Forrest defeated a Union force twice the size of his unit at the Battle of Brice's Crossroads in North Mississippi. Following this battle, Sherman wrote, "There will never be peace in Tennessee until Forrest is dead."

Scattered Confederate guerrilla raids still took place from time to time. Even as thousands of Mississippians continued to battle and lose their lives under the leadership of Johnston and Lee in the east, a semblance of peace prevailed in Mississippi, following the Battle of Vicksburg, notwithstanding Forrest's efforts.

"THE VERY DEVIL"

Nathan Bedford Forrest was born in Tennessee in 1821, but from age thirteen he lived most of his years in Mississippi. He educated himself and was not very literate. He became a horse trader in Hernando, in North Mississippi. Then he operated a brickyard for a while. But he made his huge fortune—more than $1,000,000—dealing in cattle, cotton, land, and enslaved Blacks.

When he was forty years old he enlisted as a private in the Confederate army, but he ended the war a lieutenant general. Sherman called him "the very devil." When Forrest won the Battle of Brice's Crossroads, he was asked for his secret of victory. He is said to have replied, "Git thar fust with the most men!"

On April 12, 1864, Forrest's men attacked Fort Pillow, a Union outpost on the Mississippi River forty miles above Memphis. It was defended by 570 federal troops, of whom slightly less than half were Black. A Black private from Mississippi named Major Williams, who was wounded after the fort surrendered, told a congressional investigation afterward about what happened: "I heard one of the officers say, 'Kill all the n-----s'; another one said, 'No, Forrest says take them and send them to their masters.' Still, they kept on shooting."

After the fort fell, many of its defenders were massacred. According to testimony, some men were held up with their arms outstretched; nails were driven through their palms to the tent frame behind them; they were then shot through the stomach or burned. There is little evidence that Forrest ordered the massacre, but he was the officer in charge and he took no action against his men.

In his farewell address to his men on May 9, 1865, he called on them to forget past bitterness and accept the outcome of the war. Two years later, while living in North Mississippi, he became Grand Wizard of the Ku Klux Klan. By 1869, perhaps because of public criticism of the Klan, he cut his connection with the organization.

He farmed near Memphis until his death in 1877. His life was an incredible combination of hard work, shrewd dealing in not-quite-honorable professions, brilliant tactics, and racism toward Black people. These characteristics all combined help explain his success as slave trader, general, and planter.

Figure 8.7. Union Forces destroy a Mississippi railroad. Library of Congress Prints and Photographs Division, LC-USZ62-132568.

VISIT A BATTLEFIELD

Seeing a battlefield close up, walking the hills and fields, reading the monuments and markers, give one a feeling of what the war actually meant to the soldiers on both sides. Vicksburg and Shiloh are the most important, but other battlefield sites well worth a visit include Ship Island, Grand Gulf, and Brice's Crossroads. Other monuments or markers indicating Civil War incidents are scattered throughout the state, at Iuka, Greenwood, Yazoo City, Biloxi, Macon, and many other sites. Find out if your area was the scene of any Civil War events.

OPPOSITION TO THE CONFEDERACY

As the war went against the South, Mississippians complained about Mississippi boys dying in Virginia to protect Richmond while Grant threatened Mississippi. In December 1862, President Davis made a trip into Tennessee, Alabama, and Mississippi to bolster support for his administration. He denounced states' rights as destructive to the Confederate cause. In February 1864, he complained to the Confederate Congress: "The zeal of the people is failing: discontent, disaffection, disloyalty are manifest among those who, through the sacrifice of others, have enjoyed quiet and safety at home; public meetings of treasonable character, in the name of state sovereignty, are being held. Desertion is frequent and becoming the order of the day. Bands of deserters have organized and now systematically plunder, burn, and rob wherever they go."

CHAPTER 8.

THE PEACE MOVEMENT IN MISSISSIPPI

Opposition to the Confederacy in Mississippi had begun with the opposition to secession itself. As Union forces won greater and greater control of Mississippi, more and more White Mississippians desired peace. Confederate forces, which had lost the western border of the state to Grant, now had considerable trouble with civilian revolts in the eastern counties.

The area that opposed the Confederacy ran from the Tennessee Hills down through the east central part of the state, through the Piney Woods to the coast. In February 1862, residents of Tishomingo County lined the banks of the Tennessee River and cheered the Union gunboats on it. Many of the residents of Northeast Mississippi took the federal loyalty oath when they could and began thinking about political reconstruction.

In Choctaw County, many deserters took shelter in the woods. In Bankston, an antiwar society appeared when the workers of a textile mill and shoe shop pledged not to fight in the war. Itawamba, Pontotoc, Attala, Winston, and Leake counties were also centers of antiwar sentiment.

In Greene County, the McLeod brothers supported Lincoln and tried to organize Blacks for the Union as early as 1861. By 1864, anti-Confederacy forces there forced Confederate soldiers entering the county to desert or accept parole. They raided government depots and burned gins, barns, bridges, and the courthouse. In Perry County, anti-Confederate forces scared the sheriff so badly that he refused to collect taxes for the Confederacy.

CAUSES FOR OPPOSITION

Some White Mississippians had been against slavery, or at least against slaveholders, well before 1860. Certain actions of the Confederacy further increased the resentment of many White Mississippians.

Many soldiers had volunteered for a fixed period—usually six months or a year. In 1862, the Confederate Congress passed the first Conscription Act, permitting authorities to draft men into the army. Many volunteers felt that this was an attempt to force them to stay in the service after their enlistments were up.

These draft laws exempted elected officials and large slaveholders. For every twenty Blacks on plantations, a White man was exempted from the draft to control them. The law also allowed draftees to hire substitutes to serve for them. All of these provisions meant that rich people could escape service while poor people had to fight.

Another factor was the conduct of some Confederate officials. Army agents traveled over the state taking what they needed from civilians and giving the victims receipts. In many cases, cavalry bands took whatever they wanted. Many soldiers returned home to protect their families from such actions.

"THE FREE STATE OF JONES"

According to some sources, the citizens of Jones County met in the Ellisville courthouse and declared themselves independent of the Confederacy. They named their county "The Free State of Jones." Other sources state that the "Free State of Jones" was an exaggeration. They claim that the revolt involved only a minority of the White citizens of the county.

The revolt was led by Newt Knight. He was a farmer and shoemaker and a Unionist who refused to serve in the Confederate army until he was drafted. Then he refused to fight and served as a hospital orderly. He went home when he heard of the abuses of the cavalry and the provisions of the "Twenty-Negro Law."

He organized a company of militia who united to protect each other's cornfields and to raid Confederate stores for arms and food. They tried to join the Union forces, but failed. Although two different Confederate forces hunted them in the spring of 1864, they survived and even voted openly in elections.

The story of Newt Knight and Jones County was picked up by journalists in the North and South, and became a source of great embarrassment. The Southern states had seceded from the Union; now they were in the position of denying the right of a county to secede from the Confederacy.

LIVING CONDITIONS DURING THE WAR

Living conditions in Mississippi quickly deteriorated when the war started. Although Mississippi was an agricultural state, it had a hard time feeding its people. Believing there would be no war, planters had not listened to the Secession Convention's pleas to plant food crops in 1861. Instead, they planted cotton.

They had counted on being able to sell their crop abroad. But when the Union navy blockaded the Gulf Coast, this left the state with cotton that could neither be sold nor all used. Droughts in 1862 and 1864 destroyed much of the corn and wheat crops. Food shortages were made more serious by a breakdown in distribution. As the war continued, the railroads fell into disrepair.

The Confederate government was unable to control excessive profiteering and hoarding on the part of some citizens. Confederate paper money became worthless and prices went out of sight. A visitor in Jackson in November 1862 observed: "Commodities grow scarcer and scarcer. Shoes here sell at $25 or $30 the pair, and boots $40 to $50; hats $15 to $20, and other things in proportion. Coffee now commands $4 per pound, and tea $25. Salt $75 to $100 per sack. Whiskey $15 per gallon."

WOMEN "MAKE DO"

At the beginning of war, most Mississippi White women had thrilled to their men's parading and going off to fight. But as the war progressed, conditions at home got worse, and their letters to soldier husbands complained of the hardships.

In the face of many shortages, the people adopted substitutes. They made coffee from parched corn, okra, or sweet potato, and tea from dried raspberry leaves. Berries and tree bark furnished inks and dyes. Plaited corn shucks made horse collars.

A major problem was the lack of salt. People also had to find substitutes for cloth, and the home manufacture of clothing began early. Palmetto leaves made good hats, and many old looms and spinning wheels were brought out and repaired.

In all these processes, women took the major role. With their husbands and brothers in the army, White women had to supervise not only the home but in many cases the farm, plantation, or business. They made flags and uniforms, knit socks, and rolled bandages. They formed soldiers' aid societies to send packages to the front and to entertain soldiers at dances and picnics. Many women worked as nurses in hospitals and as schoolteachers. A British visitor traveling in Mississippi in 1863 was amazed at the "quiet, calm, uncomplaining manner" in which Mississippi women "bore their sufferings and their grief."

TRADE BETWEEN THE LINES

Shortages made smuggling almost a necessity. Mississippi had a surplus of cotton, and the North needed cotton for its mills. The only problem was how to get the cotton to the market. Anyone who could smuggle cotton through the lines and sell it could make huge profits and still help get necessities for home. At first, both sides tried to stop the trade, but this was impossible.

GOVERNMENT DURING THE WAR

Despite the chaos caused by the war, Mississippi conducted two wartime elections, in 1861 and 1863, and the legislature met every year, although many representatives stayed away. As the war turned unfavorable for the South, the state capital was frequently relocated, moving from Jackson to Enterprise, then to Meridian, back to Jackson, again to Meridian, followed by Columbus, Macon, and finally back to Jackson.

In 1861 Governor Pettus was reelected. But by 1863, Mississippi voters turned away from the Fire-eaters and chose Charles Clark as governor. Many of his supporters hoped to achieve an honorable compromise peace with the North. By 1865, the tide had turned even more strongly away from Fire-eater leadership. As the war entered its final months, most of the political leaders and the people wanted peace and political reconstruction.

BLACKS DURING THE WAR

Some enslaved Blacks were forced to continue working throughout the war. Some even went off to war as servants of Confederate officers. But long before the Emancipation Proclamation, the Union army had been freeing Blacks, and Blacks had been taking their own freedom.

For White Mississippians, the usual fears of slave rebellion increased enormously. They tried to counter these fears by isolating Blacks from outside news and restricting them to the plantations. By September 1861, there were reports of plots in the river counties. In July 1862, the provost marshal of Natchez reported hanging forty Blacks during the preceding year. In 1863, a group of Blacks in Lafayette County revolted, drove off their overseers, and divided their master's property among themselves. Confederate troops put down slave rebellions near Holly Springs and in Amite County.

SLAVERY GRADUALLY ENDS

On January 1, 1863, Lincoln signed the Emancipation Proclamation. The movement of slaves to Union lines increased. In her novel *Jubilee*, Margaret Walker described the scene: "Behind the soldiers came still another motley lot, more than a mile of freed slaves following the army. They had bundles of rags and some had pots and pans and squawking chickens and other fowl. They were in wagons and on foot, riding mules and driving little oxcarts. There were gray-haired men and women, young mothers with their babies at the breast and streaming lines of children walking. These people were also hungry, and some were sick and diseased with running sores."

SONG OF JUBILEE

This song was sung by slaves as they left their old homes:

> Has anybody seen my master,
> With the moustache on his face?

> Go 'long the road sometime this morning,
> Like he's going to leave the place.
> He saw the smoke, way up the river,
> Where the Lincoln gunboats lay.
> He took his hat and he left mighty sudden,
> And I suppose he's run away.
> The master run—ha! ha!
> The darky stay—ho! ho!
> It must be now that the kingdom's coming,
> And the year of jubilee.

What was the "Year of Jubilee"? What were the "Lincoln gunboats"? Why did the master run away? Do you know any modern "freedom songs" from the civil rights movement?

BLACKS FIGHT FOR THE UNION

Blacks also joined the Union army in large numbers. Until 1862 they were not allowed to fight, and even then they were not welcomed in all combat units. But they worked from the beginning as cooks, teamsters, orderlies, scouts, and blacksmiths. Over 17,000 Black Mississippians served with Union armies.

Eventually they were used in combat. Some of the early Black units fought well in the Vicksburg campaign and earned the respect of White soldiers on both sides. After the fall of Vicksburg, General Grant wrote to Lincoln: "By arming the Negro, we have added a powerful ally. They will make good soldiers and taking them from the enemy weakens him in the same proportion they strengthen us." Later, Black troops took part in many of the small battles in Mississippi, including such as Yazoo City.

The arming of Black soldiers had deep meaning for race relations in Mississippi and America. It would be difficult to return armed soldiers to slavery or to second-class citizenship. Also, the performance of Black men under battle conditions helped abolitionists of both races to argue that Blacks were fully human and deserved equal human rights after the war. And the fact that Blacks had fought in the war meant that they had participated in freeing themselves. White people on both sides had to change their opinions about Blacks to fit the new circumstances.

BLACKS AND THE CONFEDERACY

Some Blacks went with their masters to serve with the Confederate army. They were used as cooks, teamsters, servants, and laborers. As the Confederacy faced manpower shortages, there were proposals to arm enslaved Blacks and use them as soldiers. President Davis, who had at first opposed the arming of slaves, later supported the idea. Others still opposed it; one high Confederate official said, "If slaves will make good soldiers, our whole theory of slavery is wrong." In March 1865, the Confederate Congress finally authorized the use of Black soldiers. It was too late, however, for the war ended a month later.

GRANT AND THE FREEDMEN

As the Union army marched through Mississippi in late 1862 and early 1863, more and more formerly enslaved Blacks sought freedom within its lines. This mass of people posed a large problem to the Union generals. Equally a problem was the army's gradual accumulation of lands abandoned by Confederate plantation owners.

In November 1863, General Grant and chaplain John Eaton established contraband camps along the Mississippi River to address the growing numbers of escaped enslaved people seeking freedom. The camps' residents compelled both Lincoln and Grant to make Black freedom central to the Union's war aims. Corinth emerged as the largest and most successful of these camps when it opened in summer 1862. There, formerly enslaved people established some of Mississippi's first Black schools, and by 1863, Black men began enlisting in the Union Army. While Northern businessmen leased abandoned plantations and hired freedpeople to grow cotton and corn, this new arrangement often perpetuated exploitation. Many businessmen amassed fortunes while the freedpeople found themselves still laboring for White employers with limited actual freedom.

DAVIS BEND

The government then tried a different type of colony. It began to give land to the freedmen to operate for themselves. This bold idea could have revolutionized the South and changed the entire course of Reconstruction.

Grant chose Jefferson Davis's plantation at Davis Bend near Vicksburg for a bold experiment in Black autonomy—an ironic choice given Davis's role as Confederate president. The site had a notable history: Davis's brother Joseph had previously allowed enslaved people to operate the plantation under the management of Benjamin Montgomery, an enslaved person who proved highly capable. Whether Grant selected the location for its rich soil, its previous success under Montgomery, or its symbolic value remained unclear.

By the end of 1863, about 1,000 formerly enslaved people had established a farming community there. Under the support of Grant and Colonel Eaton, seventy

Figure 8.8. Union troops and Black civilians occupied the Davis plantation; the banner shows their feeling about being there. Library of Congress Prints and Photographs Division, LC-B8184-3170.

of the strongest workers received thirty acres each. Protected by a Black Union regiment, the settlement thrived despite Confederate raids and pressure from Northern business interests, marking an early success in Black land ownership.

Military authorities, impressed by the early results, expanded the program significantly in 1865. Five thousand acres were divided among more than 1,800 Blacks organized into 181 associations or companies. Each company had to pay for all equipment and supplies advanced by the government. Several Blacks opened general stores. They formed a school board and in May 1866 established a school. A system of self-government was set up, including a sheriff and judge in each district. Free medical services were provided to all who could not afford a regular physician.

The system was an astounding success. The year 1865 was a good one for cotton, and by its end the colonists had sold over $400,000 worth of cash crops. After paying their expenses, they cleared nearly $160,000, an average of $880 per company.

THE END OF THE DREAM

But during the winter, new developments in national politics doomed the "grand experiment." Two of the six plantations on Davis Bend had been returned to their original owners as early as 1864. On January 1, 1866, President Andrew Johnson pardoned two more of the original owners, and they received their land back.

Then in late March, Joseph Davis, brother of the president of the Confederacy, regained the two Davis's plantations.

Joseph Davis, fearing Congressional confiscation of his property, made a pragmatic decision to sell his land to a former enslaved individual, Benjamin Montgomery. While Montgomery achieved considerable success with the property, other Black farmers were denied similar opportunities. Without access to land, the broader experiment in Black autonomy came to an end.

The Davis Bend experiment might have provided a model for securing political and economic rights for newly freed Black Mississippians, had it been allowed to continue. Instead, President Johnson betrayed Reconstruction's promise by returning confiscated lands to former Confederate leaders, signaling his commitment to White Southern interests over Black economic independence.

SECESSION AND SLAVERY

The debate surrounding Mississippi's reasons for seceding from the Union at the start of the Civil War has long been a topic of discussion. While the state issued a "Declaration of Secession" in 1861 to justify its actions, the underlying causes remain complex and subject to interpretation. However, among professional historians, there is a growing consensus that challenges the conventional narrative of a multifaceted debate.

Historian Jere Nash argues that the primary motivation for secession was the preservation of White supremacy, with slavery serving as the primary tool to enforce this racial hierarchy. This perspective aligns with the unambiguous language in Mississippi's declaration, which states: "Our position is thoroughly identified with the institution of slavery—the greatest material interest of the world." It's worth noting that Mississippi had the highest proportion of enslaved people among all slaveholding states, with almost 55 percent of its total population enslaved in 1860.

The argument for slavery's centrality to secession is further supported by works such as Charles B. Dew's *Apostles of Disunion: Southern Secession Commissioners and the Causes of the Civil War*. However, this raises the question of why half of Mississippi's White population, who did not own slaves, were willing to fight and die for the cause. Nash contends that the core motivation for these individuals was also the preservation of White supremacy, rather than economic factors or states' rights.

This interpretation suggests that figures like John Pettus or L. Q. C. Lamar were primarily concerned with maintaining racial dominance rather than economic or constitutional issues. After 1875, with the end of slavery, Jim Crow laws became the new tool for enforcing White supremacy in Mississippi.

Others also argue economic dependence on slavery alone does not fully explain Mississippi's motivations. Defenders of the "Lost Cause" myth contend secession was driven by a desire to defend states' rights and maintain Southern identity. Others highlight fear of slave uprisings or loss of political power if slavery was abolished.

Ultimately, while the declaration explicitly names slavery, it does not tell the whole story. Mississippi's decision emerged from a mix of perceived economic necessity, cultural fears, political turmoil, and complex racial dynamics. Teasing out the multifaceted motivations for secession remains an ongoing scholarly endeavor. The true rationale was neither simple nor singular. But undoubtedly, the desire to perpetuate slavery was an indispensable factor that must bear the greatest moral responsibility. Any credible interpretation must place Mississippi's economic investment in slavery at the crux.

Recommended Readings

Michael B. Ballard, *The Civil War in Mississippi: Major Campaigns and Battles* (Jackson: University Press of Mississippi, 2014).

Victoria E. Bynum, *The Free State of Jones: Mississippi's Longest Civil War* (Chapel Hill: University of North Carolina Press, 2001).

Bradley R. Clampitt, *Occupied Vicksburg* (Baton Rouge: Louisiana State University Press, 2016).

Charles B. Dew, *Apostles of Disunion: Southern Secession Commissioners and the Causes of the Civil War* (Charlottesville: University of Virginia Press, 2016 and 2001).

Noralee Frankel, *Freedom's Women: Black Women and Families in Civil War Era Mississippi* (Bloomington: Indiana University Press, 1999).

Caroline E. Janney, *Ends of War: The Unfinished Fight of Lee's Army After Appomattox* (Chapel Hill: University of North Carolina Press, 2021).

Bruce Levine, *The Fall of the House of Dixie: The Civil War and the Social Revolution that Transformed the South* (New York: Random House, 2013).

James M. McPherson, *Battle Cry of Freedom: The Civil War Era* (New York: Oxford University Press, 1988).

James McPherson, *The War That Forged a Nation: Why the Civil War Still Matters* (New York: Oxford University Press, 2015).

Christopher J. Olsen, *Political Culture and Secession in Mississippi: Masculinity, Honor, and the Antiparty Tradition, 1830–1860* (New York: Oxford University Press, 2000).

Jarret Ruminski, *The Limits of Loyalty: Ordinary People in Civil War Mississippi* (Jackson: University Press of Mississippi, 2017).

Timothy B. Smith, *The Mississippi Secession Convention: Delegates and Deliberations in Politics and War, 1861–1865* (Jackson: University Press of Mississippi, 2014).

Timothy B. Smith, *Mississippi in the Civil War: The Home Front* (Jackson: University Press of Mississippi, 2010).

John W. Winkle III, *The Mississippi State Constitution* (New York: Oxford University Press, 2014).

Ben Wynne, *Mississippi's Civil War: A Narrative History* (Macon, GA: Mercer University Press, 2006).

CHAPTER 9

RECONSTRUCTION

1865–1877

AS THE CIVIL WAR ENDED, PRESIDENT LINCOLN'S ASSASSINATION LEFT A LEADership void that his successor, Andrew Johnson, struggled to fill. The nation faced the complex challenge of reuniting a divided America and resolving fundamental issues left unaddressed by the war.

The central questions of Reconstruction revolved around reintegrating Southern states into the Union's political life and defining the rights of newly freed Blacks. While Southern states had never legally left the Union, their political participation was suspended until they met conditions set by Congress in the Reconstruction Acts of 1867.

For formerly enslaved people, this era represented a unique opportunity to define and actualize freedom. By 1870, Black Americans had developed a vision of freedom centered on three fundamental rights: voting, land ownership, and education. These aspirations reflected their understanding of citizenship and economic independence in American society.

Radical Republicans successfully pushed for Black male suffrage, marking a crucial step toward full citizenship. However, land redistribution efforts were blocked by President Johnson, leaving many Black Americans economically vulnerable. Education became a realm where Black communities took initiative, establishing public schools throughout the South.

This period highlights the agency of Black Americans in shaping their futures and expanding the concept of liberty. It underscores that freedom encompassed not just legal rights, but also economic opportunities and access to education. Understanding Reconstruction through this lens provides insight into a pivotal moment when the meaning of American freedom was being redefined and expanded. It allows us to appreciate the profound social transformation that was underway, as well as the lasting impact of this period on American concepts of citizenship, equality, and freedom.

In this chapter, we explore how Mississippi and the nation struggled with defining and protecting rights for newly freed Black citizens after the Civil War.

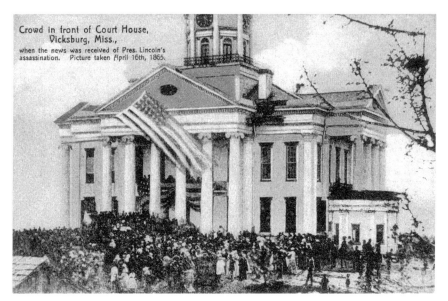

Figure 9.1. The murder of Lincoln shocked Black Mississippians. This crowd gathered at the Vicksburg courthouse to hear the news. Courtesy of the Archives and Records Services Division, Mississippi Department of Archives and History.

During Reconstruction (1865–1877), the country took major steps forward by passing the Thirteenth Amendment to end slavery, the Fourteenth Amendment to grant citizenship, and the Fifteenth Amendment to protect voting rights.

But this progress faced strong pushback, especially in the South. The federal government's early work to protect Black civil rights began to fall apart as opposition grew stronger. By 1875–1877, both Congress and the nation gave up on enforcing Reconstruction policies. This decision to stop protecting Black rights had long-lasting effects on racial equality in Mississippi and across America.

What started as a hopeful time of change ended up giving way to new forms of discrimination, particularly in Mississippi, where White opposition to Black civil rights was fierce. The shift away from Reconstruction's goals shaped life in America for many years to come.

CONDITIONS IN 1865

When the war ended, most Mississippians, whatever their feelings, welcomed peace. With the collapse of the Confederacy, Mississippi now faced the job of reorganizing its state government and determining what a political, economic, and social structure would look like that involved free Blacks. Governor Charles Clark called for the legislature to meet in Jackson on May 18 to begin this work. But before anything could be done, Clark was arrested and General E. D. Osband of the Union army took control.

The cost of war was high. The social structure and economy of Mississippi were in chaos. Roads, railroads, and levees needed repairs. Many plantations were grown up in weeds. Confederate money was worthless, and trade was at a standstill. Many towns were in partial or complete ruin. Walter Lord later noted: "By the end, Mississippi seemed but a forest of chimneys. The whole town of Okolona could be bought for $5,000. There was not a fence left within miles of Corinth, not a clock running in Natchez. The capital, Jackson, was in ashes—the Confederate Hotel as complete a wreck as the cause it honored."

FREED PEOPLE

The labor system based on slavery had been destroyed by the very war that had been fought to preserve it. In Mississippi, 400,000 enslaved Blacks were now free. Years later, one former enslaved Black recalled her first taste of freedom: "When the war ended, White man came to the field and told my mother-in-law she free as he is. She dropped her hoe and danced up to the turn row and danced right up into old Master's parlor. She went so fast she could have sat on her dress tail. That was in June. That night she sent and got all the neighbors, and they danced all night long." Black Mississippians were thankful that the "Year of Jubilee" had finally come. Long migrations began, as parents tried to find their children, separated during slavery. Mass marriages took place, as former enslaved Blacks began to establish the family life that had largely been denied them under slavery. In Vicksburg alone, between April and November 1865, more than 1,500 marriages between freed people were recorded.

But this was also a time of great suffering for Black people. Food and clothing were hard to get. Medical care, always scarce, was now almost nonexistent. Former slaveholders used violence as a tool to force Blacks to work in the fields much as they did as slaves.

WHITES FACE GREAT CHANGES

For most White people, it was no "Year of Jubilee." Of the 78,000 White Mississippians who had marched off to war, 27,500 had been killed or wounded. Many women who had been homemakers before the war were now forced to manage farms, open boarding houses, or teach school. Some farmers found themselves wiped out financially. A planter described his situation: "I think it was in the decrees of God Almighty that slavery was to be abolished in this way; and I don't murmur. We have lost our property, and we have been subjugated, but we brought it all on ourselves. Nobody that hasn't experienced it knows anything about our suffering. We are discouraged; we have nothing left to begin new with. I never

Figure 9.2. The Confederate Cemetery in Raymond, Mississippi, contains the graves of 140 Confederate soldiers killed in the Battle of Raymond, or who later died from their wounds. Library of Congress Prints and Photographs Division, LC-DIG-highsm-42622.

did a day's work in my life, and don't know how to begin. You see me in these coarse old clothes; well, I never wore coarse clothes in my life before the war."

Some Whites blamed Blacks for the troubled times following the Civil War. Freed people became a symbol of the Confederacy's defeat in the eyes of many former Confederates. Virtually all planters, accustomed to controlling Black people, resented having to treat them as free workers. Some planters refused to acknowledge the enslaved Blacks' freedom, despite the public posting of the Emancipation Proclamation as proof.

Many planters continued to employ overseers and insisted that Blacks would not work unless forced. This claim, however, was a continuation of racist stereotypes and a justification for maintaining oppressive labor practices, rather than an accurate reflection of freed people's willingness to work. Many former enslaved individuals were eager to work for fair wages and conditions but faced significant obstacles and discrimination in their efforts to do so.

This period saw a complex struggle between the desire of freed people to exercise their newly granted rights and the resistance of many Whites to accept the new social order. The persistence of such attitudes among planters and other Whites played a crucial role in shaping the difficult transition from slavery to freedom in Mississippi and throughout the South.

BAD FEELINGS

A Northern journalist, Whitelaw Reid, observed in 1865: "However these [former slaveholders] may have regarded the Negro slave, they hated the Negro freeman. However, kind they may have been to Negro property, they were virulently vindictive against a property that escaped from their control." Look up "virulent" and "vindictive" in a dictionary. Why do you think these men felt this way?

THE FREEDMEN'S BUREAU

The federal government reacted to the situation of Southern Blacks by creating the Freedmen's Bureau (officially the Bureau of Refugees, Freedmen, and Abandoned Lands). It issued supplies to thousands of needy people, regardless of color. Bureau agents established schools and hospitals for Blacks. Special courts were established to protect the rights of Black people, since state courts would not let Blacks testify against Whites.

Another key responsibility was overseeing labor relations between freedmen and plantation owners. This new requirement for signed labor contracts was a significant shift from the previous system of slavery. The Bureau developed guidelines for these contracts, which included provisions for fair wages, adequate

Figure 9.3. Freedmen's school near Vicksburg. From *Harper's Weekly*, June 1866.

supplies, and proper working conditions. Their goal was to ensure that freedmen were not exploited and received just compensation for their labor.

However, the implementation of this system faced significant challenges. Many plantation owners, impoverished by the war, lacked the cash to pay regular wages. Simultaneously, most freedmen had no land or resources of their own. This economic reality, combined with the reluctance of many White landowners to treat Black workers as truly free laborers, led to the gradual emergence of sharecropping.

Sharecropping was a system where laborers worked a portion of land in exchange for a share of the crop, rather than for wages. While initially seen as a compromise, this system often resulted in cycles of debt and dependency for many Black families, effectively limiting their economic freedom.

This evolution from slavery to wage labor to sharecropping demonstrates the complex economic challenges of Reconstruction and highlights how the promise of freedom was often constrained by economic realities and ongoing racial inequalities.

The Freedmen's Bureau received authority to distribute seized and abandoned lands, sparking hopes among newly freed people for "forty acres and a mule"—a phrase that symbolized their desire for economic independence through land ownership. This idea originated from General William T. Sherman's Special Field Order No. 15 in January 1865, which set aside 400,000 acres of confiscated Confederate land along the Georgia and South Carolina coast, to be divided into forty-acre plots for formerly enslaved families.

Though Sherman's order was geographically limited, it raised expectations for land redistribution throughout the South. President Andrew Johnson undermined the Freedmen's Bureau's mission of land reform in 1865–66. Although Congress had empowered the Bureau to acquire and distribute Confederate land to formerly enslaved people, Johnson ordered the land returned to its original White owners, effectively blocking Black economic independence.

The lack of widespread land ownership among Black farmers in post–Civil War Mississippi left many in a vulnerable economic position. This vulnerability gave rise to the sharecropping system, which emerged through complex negotiations between freedmen and White landowners. Importantly, former enslaved individuals were not merely passive victims in this arrangement; many initially viewed sharecropping as a potential path to economic independence, moving away from wage labor.

However, the reality of sharecropping fell far short of these aspirations. The system's capacity for genuine economic advancement was severely constrained, primarily due to consistently low cotton prices that rarely allowed sharecroppers to rise above basic survival. This economic stagnation stood in sharp contrast to federal land policies in the Western United States, where the government generously granted extensive land tracts to railroads and settlers.

The failure to implement widespread land redistribution in the South had long-lasting consequences, significantly affecting the economic power and independence of freed people for generations to come.

FREEDMEN'S BUREAU CONTRACTS

Read the following directive of the Freedmen's Bureau in Mississippi, dated March 23, 1865:

> In addition to just treatment, wholesome rations, comfortable clothing, quarters, fuel, and medical attention, and the opportunity for instruction of children, the planter shall pay to the laborer as follows:
>
> Male hands, first class, $10 per month; second class, $8 per month; third class, $6 per month.
>
> Female hands, first class, $8 per month; second class, $6 per month; third class $5 per month.
>
> For Boys under fourteen, $3 per month.
>
> For Girls under fourteen, $2 per month.
>
> These classes will be determined by merit and on agreement between the planter and the laborers.

Who, in your opinion, would probably be considered a "first-class" hand? A "second-class" hand? What do you think about the sex differences in payment? How much would a Black family earn in a month if the parents and their two teenage (over fourteen) daughters and one young (under fourteen) son worked? Keeping in mind that a dollar in 1866 would equal almost twenty dollars in 2023, would you be willing to work for these wages? (Remember that the wages were in addition to food, clothes, a place to live, and medical care.)

JOHNSON'S PLAN OF RECONSTRUCTION

A slaveholder and former senator and governor from Tennessee, President Johnson offered a very lenient plan to restore the defeated states. All White males, including former rebels, were given an opportunity to swear loyalty to the Union. These citizens would then elect delegates to constitutional conventions, which would abolish the Ordinance of Secession and provide for the end of slavery.

These provisions excluded Blacks because Blacks had not been eligible to vote under prewar state law. A convention of Blacks in Vicksburg protested to President Johnson. Frederick Douglass and other national leaders met with him to urge better federal protection for former enslaved Blacks, but Johnson refused, saying this was a matter to be left to the states.

THE CONSTITUTIONAL CONVENTION OF 1865

Johnson appointed William L. Sharkey temporary governor of Mississippi. Sharkey called for a constitutional convention to be held in August 1865. This convention was the first to be held in a former Confederate state. Of the ninety-eight delegates, most were former Whigs who had opposed secession in 1861. Only seven had served in the 1861 Secession Convention.

The constitutional convention in Mississippi was deeply divided over the issue of slavery's abolition. The delegates engaged in heated debates, with some advocating for a gradual emancipation process, while others demanded that the North compensate slaveholders for the loss of their "property," arguing that the war had effectively destroyed the institution of slavery.

George Potter, a delegate from Hinds County, took a particularly defiant stance. He asserted that Congress had no authority to impose demands on a "sovereign state." Potter warned that if the convention chose to abolish slavery, it would open the floodgates to further federal demands, including Black suffrage and racial equality. He urged the convention to take no action on the matter.

This debate in Mississippi held significant national importance. At the time of Mississippi's convention, the ratification process for the Thirteenth Amendment, which would officially abolish slavery throughout the United States, had stalled. Only twenty-three states had voted to approve the amendment, while twenty-seven were needed for its ratification. In August, it remained uncertain whether this threshold would be met.

The discussions and decisions made in Mississippi's constitutional convention thus had potential ramifications beyond the state's borders. The resistance to abolition in Mississippi reflected broader tensions and uncertainties about the future of slavery and race relations in the postwar South, as well as the challenges facing the ratification of the Thirteenth Amendment.

In the end, cooler heads won out. Prominent men like Judge Amos R. Johnston argued that Mississippi had been defeated in war, that abolition was a fact, and that the South was at the mercy of the federal government. Speaking of slavery, Johnston advised: "It is gone, and however much we were attached to

Figure 9.4. The convention met in what is now the "Old Capitol." Historic American Buildings Survey, Library of Congress Prints and Photographs Division, HABS MISS,25-JACK,3-.

it or however much it benefitted us—being dead, let us indulge in no useless regrets over its demise, but bury the carcass, that it may no longer offend our nostrils." When the vote was taken, slavery in Mississippi was declared abolished, eighty-seven to eleven. No one suggested political rights for Blacks. President Johnson had suggested allowing some Black men to vote, but did not insist on it.

PRESIDENTIAL ADVICE

In a telegram to Governor Sharkey, President Johnson stated:

If you could extend the elective franchise to all persons of color who can read the Constitution of the United States in English and write their names, and to all persons of color who own real estate valued at not less than two hundred and fifty dollars, and pay taxes thereon, you would completely disarm the adversary and set an example the other States will follow. This you can do with perfect safety, and you thus place the southern States, in reference to free persons of color, upon the same basis with the free States. I hope and trust your convention will do this, and, as a consequence, the radicals, who are wild upon Negro franchise, will be completely foiled in their attempt to keep the southern States from renewing their relations to the Union by not accepting their senators and representatives.

Why do you think President Johnson sent this telegram? Was he thinking of the benefits to Black people? What did he mean by "perfect safety"? Who were the "radicals" he mentioned? Why do you think the Mississippi convention ignored this message?

UNDER A NEW GOVERNMENT

Elections for new state officials were held on October 2, 1865. Former Confederate General Benjamin G. Humphreys was elected governor. Since President Johnson had not yet pardoned Humphreys, he could not take office. Therefore, Johnson promptly sent him a pardon.

The Mississippi state government was operating in a very delicate situation at this time. Northern public opinion after the war demanded two things of the rebel states: first, that they swear loyalty to the Union and agree that secession was at an end; and second, that they agree that slavery had been ended by the war. Related to the second demand was some degree of citizenship for Blacks.

The northern states themselves denied full civil rights to their own Black citizens, however, and could not logically require that the South confer full political equality on its Black residents. On the other hand, the North was not about to accept the reinstatement of slavery in the South.

President Johnson, unlike his Republican opponents, seemed unwilling to force the South to safeguard the rights of freed people. As his telegram to Governor Sharkey indicates, he merely made suggestions. Thus, if the South failed to do so, he would not require them, and the stage would be set for a major conflict between the president and Congress.

Governor Humphreys's message to the legislature set the tone for its session: "Under the pressure of federal bayonets, urged on by the misdirected sympathies of the world, the people of Mississippi have abolished the institution of slavery. The Negro is free, whether we like it or not; we must realize that fact now and forever. To be free, however, does not make him a citizen, or entitle him to social or political equality with the White man."

THE BLACK CODES

The newly elected Mississippi legislature, dominated by former Confederates and White supremacists, not only refused to ratify the Thirteenth Amendment but also enacted a series of oppressive laws known as "Black Codes," mirroring similar legislation across the former Confederate states. These codes, far more severe and comprehensive than initially apparent, created a system of de facto slavery and racial subjugation.

Under these laws, Black individuals could only sue other Black people and could only be sued by them in state courts. Their testimony would be accepted in state courts, but only in cases involving other Black individuals. Their marriages were legally recognized, though separate records were kept for these unions. They were allowed to own personal property, but with significant limitations.

While ostensibly granting some basic rights to freed people, they severely restricted freedoms and maintained White supremacy through various means: labor restrictions requiring proof of employment to avoid vagrancy charges; apprenticeship laws that bound out Black children, often to former slaveholders; mobility limitations prohibiting travel without permits; property restrictions barring land ownership outside towns; civil rights restrictions denying voting and jury service; vaguely defined behavioral codes leading to arrest and forced labor; gun ownership prohibition; criminalization of interracial marriage; and education limitations. These measures effectively created a state-sanctioned system of racial subordination, controlling every aspect of Black life and ensuring a cheap, compliant labor force. The severe nature of these codes sparked Northern outrage, pushing for more stringent Reconstruction policies and eventually leading to the Civil Rights Act of 1866 and the Fourteenth Amendment. However, the legacy of systemic racism and economic disparity established by these codes would persist long after their official repeal, shaping race relations in the South for generations to come.

MISSISSIPPI REACTS

Some White Mississippians criticized passage of these laws. They feared it would cause federal controls to be imposed on Mississippi. Others felt that Black people were being denied justice by the laws.

Defenders of the codes said they were consistent with prewar northern laws regulating the lives of free Blacks. They denied that the legislature was trying to re-enslave Blacks. The laws were necessary, they said, to force Blacks to work.

The vast majority of legislators sought simply to establish a racial hierarchy in this new, post-slavery era, both socially and especially economically. Economic motives drove the decision to secede and to fight for the Confederacy, and they still dominated the decision making of Mississippi politicians. As the *Jackson Daily News* wrote: "We must keep the ex-slave in a position of inferiority. We must pass such laws as will make him feel his inferiority."

During the two years Sharkey and Humphreys governed (1865–1867), some federal troops were stationed in Mississippi. Their job was to help protect Black rights and "to aid but not to interfere" with the state government. Sometimes these two aims conflicted, but on the whole the military and civilian authorities got along well with each other.

THE NORTH REACTS

Northerners reacted swiftly to the Black Codes. The *Chicago Tribune*, for example, wrote: "We tell the White men of Mississippi that the men of the North will convert the state of Mississippi into a frog pond before they will allow any such laws to disgrace one foot of soil in which the bones of our soldiers sleep and over which the flag of freedom waves." Reports from the South informed Congress of the Black Codes and of mounting White violence toward freed people. And under Presidential Reconstruction—the period of President Johnson's lenient treatment of the ex-Confederacy and its efforts to reimpose something close to slavery—White Southerners sent many former Confederate officials to Congress in elections that prevented Blacks from voting. Northern Republicans wanted to keep control of Congress, and the former Rebels were almost all Democrats. Northerners also could not tolerate letting some of the same men back into Congress who had led the Southern states out of the Union. Therefore, when Congress met in December 1865, Republicans blocked new Southern congressmen from taking office.

THE ASCENDANCE OF THE RADICAL REPUBLICANS

Outraged by both the Black Codes and by President Johnson's deference to the interests of former slaveholders over the demands of justice, many Northern members of Congress—labeled "Radical Republicans" by Johnson and his supporters—began demanding voting rights for Blacks. They believed that without voting rights, freedmen would be unable to defend themselves and their families in the postwar economy and society. Testimony heard in congressional committees in the spring of 1866 strengthened this belief. Over Johnson's numerous vetoes, Congress extended the Freedmen's Bureau, other Reconstruction legislation, and passed the first Civil Rights Act in US history.

Race riots in Memphis and New Orleans and the rejection of the Fourteenth Amendment by Southern legislatures further aroused Northern public opinion.

(The Mississippi legislature unanimously rejected the amendment.) The result was that in the congressional elections of 1866, the "Radical Republicans" won a sweeping victory. Clearly, the Black Codes and other examples of stubborn resistance by former Confederates had backfired.

In January and February 1867, probably in reaction to the Republican triumph, the Mississippi Legislature repealed some of its Black Codes. But the action came too late. The Radical Republicans were now in charge of Reconstruction.

CONGRESS TAKES CONTROL

In March 1867, Congress passed a series of Reconstruction Acts. These acts nullified the Southern state governments that had been reorganized under Presidential Reconstruction. In their place, Congress created five military districts that in effect reoccupied almost all of the states of the ex-Confederacy, including Mississippi. Mississippi and Arkansas comprised the Fourth Military District, with General E. O. C. Ord in charge.

The process of Southern states resuming full participation in the federal government after the Civil War is often mischaracterized as "rejoining, or readmission to the Union." In reality, these states never legally left the Union, as confirmed by the 1869 Supreme Court decision in *Texas v. White*, which declared secession illegal and the Union "perpetual." The Constitution did not permit states to secede unilaterally. What actually occurred was a complex process of restoring political representation for these states. During the war, Southern Congressional delegations had either resigned or been expelled. After the conflict, Congress leveraged its constitutional authority to "judge the elections, returns, and qualifications of its own members" to establish conditions for seating Southern representatives and senators. This approach gave Congress significant control over Reconstruction policies and the terms under which Southern states would regain full political representation at the federal level.

Under the Reconstruction Acts, all adult males, White or Black, who would take a new loyalty oath called the "ironclad oath," were eligible to register to vote. This expansion of suffrage was a revolutionary change in the South. After registration, voters would elect delegates to new constitutional conventions tasked with drawing up entirely new state constitutions. These new constitutions were required to guarantee civil rights to Blacks, among other provisions. Only after Congress approved a state's new constitution could that state resume full participation in the federal government, with its representatives and senators allowed to be seated in Congress. This process ensured that the Southern states met specific conditions, including ratifying the Fourteenth Amendment and establishing Black male suffrage, before regaining their full political voice in national affairs. Thus, rather than "rejoining the Union," Southern states underwent a carefully managed process of meeting Congressional requirements to restore their delegations' place in the federal legislature.

WHITES REACT TO CONGRESSIONAL RECONSTRUCTION

Many White Southerners, despite having engaged in treason and instigating a devastating war that claimed 600,000 American lives in defense of slavery, ironically felt they were being punished unfairly in the war's aftermath. These same individuals, who had fought to maintain a brutal system of human bondage, vehemently denounced equal citizenship for Black Americans. They claimed, with cruel hypocrisy, that Black participation in government would lead to the "ruination" of the South—a South they themselves had already brought to ruin through their actions to preserve the institution of slavery. Walter Lord has described this ideology: "To the ordinary White Mississippian, political equality automatically led to social equality, which in turn automatically led to race-mixing. It was inevitable—and unthinkable. To a people brought up to believe that Negroes were genetically inferior, the mere hint of 'mongrelization' was appalling." On the other hand, a prominent group of White men argued that Mississippi should accept the Reconstruction Acts. They pointed out that Mississippi could not bargain but had to accept whatever terms Congress imposed. And so the arguments continued—during Reconstruction and beyond—between the "irreconcilables" and more moderate-thinking men.

THE ELECTION OF 1867

In 1867, Mississippi held its election for delegates to its state constitutional convention. Those White Mississippians who opposed racial equality decided to boycott politics. They preferred to leave the state under martial law.

For the first time, Black men in Mississippi could vote. Despite intimidation, more Blacks than Whites registered to vote: 79,179 to 58,385.

"CARPETBAGGERS" AND "SCALAWAGS"

People who came from outside Mississippi to invest in the new, postwar economy, run for office, or provide humanitarian assistance were called "carpetbaggers." Most of them supported the Reconstruction policies of the Radical Republicans. White conservatives charged that these "outsiders" brought their entire possessions to the South in a carpetbag (suitcase) and came hoping to get rich.

Native-born White Mississippians who voted Republican were called "scalawags." These men were more likely to have opposed secession and war and to resent the political dominance of plantation owners. Even if they were not committed to racial equality, they decided to back the Republican Party, which was more supportive of building fairer political and economic systems. Their opponents condemned them as traitors to their race.

THE CONSTITUTION OF 1868

The newly elected delegates to the constitutional convention met in Jackson on January 7, 1868. There were twenty-six "carpetbaggers," thirty-three "scalawags," nineteen conservatives, and seventeen Blacks in attendance. Despite the small share of Black delegates, some newspapers called it the "Black and Tan Convention." Later the term was used to discredit the constitution that was written by the group.

The 1868 Mississippi Constitution marked a significant departure from previous state constitutions, embracing democratic principles more aligned with those of northern states. This new constitution represented the most democratic framework the colonial province, territory, or state had ever experienced. It enshrined the principle of equal civil and political rights for all citizens residing in Mississippi who were also citizens of the United States. The document guaranteed fundamental rights such as trial by jury, freedom of speech, press, assembly, and petition. Notably, it eliminated property qualifications for jury service, holding office, or voting, making civic participation more accessible to a broader range of citizens.

A groundbreaking feature of the 1868 Constitution was its provision for a system of free public education, the first in Mississippi's history. The state legislature was to be apportioned based on total population, ensuring fairer representation. The constitution also prohibited discrimination in the use of public facilities and affirmed every citizen's right to travel on public conveyances. As delegate A. T. Morgan observed, "This new constitution dodged nothing. Under its provisions the Negro was a man, and all men were to be equal in their right to life, liberty and the pursuit of happiness."

Perhaps most significantly, the 1868 Constitution stood out among Mississippi's four historical constitutions as the only one submitted to the people for a ratification vote. This democratic process of ratification underscored the document's commitment to popular sovereignty and represented a stark contrast to the more exclusive methods of constitutional adoption in the state's past. By involving the citizenry directly in the approval of their governing document, the 1868 Constitution not only promoted democratic principles in its content but also in the very process of its establishment.

OPPOSITION TO THE NEW CONSTITUTION

A constitution providing equal rights, greater public services, and education for all was clearly an improvement over the previous one. Thus, conservatives condemned it. The *Vicksburg Daily Times* was particularly bitter toward White Republicans: "It is a contest which must determine whether Mississippi shall be ruled by Negroes and Radicals, or by White men, and in such a contest, NO REAL WHITE MAN will refuse to stand by and sustain his own race and color! If there is a White man who refuses to affiliate with his own race, in maintaining the rightful supremacy of White men in the South, we have no use for that man." A test oath for voters required that they swear that they had not "given encouragement" to the Confederacy at any time and that they believed in "the civil and political equality of all men." The oath caused fiery arguments when the new constitution was submitted to the people for approval.

THE ELECTION OF 1868

White conservatives formed the "Democratic White Men's Party of Mississippi" in order to defeat the ratification of the newly drafted constitution. The conclusion of its platform read: "Resolved, That the nefarious design of the Republican party in Congress, to place the White men of the Southern States under the governmental control of their late slaves, and degrade the Caucasian race as the inferiors of the African Negro, is a crime against the civilization of the age, which needs only to be mentioned to be scorned by all intelligent minds." In the elections held that year, Humphreys won the governorship again, Republicans gained control of the state legislature, and conservative Democrats secured four of the five congressional seats. However, these results were effectively nullified when Mississippi voters rejected the new constitution by a margin of 63,860 to 56,234.

This rejection was primarily orchestrated by White leaders who opposed two key provisions in the proposed constitution. These provisions would have disqualified a significant portion of the White population from voting and holding public office, likely due to their involvement in the Confederacy. Despite being outnumbered by Black voters, White opponents of the constitution succeeded in their efforts. This success was largely due to federal officials' failure to enforce a fair election, allowing for voter suppression and intimidation tactics.

As a result of the constitution's rejection, the newly elected officials could not take office, since the legal framework under which they were to govern had not been approved. Consequently, martial rule continued in Mississippi, maintaining federal control over the state's governance.

MISSISSIPPI RATIFIES ITS NEW STATE CONSTITUTION

President Ulysses S. Grant appointed General Adelbert Ames as both military commander and provisional governor of Mississippi. Grant then ordered another vote on the state constitution, which included separate ballots for two controversial oath provisions in addition to the main body of the constitution.

The first oath, often referred to as the "ironclad oath," required voters to swear that they had never voluntarily supported the Confederacy. This oath was particularly controversial as it would have disenfranchised many White Mississippians who had supported the Confederacy. The second oath was likely a modified version of the ironclad oath, possibly allowing for some exceptions or a less stringent declaration of past loyalty. Both oaths were aimed at restricting voting rights and officeholding for former Confederates, ensuring that those who had rebelled against the Union would not immediately regain political power.

During this vote, both oath provisions were defeated. Despite the rejection of these oath requirements, the rest of the constitution won approval by a large majority and went into effect.

However, the passage of the new constitution was just one step in Mississippi's path to fully restoring its political rights and congressional representation. Two additional requirements remained: ratification of both the Fourteenth and Fifteenth Amendments to the US Constitution. These ratifications would be undertaken by the newly elected state legislature in January 1870.

THE ELECTION OF 1869

During the same time the constitution was being ratified, new elections were held for state officials. There were two candidates for governor, both Republicans. The National Union Republican Party was formed by conservatives, including many White Democrats. The party picked Judge Louis Dent, a Northerner who was also President Grant's brother-in-law. The regular Republican Party's candidate was James L. Alcorn, a native Kentuckian and wealthy Coahoma County planter.

Alcorn, a former Whig, directed his campaign toward the poor Black and poor White citizens of Mississippi. He called for a reorganization of political parties in the state. He wanted to avoid the danger of a White party controlled by White conservatives and a Black party dominated by Northern Republicans. The only way to prevent ruin, he said, was to unite with and lead the freedmen. Alcorn explained: "A colored man comes, as well as the White man, within the scope of my proposed negotiation. I propose to vote with him; to discuss Political affairs with him; to sit, if need be, in political council with him and form a platform

Figure 9.5. James L. Alcorn. Library of Congress, Manuscript Division, Brady-Handy Collection, LC-DIG-cwpbh-00580.

acceptable alike to him, to me, and to you, to pluck our common liberty and our common prosperity out of the jaws of inevitable ruin." Alcorn won, 76,186 to 38,097. Military rule was over in Mississippi.

THE RESEATING OF MISSISSIPPI'S CONGRESSIONAL DELEGATION

The composition and actions of Mississippi's state legislature underwent significant changes during the Reconstruction era. In 1870, the newly seated legislature reflected a dramatic shift in political power from the pre-Reconstruction period. According to Vernon Lane Wharton's *The Negro in Mississippi, 1865–1890*, the House of Representatives, consisting of 107 members, saw Republicans holding a strong majority. Specifically, the House comprised eighty-two Republicans, thirty of whom were Black, and twenty-five Democrats, all of whom were White. The thirty-three-member Senate included five Black senators, further illustrating the changed political landscape.

This new legislative body stood in stark contrast to its predecessor. The pre-Reconstruction legislature, dominated by White Democrats, had refused to ratify the Thirteenth Amendment, which abolished slavery. This refusal led to a prolonged delay in Mississippi's ratification of the amendment; it was only symbolically ratified on March 16, 1995, and officially certified in 2013.

In contrast, the post-Reconstruction legislature, with its Republican majority including Black representatives, took a markedly different approach to civil rights legislation and ratified both the Fourteenth and Fifteenth Amendments.

Figure 9.6. In this Thomas Nast cartoon, Jefferson Davis reacts to the seating of Revels. From *Harper's Weekly*, April 1870.

The legislature also selected three United States senators: Hiram Rhodes Revels, Adelbert Ames, and James L. Alcorn. Revels, elected to fill Albert G. Brown's unexpired term, served from February 1870 to March 1871, becoming the first Black US senator and notably occupying Jefferson Davis's former Senate desk. Ames, a former Union general and military governor of Mississippi, was elected to serve from 1870 to 1874, while Alcorn was chosen for a full term beginning in 1871. This rapid succession of senators, resulting from the need to fill vacancies and unexpired terms alongside regular elections, reflected the complex political transitions of the Reconstruction era in Mississippi. It's important to note that despite these overlapping appointments, Mississippi never exceeded the constitutional limit of two serving senators at any given time. These elections marked a significant shift in Mississippi's political landscape, introducing both Black representation and Northern Republicans like Ames into positions of power in the state.

REPUBLICAN RULE, 1870–1876

In his inaugural address in January 1870, Governor Alcorn outlined two basic problems that faced his administration. "Under the new order of things," he said, the Republicans had to "extend very greatly the breadth of duty of the State Government," and they had to make "the colored man the equal, before the law, of any other man."

True to his word, Alcorn increased government services. The new administration rebuilt railroads, bridges, and public facilities; repaired levees; and built schools, hospitals, and insane asylums. Therefore, government expenses rose. In addition, there were now more citizens to be served.

In 1870, the state legislature passed a Civil Rights Act prohibiting discrimination in public places and on public vehicles. The added expenses of government meant higher taxes on land, which increased conservative resentment.

AID FOR EDUCATION

The School Law of 1870 marked a significant milestone in Mississippi's educational history, establishing the state's first public school system. This law introduced a tiered salary structure for teachers: $90 per month for first class, $70 for second class, and $50 for third class.

However, the implementation of this system faced severe challenges due to racial tensions. White conservatives vehemently opposed teachers who educated Black students, regardless of the teachers' origins. These educators often faced social ostracism from the White community, forcing them to seek lodging with Black families—a situation that further inflamed White anger. In some cases,

Figure 9.7. "The Mansion" at Tougaloo College, founded in 1869. Courtesy of National Park Service, National Register of Historic Places Collection.

this hostility escalated to violence, with Black schools being burned and teachers driven away, though most schools managed to remain operational.

During this period, the demand for higher education grew among both Black and White Mississippians. However, racial segregation remained contentious, with some Whites resisting integration at the University of Mississippi. In the 1860s, Shaw University in Holly Springs—renamed Rust College in 1890—was the only school available for Black students. The state-operated Normal School originated from Shaw University but later became independent. Among the more prominent institutions, Tougaloo College, founded in 1869, thrived despite limited state funding, which ceased in 1891.

A major challenge in these institutions was the lack of Black instructors. To address this need—and to avoid integrating the University of Mississippi—Governor James L. Alcorn supported the establishment of Alcorn University (now, Alcorn State University) in 1871. As the first publicly funded historically Black land-grant institution in the United States, Alcorn was founded under the Morrill Act of 1862, which provided land to states for colleges specializing in agriculture, science, and engineering.

BLACK PARTICIPATION IN RECONSTRUCTION GOVERNMENT

While the vote provided freed people some political influence, they did not control the state government. No Black was ever elected governor, and the state's delegation to Congress was always predominantly White. The only Black US

Figures 9.8–9.10. Mississippi's three Black Reconstruction congressmen: Hiram Revels, Blanche K. Bruce, and John Roy Lynch.

senators during Reconstruction, however, were from Mississippi: Hiram Revels and Blanche K. Bruce.

After the 1873 elections, Blacks held the offices of lieutenant governor, secretary of state, superintendent of education, and speaker of the House. They also served in the state legislature and filled some city and county offices such as alderman, sheriff, and justice of the peace.

Many of the Black leaders in Mississippi were educated; several were college graduates. They were reasonable in their use of political power and in their actions toward White Mississippians. All they asked was equal rights before the law.

TROUBLE WITH THE KU KLUX KLAN

A major problem of the Alcorn administration was the terrorism of the Ku Klux Klan. Organized in Pulaski, Tennessee, in December 1865, the Klan became an instrument of political terror throughout the South. Its stated purpose was to promote White supremacy and to "preserve the Southern way of life." There were secret handshakes and other signs of recognition. The elaborate rituals and oaths appealed to many Whites.

The Klan and other White supremacist organizations served as violent enforcers for the Democratic Party's political agenda. Their terrorism was not random

Figure 9.11. Klan outfits captured in Mississippi in 1872. From *Harper's Weekly*, January 1872.

but strategically targeted to help Democrats "redeem" Mississippi by returning control to White hands. This campaign of violence was, at its core, a partisan political weapon. Blacks and White Republicans were beaten and sometimes killed. The Klan burned a number of Black schools and churches. In 1871, Congress investigated the Klan and other terrorist organizations in the South. As a result, Congress passed laws extending federal law over all citizens' civil and political rights. It now became a federal offense to wear masks for purposes of intimidation.

As the Klan's violence increased, moderate Whites withdrew from it, but the harassment of and assaults on Blacks and White Republicans continued. Other groups, such as the Knights of the White Camellia, the Sons of Midnight, and the White League, continued to ride throughout the Reconstruction period. The formation and activities of these groups were driven by a unified objective: the restoration of White supremacy.

"WAVING THE BLOODY SHIRT"

One of the most famous incidents of "kukluxing," in the entire South was the whipping by the Klan of Colonel A. P. Huggins near Aberdeen. Huggins was a Northern Republican, a former Union soldier who had stayed in Mississippi after the war. In 1870 he was superintendent of public schools in Monroe County. When he refused to obey a Klan warning to leave the state, he was given seventy-five lashes. His bloody nightshirt was taken to Washington as proof of Klan terrorism in the South. This incident led to the expression "waving the bloody shirt."

THE MERIDIAN "RIOT"

The first indication that violence might succeed in defeating Reconstruction in Mississippi was the Meridian riot of 1871. When a fire broke out in the town, friction between Blacks and White conservatives came to the surface. Whites accused three Black leaders of making inflammatory speeches.

During the trial, gunfire broke out in the crowded courtroom. The Ku Klux Klan assassinated the White Republican judge, and the three Black defendants were also killed. In the days that followed, armed White Klansmen launched a violent campaign, hunting down and killing approximately thirty Black individuals. The violence forced Republican mayor William Sturgis to flee town, abandoning his office.

The riot ended Republican rule in Meridian. Thus, the episode was less a "riot" between two groups of people than a wave of White-on-Black violence and intimidation that had the political result of a coup. And it was a forecast of things to come. Whites realized that the Blacks, largely unarmed and poor, could not resist armed violence. From this time on, any unpleasant incident might produce another "riot."

AMES AGAINST ALCORN

In 1871 Governor Alcorn resigned from office to join Adelbert Ames in the United States Senate. He was succeeded by his lieutenant governor, Ridgley C. Powers, a Northern Republican planter from Noxubee County. The political landscape of post-Reconstruction Mississippi was marked by intense rivalries, even within the Republican Party. The Party split when Alcorn became involved in bitter arguments with Ames. Ames accused Alcorn of not protecting Black Mississippians, of cooperating with the White conservatives, and of allowing the Ku Klux Klan to operate in the state. He called for federal troops in Mississippi to maintain law and order. Alcorn countercharged that Ames was not a citizen of the state, that he owned no property in Mississippi, and that he never intended to remain in Mississippi. The feuding culminated with their opposition during the governor's race.

Ames, representing the more radical wing of the Republican Party that advocated for stronger civil rights measures, secured the endorsement of the Republican state convention. Alcorn, who took a more conservative approach that often aligned with White Southern interests, broke away and formed a separate ticket with his followers.

The election highlighted the fractures not only within the Republican Party but also among Democrats. Some Democrats, viewing Alcorn as the lesser of two evils, threw their support behind him instead of nominating their own candidate. Other Democrats, unwilling to back either Republican, chose to abstain from the election entirely.

The final tally saw Ames victorious with 69,870 votes to Alcorn's 50,490. However, Ames's victory came at a cost. Rather than unifying the party, the election deepened the existing divisions within Republican ranks. These divisions would prove detrimental to the party's long-term prospects in Mississippi, as they weakened the Republicans' ability to present a united front against the growing power of White conservative Democrats.

CONSERVATIVE OPPOSITION

Mississippi, like all other Southern states, struggled to raise revenues. Having bound up most of its wealth in the form of property in slaves, emancipation meant that the only major taxable form of wealth was land. Thus, the Republican

Party could only succeed in making good on the potential of the new state constitution and its own campaign promises by funding expanded public services by raising taxes on land. This meant angering the often financially strapped poorer White owners of small farms. After Ames's election, many "White Men's Clubs" were formed throughout the state. In the summer of 1874, "Taxpayers' Leagues" were organized. Opponents of Republican rule complained of the high costs of government and the ensuing high taxes. Republicans pointed out that demand for government services was great and Mississippi was in better financial condition than other Southern states.

Many Whites complained about the Black participation in the new administration. The lieutenant governor, the secretary of state, the commissioner of immigration and agriculture, legislators, and the presiding officers of both houses of the legislature were Black. These Whites felt the only way to combat high taxes and "Negro rule" was to return White Democrats to office.

CITY ELECTIONS IN VICKSBURG

One of their first opportunities to translate this plan into action occurred in Vicksburg in the summer of 1874. White Democrats in Vicksburg organized a "People's Party" to defeat the Republican city government. In the days before the election, both Democratic and Republican rifle clubs paraded in the streets with their weapons openly displayed. It was rumored that a Black militia company from Louisiana was headed to Vicksburg to intimidate the Whites from voting. White men in Yazoo City armed themselves and prepared to go to Vicksburg. As the August election approached, tensions rose to a fever pitch.

Governor Ames asked for help from the federal authorities, but President Grant refused to intervene. When the Democratic candidates won the election, Republicans charged that the Democrats had used intimidation to win. The Vicksburg election, with its tense atmosphere and intimidation of Republican voters, became the model for White conservatives statewide.

THE VICKSBURG RIOT

In December 1874, Democrats used violence to seize control of Warren County. A mob of 500 White men marched on the Vicksburg courthouse, forcing Black sheriff Peter Crosby—the highest-ranking county official—to flee to Jackson. When Crosby returned with Governor Ames's support to reclaim his position, Black citizens throughout the county mobilized to defend him. On December 7, 1874, when African Americans marched toward Vicksburg in support of Crosby, they were confronted by an armed White mob. Though Black citizens agreed to

Figure 9.12. This sketch shows armed White citizens rallying at the Vicksburg courthouse in 1875. From *Harper's Weekly*, December 1876.

withdraw, White vigilantes charged them, sparking violence. The initial clash left two Whites and roughly thirty-five Black people dead. In the days that followed, armed White bands swept through the countryside, hunting down and killing innocent Black residents. While historian Vernon Lane Wharton documented the initial deaths (the thirty-five), total estimates of Black citizens killed range significantly from fifty to three hundred. Crosby fled to Jackson and was reinstated as sheriff, but he soon faced further challenges. After hiring a White deputy, an argument arose when the deputy refused to follow his directives, culminating in the deputy shooting Crosby in the head. While Crosby survived, he was eventually removed from his position as sheriff.

The massacre achieved its political aims: it forced out the democratically elected Republican officials (many of whom were Black) and restored Democratic White supremacist control of Vicksburg and Warren County.

"THE COUNTERREVOLUTION OF 1875"

Following the Vicksburg riot, White conservatives grew increasingly aggressive in their efforts to supplant peaceful democratic electoral processes with intimidation and violence. Their actions were emboldened by several factors weakening the Republican Party both nationally and within Mississippi.

At the national level, the Panic of 1873—a severe financial crisis that sparked a prolonged economic depression in the United States and Europe—severely damaged public confidence in the Republican-led government. This economic turmoil, combined with major scandals in President Grant's administration, significantly undermined the reputation of the national Republican Party.

Within Mississippi, conservatives found further encouragement in the growing divisions within the state Republican Party. Several prominent Republican leaders, including Hiram Revels, had begun to distance themselves from Governor Adelbert Ames and openly criticize his policies. This internal rift provided additional ammunition for conservative efforts to challenge Republican control in the state.

Word now spread of a "revolution," and restoring White supremacy became the central issue in the coming election. Mounted riflemen, wearing red shirts, drilled and held torchlight parades at night to scare Black residents, and especially Black voters. Cannons were fired near Republican rallies. Employers threatened to dismiss those who voted Republican. One Democrat warned Blacks that "whoever eats the White man's food must vote with the White man or refrain from voting at all."

Democratic forces pressured White Republicans, too. Armed bands of Whites threatened Republican candidates. In one town, Democrats made coffins for prominent Republicans and placed black paper on their doors (signaling a house in mourning). Many White Republicans retired from politics. Others fled. Only a few brave ones stood with their Black political allies.

MORE VIOLENCE

There were vicious race riots at Water Valley, Louisville, Macon, Yazoo City, Friar's Point, Columbus, and Rolling Fork. Several Blacks were killed when Whites broke up a Fourth of July parade in Vicksburg.

On September 4, 1875, a joint political debate was held at Clinton. After the Democratic speaker spoke, firing broke out. Republicans charged a group of drunken Whites with starting it, while Democrats blamed Blacks. In the fight that followed, several Blacks and Whites were killed. The news spread rapidly, and special trains of armed Whites came from Jackson, Vicksburg, and Bolton. They instituted a reign of terror. For several days, they hunted Blacks around Clinton, murdering from twenty to fifty of them. Many Blacks fled to Jackson; others hid for days in woods and swamps.

In Monroe County, the Ku Klux Klan brutally targeted Jack Dupree, a Black Republican leader, as a symbol of the threat Blacks imposed. Dragged from his home, Dupree was forced to kneel before his pregnant wife and publicly executed to terrorize African Americans into political silence. His killers went unpunished, signaling that Black political rights could be violently suppressed without consequences during Reconstruction. Governor Ames, abandoned by federal support, faced rejection from President Grant, who stated, "The whole public are tired out with these annual autumnal outbreaks in the South, and the great majority are ready now to condemn any interference on the part of the government." Left to act alone, Ames organized Black militias, further provoking White hostility. An October 15 agreement to disband the militias in exchange for a fair election failed, as Democrats continued violence and intimidation unchecked.

"HE HAD TO DIE"

Charles Caldwell had to die. He had to die because he was a Republican, because he was a leader, and because he was Black.

He was no ordinary man. Those who liked him described him as strong, fearless, a dead shot. Those who did not like him called him "a notorious and turbulent Negro" and "a desperate character." But even they admitted that he was "a man of great courage."

Born a slave in Hinds County, Caldwell lived all his life near Clinton. He educated himself and worked as a blacksmith until Emancipation gave him a chance to do other things. Hinds County elected him to the 1868 Constitutional Convention; there he helped draft the new state constitution. He then served in the Mississippi Senate and became a top officer in the state militia.

In the violent days following the Clinton riot in September 1875, bands of armed White men terrorized both Black and White Republicans in Hinds County. A group of Whites told Caldwell's wife that they were going to kill her husband "if it [takes] two years, or one year, or six; no difference; we are going to kill him anyhow. We have orders to kill him, and we are going to do it, because he belongs to this Republican Party, and sticks up for these Negroes."

They got their chance on Christmas Night, 1875. Those who planned his death lured him into a store for a "friendly" Christmas drink. There he was ambushed and shot in the back. Bleeding heavily, he was carried outside to the street. A crowd of White men gathered, drawing their pistols. Charles Caldwell looked up at them and defiantly spoke his last words: "Remember, when you kill me, you kill a gentleman and a brave man. Never say you killed a coward. I want you to remember it when I am gone."

The roar of blasting pistols shattered the quiet of that Christmas Night in Clinton. Charles Caldwell, a leader of his people, was dead.

VIOLENCE WITHOUT END: THE CARROLL COUNTY MASSACRE

The wave of deadly massacres extended beyond the 1870s, reaching into the 1880s when Carroll County's courthouse turned into a site of bloodshed. A disagreement over spilled syrup in Carrollton escalated into yet another racial massacre. After the Brown brothers—of mixed Black and Native American ancestry—filed charges against White attorney James Liddell for attempted murder following an incident where both Liddell and one of the Brown brothers were wounded during a shootout, with the Browns claiming Liddell shot first, armed White men took deadly revenge. On March 17, 1886, more than fifty Whites stormed the courthouse during the trial and opened fire on Black attendees. Those who tried escaping through windows were shot by gunmen positioned outside. Twenty-three Black citizens, including the Brown brothers, were killed. Not one White assailant was injured or faced charges.

DEMOCRATIC CORRESPONDENCE

These two telegrams between Democrats show their intentions regarding the "peace agreement" of October 15:

W. J. Taylor, Goodman, Miss., October 28, 1875, to James Z. George: "Can you send us cannon, good size for display at Lexington? Want it Friday night. Answer quick."

James Z. George, October 28, to W. J. Taylor: "We telegraphed to N. O. to have cannon sent you, paying transportation both ways. You must provide ammunition."

Chances for a fair election were fading. During this time, a Northern correspondent saw Ames and reported: "The governor has but faint hopes of the Republicans' carrying the State. He takes a gloomy view of the Black man's future."

THE "MISSISSIPPI PLAN"

The sun rose on Election Day. There was trouble at Forest, Okolona, Grenada, and Port Gibson. At Aberdeen, a White militia company from Alabama paraded and a cannon was aimed on the polls all day. In some places, armed White men, supposedly going hunting, "accidentally" fired shots into the air near Blacks. At

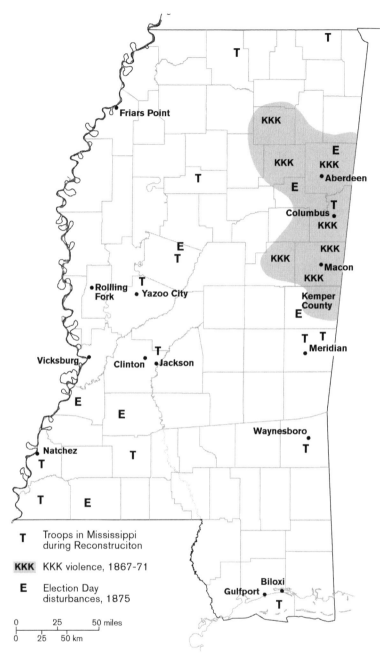

Map 24. Reconstruction Incidents

one precinct in Claiborne County, Whites stacked arms near the polls and dug trenches as if in preparation for war.

The Democrats carried the state by more than 30,000 votes, electing a majority of legislators and all but two congressmen. They won local elections in sixty-two of the seventy-four counties. Two years before, in 1873, Democrats had carried only thirty-nine counties. In Yazoo County, where Republicans had received 2,433 votes in 1873, only seven Republican votes were reported. Only twelve Republican votes were tallied in Tishomingo County, and only four in Kemper County.

The tactics employed by White Democrats during the 1875 Mississippi election campaign became known as the "Mississippi Plan." While these methods included intimidation and violence, recent historical analysis by Jere Nash suggests that such terror tactics were less effective than previously thought in deterring Black voters. Instead, the Democratic victory was largely achieved through widespread electoral fraud, particularly the manipulation of ballot counts at precinct levels.

Despite facing threats and violence, Black men in Mississippi demonstrated remarkable courage and persistence, turning out to vote in numbers comparable to previous elections. This resilience echoed their earlier response to Ku Klux Klan activities between 1870 and 1873. However, without federal protection at polling locations, Democratic operatives, led by figures like J. Z. George, were able to manipulate election results effectively.

The perceived success of these fraudulent tactics in Mississippi inspired White conservatives in other Southern states, who adopted similar methods to challenge and ultimately dismantle their biracial Republican governments.

Even before federal troops were withdrawn in 1877 under President Hayes with his compromise, Mississippi had already developed methods to suppress Black voters that would later spread throughout the South.

SIGNIFICANT RECONSTRUCTION-ERA EVENTS AND CONFLICTS IN MISSISSIPPI (1865–1877)

Aberdeen
1870: Whipping of A. Huggins, known as the "Bloody Shirt" affair.
1875: Disturbance during Election Day.

Clinton
1875: Race riot that includes the murder of Charles Caldwell and other Black leaders.

Columbus
1875: Election-eve riot by Whites, resulting in the deaths of four Black individuals.

Friars Point
1875: Race riot. Black Sheriff John Brown was removed from office, led by former governor James Alcorn.

Jackson
1865: Constitutional convention convenes; Black Codes enacted.
1868: Constitutional convention; new state constitution ratified in 1869.
1868–1875: Jackson serves as the seat of Reconstruction government.
1876: The impeachment trial of Governor Adelbert Ames marks the end of Republican control as Conservatives assume power. Republican governance in Jackson continues until 1888.

Kemper County
1877: The "Chisholm Massacre" occurs, marking violent retaliation in the aftermath of Reconstruction.

Macon
1875: White Alabamians kill twelve Blacks at a church meeting.

Meridian
1871: Riot breaks out, followed by days of violence and the killing of Black residents.

Rolling Fork
1875: Race riot.

Vicksburg
1865: Black convention held to protest presidential Reconstruction policies.
1866–1870: Site of military headquarters during Reconstruction.
1874: Riot following heated July city elections; subsequent December unrest leads to killings of Black residents.
1874: The attempt to remove Sheriff Peter Crosby and the killing of Blacks.

Yazoo City
1875: Race riot. Several Black political leaders lynched.

AFTERMATH OF THE "MISSISSIPPI PLAN"

The newly empowered Democratic legislature impeached three Republican leaders: Governor Adelbert Ames, Black Lieutenant Governor Alexander K. Davis, and Superintendent of Education Thomas W. Cardozo. Lieutenant Governor Davis was quickly convicted and removed from office to prevent a Black official from assuming the governorship after Ames's departure. Both Cardozo and Ames resigned during their impeachment proceedings and departed Mississippi. John M. Stone, president pro tempore of the Senate, now became governor.

Mississippi was again under the control of conservative Whites, who had successfully deployed the Democratic Party.

Republicans condemned the violence used by the Democrats. A prominent White Republican in Mississippi called the methods "armed resistance and wholesale riot and murder." President Grant wrote in 1876: "Mississippi is governed today by officials chosen through fraud and violence."

Ironically, Mississippi Democrats justified the campaign as a moral crusade. A campaign leader later wrote: "We were forced to a choice between the evils of Negro rule and the evils of the questionable practices to overthrow it. We chose what we thought was the lesser evil, and it is now not to be regretted."

LASTING MYTHS

Out of Reconstruction have come several myths, including that of a helpless South suffering under unbearable military rule for a decade. Martial law in Mississippi lasted less than three years, and the number of troops stationed in the state never exceeded 6,900. In 1869, there were only 716 soldiers in Mississippi. Thus, old stories of "bluecoats on every corner" are false.

Some writers claimed that all Reconstruction governments in the South were corrupt. It is true that some White Republicans stole; so did some Black officials, and so, indeed, did some White Democrats. Vernon Wharton, in his work on Reconstruction, found no difference between Democratic and Republican counties in Mississippi in this regard. There were no major scandals in Mississippi during Reconstruction; major embezzlements of funds by state treasurers occurred in 1866, 1890, and 1902, all of them Democrats.

Another myth is that of domination by Blacks. Although Black people started exercising their rights during Reconstruction, nowhere did they hold power in proportion to their voting strength. On the local level in Mississippi, there was only one Black mayor (in Natchez) and only twelve of the seventy-four sheriffs were Black.

All of these myths appeared in the most popular book on Mississippi history for many years, John K. Bettersworth's *Mississippi: A History*. He wrote:

> The war was over, but the fighting was not; for reconstruction was a worse battle than the war ever was. Slavery was gone, but the Negro problem was not gone. To make matters worse, political adventurers from the North came in to make their fortunes off the prostrate state.... Fortunately, time was on the side of the Mississippians; and, by 1875, the old political order had returned. Once again, Mississippi was for the Mississippians, and now Whites and Blacks could set about the task of getting along together in the "New South" as they had in the "Old."

Even more inaccurately, Bettersworth concludes the passage by suggesting that the state was racially unified behind the "task" of replacing biracial democracy with something far worse, and "getting along together" as they had during slavery (the "Old" South). Myths are stubborn, but they are stubborn because they are repeated. When those who repeat the act are considered trustworthy authorities, damaging myths live for decades and decades.

A BOLD LEADER AMONG THE TUMULT OF RECONSTRUCTION

JOHN ROY LYNCH

Born near Vidalia, Louisiana, in 1847, the son of an enslaved woman and a White man who oversaw Tacony Plantation. Lynch worked on the plantation until he was freed at the age of sixteen. After working with the Union Army in Natchez, he soon began helping manage a photographer's studio there, and attended night school. Taking to politics at a young age, he was only twenty-two when appointed by military Governor Ames to a position as a Justice of the Peace in Natchez. Lynch became active in Republican politics and quickly won election to the state House in 1869, at only twenty-two years of age. At the tender age of twenty-five, he was elected by his fellow House members to the powerful position of speaker, and soon he won election to Mississippi's Sixth Congressional District. He was an important voice in helping nominate and elect Governor Ames; he even won reelection to Congress in 1874 despite substantial election violence against his Republican supporters.

Defeated by Democratic redistricting in 1876, he mounted a comeback, winning a congressional seat with the help of the US House Committee on Elections, which ruled that

Figure 9.13. John Roy Lynch.

he had been cheated out of his seat in an 1880 election. While in Congress, Lynch testified and spoke on behalf of the 1875 Civil Rights Act. He even served as the temporary chair of the 1884 Republican National Convention.

Outside of politics, Lynch earned a law degree and practiced law in Washington, DC, and entered the US Army and served tours of duty as an officer stateside, in Cuba, and in the Philippines.

Later in life, Lynch wrote several books and articles. The most important one published during his life, *The Facts of Reconstruction* (1913), was one of the first to push back against the myth of Reconstruction then in its ascendancy. This book remains an important window into Reconstruction more than one century later.

Lynch died in 1939 and, befitting a former member of Congress and military officer, was buried with military honors in Washington's Arlington National Cemetery.

THE FAILURE OF RECONSTRUCTION

Gradually, White northerners lost interest in building democracy in the former Confederacy. The North was now involved in industrial development. Northern businessmen wished to carry on trade with the South, and they urged an end to government intervention. Grant was simply echoing national sentiment when he said the nation was "tired out."

Finally, in 1877, President Rutherford B. Hayes withdrew the last of the federal troops from the South. Rights of property had been judged more important than the rights of human beings. The Black man in the South was abandoned to the mercy of his former owners. The dream of the freedmen was dead, or was to lie sleeping. Thus, the tragedy of Reconstruction is not that it brought suffering to the South, but that it failed to bring equality to its Black citizens and democracy to Blacks and Whites alike.

REDEMPTION

White Mississippians framed the end of Reconstruction in religious terms, calling it "redemption" and labeling themselves as "redeemers" who had reclaimed control from Black political participation and federal oversight. In *Lanterns on the Levee*, William Alexander Percy described how his father's generation fought to keep the Mississippi Delta under White control: "They stole ballot boxes to prevent Black officials from being elected, knowing that fair vote counts would have put Black people in every county office. They also helped create the 1890 constitution that legally stripped Black citizens of their right to vote."

THE NAME OF THE ERA

Do you think the term "Reconstruction" is a good term for the postwar years? What better term might be applied? What problems were solved during Reconstruction? What problems emerged from this period?

Recommended Readings

Aaron D. Anderson, *Builders of a New South: Merchants, Capital, and the Remaking of Natchez, 1865–1914* (Jackson: University Press of Mississippi, 2013).

Justin Behrend, *Reconstructing Democracy: Grassroots Black Politics in the Deep South after the Civil War* (Athens: University of Georgia Press, 2015).

Nancy D. Bercaw, *Gendered Freedoms: Race, Rights, and the Politics of Household in the Delta, 1861–1875* (Gainesville: University Press of Florida, 2003).

David W. Blight, *Race and Reunion: The Civil War in American Memory* (Boston: Harvard University Press, 2001).

John Cimprich, *Navigating Liberty: Black Refugees and Antislavery Reformers in the Civil War South* (Baton Rouge: Louisiana State University Press, 2023).

James C. Cobb, *The Most Southern Place on Earth: The Mississippi Delta and the Roots of Regional Identity* (New York: Oxford University Press, 1992).

Thulani Davis, *The Emancipation Circuit: Black Activism Forging a Culture of Freedom* (Durham, NC: Duke University Press, 2022).

W. E. B. Du Bois, *Black Reconstruction in America: An Essay toward a History of the Part which Black Folk Played in the Attempt to Reconstruct Democracy in America, 1860–1880* (New York: Free Press, 1988 [1935]).

Philip Dray, *Capitol Men: The Epic Story of Reconstruction Through the Lives of the First Black Congressmen* (Boston: Houghton Mifflin, 2008).

Douglas R. Egerton, *The Wars of Reconstruction: The Brief, Violent History of America's Most Progressive Era* (New York: Bloomsbury Press, 2014).

Eric Foner, *Reconstruction: America's Unfinished Revolution, 1863–1877* (New York: Harper & Row, 1988).

Noralee Frankel, *Freedom's Women: Black Women and Families in Civil War Era Mississippi* (Bloomington: Indiana University Press, 1999).

Henry Louis Gates Jr., *Stone the Road: Reconstruction, White Supremacy, and the Rise of Jim Crow* (New York: Penguin, 2019).

Allen C. Guelzo, *Fateful Lightning: A New History of the Civil War and Reconstruction* (New York: Oxford University Press, 2012).

Steven Hahn, *A Nation Under Our Feet: Black Political Struggles in the Rural South from Slavery to the Great Migration* (Cambridge, MA: Harvard University Press, 2005).

William C. Harris, *The Day of the Carpetbagger: Republican Reconstruction in Mississippi* (Baton Rouge: Louisiana State University Press, 1979).

William C. Harris, *Presidential Reconstruction in Mississippi* (Baton Rouge: Louisiana State University Press, 1967).

Nicholas Lemann, *Redemption: The Last Battle of the Civil War* (New York: Farrar, Straus and Giroux, 2006). This book provides a detailed account of the effective political violence used by Democratic forces that climaxed in the bloody elections of 1875.

John Roy Lynch, *The Facts of Reconstruction* (New York: Neale, 1914).

John Roy Lynch, *Reminiscences of an Active Life: The Autobiography of John Roy Lynch*, edited by John Hope Franklin (Chicago: University of Chicago Press, 1970 [1937]).

Matthew Lynch, ed., *Before Obama: A Reappraisal of Black Reconstruction-Era Politicians* (Santa Barbara: Praeger, 2012).

Elaine Frantz Parsons, *Ku-Klux: The Birth of the Klan During Reconstruction* (Chapel Hill: University of North Carolina Press, 2015).

John David Smith and J. Vincent Lowery, *The Dunning School: Historians, Race, and the Meaning of Reconstruction* (Lexington: University Press of Kentucky, 2013).

Christopher M. Span, *From Cotton Field to Schoolhouse: African American Education in Mississippi, 1862–1875* (Chapel Hill: University of North Carolina Press, 2009).

Julius Thompson, *The Black Press in Mississippi, 1865–1985* (Gainesville: University Press of Florida, 1993).

Michael Wayne, *The Reshaping of Plantation Society: The Natchez District, 1860–1880* (Baton Rouge: Louisiana State University Press, 1983).

Vernon Lane Wharton, *The Negro in Mississippi, 1865–1900* (New York: Harper & Row, 1965 [1947]).

Richard White, *The Republic for White It Stands: The United States During Reconstruction and the Gilded Age, 1865–1896* (New York: Oxford University Press, 2017).

CHAPTER 10

CONSERVATIVE REACTION

1876–1890

FOLLOWING THE END OF RECONSTRUCTION IN MISSISSIPPI, THE EXISTING PARTY system collapsed. The Republican Party, which had been in power during Reconstruction, was deeply divided and unable to effectively oppose the Democratic Party, which had positioned itself as the party of White supremacy. By the turn of the century, this shift in the political landscape led to the emergence of the "Solid South," a term used to describe the dominance of the Democratic Party in the Southern states, including Mississippi.

The new power structure in Mississippi was controlled by a small but influential group of White Democrats, known as "Conservatives," "Redeemers," or "Bourbons." This group included the planters who had previously held power before the Civil War, as well as new planters who had emerged in the Delta region. However, as the state's economy and society evolved, influence shifted from rural areas to towns, giving rise to a new generation of leaders, including merchants, bankers, and lawyers.

Despite the changes in political leadership, many Mississippians continued to face significant challenges, including poverty, disease, and limited access to education. Agriculture, the backbone of the state's economy, was not providing sufficient income for many farmers, and children growing up in rural areas often had limited access to schooling and literacy. These challenges were particularly acute for Black Mississippians, who faced ongoing discrimination and segregation, as well as economic and political marginalization. The political and social changes of the post-Reconstruction era reinforced and perpetuated the state's existing inequalities.

OLIGARCHY IN CONTROL

Political power in Mississippi rested with a small elite group—an oligarchy—that dominated state government. Most citizens, Black or White, had little voice in their own government. A few men controlled the Democratic Party conventions which nominated candidates for state office. Thus, they controlled the party. And since there was no longer an effective Republican Party to challenge them, they controlled the state.

For twenty years after Reconstruction, John M. Stone and Robert Lowry shared the governor's office with each other. County politicians passed positions among themselves and stayed in office for years. Throughout the state, little was done without approval of the two chief Bourbon leaders, J. Z. George and L. Q. C. Lamar.

A POWERFUL POLITICIAN

The most powerful man in Mississippi politics after Reconstruction was Lucius Quintus Cincinnatus (L. Q. C.) Lamar. In 1849, Lamar moved from his native Georgia to Oxford, where his father-in-law was president of the new University of Mississippi. He practiced law and taught at the school.

In 1851, Lamar supported Jefferson Davis for governor. When Unionist candidate Henry S. Foote came to Oxford, Lamar took him on in debate. Although Davis lost the election, Lamar had caught the public's eye.

In 1857, Lamar beat James L. Alcorn, a Whig, for Congress. He left his plantation and went to Washington. There he supported the South's position on slavery, but he knew that secession would mean war. "When the sun of the Union sets," he wrote," it will go down in blood." He resigned from Congress with the rest of the Mississippi delegation, returned home, and drafted the Ordinance of Secession adopted by the state convention in January 1861.

Serving in the Confederate army until his health failed, Lamar was then appointed special envoy to Russia, England, and France. In 1872 he was elected to Congress, the only Democratic representative from Mississippi. He realized that if northern public

Figure 10.1. L. Q. C. Lamar. Library of Congress, Manuscript Division, Brady-Handy Collection, LC-DIG-cwpbh-03965.

opinion could be softened toward the White South, Republican power in Southern states could be eroded. When Senator Charles Sumner of Massachusetts died in 1874, Lamar got his golden opportunity. Before a packed chamber, he praised the sincerity and idealism of Sumner, who had championed the cause of Black equality. Lamar made a dramatic appeal for an end to sectional hatred, and concluded by saying, "My countrymen, know one another and you will love one another." Later Lamar spoke throughout the North on behalf of the Democratic Party, explaining to audiences White Southern attitudes.

Lamar played a major role in Mississippi's "Revolution of 1875," by which Democrats relied on White supremacist partisan violence to triumph in state elections. The 1876 legislature then chose him to be United States senator. Although as senator and, after 1885, as secretary of the interior, he spent most of his time in Washington, he remained the "kingpin" of state politics. As historian Albert D. Kirwin put it, "The fate of candidates for office seemed to rest in his hands; his approval was almost sufficient to guarantee election, his disapproval, to ensure defeat."

From 1888 until his death in 1893, Lamar served as associate justice of the United States Supreme Court. Lawyer, teacher, congressman, soldier, senator, cabinet member, judge—no other Mississippian ever held so much power on the state level and had so much influence on the national scene as L. Q. C. Lamar.

ECONOMIC POLICIES

Conservative leaders believed in low government costs and low taxes. They abolished several state offices and set salaries of public officials at a low level. State expenses were cut from $1,130,000 in 1875 to $547,000 in the next year. As a result, government services were sharply reduced.

The conservatives strongly supported industry. They appealed to northern investors by highlighting the fact that the state's workers were low-paid and unorganized by labor unions. They gave tax breaks to corporations. Still, Mississippi's economy failed to grow. By 1883, there were only fourteen plants and mills in the state. Railroads did grow, and a state railroad commission was established in 1884 to regulate freight and passenger rates. Mississippi continued to be overwhelmingly rural.

CORRUPTION IN GOVERNMENT

While Mississippi's conservatives claimed they had "restored" honest government after what they called Reconstruction's corruption, the reality proved different. Elections continued to be filled with fraud and violence. These claims of superior governance were exposed when State Treasurer William L. Hemingway, after fourteen years in office, was caught stealing $315,612—an amount far larger than any theft during Reconstruction. His mere five-year prison sentence further revealed the double standard in how corruption was handled under conservative rule.

THE NEEDS OF THE PEOPLE

In exchange for economy in government, Mississippians paid a higher price. Tax policies favored the rich more than the poor. Care for the poor, the sick, and the blind was maintained at very low levels. The laissez-faire government of the conservatives usually left such social concerns to relatives or private charities.

State government did advance health care. It established an East Mississippi Insane Hospital at Meridian and a State Board of Health. In 1878, state authorities fought a yellow fever epidemic that took more than 3,000 lives. Doctors, unaware that yellow fever was caused by a mosquito-carried virus, were helpless. A few towns lost over one-half of their population.

The state also gave much attention to flood control in the Delta. The prewar system of levees along the Mississippi River had been heavily damaged during the war, and the flood of 1867 had completed its destruction. During Reconstruction, levee boards tried to rebuild the levees but made little progress. During the 1880s, levee construction increased; Governor Robert Lowry reported in 1890 that the Yazoo-Mississippi levee system was better than ever.

Figure 10.2. Memorial to victims of the yellow fever epidemic in Mississippi. Library of Congress Prints and Photographs Division, LC-DIG-highsm-37211.

EDUCATION

The public school system received a severe setback. Unlike Reconstruction leaders, the new state leaders did not give public education a high priority. For example, the 1872 legislature appropriated $1,136,987 for 148,000 pupils, while the Democrats in 1881 cut back to $757,757 for 237,288 pupils. National per pupil spending was ten times as much. White teachers' salaries dropped from $55.47 per month in 1875 to $28.74 in 1885. Black teachers received even less. With many children not attending school, Mississippi had a high rate of illiteracy.

In 1878, the Agricultural and Mechanical College (now Mississippi State University) was founded at Starkville. The Mississippi Industrial Institute and College, the first state-supported college for women in the nation, was founded at Columbus in 1884. Unfortunately, state-supported colleges sat far below national standards. Other colleges were established by church groups: Natchez Seminary, 1877 (now, Jackson State University), Belhaven College (1883), Natchez College (1885), Campbell College (1887), and Millsaps College (1890). Alcorn College, Rust, and Blue Mountain had been founded during Reconstruction.

THE LOOPHOLE: HOW MISSISSIPPI REINVENTED SLAVERY THROUGH CONVICT LEASING

Convict leasing emerged as a new form of forced labor after the Civil War. This system allowed private employers to lease prisoners from the state, exploiting a loophole in the Thirteenth Amendment that banned slavery "except as punishment for a crime." While supposedly prisoners were working off their sentences, in reality, this was legalized slavery—private businesses paid the state for prison labor, but prisoners received no compensation.

The system targeted newly freed African Americans facing severe economic hardships. In 1876, Mississippi's Democratic legislature passed the "pig law," making theft of farm animals or any property valued at $10 or more a felony punishable by up to five years in prison. Many impoverished Black citizens, with few employment opportunities, had resorted to taking freely roaming farm animals for food. The law's impact was dramatic: the prison population quadrupled from 250 in 1875 to 1,000 in 1887.

Conditions under convict leasing were brutal. The business owners who leased prisoners, focused only on maximizing profit, showed no concern for prisoners' welfare. A Mississippi grand jury reported on conditions of prisoners in 1887 and found, "prisoners covered in scars, blisters, and open wounds from severe beatings. Most of them had their backs cut in great wales, scars and blisters, some with skin peeling off in pieces." Workers were forced to wade through snake-infested swamps and work sugar cane fields while chained together, their

Figure 10.3. Convict chain gang hoeing a field at Parchman Farm. Courtesy of the Archives and Records Services Division, Mississippi Department of Archives and History.

feet bare and flesh cut by shackles. Chained in lines, they were forced to urinate and defecate in the same swamp water they were forced to drink, creating a deadly cycle of disease and suffering. Without access to proper sanitation, this contaminated water became their only source of hydration. They faced constant exposure to parasites, snakes, and disease.

Some reforms followed. By 1889, annual prisoner deaths decreased from sixty to nineteen. The 1890 Mississippi Constitution called for abolishing convict leasing in favor of state-run farms, though the system continued into the early 1900s, marked by corruption including a $400,000 scandal during Governor McLaurin's administration (1896–1900).

When convict leasing finally ended, Mississippi established Parchman Farm, but this state penitentiary operated much like a traditional plantation. Guards used a leather strap called "Black Annie" for public whippings, maintaining the brutal disciplinary practices of slavery and convict leasing. Parchman effectively transformed state imprisonment into another form of plantation labor. Governor Vardaman remarked, "It operates like a well-run plantation."

Parchman Prison's current conditions closely reflect its origins as a penal farm. Inmates continue to labor in prison factories and agricultural operations, earning wages far below the minimum standard. The economic exploitation is evident—according to the Mississippi Department of Corrections' 2022 Work Annual Report, inmate labor generated nearly $5 million in revenue. While one report claims that some prisoners receive minimum wage, the reality is that this system sustains a form of forced labor reminiscent of its plantation-era foundations.

FARMER DISCONTENT

During the 1870s and 1880s, farmers in the hill sections knew something was wrong. While many townsfolk, bankers, railroad lawyers, and merchants seemed to prosper, they suffered. They saw the soil on their hillside farms wearing out, and they were barely providing for their families. Cotton prices fell from twelve cents per pound in 1870 to nine cents in 1884 and eventually reached a low of four cents in 1898. They became mired deeper and deeper in debt. Sharecroppers throughout the state were even worse off. Mississippi's per capita income in 1880 was only $82, among the lowest in the nation.

White farmer discontent in Mississippi took several forms. Farmer organizations such as the Grange and the Farmers' Alliance set up self-help programs and ran candidates against the Bourbons, who seemed to care so little for small farmers. Many small farmers backed the Greenback Party, which endorsed the use of paper money to help those in debt.

Other Whites called themselves Independents and challenged Bourbon control of the Democratic Party. They campaigned for the end of convict leasing, the regulation of railroads, and monetary policies that favored debtors. They appealed to Black farmers to join them.

This frightened conservatives. If White and Black farmers united politically, the conservatives would lose power. They appealed to White voters not to desert the "White man's party." Such a thing, they said, might bring back the "Negro Domination" of Reconstruction days, and must be avoided at all costs.

FUSION

At the same time, the conservatives turned to the Black vote in their struggle against the White Independents. In those counties where Blacks were the majority, "fusion" had been practiced since the end of Reconstruction. Fusion meant that a few local offices and perhaps one of the county's positions in the state legislature would be given to Blacks. In return, conservative Whites relied on Black votes to help them stay in power.

Thus, fusion undercut any chance for a real union of Blacks and Whites. In a way, Black fusion politicians "sold out" for personal power and gain. But they felt the "Revolution of 1875" had shown that real Black influence was now impossible in Mississippi.

By using fusion in the Black counties, by appealing to White racism in White counties, and by using fraud and intimidation wherever necessary, the Bourbons weathered the Independent revolts of the 1880s.

BLACK POLITICAL RIGHTS AND WHITE SUPREMACY

After the "Revolution of 1875," some Republican leaders in Mississippi advised Blacks to forget politics, at least temporarily. A Greenville Republican even advised Blacks to join the White Democrats: "It will give you rest from annoyance, if you declare yourselves Democrats, and they will let you alone to attend your crops, to pull your fodder and dig your sweet potatoes in peace."

However, Blacks did not join the Democratic party in large numbers. White politicians used various devices to control the Black vote. Among these were gerrymandering, the practice of manipulating the boundaries of districts for the purpose of advantaging one party or group over another. For example, the Third Congressional District, called the "Shoestring District," stretched from Tennessee to Louisiana along the Mississippi River. It contained mostly Black voters and left the other six districts mostly White. This was an impressive political feat in a majority-Black state.

WHITE INTIMIDATION CONTINUES

Although Whites preferred legal methods, some were willing to use any means to eliminate Blacks from politics. These practices came to be known as "bulldozing." They included intimidation, threats of loss of jobs, stuffing ballot boxes, miscounting ballots, and bribery. In practically every election, Whites used violence against Black voters. A White Republican of Yazoo City complained to Governor Stone in November 1879: "Voters have been refused admission to the polls to vote by a lawless band and by force. Others have had tickets contrary to their wishes forced upon them and voted. More outrageous and unlawful conduct at the polls and around them I never witnessed or read in all my life. I wish you could have been here to see it. The election is a farce and a shame." Violence during the Copiah County elections in 1883 and the Jackson city elections in 1888 caused Congress to investigate, but nothing came of it. In Jackson, where a biracial Republican organization had held control since 1866, a city newspaper called for the White Democrats to overthrow "Negro rule." A resolution of the "Young White Men League" warned Blacks that they would be harmed if they attempted to vote. Only one Black man even tried to vote.

BLACK SENATOR FROM MISSISSIPPI

After 1876, because of the violence and fraud used against Republican voters, only one Black Mississippian remained in Congress. He was Blanche K. Bruce.

Born a slave in Virginia, Bruce was taught to read and write by his master's son. During the Civil War he made his way to Missouri and became a teacher. After attending Oberlin College, he moved to Mississippi. He bought land for a plantation in Bolivar County and was elected tax assessor, sheriff, and later county superintendent of schools.

In 1874, the Mississippi legislature elected him to the United States Senate, joining James L. Alcorn. Bruce later recalled the scene:

> When I came up to the Senate I knew no one except Senator Alcorn, who was my colleague. When the names of the new Senators were called out for them to go up and take the oath, all the others except myself were escorted by their colleagues. Mr. Alcorn made no motion to escort me, but was buried behind a newspaper, and I concluded I would go it alone. I had got about half way up the aisle when a tall gentleman stepped up to me and said: "Excuse me, Mr. Bruce, I did not until this moment see that you were without an escort. Permit me. My name is Conkling," and he linked his arm in mine and we marched up to the desk together.

When Bruce's only child was born, he was named Roscoe Conkling Bruce, honoring Senator Conkling of New York for his friendship.

Bruce's first speech in the Senate dealt with the frauds of the 1875 Mississippi election. However, Bruce was not concerned solely with the rights of Black people. He spoke movingly of the mistreatment of Native Americans, and, saying he was the representative of "a people who but a few years ago were disqualified from enjoying the privilege of American citizenship," he voted against the Chinese Exclusion Bill. He also worked to allow all Southern Whites to vote and helped build better levees along the Mississippi River.

His term ended in 1881. The Mississippi legislature, now under White conservative control, replaced him with James Z. George. Later Bruce was appointed Register of the US Treasury, among other positions, and served as temporary chairman of the 1880 National Republican Convention. Toward the end of his Senate term, Bruce remarked to a friend that he would be the last Black man to serve in the Senate. For eighty-five years he was right. In 1966, Edward Brooke was elected by Massachusetts, marking the return of a Black individual to the United States Senate.

THE EXODUS OF 1879

In 1879, thousands of African Americans, mostly from Mississippi and Louisiana, left their homes and moved west to Kansas and Oklahoma. There were several causes. Their political rights were being stripped away. A combination of drought, low prices, and the yellow fever epidemic caused misery. Many tenant farmers, trapped in the exploitative system of sharecropping, desperately sought ways to break free. Sharecroppers were agricultural laborers who worked land owned by others, typically receiving a share of the crop as payment instead of wages. This arrangement often led to a cycle of debt and poverty, as sharecroppers frequently had to borrow money for seeds and supplies, with high interest rates keeping them perpetually indebted to landowners. Blacks continued to live in fear of White violence. Finally, land agents from Kansas painted glowing pictures of a "Utopia" in the West where Blacks might start anew.

About 30,000 Blacks—6,000 from Mississippi—made their way to Kansas in the winter of 1879. Most of those who made it suffered from cold weather and hunger. One wrote of hard times in Kansas: "Negroes are not any more respected in Kansas than they are in Mississippi." Another wrote to Blacks back in Mississippi: "You had better stay where you are. There are some who have come here and are now sick, and cannot help their selves, wishing that they were back home."

Most of the Black people who left Mississippi for Kansas returned home within a few years. The real Black exodus from Mississippi began during World War I.

Figure 10.4. Blacks go West from Vicksburg in the Exodus. From *Harper's Weekly*, May 1879.

CHAPTER 10.

STRANGE FRUIT: THE LYNCHING OF BLACKS

Southern trees bear a strange fruit, blood on the leaves and blood at the root. Black bodies swinging in the Southern breeze, strange fruit hanging from the poplar trees.

—"STRANGE FRUIT," WRITTEN BY ABEL MEEROPOL AND RECORDED IN 1939 BY BILLIE HOLIDAY

Lynching was the ultimate weapon to keep Blacks under control. It had a long history. In frontier America, law enforcement was weak. In order to protect their society, frontier settlers took the law into their own hands.

Most of the lynching victims in the South before the Civil War had been White. But after the Civil War, Blacks became the prime target of Southern mob violence. In the minds of many White Mississippians, the Black man had become the symbol of the defeat of the Confederacy. Lynching, which originally had meant whipping or tarring and feathering, came to mean death by hanging. The National Association for the Advancement of Colored People (NAACP) laid bare the true nature of lynching with a precise definition: "a murder committed by three or more people who simply ignored justice altogether." It was mob rule in its purest form—trampling the basic right to trial by jury. Although lynchings occurred throughout the United States, most of them took place in the Deep South. More lynchings have been recorded in Mississippi than in any other state.

The systemic violence of lynching, combined with the haunting imagery evoked by Billie Holiday's rendition of *"Strange Fruit,"* highlights how deeply these acts of terror were embedded in Southern society. Lynching served as both a stark warning to anyone who might challenge racial hierarchies and a public spectacle of dominance, intended to reinforce White supremacy through fear and brutality.

THE IDEOLOGY OF LYNCHING

Though Whites often claimed lynching protected White women, Frederick Douglass proved this excuse was false by pointing out a telling fact: during the Civil War, when White men were away fighting, there were no mass accusations of Black men assaulting White women. These accusations only surged during Reconstruction, revealing lynching's true purpose: maintaining White control through terror.

As is indicated in maps 25, 26, and 27, lynchings emerged most frequently in areas where Black advancement threatened White dominance. Political scientist

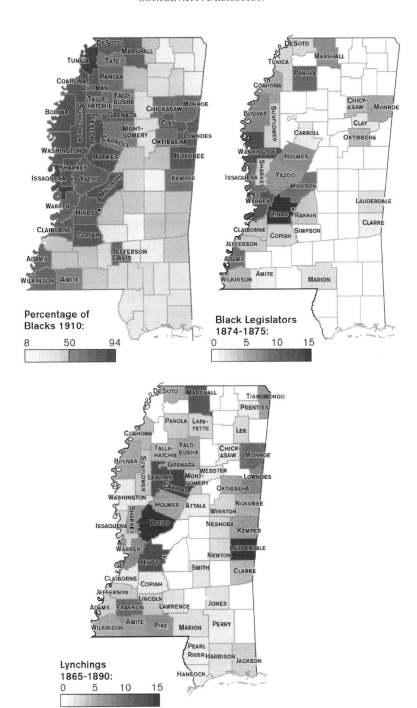

Map 25. Percentage of Blacks 1910
Map 26. Black Legislators, 1874–1875
Map 27. Lynchings, 1865–1890

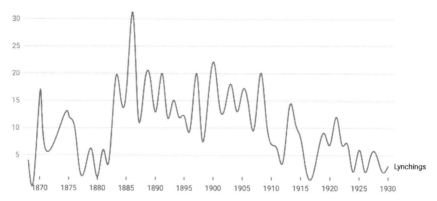

Figure 10.5. Confirmed Black lynchings from 1865–1930.

V. O. Key Jr.'s research showed that these killings clustered in counties with large Black populations and areas that had elected Black officials during Reconstruction. The violence intensified in the mid- to late 1880s, targeting successful Black communities as African Americans gained economic independence.

The victims were often killed for the smallest perceived infractions against racial customs. Keith Bowen was lynched in 1889 simply for trying to enter a room where White women were sitting, with no other accusations against him. In 1916, Jeff Brown was murdered in Cedarbluff merely for accidentally bumping into a White girl while rushing to catch a train. These examples show how lynching served primarily to enforce White supremacy through terror and intimidation.

Governor James K. Vardaman openly endorsed racial violence, declaring that, "If it is necessary, every Negro in the state will be lynched; it will be done to maintain White supremacy." The White population's acceptance of lynching, and the fact that known lynchers were rarely punished, demonstrated how deeply this form of racial terrorism was embedded in Mississippi's power structure. During Vardaman's campaign for political office starting around 1900 and throughout his administration (1904–1908), Figure 10.5 reveals that Mississippi experienced a surge in brutal racial violence, with lynchings averaging horrific levels. Both his inflammatory rhetoric as a candidate and his policies as governor helped create an atmosphere where mob violence against African Americans became increasingly savage and public.

Vardaman's words emboldened White mobs to commit increasingly barbaric acts of violence. In 1904 in Sunflower County, a White mob captured Luther Holbert and a woman named Mary. The mob mutilated their bodies, distributing ears and fingers as souvenirs, and forced two Black men to drag them to their execution. Mary was burned alive while Holbert was forced to watch before suffering the same fate. Decades later in 1937, Elias "Bootjack" McDaniels and

Figure 10.6. A Mississippi lynching, captured by the camera. Bettman Archive/Getty Images.

Roosevelt "Red" Townes were tortured with blowtorches and killed in Duck Hill during a public spectacle that White men, women, and children gathered to witness—an atrocity they cruelly termed a "negro barbecue."

In the end, Vardaman's public support for lynching, segregation, and Black disenfranchisement drove many to seek safety in other Southern states and Northern cities. About 100,000 Black Mississippians fled the state during his governorship (1904–1908), seeking escape from racial terror and economic oppression.

JIM CROW

Jim Crow—named after a demeaning character from minstrel shows—was the system of laws and practices that enforced racial segregation and discrimination. While racial oppression defined both slavery and the post-Reconstruction period, formal legal segregation emerged later. Most Mississippi laws mandating racial separation were not enacted until the late 1880s and 1890s, when the state government systematically created legal barriers between races.

Of course, discrimination and segregation had existed before this period. White Mississippians carried over the racial attitudes they had developed during slavery days. Nevertheless, the conservative leaders did not go beyond providing for separate schools in 1878 and forbidding intermarriage in 1880. It was not unusual to see Black people admitted to most parks, theaters, streetcars, and trains along with White people. They served on juries (although not in great numbers) and even shared cemeteries with Whites. Only in hotels was there open discrimination. Many restaurants served both races in the same room. But by 1890, segregation was becoming the pattern.

Prior to the Civil War, many White churches maintained segregated seating, with enslaved Black worshippers often restricted to balconies or designated areas. Following emancipation, Black congregants faced increasing exclusion from White churches. At the same time, many freed people sought to establish their own independent congregations. This led to a widespread racial separation of churches during Reconstruction that became even more pronounced in the late nineteenth century.

THE COURT APPROVES SEGREGATION

In 1883, the US Supreme Court removed the only real legal barrier to racial segregation when it ruled the Civil Rights Act of 1875 unconstitutional, holding that the constitution did not empower Congress to prohibit private individuals from committing racial discrimination. The Court declared that the Fourteenth Amendment only allowed the federal government to block discrimination emanating from governmental authorities. Blacks who were refused accommodations could not be protected by federal courts. Only one justice dissented: former slaveholder John Marshall Harlan attacked the decision for destroying the "substance and spirit" of the Reconstruction amendment.

Between 1887 and 1907, every Southern state separated the races on railroad cars. Florida was first in 1887; Mississippi followed in 1888. A Black boycott of Jim Crow streetcars in Mississippi failed to reverse the policy. Mississippi was the first state to require separate waiting rooms. In the case of *Louisville, New Orleans, and Texas Railroad Company v. Mississippi* in 1890, the US Supreme Court ruled that a state could constitutionally require segregation on railroads. Given a legal green light, the states of the former Confederacy and several others expanded Jim Crow to streetcars, parks, playgrounds, waiting rooms, and elevators. Even "Jim Crow Bibles" were used in courtrooms.

THE PLESSY V. FERGUSON DECISION

In the 1896 case of *Plessy v. Ferguson*, the US Supreme Court ruled that to require separate facilities for Blacks did not imply that Black people were inferior and did not violate the Fourteenth Amendment. Read carefully the argument of the Court:

> The object of the Fourteenth Amendment was undoubtedly to enforce the absolute equality of the two races before the law, but in the nature of things

it could not have been intended to abolish distinctions based upon color, or to enforce social, as distinguished from political, equality or a commingling of the two races upon terms unsatisfactory to either. Laws permitting, and even requiring their separation in places where they are liable to be brought into contact do not necessarily imply the inferiority of either race to the other, and have been generally, if not universally, recognized as within the competency of the state legislatures in the exercise of their police power.

In his dissent, Justice Harlan rejected this line of thought: "Our Constitution is color-blind, and neither knows nor tolerates classes among citizens. In respect of civil rights, all citizens are equal before the law. The law regards man as man, and takes no account of his surroundings or of his color when his civil rights as guaranteed by the supreme law of the land are involved. The arbitrary separation of citizens on the basis of race is a badge of servitude wholly inconsistent with the civil freedom and the equality before the law established by the Constitution." It should be noted that while Justice Harlan argued against segregation and for equal rights under the law, he also stated that "the white race deems itself to be the dominant race in this country in terms of prestige, achievements, education, wealth, and power." He expressed his belief that this would continue if the White race remained true to its heritage and upheld the principles of constitutional liberty. This statement, implying the superiority of the White race, has been criticized for its racial prejudice. However, it is still important to note that Harlan's overall dissent is a defense of civil rights.

SEGREGATION REPLACES SLAVERY

In the aftermath of the *Plessy* decision, segregation replaced slavery as the chief means of maintaining White control of society, politics, and economics. Segregation was a social arrangement that expressed the feelings of Whites that Blacks were inferior. An elaborate racial etiquette was developed. All parts of society, including schools and churches, reinforced the system.

Under segregation, whenever both races were involved in similar tasks (such as learning arithmetic in school), they were kept separate. When the relationship between Whites and Blacks was clearly "superior" to "inferior" (such as White housewives and Black maids), the races were allowed to mingle in close physical contact.

Thus, Jim Crow became another burden that Black people had to bear. In 1937 sociologist Bertram Doyle wrote with great accuracy: "Tradition thus assigns the Negro his place in the South, law defines it, sentiment supports it, custom and habit continue it, and prejudice maintains it in those instances where it seems to be breaking down."

Recommended Readings

Stephen Cresswell, *Rednecks, Redeemers, and Race: Mississippi after Reconstruction, 1877–1917* (Jackson: University Press of Mississippi, 2006).

Bertram Wilbur Doyle, *The Etiquette of Racial Relations in the South* (Chicago: University of Chicago Press, 1937).

Lawrence Otis Graham, *The Senator and the Socialite: The True Story of America's First Black Dynasty* (New York: HarperCollins, 2006). This book is a biography of Mississippi Senator Blanche K. Bruce.

Albert D. Kirwan, *Revolt of the Rednecks: Mississippi Politics, 1876–1925* (Lexington: University Press of Kentucky, 1951).

Neil R. McMillen, *Dark Journey: Black Mississippians in the Age of Jim Crow* (Urbana: University of Illinois Press, 1990).

James B. Murphy, *L. Q. C. Lamar: Pragmatic Patriot* (Baton Rouge: Louisiana State University Press, 1973).

David M. Oshinsky, *"Worse Than Slavery": Parchman Farm and the Ordeal of Jim Crow Justice* (New York: Free Press Paperbacks, 1996).

Nill Irvin Painter, *Exodusters: Black Migration to Kansas after Reconstruction* (New York: W. W. Norton, 1986).

Timothy B. Smith, *James Z. George: Mississippi's Great Commoner* (Jackson: University Press of Mississippi, 2012).

Stewart E. Tolnay and E. M. Beck, *A Festival of Violence: An Analysis of Southern Lynchings 1882–1930* (Urbana and Chicago: University of Illinois Press, 1995).

CHAPTER 11

THE NADIR OF RACE RELATIONS

FIFTEEN YEARS HAD PASSED SINCE THE END OF RECONSTRUCTION IN MISSISsippi. The split between hill farmers and conservative leaders within the Democratic Party was growing. However, a breakdown of White unity frightened many Whites, especially political and economic elites. Some way must be found, they said, to allow Whites to split politically without endangering White control of the state. The new 1890 Constitution seemed to be the answer. Its new voting requirements disfranchised most Blacks. Soon, other Southern states had followed Mississippi's lead and denied Blacks the political rights guaranteed to them by the Fourteenth and Fifteenth Amendments.

This chapter discusses the disfranchisement of most Black and some White Mississippians, the failure of the Populist movement to unite poor White and poor Black farmers, and the rise of new political leaders representing the White common man.

NEGROPHOBIA: THE FEAR OF "NEGRO DOMINATION"

Conservative politicians warned White voters about the dangers of a return to "carpetbag days." Some, including Senator James Z. George, predicted a 500,000 Black majority in Mississippi by 1890. Therefore, according to the Bourbons, Whites had to stay united behind their Democratic Party leaders. "Unless something is done," a reader wrote the *Jackson Clarion-Ledger*, "we will everlastingly be under the heel of the Negro."

These worries were like the old fears of slave uprisings in Mississippi, and the rumors of revolts by freed Blacks during the Civil War and the time of Reconstruction. The 1890 census, however, showed them to be exaggerated.

THE DEMAND FOR DISFRANCHISEMENT

Pressures against Black voting had been building up for years. White control had been maintained throughout the 1880s by fusion and bulldozing. However, many Whites felt uneasy about using illegal methods. The *Jackson Clarion-Ledger* said, "We have grown weary of shotguns and fraud." The time had come, many Whites said, to keep Blacks from voting by "legal" and "constitutional" means. A letter in the *Port Gibson Southern Reveille* explained: "The old men of the present generation can't afford to die and leave their children with shot guns in their hands, a lie in their mouths, and perjury on their souls, in order to defeat the Negroes. The constitution can be made so that this will not be necessary."

THE CALL FOR A NEW CONSTITUTION

In June 1890, a bill was introduced in Congress to provide federal supervision of congressional elections. This threat of federal intervention to protect Black voters in the South scared many Whites. Blacks must be removed from politics "legally" to avoid a "second Reconstruction."

Many other reasons were given in support of a new constitution. Voters in White counties wanted to take away the power of Delta politicians who "exploited" the votes of a small number of Blacks to stay in power. Prohibitionists wanted to outlaw alcoholic beverages. Others wanted a new constitution in order to have judges elected by the people, halt convict leasing, or regulate corporations.

The Constitution of 1868 contained few provisions that could be attacked. Many Whites were simply opposed to it because it had been written during Reconstruction. The *Jackson New Mississippian* said that it had been drawn up by "a conglomeration of White and yellow adventurers, camp followers, carpetbaggers, [and] war bummers." It wanted a constitution drawn up by White men only.

OPPOSITION

Many Whites did not want a new constitution. They agreed with former Governor James L. Alcorn when he advised "leaving well enough alone." After all, they said, the Black vote had already been made ineffective. Others were afraid that any property or educational qualifications would keep many Whites as well as Blacks from voting. Still others worried that a new constitution might arouse Northern opinion and bring about federal intervention in Mississippi's elections.

Governor Robert Lowry had vetoed a constitutional convention call in 1888, but the new governor, John M. Stone, favored a new constitution. In 1890 the legislature called for a constitutional convention to meet in Jackson.

THE CONSTITUTIONAL CONVENTION OF 1890

Of the 134 delegates in the 1890 Constitutional Convention, 130 were Democrats. Isaiah T. Montgomery of Bolivar County was the only Black delegate. S. S. Calhoon, a Hinds County planter and lawyer, was elected president of the convention.

The first problem considered by the important Committee on Elective Franchise, Apportionment, and Elections was apportionment. White counties were being outvoted by Whites in Black counties. J. Z. George's reapportionment plan was adopted. It increased the number of representatives in the House by thirteen, with all thirteen going to White counties.

This action did not effectively cut the Delta's power, however. After 1890, there were still sixty-nine representatives from Black counties and sixty-four from White counties. Not until the 1920s did the White counties achieve a majority position in state government.

"THE COMMONER"

Coming home from Washington, DC, to play the leading role in the 1890 Constitutional Convention was US Senator James Z. George. A native of Georgia, George was raised in Carroll County, Mississippi, and became a self-taught lawyer. He served as a private in the Mexican War, was later elected to the 1861 Secession Convention, and served on L. Q. C. Lamar's committee to draft the Ordinance of Secession. When fighting broke out, he joined the Confederate army. He was captured and held as a prisoner of war for twenty-five months.

George played a leading role in the "Revolution of 1875" in Mississippi. As chairman of the statewide Democratic Executive Committee, he met with Governor Ames two weeks before the election to arrange a truce. His leadership in restoring White supremacy through illegal practices, including violence, won him great popularity among White Democratic voters and guaranteed his political future.

George was instrumental in chartering Mississippi A&M (now Mississippi State University) in 1878. The next year he was chosen chief justice of the Mississippi Supreme Court. In 1881 he resigned to accept the position of United States senator, remaining in the Senate until his death in 1897.

In the Senate he served on a number of important committees. He was considered the "Father of the Department of Agriculture," and he coauthored the Sherman Anti-Trust Act of 1890, which opposed business monopolies.

George spent much of his time defending the South's policies after Reconstruction. His first Senate speech defended the campaign tactics of Mississippi Democrats in the election of 1875. In a major speech in 1882, he spoke in favor of Chinese exclusion. On December 31, 1890, he addressed the Senate for four and a half hours defending the new Mississippi Constitution.

Although as a lawyer he usually defended corporations and railroads, his speech was simple and his dress was plain. His supporters called him "The Commoner." After his death, he was honored as one of Mississippi's major leaders. In 1931, Mississippi presented, as its contribution to the Hall of Fame in Washington, DC, statues of Jefferson Davis and J. Z. George.

VOTING RESTRICTIONS

Various schemes for restricting the Black vote were discussed. Delta leaders wanted to limit the Black vote without sacrificing their political power. They supported educational and property qualifications. Hill-county leaders opposed these restrictions because they would block thousands of poor and/or illiterate Whites from the polls.

The franchise committee's report established new voting requirements that systematically disenfranchised Black voters. While initially granting voting rights to all adult males (except "idiots, the insane, and American Indians"), the committee then created multiple barriers to voting. They required two years of state residence and one year in the election district. Voters had to register at least four months before an election and pay a $2 poll tax two years in advance, producing the receipt at voting time. It disqualified anyone who could not read or understand materials that were read to them. Most significantly, the committee disqualified anyone convicted of specific crimes, such as burglary, theft, arson, perjury, forgery, receiving stolen goods, or bigamy. This list intentionally focused on crimes linked to poverty and economic hardship, disproportionately impacting Black residents, while deliberately omitting violent offenses like murder, frequently carried out by White supremacist terrorists. This selective criminalization revealed the law's true intent: to prevent Black citizens from voting while preserving White political power.

VOTER DISQUALIFICATION

Were the provisions of the 1890 Constitution fair? Which of them have been repealed? How did these provisions affect your ancestors if they lived in Mississippi at this time?

THE DEBATE OVER DISFRANCHISEMENT

The disfranchising provisions were hotly debated on the convention floor and outside the halls. The *Natchez Democrat* said the "understanding" clause was drawn up to give corrupt officials an opportunity to restrict White as well as Black voters. Mississippi was the only state, said the *Port Gibson Southern Reveille*, to make its constitution "an instrument of fraud."

Supporters of the clauses argued that the increased residence requirement would disfranchise many Blacks, since they moved more often than Whites. Early voter registration and the poll tax would keep many poor people from registering. In effect, supporters argued, these provisions would not discriminate directly against Blacks, but against what were called their "racial characteristics." Thus, they said, the Fifteenth Amendment—which protected individuals from having their ability to vote restricted explicitly because of their race—would not be violated.

S. S. Calhoon left no doubt about the purpose of the disfranchising provisions or, indeed, of the convention. "Let's tell the truth if it bursts the bottom of the Universe," he told the delegates. "We came here to exclude the Negro. Nothing short of this will answer." James K. Vardaman was more explicit. He declared, "There is no use to equivocate or lie about the matter. Mississippi's constitutional convention of 1890 was held for no other purpose than to eliminate the n----- from politics."

APPROVAL

The people of Mississippi were not allowed to vote on the new constitution. A majority of the convention declared it to be in effect without a vote. Many political elites did not want to run the risk of the constitution being rejected. The *Winona Times* said there were enough Whites opposed to it that, combined with the Black vote, it would be defeated. "Its submission means its defeat," said the *Winona Times*. Later, the disfranchising features of the Constitution of 1890 were upheld by the Mississippi Supreme Court and later by the United States Supreme Court, which for several decades decided that the Constitution did not provide for a right to vote.

Not just the South, but the entire nation was moving backward in race relations. Three events at the end of 1890 ushered in what historians termed "the nadir" (or lowest point) in US race relations. One was Mississippi's new constitution, which obviously conflicted with the Fourteenth and Fifteenth Amendments to the US Constitution. Since the national government did nothing to oppose it, it became known as the "Mississippi Plan," and other Southern states followed suit, including Oklahoma in 1907. Second, the voting rights bill mentioned earlier went down to a one-vote defeat in the US Senate. After its demise, Democrats taunted

Republicans for their support of Black voting rights. But now, Republicans moved away from that cause, and Blacks found themselves without real allies. Third, at the Battle of Wounded Knee in South Dakota, now more accurately known as the Massacre at Wounded Knee, Lakota (Sioux) Indians, already surrendered, were mowed down by machine-gun fire. Native Americans went into their nadir as well. Of course, from the perspective of many racist Whites, "relations" between the races can be very good while racial inequality and injustice run rampant. Thus, the "nadir" is best thought of not as describing the "relations" between the races, but the commitment of American society and government toward justice. In terms of justice, this certainly was the nadir in the post-slavery era.

ISAIAH MONTGOMERY AND THE END OF BLACK SUFFRAGE: STATESMAN OR TRAITOR?

Isaiah Montgomery was one of only two Republicans at the 1890 Mississippi Constitutional Convention and the sole Black delegate. In this historic yet contentious role, he cast a vote that would forever define—and complicate—his legacy.

Supporting measures like literacy tests and poll taxes, Montgomery helped strip Black Mississippians of their hard-won voting rights. He defended his decision by claiming these restrictions were based on class rather than race, arguing that Black citizens could eventually regain voting rights by overcoming poverty and illiteracy. This reasoning rang hollow, as these were the very conditions that White supremacist policies helped create and maintain. To many in the Black community, Montgomery's actions represented a betrayal—a surrender to White supremacy disguised as pragmatic compromise.

The motivations behind Montgomery's stance remain a puzzle. Some point to the assassination a few weeks earlier of F. M. B. "Marsh" Cook, a White Republican who had opposed disenfranchisement, as proof of the lethal risks of defiance. Others believe Montgomery traded his support for

Figure 11.1. Isaiah T. Montgomery, founder of Mound Bayou. Library of Congress Prints and Photographs Division, LC-DIG-bellcm-00606.

financial backing for Mound Bayou, the all-Black town he founded, or sought to shield his community from even greater violence. Whatever the reasoning, his decision left him admired by Whites but alienated from many Black contemporaries, his name forever tied to one of the most contentious chapters in Mississippi's racial and political history.

ISAIAH MONTGOMERY AND THE BLACK TOWN OF MOUND BAYOU

Isaiah T. Montgomery was born, enslaved, in 1847 on Joseph Davis's plantation at Davis Bend. His father, Ben Montgomery, a brilliant man who had made several inventions while enslaved, taught him to read. He then became Joseph Davis's private secretary. Davis provided the Montgomerys more autonomy than other enslaved Blacks.

After the Davis family fled during the Civil War, the Montgomerys managed and later purchased the plantation, building it into the South's third-largest cotton producer by 1873. However, when the Mississippi River turned Davis Bend into an island and financial troubles mounted, Isaiah had to abandon the property. After exploring opportunities in Kansas, he returned to Mississippi to pursue other ventures.

In 1886, Isaiah and his cousin, Benjamin T. Green, established Mound Bayou on 840 acres in the Mississippi Delta. As the South's first all-Black town, it aimed to provide a safe and prosperous community for Blacks amid widespread racism.

Figure 11.2. Mound Bayou. Library of Congress Prints and Photographs Division, LC-USF34-032053-D.

By the second decade of the twentieth century, Mound Bayou's population had grown significantly. The town boasted thirteen stores, several small shops, a sawmill, three cotton mills, the leading Black-owned bank in Mississippi, and ten churches. It also had a privately maintained high school with 200 pupils, a rarity for Blacks at the time. The town's success attracted the attention of Booker T. Washington, Black America's most well-known leader, who praised Mound Bayou as a model for Black economic achievement. The town also enjoyed political autonomy, as it was governed by Black officials initially appointed by Montgomery. Mound Bayou's progress even drew the attention of President Theodore Roosevelt, who visited the town to witness its accomplishments. Years later, Mound Bayou experienced economic difficulties but managed to recover. As of 2025, it was one of the poorest towns in the country with a poverty rate of 46.3 percent.

DISFRANCHISEMENT IN OPERATION

After the ratification of the 1890 state constitution, its new voting restrictions went into effect and greatly reduced the number of registered Black voters. When the new voting rolls were collected in 1892, only 8,600 of 147,000 voting-age eligible Black men were registered. But despite the new regulations, a few unregistered Blacks were allowed to vote in some state and local elections when White political elites needed their votes to remain in office.

Although the convention had promised that no Whites would be denied the vote, thousands of Whites were excluded. Of 120,000 voting-age eligible White voters in Mississippi in 1890, only 68,000 were registered in 1892.

The poll tax discouraged poor people from registering. If a voter fell behind in his poll-tax payments, the amount soon added up to more than he could pay. Also, the voter had to pay the tax months in advance of an election, before he even knew the candidates or the issues. In other words, candidates had no ability to inspire unregistered voters to become interested in politics and decide to register.

DEMOCRACY IN THE JURY BOX: THE CORNELIUS JONES CASE

Most African Americans opposed Isaiah Montgomery's support for Black disfranchisement. Cornelius Jones, a lawyer and legislator, challenged Mississippi's new laws with a unique argument: since Blacks were barred from voting, they couldn't serve on juries, violating defendants' constitutional rights. As the first African American to argue before the US Supreme Court, Jones faced a Mississippi Supreme Court that claimed crimes "more inclined to be committed by Blacks" should disqualify voting rights. In *Williams v. Mississippi*, the US Supreme Court ruled that "it has not been shown that their actual administration was evil, only that evil was possible under them," requiring proof of intentional discrimination—an almost impossible task.

While Black men like Jones fought disenfranchisement through legal channels, women in Mississippi faced their own battles for political rights.

WOMEN ACTIVISTS

Delegates at the 1890 Convention considered giving women the right to vote but decided against it. However, this denial of political rights did not stop Mississippi women from being active citizens. Eliza Jane Poitevent and Ida B. Wells were two such individuals who were well respected in the field of journalism.

When she was twenty-seven years old, Eliza Jane Poitevent became the first woman owner-publisher of a major daily newspaper in the United States. Born in 1849 in Hancock County, she later expressed her love of nature in poetry written under the name "Pearl Rivers."

Her work captured the attention of A. M. Holbrook, owner of the *New Orleans Daily Picayune*, who offered her the job of literary editor at $25 per week. She married Holbrook in 1872 and inherited the paper when he died four years later. The paper was deep in debt, but Mrs. Holbrook saved it. Later she employed another woman, Elizabeth Meriwether Gilmer, who started the Dorothy Dix advice column, similar to the columns that have become so popular today.

Figure 11.3. Ida B. Wells. Library of Congress Prints and Photographs Division, LC-USZ62-107756.

Figure 11.4. Eliza Jane Poitevent. From *Some Notables of New Orleans: Biographical and Descriptive Sketches of the Artists of New Orleans and Their Work* by May W. Mount, 1896.

Ida B. Wells was born in Holly Springs in the summer of 1864. Both her parents had been enslaved. When she was fourteen, her parents died in the yellow fever epidemic of 1878, and she took care of her four younger brothers and sisters. She put herself through school, attending Rust College and also Fisk University.

After college, she taught in county schools in Mississippi and Tennessee. However, after speaking out against injustices to her people, she was fired from her teaching position. She became editor and part-owner of the *Memphis Free Speech* and wrote a pamphlet called *The Red Record* condemning lynching. When White supremacists threatened to kill her and chased her out of Memphis, she spoke in northern cities and in Europe. In 1898 she told President McKinley, "We refuse to believe this country, so powerful to defend its citizens abroad, is unable to protect its citizens at home."

Wells married a Chicago lawyer, and in 1908 she organized the Negro Fellowship League. She spent the rest of her life working for civil rights for women and Blacks until her death in 1931.

POLITICS AFTER 1890

After 1890, the narrative grew that eliminating the Black men from voting helped "purify" Mississippi politics. However, there was as much violence and fraud as before. Some also claimed that eliminating Blacks from politics would stimulate White participation. Instead, Whites took less interest in elections than before, and an even tighter oligarchy resulted. "Courthouse gangs" (those who controlled government, such as sheriffs) dominated many counties. Political issues did not come to the surface because Mississippi was now locked into a one-party system. Only within the Democratic Party was there room for disagreement on some issues.

PANIC AND POPULISM

During the 1890s, prices for farmers' crops remained low. An economic crisis known as the Panic of 1893 caused still more hardship. Farmers, angry at Bourbon economic policies, cried out for relief, but these conservatives remained indifferent. Therefore, many farmers joined forces with the Populist Party. The Populists supported all farmers, Black and White. Frank Burkitt of Chickasaw County was the Populist leader in Mississippi.

In 1891, Burkitt ran for the United States Senate against James Z. George, and in 1895 against A. J. McLaurin for governor. He lost both times. Populist candidates opposed Democratic candidates in the congressional elections of 1892, 1894, and 1896. Although no Populist candidate won, the party garnered more than one-third of the vote.

The Mississippi Republican Party failed to run candidates but supported the Populist candidates. This led to charges of a Republican-Populist alliance. Democratic orators claimed that a Populist victory would mean "Black rule." Democratic Party activists and voters who left the party were condemned. A typical comment came from the *Bolivar County Democrat*: "We cannot believe that many of them will turn their backs on the White Democrats of the county and join the Black brigade in the struggle for Negro supremacy in our county. . . . The White people have determined to rule Bolivar County, and no combination of Republicans, populists, and soreheads can defeat them."

THE COLLAPSE OF POPULISM

The Populist movement collapsed in Mississippi under this pressure. It had posed a real threat to the Democratic Party. If poor White and poor Black farmers had united politically, theirs would have been an unbeatable combination. But racial prejudice was strong, and it could not be overcome. Everything else faded into the background when the threat of "Negro domination" was brought up.

Between 1890 and 1915, Confederate memorials were built throughout Mississippi. Right after the Civil War, most people had not wanted to remember or celebrate it, but now times had changed. The "Lost Cause"—the myth that the Civil War was unwinnable for the South but still a noble effort motivated by honorable principles—was not really lost, and the memorials helped foster it, increasing feelings of White supremacy and White solidarity.

Figure 11.5. Almost every Mississippi county seat has a statue like this one, built in 1919 in Pontotoc. Library of Congress Prints and Photographs Division, LC-DIG-highsm-47278.

This is not how Jefferson Davis envisioned honoring the past. In 1888, during a speech he gave, he stated, "The past is dead; let it bury its dead, its hopes and its aspirations. Before you lies the future, a future full of golden promise, a future of expanding national glory, before which all the world shall stand amazed. Let me beseech you to lay aside all rancor, all bitter sectional feeling, and to make your places in the ranks of those who will bring about a consummation devoutly to be wished—a reunited country."

DEFEAT OF THE FARMERS

Do you think things would have been different in Mississippi if the Populists had won? Why did poor Whites stay politically powerless rather than ally with Blacks to gain power for both groups?

THE PRIMARY LAW

The turn of the century saw the death of the nominating convention and the birth of the primary system. Since the end of Reconstruction, the conservatives had held tight control of the conventions at which candidates were nominated to represent the Democratic Party. Those outside the ruling group looked to a new system, the party primary—whereby voters would select who would serve as their party's nominee—as the only way to break this power. The system by which the Democratic Party would choose its candidates was critical; now that Mississippi was a one-party state, the only meaningful choices occurred within the Democratic Party.

Although the 1890 Constitution gave the legislature the power to pass a primary law, it did not pass one until 1902. State politics then underwent a major change. The primary law weakened the control of the oligarchy. Under the convention system, a candidate had only to win the support of convention delegates. Now, with primaries, he had to have popular appeal.

For the first time since Reconstruction, statewide campaigns were competitive. Now the hill farmers came into their own. The way was now paved for James K. Vardaman, their leader, who used the explosive issues of racism and lower-class resentment against the "establishment."

THE GREAT WHITE CHIEF

Known as the "Great White Chief," Vardaman had twice been defeated for the Democratic nomination for governor in Mississippi under the convention system. A colorful campaigner, he also used his *Greenwood Commonwealth* to spread his views.

Vardaman wrote vicious attacks against Black people. Calling Black suffrage a "crime," he advocated repealing the Fifteenth Amendment and modifying the Fourteenth, which had promised Blacks equal citizenship. The Black man, Vardaman said, was a "curse" to America, unfit for citizenship. He urged lynching as the only "cure" for the Black man's supposed desire for White women. Poor White constituents in the hill country, lacking education and access to accurate information, blindly embraced his demagogic rhetoric despite his inability to actually change constitutional amendments.

THE ELECTION OF 1903

Campaigning in 1903 for governor, Vardaman traveled up and down the state preaching racist hate. A master showman in a White suit and Black hat, with long black hair flowing down to his shoulders, Vardaman thrilled his audiences. He proposed to force many Black schools, already inadequate, to close down entirely. Why should Mississippi educate Blacks to qualify them to vote? he asked. He stated, "the only effect of Negro education is to spoil a good field hand...." For Vardaman, these schools were a waste of money and only made Blacks dissatisfied with their place in Jim Crow Mississippi.

Vardaman's campaign was helped by national events. President Theodore Roosevelt had offended White Southerners by hosting Booker T. Washington to a lunch at the White House.

When local White leaders in Indianola, Mississippi, pressured African American postmistress Minnie Cox to resign, President Theodore Roosevelt refused to accept her forced departure. Instead, he shut down the town's post office, making it clear he would not tolerate racial intimidation.

Cox and her husband, Wayne, were respected Black leaders and founders of one of the nation's first Black-owned life insurance companies. Their success made them targets of White hostility.

Roosevelt's actions outraged White supremacist politician James K. Vardaman, who launched a racist attack on the president, calling him a "bronco-busting N----- lover." His inflammatory rhetoric energized White farming audiences, helping him easily win the election and further deepening racial tensions in Mississippi.

Figure 11.6. Vardaman was the first governor to take office in the new Capitol, completed in 1903. Library of Congress Prints and Photographs Division, LC-DIG-highsm-46990.

RACE AS AN ISSUE

Can you think of any recent Mississippi politicians who have used the race issue as Vardaman did? What is meant by "dog whistle"? Can you think of any instances when candidates used a dog whistle to disguise issues related to race?

VARDAMAN'S ADMINISTRATION, 1904–1908

Vardaman's racial politics were particularly evident in his approach to education. He opposed using any tax money, whether collected from Black or White citizens, to fund Black schools. Instead, he advocated for a fully segregated system where Black communities would have to fund their own schools entirely. While the legislature rejected this proposal, their reasoning was cynical: they noted that

Black taxpayers were already effectively subsidizing White schools since only minimal funds were being appropriated to Black education.

Vardaman's hostility to Black education reached its peak when he vetoed funding for the State Normal School, a teacher training institution established during Reconstruction to promote education and literacy among formerly enslaved people. And while he earned praise for dismantling the convict leasing system, his alternative—Parchman Farm (the state penitentiary)—effectively recreated plantation conditions for Blacks under state control. Indeed, Vardaman referred to Parchman as running like "a well-run plantation."

Beyond his racist policies, Vardaman pursued progressive reforms in other areas. He broke the American Book Company's monopoly by creating a state textbook commission. Through his efforts, Mississippi also regulated insurance companies, railroads, banks, and utilities. He asked the legislature for, but could not get, child-labor regulations, a state school for deaf-mutes, and a state highway commission. At the same time, he vetoed legislation permitting corporations to acquire big holdings and permitting railroad mergers.

Figures 11.7–11.9. In East Mississippi, this (virgin forests) led to this (lumber boom) and to this (erosion). Figure 11.7, courtesy of the Archives and Records Services Division, Mississippi Department of Archives and History; figure 11.8, courtesy of Library of Congress Prints and Photographs Division, LC-USF34-031899-D; and figure 11.9, courtesy of Library of Congress, Prints & Photographs Division, Farm Security Administration/Office of War Information Black-and-White Negatives, LC-DIG-fsa-8c52279.

Economic conditions improved briefly because of a boom in lumbering. Out-of-state corporations employed thousands of Mississippians to cut down the virgin trees of the Piney Woods and parts of the Delta. By the end of Vardaman's administration, Mississippi ranked third in the country in lumber production.

THE WHITECAPS

Unsurprisingly, given the fact that Blacks had been stripped of the possibility of wielding political influence, Mississippi made little progress in the cause of racial justice. In the 1890s, White terrorist groups known as Whitecaps sprang up partly as a result of the agricultural depression. White farmers in debt to merchants struck back at these merchants for having their farms taken away by burning their stores and gins. They also terrorized Black tenant farmers and the Black employees of lumber companies.

After the turn of the century, the terror continued, particularly in Southwest Mississippi. Whitecappers whipped Blacks, burned their churches, and threatened them with death. A Black man from Waldo wrote Governor Vardaman: "A crowd of lawless rough brutal men has beaten and run off all the Negroes in this community without cause. All we know as reason that it was done is because they are Negroes. It was done in the night and we could not help it. We are expecting someone to be killed any time. The sheriff cannot do much or has not. He seems to be afraid or careless." Though Governor Vardaman hired a detective to investigate White vigilante violence in Lincoln and Franklin Counties, his response proved largely symbolic. While 312 "white cappers" were found guilty, they received minimal punishment: just a $25 fine and a three-month suspended sentence. Even the single defendant sentenced to life imprisonment was eventually pardoned by Vardaman himself.

With no real protection from the law, many Black families moved to places like Texas to escape the Whitecappers. By World War I, Whitecapping died out in Mississippi, but it left behind a legacy of terror and fear. Lacking political power, White law enforcement officials had little motivation to use their offices to protect Black citizens whom they were supposed to serve.

BLACKS STRUGGLE FOR PROGRESS

Despite disfranchisement, lynching, Jim Crow, and Whitecapping, Blacks made some progress. At the turn of the century, Blacks owned far less property than their share of the population might indicate, but they did own small businesses, drug firms, cafes, and even theaters and banks. Black people also worked in skilled trades as bakers, masons, smiths, and carpenters. This was the age of Booker T. Washington, who emphasized vocational education and economic self-help.

Figure 11.10. Although progress was made after 1900, this school was still being used in Lafayette County in 1962. Martin J. Dain Collection (MUM00702) Archives and Special Collections. University of Mississippi Libraries.

In 1900 Washington organized the National Negro Business League. The President of the Mississippi chapter, Charles Banks of Mound Bayou, was national vice-president. Large organizations founded in Mississippi in this era included the Knights of Pythias, the Knights and Daughters of Tabor, and the Church of God in Christ. Some of these organizations were mutual-aid societies, providing for burial, health care, and education. Blacks also established several schools during this period: Mary Holmes (1892), Okolona (1902), Utica Junior College (1903), Mississippi Industrial (1905), and Prentiss Institute (1907).

WASHINGTON'S STRATEGY AND MISSISSIPPI HISTORY

Booker T. Washington suggested that Blacks should focus on economics and forgo, for a time, their social and political rights. W. E. B. Du Bois believed Blacks should organize to get all their rights, social and political as well as economic. What happened to Blacks economically in the years when their civil rights and voting rights were stripped away? Did Washington's philosophy work?

VARDAMAN RUNS FOR THE SENATE

In 1907, Governor Vardaman and Congressman John Sharp Williams ran for the United States Senate. Vardaman and his followers saw the question of Black domination in Mississippi as the main issue. Williams had been educated in American and European universities and was in some ways the opposite of the "champion of the people." He made it clear that he did not differ with Vardaman on White supremacy, but he condemned Vardaman's use of Blacks as an issue.

The vote was so close that it was not until ten days after the primary that the results were known. Out of 118,344 votes, Williams won by only 648. The "Great White Chief" had lost!

PROGRESSIVE REFORMS CONTINUE

Under the next two governors, Edmund F. Noel and Earl Brewer, the legislature gave more money to schools, making possible better buildings and higher teachers' salaries. Provisions were made for rural pupil transportation (busing), consolidation of rural schools, and new county agricultural high schools. In 1910 the major colleges were placed under a single board of trustees, and Mississippi Normal College (later the University of Southern Mississippi) was established in Hattiesburg to train White teachers.

Scientific agriculture was encouraged, and help was given to farmers to fight the boll weevil and the livestock tick. A new state charity hospital, a child-labor law, a pure-food law, and a Bureau of Vital Statistics modestly improved the quality of life for Mississippians. Also in this period, Mississippi prohibited alcoholic beverages.

THE "SECRET CAUCUS"

In December 1909, Senator A. J. McLaurin died. Former governor Vardaman immediately declared himself a candidate for the rest of McLaurin's term. The legislature had the job of picking a successor. Many people felt that if a number of anti-Vardaman candidates ran for the office, they could keep the "Great White Chief" from winning until they could unite behind one of their group.

Six different candidates announced to run against Vardaman. The anti-Vardaman coalition did not disagree with Vardaman's basic ideology; each of them supported White supremacy. On the first ballot, Vardaman led with seventy-one votes. The opposition controlled a total of ninety-nine votes, which was more than enough to win if they could stick together. The struggle dragged on for seven weeks.

One of Vardaman's opponents was the able Delta planter and lawyer LeRoy Percy of Greenville. On February 10, 1910, on the forty-eighth ballot, Percy passed

Figure 11.11. Towns grew. This is downtown Jackson in a flood, about 1915. Courtesy of the Archives and Records Services Division, Mississippi Department of Archives and History.

the fifty mark for the first time. Twelve days later, the moment came: all the opposition candidates except Percy withdrew. The strategy worked. Percy was nominated, eighty-seven to eighty-two.

ENTER BILBO

At this point, State Senator Theodore G. Bilbo, a Vardaman man, charged that he had set a trap and had taken a bribe from a Percy supporter to switch his vote. The charge was a bombshell! A legislative investigation showed problems in Bilbo's testimony. It turned out that some of the money Bilbo said he took was issued after the event. The Mississippi Senate condemned Bilbo and demanded that he resign. But Bilbo did not step down. He began to build a political career that lasted for decades.

THE ELECTION OF 1911

Percy served a few months in the United States Senate. Then he came home to Mississippi to defend his record in a primary against Vardaman. Bilbo ran for lieutenant governor.

The campaign was the most vicious in the state's history. Hill farmers expressed their long-standing dislike of the Delta. They called Percy "LeRoyal" and

Figure 11.12. James K. Vardaman. Library of Congress Prints and Photographs Division, LC-B2-2560-9.

Figure 11.13. Governor Paul B. Johnson Jr. signing an act repealing statewide prohibition. Prohibition lasted in Mississippi until 1966. Courtesy of the Archives and Records Services Division, Mississippi Department of Archives and History.

mercilessly heckled him. They denounced him as an aristocrat and corporation lawyer. On one occasion, Percy lost his temper and called a Vardaman-Bilbo crowd "cattle" and "rednecks." But despite Percy's view of them, the hill voters picked Vardaman for a term in the United States Senate.

All over the South, Vardamans and Bilbos were taking control away from the old ruling class. The old oligarchy had been indifferent to the needs of ordinary people. Poor Whites, like poor Blacks, faced real problems. The great failure of Southern politics after the turn of the century has been that, while men like Vardaman and Bilbo promised much, they did not always deliver. When they did, the "progressive" gains made in the name of the common citizen were for White people only.

Recommended Readings

Omar H. Ali, *In the Lion's Mouth: Black Populism in the New South, 1886–1900* (Jackson: University Press of Mississippi, 2010).

Stephen Cresswell, *Rednecks, Redeemers, and Race: Mississippi after Reconstruction, 1877–1917* (Jackson: University Press of Mississippi, 2006).

Stephen Cresswell, *Multiparty Politics in Mississippi, 1877–1902* (Jackson: University Press of Mississippi, 1995).

Terence Finnegan, *A Deed So Accused: Lynching in Mississippi and South Carolina, 1881–1940* (Charlottesville: University of Virginia Press, 2013).

Janet Sharp Herman, *The Pursuit of a Dream* (Jackson: University Press of Mississippi, 1999).

William F. Holmes, *The White Chief: James Kimble Vardaman* (Baton Rouge: Louisiana State University Press, 1970).

Valdimer Orlando Key Jr., *Southern Politics in State and Nation* (New York: Alfred A. Knopf, 1949).

Neil R. McMillen, *Dark Journey: Black Mississippians in the Age of Jim Crow* (Urbana: University of Illinois Press, 1989).

Dorothy Overstreet Pratt, *Sowing the Wind: The Mississippi Constitutional Convention of 1890* (Jackson: University Press of Mississippi, 2017).

Joseph A. Ranney, *A Legal History of Mississippi: Race, Class, and the Struggle for Opportunity* (Jackson: University Press of Mississippi, 2019).

Julius E. Thompson, *Lynchings in Mississippi: A History, 1865–1965* (Jefferson, NC: McFarland, 2007).

Stewart E. Tolnay and E. M. Beck, *A Festival of Violence: An Analysis of Southern Lynchings, 1882–1930* (Urbana and Chicago: University of Illinois Press, 1995).

CHAPTER 12

HARD TIMES

1910–1940

IN THE EARLY YEARS OF THE TWENTIETH CENTURY, COTTON WAS STILL MISSIS-sippi's main crop. It was grown on both small farms and large plantations, but most of the good cotton land was on large plantations. Different modes of farm work by landless Blacks and Whites had replaced slavery.

At the same time, education did not provide a way out for most of the state's children. Each town and rural district struggled under the burden of maintaining a dual school system, separate and unequal, for Whites and for Blacks. Neither race received adequate schooling compared with residents of other states. Lumbering and woodworking, the state's largest industry, declined after 1920 because much of the virgin forests had been cut. And before these problems could be solved, the greatest flood in American history up to that time left thousands of Mississippians in misery.

By the early 1900s it was more economical to divide large plantations into smaller plots managed by tenants. The tenant farmed the plantation owner's land, kept part of the crop for himself, and paid the plantation owner with money or the rest of the crop.

THREE KINDS OF TENANTS

There were three different kinds of tenants: sharecroppers, share-tenants, and renters. The sharecropper agreed with the owner to work a certain acreage of the plantation. The owner furnished the land, farm tools, work animals, and fertilizer; the sharecropper provided the labor. After harvesting, the sharecropper had to give the owner one-half or more of the crop as payment for use of the land and equipment. With what he had left over, the sharecropper had to pay for the food and household goods he had bought on credit during the work season.

The share-tenant owned his own tools, work animals, and fertilizer. He had only to pay the owner about one-third of his crop for the use of the land. Like the sharecropper, he had to pay for his goods with what was left over.

The renter, who had enough money to rent a piece of land from the owner, used his own equipment to work the land. He paid the owner a fixed price for the land but was able to keep the entire crop.

In 1930, approximately 60 percent of the 226,000 tenant families in Mississippi were sharecroppers—the poorest and most economically insecure type of farmworker. In addition, some farm laborers were paid cash to farm or perform particular jobs. These workers were called wage laborers.

THE UPS AND DOWNS OF COTTON

Cotton prices held firm through 1911, but the next twenty years brought disaster. In 1914 the price of cotton dropped to five cents per pound. This decline caused farmers (especially sharecroppers) to go deeper in debt to merchants and forced some banks to close.

When the United States entered World War I in 1917, many farmers were able to recover. The Army required massive amounts of cotton for its uniforms. From 1914 to 1919, the average price of cotton increased nearly 300 percent. This meant more money for everybody—merchants, landlords, and sharecroppers.

But at the end of the war, cotton prices crashed to frightening lows. In areas of the Delta where cotton had briefly reached 85 cents per pound, prices fell as low as 10 to 11 cents. Small banks had to close. Farm owners, unable to meet mortgage payments, lost their farms and were forced to become tenants. The number of landowners declined 10 percent, while the number of sharecroppers increased by almost two-thirds.

Prices picked up, only to crash again in 1924 and 1926. By 1929, Mississippi's farmers began to recover. Then the next year brought a drought and a national depression. The poverty that usually inflicted Mississippi farming was back with a vengeance.

LIVING CONDITIONS OF THE SHARECROPPER

Living conditions for the sharecropper were generally poor. Most of the unpainted wooden houses scattered over the plantation had only three rooms. With families of from five to fifteen people living in them, these houses were terribly crowded. Few doors had screens and almost no houses had indoor plumbing. Sharecroppers usually heated their homes with wood or coal stoves.

The sharecropper's diet centered around flour, cornmeal, sorghum, salt pork, lard, and dry peas. Many sharecroppers tried to grow vegetables to improve their diet, but some landowners discouraged gardening because they preferred to maximize the share of land devoted to cotton. A better-than-average sharecropper's menu included other items such as chitterlings ("chitlins," or pig intestines), rabbit, molasses, butter, milk, and sweet potato pie. The poorest sharecroppers, however, lived on only two meals a day—rice, cornbread, and coffee for breakfast, and peas and cornbread for dinner. Men wore basic denim overalls, and women wore cheap cotton dresses. Since feed and flour sacks were used to make shirts, dresses, sheets, and diapers, many mills put their products into colorful sacks to boost sales.

THE SHARECROPPER'S YEAR

The sharecropper's year began in the spring at "furnish time." In early March, the landlord began to furnish the sharecropper with food, clothes, and farming supplies, usually from the plantation commissary. From March through July, the sharecropping family planted and cultivated the cotton. They harvested the crop from September through November.

After harvesting, the sharecropper paid the landlord his share of the crop and paid for all food and supplies the landlord had furnished him. Many landlords took advantage of their illiterate tenants by cheating them at settlement time.

By winter the tenants' resources were usually exhausted, and "slim rations" began. From December through March, there was very little crop work to be done. Men did odd jobs on the farm or in town, and women sometimes hired themselves out as maids. With little chance to make money during these months, many families could not make ends meet. They were forced to depend upon the landlord for loans to see them through. This cycle of debt left them tied to the landlord and kept them from improving their condition.

FAMILY LABOR

Women built fires and hauled water, cooked the meals, washed clothes, cleaned house, and watched over children. They did all of this as best they could and without the aid of electricity, plumbing, or central heating. If the family were allowed to use a small patch of land as a garden, the woman of the home was in charge of it. During crop seasons, she worked in the fields beside her husband and children.

Older children worked hard, too. Their jobs included building the fire, hauling the water, beating biscuits and cleaning greens and other food-preparation tasks, looking after their younger siblings, and helping out in the fields at chopping and picking times.

Figure 12.1. A planter and his tenants in the Mississippi Delta in 1936. Library of Congress Prints and Photographs Division, LC-USF34-009596-C.

THE EFFECTS OF TENANCY

When sharecropping began, during and after Reconstruction, some people thought the landlord-tenant system would work well. It could have been a way, though a hard one, for landless Blacks and Whites to advance to a better economic position. Ideally, the tenants would be able to save a little money or store away extra crops to help pay their debts, or possibly buy some land of their own. But this happened only rarely.

The traditions developed during slavery influenced the tenant system. Although Blacks were no longer physically enslaved, they were still in economic bondage. The Black sharecropper started as a laborer and was now bound to the land, his debts, and his landlord.

More and more Whites, too, were now landless farmers, forced to choose between unemployment and sharecropping. In 1900, one-fifth of tenant farmers were White; by 1930 this share had risen to one-third. Since most people were poor and needed work, a sharecropper who demanded higher pay could always be replaced by someone who would work for less. People began to realize that the tenant system, designed partly to keep Blacks on the bottom of the scale, hurt many Whites as well.

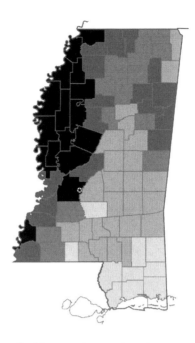

Map 28. Tenant Farmers, 1925

% of farmers who were tenants
- more than 90%
- 65-90%
- 50-65%
- 30-50%
- less than 30%

PLANTERS AND PECKERWOODS

Without fear of oversimplifying, Mississippi's political history is marked by a deep divide between the prosperous Delta and the struggling hill country. In his 1949 analysis, political scientist V. O. Key described hill country Whites—using terms like "rednecks," "peckerwoods," and "peckerheads"—as living in "another world." The hill country's poor soil left farmers in constant poverty, creating deep resentment. This bitterness grew when, as Key noted, hill country Whites saw that "often Negroes have the best tenant shacks" in the Delta, intensifying both economic and racial tensions.

The divide extended to education. Delta legislators supported better schooling for Black residents, but their motives were purely economic. They sought to prevent Black workers from leaving for better opportunities in the North and West. Meanwhile, hill country schools remained underfunded. In 1946, the Delta Council's policy committee advocated for more Black school buildings.[1] After negotiating with hill country legislators, they passed a bill increasing school construction funds. These improvements for Black Mississippians, while Delta Whites prospered and hill country Whites struggled, fueled resentment that often erupted into racial violence against Black citizens.

SHARECROPPING CAUSES DEPENDENCE

Because the landlord supervised the sharecropper so closely, the sharecropper had very little choice in determining his living habits. Sharecroppers often relied on landlords for help securing medical care, protection from violent White supremacists, and other necessities. Dependence on landlords for services usually provided by the state gave landlords even more leverage in this "paternalistic" relationship, with which they demanded greater social deference from their tenants.[2] The cycle of debt left them tied to their landlord and prevented them from improving their condition.

From time to time, sharecroppers tried to unite to get a fairer share of the results of their work. In the 1930s, there were efforts to organize tenant unions in Mississippi similar to those in Alabama and Arkansas, but they failed, often due to the repression of county and state officials in league with large landowners. Without hope for improvement, many sharecroppers gave up the struggle.

THE GREAT MIGRATION BEGINS

The sharecroppers' problem seemed impossible to solve. When World War I began, new factories opened in Northern cities. Mississippians, Black and White, moved northward, with many making their way to Chicago and other destinations in the Midwest. After the war, the continuing problems of sharecropping and segregation caused Blacks to continue to leave. This migration provided the main outlet for Black frustration and protest. While less studied by historians, the size of the out-migration of White Mississippians and other Southern Whites was more than twice as great.

FAMILY LIFE IN HARD TIMES

Compare sharecropping with slavery. In what ways were the systems alike? How were they different? What part did poor Whites play in each system? Would you have left Mississippi if all you could do was work on someone else's land? Even if your family stayed behind? How did your ancestors earn a living in the 1930s? What did they do for recreation? Do they remember hard times?

THE LANDLORD'S PROBLEMS

The landlord also faced hard times and took great risks. In order to stock his commissary, he borrowed money from a town bank. The banker accepted the promise of cotton as payment: this was called a crop lien. Similarly, the landlord accepted cotton as the only payment for his loans to the sharecropper. This dependence on cotton as the only source of money caused the collapse of some plantations. One Southern congressman described the situation as follows:

> The landlord is in almost as bad shape as the tenant. He owed for the supplies. He had to take what he received at the end of the season and turn it over to the merchant, or to the bank to pay them what he owed. He has been unable to pay in full, so that he cannot advance them another year. Many of these people, especially the Negro tenants, are now in the middle of the winter, practically without food and without clothes, and without anything else, and how are they going to live? . . . Many White people are in the same kind of a situation. They beg around among their neighbors. The neighbors are poor and they have no means of helping them. They stray here and there.

Bad crops and low prices combined to produce a situation few individual landowners could manage. If cotton production was low or if the price fell, the sharecropper could not pay the commissary owner. Then the commissary owner could not pay the bank. As a result of unpaid mortgages and loans, an absentee landlord would take over the plantation.

Absentee landlords often looked for a quick profit. Emphasizing high production at low costs, they hired managers to operate the land. The British-owned Delta and Pine Land Company (D&PL) initially explored the South's timber industry but soon discovered a more lucrative opportunity in cotton production. Seeking to address Britain's cotton shortages, they purchased 38,000 acres near Scott in the Mississippi Delta region, establishing the state's largest plantation. They did not fit the stereotype of get-rich-quick owners, but emphasized good management. While the company's profits fluctuated in its early years, they eventually achieved significant success through careful planning and agricultural expertise.

THE BOLL-WEEVIL INVASION

In 1907, the boll weevil invaded Mississippi from the Southwest and gave many farmers another reason to change their minds about cotton. Farmers in the area between the Piney Woods and the Natchez Bluffs turned to beans, tomatoes, and cabbages. Near the Gulf Coast, Tung-tree orchards supplied farmers with added

HARD TIMES 221

Figure 12.2. Small landowners also faced hard times. This photo is from Lowndes County in 1911. National Child Labor Committee collection, Library of Congress, Prints and Photographs Division, LC-DIG-nclc-02128.

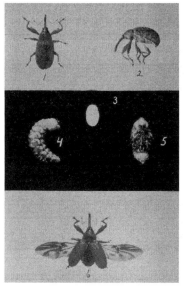

Figure 12.3. The boll weevil destroys cotton by laying its eggs in the boll of the cotton plant. Later the boll dies and with it the cotton crop. Bureau of Entomology, US Department of Agriculture.

income for a time. Prairie farmers switched to peas and other crops to make up for the loss of cotton. The dairy industry also grew.

But the truck-farming and dairy sections of Mississippi included only about twelve of the state's eighty-two counties. The rest of the state continued growing cotton until after World War II. Farmers found ways to control the boll weevil with poisons and improved their cotton crops through fertilizers, erosion control, and crop rotation. But in some counties, cotton never came back.

INDUSTRY FAILS TO GROW

Industry did not provide an answer to Mississippi's farm problems. Since the state was poor, it provided a poor market for finished products. And since it was rural, it could not attract urban industrial managers. Finally, since its people were relatively uneducated, it could not offer industry a skilled workforce.

Lumber was Mississippi's greatest resource, after the land itself. But more than half of the state's virgin forests, cut down in a few years mostly by outside corporations, were only a memory by 1920. As the Works Progress Administration (WPA) guide to Mississippi put it, describing the Piney Woods: "Until lumbering built a few fair-sized towns out of the wilderness, it was a pioneer country; and now that the forests have been ravished, and the cheaply built mill-houses are rotting, as the unused mill machinery rusts about them, it is pioneer country once more."

Figure 12.4. WPA poster.

EDUCATION

In the early 1900s, the education of most Mississippi children was inadequate. In 1901 public high schools were established in towns. However, since less than 10 percent of the children of the state lived in towns, the great majority of the children did not attend public high schools.

The 1906 legislature passed a law to establish rural public schools. Classwork centered on preparing students to be professionals: lawyers, doctors, teachers, and engineers. Although most Mississippians were farmers, there were agricultural high schools until 1910. As late as 1914, there were only 8,500 students in public high schools. Only twenty-nine schools in the state had four or more full-time teachers.

SHARECROPPING HURTS SCHOOLS

The sharecropping system also crippled quality education. Children were encouraged to work throughout the year without regard for the importance of completing the school year. Many rural schools closed as early as February so children could work in the fields. Mississippi ranked last in the nation in average days of school attendance per child (about ninety-eight days per year).

Mississippi also ranked at the bottom in overall financial support for education. The state spent about the same proportion of its income for schools as many other states. However, because its income was lower, the amount provided for education was smaller than in any other state.

"GOVERNOR OF ALL THE PEOPLE"

One Mississippian who cared deeply about the schools and their problems was Paul B. Johnson Sr. He was born on a farm in Scott County in 1880, and his own education began part-time in a one-room schoolhouse. Later he earned a law degree, ran for Congress against Governor Bilbo in 1918, and beat him. Twenty-two years later, now with Bilbo's support, he was elected governor, succeeding Hugh White.

Johnson's philosophy emphasized the "average man and woman." He supported relief funds for the old, free hospitalization for the poor, and antitrust laws against business monopolies. He also believed that women should be allowed to hold political office.

Placing great value on the need for education, Johnson said, "No educated man can be enslaved, for he knows his rights and is willing to fight for them." During his

Figure 12.5. Paul Johnson (right) takes the oath of office, January 16, 1940. Courtesy of the Archives and Records Services Division, Mississippi Department archives and History.

term of office, he signed the free-textbook law, which was to provide textbooks equally to all students in the state. Because of it, many Black families, who had watched the state government pass many previous laws for White benefit only, developed a deep respect for Johnson.

Johnson also helped bring Jackson College, now Jackson State University, under state control. Otherwise this institution, in financial trouble during the Depression, would have gone out of existence. Because of these actions, Blacks presented him with a portrait of himself with the citation:

PRESENTED TO THE HONORABLE PAUL BURNEY JOHNSON, GOVERNOR OF ALL THE PEOPLE OF THE STATE OF MISSISSIPPI, BY THE NEGRO CITIZENS OF MISSISSIPPI.

Governor Johnson once stated his aim in life: "It is my ambition to build for myself a lasting monument in the hearts and minds of the people of Mississippi, that I may be remembered as a useful citizen." He died before finishing his term of office. But his ambition has been fulfilled.

THE FIGHT FOR BLACK EDUCATION IN JIM CROW MISSISSIPPI

Under Jim Crow's "separate but equal" lie, Mississippi created two vastly different school systems. Black communities in the state faced significant disparities in educational opportunities compared to their White counterparts. The 1937 statistics tell the story: Whites had twenty agricultural high schools while Blacks had only three; Whites had 850 consolidated high schools with free transportation while Blacks had just forty, with only half providing transportation; Whites had 510 approved four-year high schools compared to only fifty-four for Blacks. To add to these inequities, Black teachers earned 3.5 times less than White teachers.

In response to the lack of educational opportunities, Black communities took the initiative to establish private schools. In 1903, William H. Holtzclaw founded the Utica Normal and Industrial Institute (now Hinds Community College–Utica Campus), following Booker T. Washington's Tuskegee model. The school became known for its choir performances in Europe and its Negro Farmers Conference promoting Black land ownership. Similarly, Lawrence C. Jones established Piney Woods School in 1910, inspiring the creation of similar schools in Clinton, Mound Bayou, and Meridian. These institutions provided crucial educational opportunities when the state would not.

To support these private schools, philanthropic organizations such as the Rosenwald Fund, the Phelps-Stokes Fund, and the Jeanes Foundation provided funding. However, even with this financial assistance, the schools were not immune to interference from White individuals. In one egregious case, it was discovered that a White person was embezzling 10 percent of the funds allocated by the foundations, further undermining the efforts of the Black community to provide quality education for their children.

EQUAL EDUCATION

Table 12.1 demonstrates that Mississippi's schools were far from the "separate but equal" ideal. Instead, they exhibited significant inequalities. Read the Fourteenth Amendment to the United States Constitution. Were these school systems constitutional?

Table 12.1. School Disparities by Race, 1940		
	White Schools	Black Schools
Money Spent per Student	$41.71	$7.24
Length of School Year	160 Days	124 Days
Average College Education of Teachers	3.5 Years	1.5 Years
Teacher Salaries	$750	$237

Sources: Report of the State Superintendent, 1942–1943; Joint Committee, Progress of the Education of Negroes 1870–1950.

Figures 12.6–12.7. White school (above) and Black school (right) in Tishomingo County about 1935. Courtesy of the Archives and Records Services Division, Mississippi Department of Archives and History.

MISSISSIPPI'S PIONEERING ROLE IN COMMUNITY COLLEGE EDUCATION

These deep inequities in education extended beyond primary and secondary schools. While Black students faced chronic underfunding and limited resources, Mississippi was simultaneously expanding educational opportunities for White students. One major development was the state's role in pioneering community college education. In 1922, Mississippi established the nation's first statewide system of public junior colleges, further reinforcing the divide in access to higher education. The movement began through the 1908 County Agricultural High School Law, which allowed agricultural high schools to offer college courses. Pearl River County Agricultural High School (now Pearl River Community College) led the way in 1921, followed by Hinds County Agricultural High School (now Hinds Community College).

In 1949, Coahoma Community College in Clarksdale became Mississippi's first public Black community college, growing from Coahoma Agricultural High School to provide crucial educational opportunities for Black students during segregation. Before Coahoma's founding, Holmes Seminary in West Point (eventually Holmes Junior College), Okolona Industrial School in Okolona, and Southern Christian Institute in Edwards were supported by different church organizations.

Community colleges have been a cornerstone in shaping Mississippi's workforce, offering a diverse range of programs tailored to the state's educational and economic needs. These institutions provide pathways for academic transfer to four-year universities, vocational training, and technical certifications in fields such as healthcare, information technology, advanced manufacturing, and skilled trades. Additionally, they support adult education and workforce development, equipping students with the skills needed for emerging industries and local job markets. As of 2024, 45 percent of Mississippi's college students were enrolled in community colleges, underscoring their vital role in delivering accessible, affordable, and practical education to residents across the state.

ENTER THE AUTOMOBILE

As Mississippi expanded educational opportunities through its groundbreaking community colleges, another transformative force began reshaping the state: the automobile. The automobile caused great changes in the culture and society of the state. It provided an additional means for the northward migration of former sharecroppers. Mobility from town to town within the state also increased. Thriving business districts in small towns began to look abandoned. Residents still lived in towns but drove to nearby centers to shop and work.

While the automobile was changing life on land, Mississippi's mighty river was about to remind everyone of its awesome power.

Figure 12.8. Downtown Merigold sat largely empty for a long stretch of time due to the cotton slump of the 1920s, Black migration, and the advent of the automobile. Today, it is a bedroom community for Cleveland and houses several vibrant restaurants and event venues. © Hey Joe's.

THE GREAT FLOOD OF 1927

The Mississippi River, sometimes referred to as "Father Mississippi," has always played a major role in the development of our state. The flood in 1890 led to a better levee system. But in 1927, the Mississippi's waters created one of the greatest disasters of our nation's history.

From the late summer of 1926 through the spring of 1927, there were heavy rains in the Mississippi River Valley. Then, on the morning of April 21, the levee broke at Stops Landing, eighteen miles north of Greenville. Even though 1,500 men worked all night to strengthen the levee with sandbags, it was evident that nothing could prevent imminent disaster. The waters rushed on, flooding the lower half of the Delta.

LIFE ON THE LEVEES

Lyle Saxon described the scene:

> We gathered together on the levee-top—White and Black men, rich and poor—or, rather, yesterday we were rich and poor; tonight we are equal in misery, for the Mississippi has taken everything from us.

Figure 12.9. Life on the Levee. Library of Congress Prints and Photographs Division, LC-USZ62-77187.

The broken levee-top is like a long narrow island. Twenty feet wide, perhaps, and water rushing on both sides—Black water that extends out in all directions, mile after mile, dotted now with wreckage of our homes and covering the land endlessly.

We sit upon the ground, in groups, afraid to sleep, too miserable to cry, waiting, with forlorn hope, for a rescue boat.

We have no water except the yellow, foul stuff that is all about us. We drink sparingly of it, grimacing, wiping our lips. There is no food. There is no wood. We have no fire. . . .

THE RED CROSS

The Red Cross established eighteen refugee camps in Mississippi to serve the affected areas. They gave emergency aid to 70,000 people. Another 88,000 received aid outside the Red Cross camps.

Of the 185,500 Mississippians displaced from their homes by the flood, 142,000 were Black. Early in the disaster, while White women and children were taken to safety, Black people were forced to remain in camps—some even at gunpoint—and work under the eyes of White administrators. LeRoy Percy, a Delta planter, tried to justify this treatment: "If we depopulate the Delta of its labor, we should be doing it a grave disservice."

Figure 12.10. The railroad at Rolling Fork. Courtesy of the Archives and Records Services Division, Mississippi Department of Archives and History.

Figure 12.11. A refugee camp. Library of Congress Prints and Photographs Division, LC-DIG-ds-01294.

Although Blacks were asked and sometimes forced to unload the relief supplies, Red Cross aid was often channeled only to Whites displaced by the flood.

At one point, dissatisfied with their treatment, Blacks refused to work. The National Guard was called in to force them back to work. In his novella *Down by the Riverside*, Richard Wright described the scene:

> He took a gourd from the wall and dipped some muddy water out of a bucket. It tasted thick and bitter, and he could not swallow it. He hung the gourd back and spat the water into a corner. He cocked his head, listening. It seemed he had heard a shot. There it was again. Something happening in town, he thought. Over the yellow water he heard another shot, thin, dry, far away. Must be trouble, must be trouble somewhere. He had heard that the White folks were threatening to conscript all Negroes they could lay their hands on to pile sand and cement bags on the levee. And they were talking about bringing in soldiers too. They were afraid of stores and homes being looted. Yes, it was hard to tell just what was happening in town. Shucks, in times like these they'll shoot a n----- down just like a dog n think nothing of it. That shooting might mean anything. But likely as not tis jus some po Black man gone.

By request, the Red Cross set up a Colored Advisory Commission to visit displaced persons and help correct some of the injustices. Langston Hughes, the legendary Black writer, described its establishment: "Some of the camps were almost like concentration camps. Some were surrounded by National Guardsmen. Negroes were not allowed outside the gates without permission of their landlords, who were waiting for the waters to subside so they could force these refugees back into semi-slavery. In some camps the inmates had to pay for Red Cross supplies that were supposed to be free. . . . Eventually some of the abuses were corrected."

SOCIAL COHESION

Usually in times of disaster or crisis, members of a community will join together to help each other in the face of a common threat. Sociologists explain this behavior by referring to a community's "social cohesion." The way the rest of the nation joined together to help flood victims is an example of this.

Unfortunately, social cohesion did not last long in Mississippi during the flood. Blacks received poor treatment, and cooperation between the races was strained. Hughes stated that "the treatment of the flood victims was based on race, a classic example of southern custom."

The flood of 1927 showed a vast split in Mississippi society, a split between planter and sharecropper, between White schools and Black schools. As David

Cohn put it: "In war or peace, in danger or stress, whatever may come to the Delta, the Negro looms as an all-important factor. In flood times, when great strains were thrown upon the community, incidents both amusing and tragic revealed the inseparable gulf between the races and the difficulties of bridging it even momentarily in times of common danger and suffering."

Notes

1. The Delta Council was a combination of a farm bureau and chamber of commerce.
2. Lee J. Alston and Joseph P. Ferrie, Southern Paternalism and the American Welfare State: Economics, Politics, and Institutions in the South, 1865–1965 (New York: Cambridge University Press, 1999).

Recommended Readings

John M. Barry, *Rising Tide: The Great Mississippi Flood of 1927 and How It Changed America* (New York: Simon & Schuster, 1997).

James C. Cobb, *The Most Southern Place on Earth: The Mississippi Delta and the Roots of Regional Identity* (New York: Oxford University Press, 1992).

David L. Cohn, *Where I Was Born and Raised* (Boston: Houghton, Mifflin, 1948).

Gene Dattel, *Cotton and Race in the Making of America: The Human Costs of Economic Power* (Chicago: Ivan R. Dee, 2009).

Valdimer Orlando Key Jr., *Southern Politics in State and Nation* (Knoxville: University of Tennessee Press, 1996).

William Alexander Percy, *Lanterns on the Levee: Recollections of a Planter's Son* (Baton Rouge: Louisiana State University Press, 2006 [1941]).

Nan Elizabeth Woodruff, *American Congo: The African American Freedom Struggle in the Delta* (Cambridge, MA: Harvard University Press, 2003).

Works Progress Administration, *Mississippi: The WPA Guide to the Magnolia State*, introduction by Robert S. McElvaine (Jackson: University Press of Mississippi, 2009 [1938]).

Gavin Wright, *Old South, New South: Revolutions in the Southern Economy since the Civil War* (New York: Basic Books, 1986).

Richard Wright, "Down by the Riverside," in *Early Works: Lawd Today!, Uncle Tom's Children,* and *Native Son* (New York: Library of America, 1991 [1938]).

CHAPTER 13

TOWARD A NEW POLITICS

1916–1954

LEADERS OF MISSISSIPPI FACED GRAVE ECONOMIC PROBLEMS BETWEEN THE two world wars. The farm problem of the 1920s became the general economic disaster of the Great Depression. Some Mississippi politicians faced these problems openly and constructively. Others made impressive speeches backed by little real action.

The state's major leaders during this period were White men. Women were granted the vote in 1920, but their participation made no immediate impact. Blacks were kept out of politics by the 1890 Constitution and the "White primaries." Both in Mississippi and nationally, Black politicians and voters sided with the Republican Party, the Party of Lincoln. In the 1930s, in response to overtures by northern Democrats and President Franklin Delano Roosevelt's New Deal policies they shifted to the Democratic Party. Meanwhile, the Republicans and President Dwight D. Eisenhower began to attract White support. Finally, in the years after World War II, national leaders of the Democratic Party indicated that they would push for greater Black participation in politics and social structure throughout the South, including Mississippi. As 1954 approached, challenges to the old system of segregated social life and segregated politics began to arise.

WORLD WAR I

In 1917, when America became involved in World War I, many Mississippians responded to the call to arms. Camp Shelby near Hattiesburg housed and trained 30,000 recruits, while Payne Field, an aviation camp near West Point, trained many servicemen. Throughout the state, industries switched to the production of war goods. Many Mississippians served with courage and dignity in our country's struggle in the war, while others, with equal courage, opposed the war and America's role in it.

BLACK POLITICS AND CIVIL RIGHTS

In the decades following World War I, Mississippi, like much of the South, remained deeply entrenched in racial segregation. The state continued to operate under the constitution adopted in 1890, which enshrined Jim Crow laws. These laws kept the races separate, severely limited Black voting rights, and resulted in unequal public facilities for Blacks and Whites.

During this period, Black Mississippians, blocked from the Democratic Party, attempted to revitalize the state's Republican Party. A biracial ("Black and Tan") Republican Party, headed by Perry Howard, a Black lawyer, emerged. However, this party wielded little power in Mississippi due to the state's racist voter registration system, entrenched customs, and threats of violence that effectively barred most Blacks from voting. The party's activities were largely limited to quadrennial appearances at the Republican National Convention and campaigning in the North to encourage northern Blacks to support Republican presidential candidates. Simultaneously, a "Lily-White" faction of the Republican Party, consisting entirely of White members, attracted only a small following.

By 1956, the national landscape of party politics began to shift. Under the leadership of President Dwight D. Eisenhower (1953–1961), the National Republican Party adopted a new strategy to expand its influence in the South. Unlike previous attempts, this approach specifically targeted White voters, marking a significant change in the party's regional tactics and setting the stage for future political realignments in Mississippi and across the South.

Meanwhile, in Mississippi, grassroots efforts to combat racial injustice were gaining momentum. The Vicksburg chapter of the National Association for the Advancement of Colored People (NAACP), the oldest in the state, was at the forefront of addressing racism and discrimination. This chapter set out to tackle various issues affecting the Black community, with key objectives including:

1. To end legal injustices against Negroes.
2. To stamp out racial discrimination.
3. To prevent lynching of Black people.
4. To assure every citizen of color the common rights of American citizenship.
5. To secure an equal opportunity for public education.

A group of White women organized a movement to improve race relations. Led by Bessie C. Alford of McComb, they set up the Mississippi chapter of the Association of Southern Women for the Prevention of Lynching. By 1939, they had collected pledges from Whites opposed to lynching in all eighty-two counties. Fifty-four county sheriffs had signed. Their program of action became a model for this regional organization and was called the "Mississippi Plan."

POLITICS AND ECONOMIC PROBLEMS

Life was hard for Mississippians throughout the state. Tuberculosis and other diseases were widespread. Farm prices rose and fell but usually were at a low level. Most Mississippians lived in rural areas, and very few of them had telephones, electricity, or running water.

Some leaders of the state took White people's minds off these problems by raising emotional issues, such as fear of a Black takeover. This type of politician still exists. Termed a "demagogue," they avoid the real issues and instead attempt to win votes by making emotional appeals, primarily those based on fear. Impressed by a politician's personality, many people vote for him, but in the end, these supporters continue to suffer from their old problems.

"THE MAN" BILBO

Some people named their sons after him; others hated him. He was called both the "Bubonic Plague" and "The Man of the People."

Theodore G. Bilbo was born on a small farm near Poplarville in 1877. He attended elementary and high schools in Poplarville and worked at odd jobs during his youth. Although he later claimed to be uneducated in order to seem to have more in common with his followers, Bilbo attended the University of Nashville, Vanderbilt Law School, and the University of Michigan.

After opening a law firm in Poplarville, he served in the State Senate from 1908 to 1912. After being implicated in a bribery scandal, the legislature asked Bilbo to resign. He refused, was elected lieutenant governor in 1911, and served as governor from 1916 to 1920. As governor, Bilbo pushed for the consolidation of rural schools, the establishment of a bureau of vital statistics, a state tuberculosis hospital, and industrial schools.

From 1920 to 1928 Bilbo held no office and was reported

Figure 13.1. Sen. Theodore Bilbo. Library of Congress Prints and Photographs Division, LC-DIG-hec-26634.

to have no income. In 1928, "The Man" returned to politics and was again elected governor. Many state educators had opposed Bilbo throughout his career. He now had a chance to purge them from the state's schools. He fired hundreds of college teachers and administrators and replaced them with his friends and supporters.

During his second term as governor, the state established state commissions for the blind and for malaria control. However, the Depression soon struck. At the end of Bilbo's second administration the state was $11,500,000 in debt.

In 1934, "The Man" ran for the United States Senate. Two young reporters described his campaign:

> Clad in a pinkish suit that would have put a bookmaker to shame, Bilbo made a striking appearance as he stepped to the front of the platform. . . . He promised everything but a guaranteed entry to Heaven, and this wasn't necessary because his election would bring Heaven to earth.

Bilbo easily defeated his opponents and was elected senator. As senator, he was not merely a demagogue, for he did support most New Deal legislation designed to help alleviate America's economic problems. On the other hand, Bilbo tried to send Blacks "back to Africa," opposed anti-lynching and anti-poll-tax bills, and spent much of his energy preaching race hatred and White supremacy.

In his reelection campaign of 1946, Bilbo advised: "Do not let a single n----- vote. If you let a few register and vote this year, next year there will be twice as many, and the first thing you know the whole thing will be out of hand." His efforts to prevent Black voting were investigated by a special Senate committee that held hearings in the state. Bilbo denied that his speeches threatened Blacks or encouraged White violence. But some Black people testified against Bilbo, showing the bloody clothes that they had worn when they were beaten while trying to vote.

Another Senate committee looked into Bilbo's dealings with war contractors and found that he had misused his office for personal gain. The Senate refused to seat him. In the midst of the ensuing debate over his political fate, Bilbo's health rapidly deteriorated, forcing him to return to his home in the South. In a twist of fate that some viewed as poetic justice, given his notorious reputation for inflammatory rhetoric, Bilbo succumbed to oral cancer of the mouth on August 21, 1947.

DEPRESSION AND THE NEW DEAL

Mississippians struggled through the Great Depression of the 1930s. Since Mississippi was an agricultural state, it suffered when unemployed workers had no money to pay for its produce. Farmers managed to barely survive, earning roughly half of their already low usual income. Many farmers who could not pay their bills had their land repossessed by the banks who owned their mortgages.

A state sales tax, perhaps the first in the nation, was passed in 1932, during Governor "Mike" Conner's administration. Its supporters called it the most effective way to tax Blacks and poor Whites, and it became another economic burden for the people.

Beginning in 1933, President Franklin D. Roosevelt took steps to remedy the Depression throughout the country. He set up "New Deal" programs designed to help the farmers by regulating farm production and providing equipment, credit, and homes.

MISSISSIPPI WELCOMES THE NEW DEAL

Although these programs called for government regulation of industry and agriculture, Mississippians accepted the New Deal as a way to fight the extremely poor conditions. Long-time editor of the *Jackson Daily News* Fred Sullens recognized that "something must be done, and it must be done very soon, and it must be something drastic, far-reaching, bold, and determined." He explained to Mississippians that only the national government could handle such a big job.

The Agricultural Adjustment Administration (AAA) set up a program to increase farm prices by limiting production. When farmers were told to plow under their cotton in order to raise its price, Sullens spoke up: "Unless the farmer

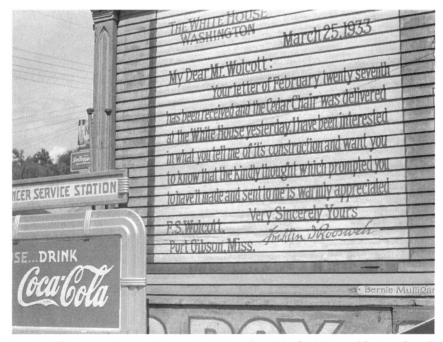

Figure 13.2. This photo indicates one Mississippian's support for the New Deal. Library of Congress, Prints & Photographs Division, Farm Security Administration/Office of War Information Black-and-White Negatives, LC-USF34-054772-D.

Figure 13.3. In some towns, even moving services were a White job. This ad is from Grenada.

cooperates with the government movement, he is hopelessly lost—and deserves to be." However, much of the federal aid to agriculture worked to the benefit of the large planters and did not help the landless tenants. The planters had a close friend in Washington; one of the key implementers of the AAA was Mississippi native Oscar Johnston, the president of the state's largest plantations, the British-owned Delta and Pine Land Company.

Since 1900, Black Mississippians had gradually been pushed out of jobs as carpenters, barbers, butchers, mailmen, and others. In 1937, bills were introduced in Congress calling for fair labor practices and an end to lynching. Thus, much New Deal legislation threatened the economic interests of wealthy White Mississippians and frightened many others about the prospect of stronger and more assertive federal government. Editor Sullens had already begun to lose his enthusiasm for the New Deal in 1935 with the government's increased spending and regulation. By 1938, torn between loyalty to the Democratic administration and personal beliefs, Sullens and other White Mississippians were bitterly criticizing the New Deal programs.

A GLIMMER OF HOPE: THE RESETTLEMENT ADMINISTRATION AND BLACK FARMERS IN MISSISSIPPI

The New Deal's Resettlement Administration (RA), created in 1935, offered a glimmer of hope to Black farmers by providing land, credit, and farming assistance to help them escape sharecropping. However, deep-seated racism meant White applicants often received better land and more resources, leaving Black

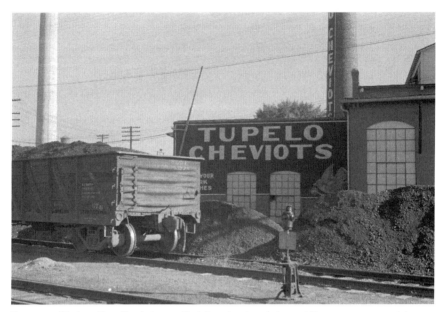

Figure 13.4. Woolen mills at Tupelo in 1935. Such factories, though they paid low wages, were crucial to the survival of many families and towns. Library of Congress, Prints & Photographs Division, Farm Security Administration/Office of War Information Black-and-White Negatives, LC-USF33-002054-M3.

farmers at a disadvantage. While a few Black families secured land, the program largely benefited White farmers. The RA merged into the Farm Security Administration (FSA) in 1937, but its brief existence revealed how racial bias shaped federal aid, leaving Black farmers to continue their fight for equality and justice.

HUGH L. WHITE

Mississippi elected an industry-minded governor late in the Depression. Hugh White launched his "Balance Agriculture With Industry" (BAWI) program upon entering office in 1936. BAWI was designed both to industrialize Mississippi and to preserve the interests of agriculture. It attracted some outside industry into the state through special low taxes and locally financed factory construction. The BAWI program helped Mississippi take the first major steps toward industrialization.

PAT HARRISON

Pat Harrison, United States senator from Mississippi throughout the Depression, was one of the most respected men in the Democratic Party. He was known for his dynamic campaigns, his ability to win over an audience, and his friendly personality. Harrison never lost an election for public office in the state. As a loyal party leader and early supporter of Roosevelt, Senator Harrison backed most New Deal legislation enthusiastically.

Like Sullens, Harrison broke with the New Deal when it proposed laws against lynching, against the poll tax—the key tool used to prevent the poorest Blacks and poor Whites from voting—and in favor of wage-and-hour controls. President Roosevelt, reliant on his support in the Senate, praised him despite this opposition: "Pat Harrison has done more for Mississippi than any other man in the United States Congress." Harrison served in the Senate for twenty-three years, dying in office on the eve of World War II.

SENATORS EASTLAND AND STENNIS

Harrison's death brought James O. Eastland to the Senate. Eastland rose in popularity as a leader of another "states' rights" movement emerging among Southern White conservatives, and was elected time and time again. Through the seniority system, whereby senators who have served longest are rewarded with the most power through valuable committee chairmanships, Eastland became chairman of the powerful Judiciary Committee in 1956.

After Bilbo's death, a special election was held in which White voters elected John C. Stennis, a DeKalb lawyer and state judge, to fill the unexpired term. Stennis gained power in the Senate through his work on the Armed Forces Committee. Especially in comparison to the demagogic and coarse Eastland, Stennis's fellow senators respected his honesty and integrity, and selected him to chair the Senate Ethics Committee.

WORLD WAR II

With the outbreak of World War II, Mississippians again rallied to the nation's defense. Camp Shelby grew into one of the country's largest training centers, while Camp McCain in Grenada County and Keesler Air Force Base in Biloxi prepared our armed forces. Mississippi also hosted military hospitals, defense plants, and prisoner-of-war camps during this time.

Ingalls Shipbuilding Company at Pascagoula built eighty all-purpose ships for carrying men, ammunition, and other war goods. Mississippians established the Mississippi War Fund and bought war bonds to boost the national treasury. During World War II, 238,000 Mississippians participated in the armed forces. Six earned Congressional Medals of Honor.

Figure 13.5. This poster in downtown Jackson shows Mississippi's mobilization for the war effort. Courtesy of the Archives and Records Services Division, Mississippi Department of Archives and History.

THE WHITES-ONLY DEMOCRATIC PRIMARY

Until 1944, Mississippi held its November general elections after a Democratic primary in which only White people were allowed to vote. Since there was only one real political party in Mississippi—the Democratic Party—whoever won the primary automatically won the general election because he had no opponent. This meant that even if Blacks registered, they could only vote in the November elections after Whites had decided who would win.

In the 1944 case *Smith v. Allwright*, the United States Supreme Court declared the White primary unconstitutional because it denied political participation on the basis of race. "One thing is certain, however," said the *Jackson Clarion-Ledger*, "this decision will not be accepted in Mississippi and Mississippi Democrats will not voluntarily open their primaries to any, but White voters." While White leaders throughout the state pledged to ignore the Court's decision, Blacks were organizing to vote.

EARLY BLACK VOTER REGISTRATION

In the early 1940s, the Committee of One Hundred for the General Improvement of the Condition of the Colored People in Mississippi had urged Blacks to vote in the election for United States senator. In 1946, the statewide Progressive Voters League was established. League President T. B. Wilson stated that it was an organization of Black Mississippi citizens—many of them military veterans—designed to encourage voter registration and political participation. The league and other local organizations successfully registered Black citizens in some parts of the state. The League was responsible for registering some 2,000 Blacks.

Their progress was halted by Bilbo's 1946 campaign. Bilbo stated, "I'm calling on every red-blooded American who believes in the superiority and integrity of the White race to get out and see that no n-----s vote." He added, "And the best time to do it is the night before." On election day came reports of murders in Choctaw County and Gulfport, beatings in Canton, and threats and intimidation in McComb, Prentiss, Natchez, Bolivar County, and Louisville.

DEMOCRATS AND CIVIL RIGHTS

The Senate's reaction to Bilbo's campaign showed that the National Democratic Party was beginning to change its views on the subject of civil and political rights for all Americans. Because some party leaders were genuinely concerned, and because of the growing political influence of Black voters, especially in the Midwest, in the wake of the Great Migration, the National Democratic Party very gradually made rights for all Americans, Black and White, one of its principles.

In October 1947, President Truman's Committee on Civil Rights recommended a program to protect the civil rights of minorities. Southern Democrats were outraged, and called for a revolt against the National Democratic Party. Mississippi Governor Fielding Wright attacked the proposals of the committee and said he would break with the national party if its leaders continued to support legislation "aimed to wreck the South and our institutions." Nevertheless, Truman urged Congress to pass some of the committee's proposals.

THE "DIXIECRAT" REVOLT OF 1948

When the Democratic National Convention met to choose a presidential candidate and party platform, a middle-of-the road stand on civil rights was recommended. Stubborn White Southerners refused to accept this compromise, and Northern leaders then persuaded the convention to adopt a firmer civil rights position than the one first proposed. At this point, the entire Mississippi delegation and half of the delegates from Alabama walked out of the convention.

The States' Rights Party, nicknamed the "Dixiecrats," then called its own convention and endorsed Strom Thurmond of South Carolina for president and Fielding Wright for vice-president. They also adopted a declaration of principles, which denounced the Democratic party's platform. In 1948, Mississippi voters encountered a ballot that left off the names of President Harry Truman and his running mate, Alben Barkley; thus, the state's electoral college votes went to the States' Rights Party, which was very popular among White Mississippians.

EQUALIZATION

In the late 1940s and early 1950s, Mississippi stood at a crossroads of racial politics and education. Black political leaders were beginning to recognize the potential of national forces like the Democratic Party and the federal government as tools for change in their home state. This shift in perspective coincided with a growing push for educational equality.

In the spring of 1948, Gladys Noel Bates, a Black teacher at Jackson's Smith Robertson School, took a courageous stand by filing a lawsuit against the school board. She claimed that the board was denying her and her colleagues pay equal to that of similarly qualified White teachers. In retaliation, the school board fired Bates. After her dismissal, another teacher, R. Jess Brown, joined the case as a plaintiff. Although the plaintiffs lost on a technicality, the judge later acknowledged that he would have ruled in their favor if not for this legal hurdle.

In response to this mounting pressure, Governor Hugh White proposed a school "equalization" program in 1953. This $50 million initiative aimed to make Black schools equal to White schools while maintaining racial segregation. The program's first step was to increase Black teachers' salaries, a move that addressed one aspect of the educational disparities but fell short of true integration.

This period marked a crucial turning point in Mississippi's educational landscape. While the equalization program attempted to preserve segregation, it also represented an acknowledgment of the glaring inequalities in the state's educational system. However, these efforts at "separate but equal" would soon be challenged by the landmark *Brown v. Board of Education* decision in 1954, which would declare state-mandated segregation in public schools and other settings unconstitutional.

The Bureau of Economics' data revealed stark disparities between Black and White schools across multiple categories in Mississippi, painting a clear picture of the educational inequalities that existed. Based on statewide figures, the funding allocation per child showed a significant gap: The state allocated $117.43 per pupil for White students, while only $35.27 was allocated for Black students.

Figure 13.6. A man entering a segregated movie theater in Belzoni. Library of Congress, Prints & Photographs Division, Farm Security Administration/Office of War Information Black-and-White Negatives, LC-USF331-030577-M2.

This disparity was even more pronounced in the Mississippi Delta region, where White students were allocated an astounding $464.49 per child, compared to a mere $13.71 for Black students.

The inequality extended beyond per-pupil funding to teacher compensation as well. White teachers earned an average salary of $1,884, while Black teachers received an average of just $760. Although it's noted that White teachers generally had higher levels of education, the scale of this salary gap suggests that educational qualifications alone cannot account for such a wide discrepancy.

Governor White of Mississippi believed that improving segregated schools would satisfy the Black community's demands for educational equity. While some Black Mississippians might have accepted truly equal but separate schools, most Black leaders viewed segregation as a tool for White control over Black lives.

In a letter to the governor, the Mississippi Teachers Association insisted that if school equalization were to be implemented, it must include equal power for Blacks, including supervisory roles at the state level. This demand highlighted the broader desire for genuine equality beyond mere facilities.

MAINTAINING SEGREGATION IN HIGHER EDUCATION

The state's approach to higher education for Black students also reflected this complex landscape. Despite the large Black population in the Mississippi Delta, access to higher education for Black students was limited to one college, Coahoma Community College. There was initial consideration to relocate all-Black, Alcorn A&M College to the Delta. However, the state ultimately decided to establish Mississippi Vocational College in 1950, later renamed Mississippi Valley State University. Some argue that this decision, championed by prominent White state legislator Walter Sillers Jr., was intended to prevent Black students in the Delta from attending the all-White Delta State Teaching College (now Delta State University).

To maintain segregation in higher education, Mississippi and fifteen other states signed the Southern Regional Education Compact in 1949. This agreement provided opportunities for Black students interested in medical school to attend schools outside of Mississippi. Southern states who were part of the compact were clearly trying to circumvent the 1948 decision *Sipuel v. Board of Regents of the University of Oklahoma*, in which the Supreme Court demanded the admission of a Black woman to Oklahoma's flagship law school, whose racist practices they ruled unconstitutional.

The Southern Regional Education Compact eventually came to a demise. However, states that learned from that experience began offering what Crystal R. Sanders has called "segregation scholarships." These scholarships were for Black students to attend out-of-state graduate and professional schools, particularly located in the North.

Interestingly, many Black students, funded by these scholarships, attended prestigious institutions like the University of Chicago and the University of Michigan. As a result, numerous Black educators returned to Mississippi often more qualified than their White counterparts who had studied within the state's segregated system.

Recommended Readings

Stephen A. Berrey, *The Jim Crow Routine: Everyday Performances of Race, Civil Rights, and Segregation in Mississippi* (Chapel Hill: University of North Carolina Press, 2015).

Kimberley Johnson, *Reforming Jim Crow: Southern Politics and State in the Age Before Brown* (New York: Oxford University Press, 2010).

Valdimer Orlando Key Jr., *Southern Politics in State and Nation* (Knoxville: University of Tennessee Press, 1984 [1949]).

Dennis J. Mitchell, *Mississippi Liberal: A Biography of Frank E. Smith* (Jackson: University Press of Mississippi, 2001).

Chester M. Morgan, *Redneck Liberal: Theodore G. Bilbo and the New Deal* (Baton Rouge: Louisiana State University Press, 1985).

Lawrence J. Nelson, *King Cotton's Advocate: Oscar G. Johnston and the New Deal* (Knoxville: University of Tennessee Press, 1999).

Crystal R. Sanders, *A Forgotten Migration: Black Southerners, Segregation Scholarships, and the Debt Owed to Public HBCUs* (Chapel Hill: University of North Carolina Press, 2024).

David G. Sansing, *Making Haste Slowly: The Troubled History of Higher Education in Mississippi* (Jackson: University Press of Mississippi, 1990).

Martha H. Swain, *Pat Harrison: The New Deal Years* (Jackson: University Press of Mississippi, 1978).

Anders Walker, *The Ghost of Jim Crow: How Southern Moderates Used "Brown v. Board of Education" to Stall Civil Rights* (New York: Oxford University Press, 2009).

Maarten Zwiers, *Senator James Eastland: Mississippi's Jim Crow Democrat* (Baton Rouge: Louisiana State University Press, 2015).

CHAPTER 14

THE STRUGGLE FOR RACIAL JUSTICE

1954–1959

THE YEARS AFTER 1954 SAW SOME OF THE MOST IMPORTANT CHANGES IN MISsissippi since Reconstruction. In 1954, the United States Supreme Court finally ruled state-required school segregation unconstitutional. A few White Mississippians agreed with the decision, but few spoke out effectively. Others organized "White Citizens' Councils" (also known as "uptown Klans" or "white-collar Klans") to intimidate officials and, especially, Black parents from desegregating the state's schools. The state enacted numerous laws to fight against integration. Meanwhile, African Americans—particularly young activists—increasingly protested segregation, voter suppression, and other forms of racial discrimination, even in the face of economic retaliation, property destruction, physical violence, and deadly attacks.

SEGREGATION OF THE RACES

In 1954, Mississippi remained firmly entrenched in a system of racial segregation that permeated every aspect of public life. The state's educational system was strictly divided along racial lines, with Black and White children attending separate schools.

This segregation extended far beyond education. Most public spaces were designated as "White only," effectively barring Black citizens from accessing many basic services and amenities. Restaurants and hotels that catered to White patrons refused service to Black customers. Even recreational facilities were segregated, with laws prohibiting Black people from entering many city parks and nearly all public swimming pools.

Cultural institutions were not exempt from this discriminatory system. For instance, Black residents were forbidden from using facilities like the main branch

> **NOTICE!**
>
> May we add our words of appreciation to Sheriff Gray for his comments regarding the improper parking situation on the Eatonville Road near the new Hub City Drag Raceway, as published in The Hattiesburg American and announced over the radio. We join with the Sheriff in helping prevent a traffic jam and safety hazard; and publicly commend him for his interest. We offer our cooperation in any and every way possible, please. The raceway is open all day; eliminations begin at approximately 2 o'clock and last until 5:00.
>
> For colored patrons—we will have an area finished in a few weeks.
>
> **HUB CITY DRAG RACEWAY CO.**

Figure 14.1. In Hattiesburg, only Whites could watch drag races.

of the Jackson Public Library. In smaller towns where only one such facility existed, Black citizens were often left without access to any such resources.

Public transportation was another arena where segregation was rigidly enforced. Black passengers were relegated to the back of buses and confined to separate train cars. They were required to use waiting rooms and restrooms specifically marked as "colored," emphasizing their second-class status.

BROWN V. BOARD OF EDUCATION

On May 17, 1954, the United States Supreme Court delivered its decision in the case of *Brown v. Board of Education of Topeka, Kansas.* Lawyers from the NAACP Legal Defense and Education Fund had brought before the Court a group of four cases challenging segregated education. They were trying to convince the Court to reverse the *Plessy v. Ferguson* decision. In that 1896 decision, the Supreme Court had ruled that "separate but equal" facilities were constitutional. Now, nearly sixty years later, the Court was asked to rule whether separate but equal schools could really be squared with a critical part of the Fourteenth Amendment: the clause requiring "equal protection under the law."

This time the nine justices concluded that "in the field of public education the doctrine of 'separate but equal' has no place. Separate educational facilities are inherently unequal. Therefore, we hold that the plaintiffs [those bringing the case to court], and others . . . are, by reason of the segregation complained of, deprived of the equal protection of the laws guaranteed by the Fourteenth Amendment." Given how state politicians rallied to the defense of Jim Crow, it would be more than fifteen years before any real steps were taken to end school segregation in Mississippi. But the *Brown* decision provided the legal means to help do so.

THE GAME THAT DEFIED SEGREGATION

The impact of *Brown* reached far beyond the classroom, as demonstrated just one year after the decision when Mississippi's Jones Junior College football team faced an unexpected challenge to segregation. The all-White team finished an undefeated season, ranking second in the nation, and secured the opportunity to face top-ranked Compton Junior College in Pasadena, California. However, Mississippi's rigid segregation policies created a dilemma: their potential opponents fielded several Black players, and Mississippi actively rejected the Supreme Court's *Brown* decision mandating school desegregation. Despite state officials demanding they forfeit the game, the Jones Junior College team defied segregationist pressure and traveled to Pasadena. Though they lost the game, their decision to play challenged Mississippi's rigid racial boundaries.

Years later, Mississippi State University would follow a similar path, defying state opposition in 1963 to face Loyola University Chicago in the NCAA basketball tournament, breaking the color line in college sports.

BLACK MISSISSIPPIANS DEMAND CHANGE

> The day is past and forever gone when White men can go behind closed doors and work out all the Negro's problems and bring them to him on a platter. As long as this is done there is going to be misunderstanding and terrible blunders are going to be made.

With these words, Dr. T. R. M. Howard of Mound Bayou opened the first annual meeting of the Mississippi Regional Council of Negro Leadership (RCNL) in 1952. His words resonated through the assembly hall in Mound Bayou, setting a tone of self-determination and empowerment.

Howard had come to Mississippi from California. He accepted the position of chief surgeon at the Taborian Hospital in Mound Bayou. This hospital, operated by the Knights and Daughters of Tabor, a Black fraternal organization, became one of the most important healthcare institutions serving African Americans in the Delta region. He started the RCNL to combat issues like segregation. In one of his campaigns, he posted signs urging, "Don't buy gas where you can't use the restroom," promoting economic resistance against discriminatory practices.

TESTING THE WATERS

Hired by Dr. T. R. M. Howard, Medgar Evers, a recent alumnus of Alcorn A & M College, had supported his family by selling insurance in the Delta. But the overwhelming poverty that he saw all around convinced him that Blacks needed to organize and demand a share of the material goods, as well as all of the rights, that most Whites already took for granted.

In 1954, inspired by the Supreme Court's *Brown v. Board of Education* ruling, Medgar Evers boldly applied to the University of Mississippi, challenging the state's segregationist policies. Initially, the university rejected his application, claiming missing recommendation letters. When Evers provided them, officials quietly changed the admission criteria to block him. Rather than endure the bureaucratic runaround, Evers shifted his focus to activism, becoming the NAACP Field Secretary and a pivotal figure in the civil rights movement.

Before Medgar Evers, one individual successfully integrated the University of Mississippi: Harry S. Murphy. In 1945, Murphy enrolled without incident under the Navy's V-12 program. His light skin allowed him to pass as White, and the Navy identified him as such, so his admission faced no opposition. Following Evers in 1955 was Charles Dubra, who applied to the law school after earning a master's degree. Dubra assured the Dean he was not an activist—he simply wanted a law degree. While the Dean supported his application, the board of trustees denied it, reflecting the deep resistance to integration even for non-activist applicants.

In 1958, Clennon King, a preacher and former Alcorn A&M professor, attempted to desegregate the University of Mississippi by applying to its graduate history program. According to Erle Johnston, director of the Mississippi State Sovereignty Commission, initially, university officials had no plans to block his enrollment. However, when King arrived, expecting resistance and media attention, the lack of both seemed to unsettle him. According to Johnston, King suddenly collapsed, crying, "Save me, save me . . . keep these people off me," though no one threatened or approached him.

This outburst gave officials the excuse they needed. Governor J. P. Coleman ordered King's removal, citing his "belligerent remarks," and had him forcibly committed to the Mississippi State Mental Hospital at Whitfield, where he was detained for weeks. Another account claims King was left waiting in an empty room for hours. When no one returned, he began yelling for help, leading to his commitment. King's ordeal starkly illustrated the extreme measures taken to maintain segregation, even against nonthreatening applicants.

Despite this ordeal, King refused to be silenced. Years later, although he was not recognized by a political party, he campaigned to run for President of the United States.

In 1959, another attempt to break Mississippi's educational color barrier came from Clyde Kennard, a poultry farmer from Eatonville who applied to Mississippi

Southern College (now the University of Southern Mississippi). Shortly after his attempt to enroll, Kennard became the target of trumped-up criminal charges. On one occasion, as he left the college campus, police arrested him, claiming he had whiskey in his car—despite witnesses confirming that his vehicle had been locked, making it impossible for officers to see inside. Undeterred, Kennard appealed his conviction through the courts. The Supreme Court put his case to the side. But before the case could gain traction, officials struck again, this time accusing him of receiving stolen goods—a charge that resulted in a seven-year prison sentence.

Behind bars, Kennard's health rapidly declined. He developed cancer, and by the time authorities granted him release, the disease had already taken its toll. He died shortly thereafter, his life cut short not just by illness, but by a system that viewed his pursuit of education as a threat. His story remains a haunting testament to the brutal lengths Mississippi officials would go to uphold segregation.

HISTORY AND THE SUPREME COURT

In 1896 the Supreme Court had ruled that segregated facilities were legal. Then in 1954 the Court ruled them unconstitutional. What are some possible explanations for the change in attitude after fifty-eight years?

WHITE REACTION TO THE BROWN DECISION

News of the decision hit Mississippi like a tornado. Headlines and news announcements reported it as the top story of the day. Fred Sullens, editor of the *Jackson Daily News*, wrote that "human blood may stain Southern soil in many places because of this decision, but the dark red stains of the blood will be on the marble steps of the US Supreme Court building."

Governor Hugh White argued more calmly: "We shall resist . . . by every legal means at our command. I want to say that there is no intention to 'defy' the Supreme Court; we are simply exercising the same legal rights to resist the most unfortunate decision that the NAACP exercised."

Walter Sillers Jr., the influential Speaker of the Mississippi House of Representatives, took an extreme position in the segregation debate by suggesting the state should completely abandon public education. As the most powerful politician in Mississippi at the time, his proposal to shut down public schools rather than integrate them demonstrated how far segregationists would go to maintain racial separation.

EASTLAND ON SEGREGATION AND MISSISSIPPI HISTORY

Senator James Eastland presented the case for segregation to the nation. On the floor of the United States Senate, he said:

> The Southern institution of racial segregation or racial separation was the correct, self-evident truth which arose from the chaos and confusion of the Reconstruction period. Separation promotes racial harmony. It permits each race to follow its own pursuits, to develop its own culture, its own institutions, its own civilization. Segregation is not discrimination. Segregation is not a badge of racial inferiority, and that it is not is recognized by both races in the Southern States. In fact, segregation is desired and supported by the vast majority of the members of both of the races in the South, who dwell side by side under harmonious conditions.

Examine Eastland's argument. How do his views compare with the description of Reconstruction? Do the events of the 1927 flood support Eastland's analysis of Mississippi society? Do you agree with him that segregation is not necessarily discrimination?

STENNIS SPEAKS OUT

Despite being often labeled a moderate conservative, Senator John Stennis's stance on segregation aligned firmly with White supremacy. Speaking to the Citizens Council in 1958, he attacked the *Brown* decision's judges, dismissing them as "social engineers and self-styled crusaders" rather than experienced jurists. He made his position on segregation clear, declaring that "To require mixing of the races will destroy the schools. The people of Mississippi will not submit to mixed schools."

BLACK REACTION TO THE DECISION

Governor White's first official action was to gather support for his school "equalization" plan. He invited ninety Black leaders from all parts of Mississippi to a meeting and asked them to support a voluntary segregation plan designed to wipe out the estimated $115,000,000 difference between White and Black school facilities. White felt that they would go along with this move to make the schools equal but keep them separate.

White began the conference by speaking of "friendly" race relations of the past in Mississippi, but several Blacks immediately spoke in favor of abolishing segregation. In an unexpected turn of events, Reverend H. H. Humes, an African American conservative figure known for his frequent alignment with White segregationists, offered a pointed critique:

> You should not be mad at us. Those were nine White men who rendered the decision. Not one colored man had anything to do with it. The real trouble is that you have given us schools too long in which we could study the earth through the floor and the stars through the roof.

White was furious. He had relied on Black conservatives like Humes to support his plan, but their resistance left him frustrated. Realizing his strategy had failed, White abruptly ended the meeting. One of the men present stated later that "for the first time I was really proud to be a Negro in Mississippi." Only one Black leader supported the governor's plan. The others, led by Dr. T. R. M. Howard of Mound Bayou, issued a statement supporting *Brown v. Board of Education*.

Black leaders then backed their statement with action. Beginning in the summer of 1954, NAACP groups in Vicksburg, Jackson, Clarksdale, Natchez, and Yazoo City filed petitions asking school boards to take steps to comply with the Supreme Court decision. The Regional Council of Negro Leadership called for the "immediate opening" of the state's graduate and professional schools to all races.

BIRTH OF THE WHITE CITIZENS' COUNCILS

While Mississippi's Black leaders were moving to break down segregation barriers, Whites were discussing what it should do. Robert Patterson, a farmer from Itta Bena, did more than merely talk. Two months after the Court decision, he met with White businessmen and planters in the Delta town of Indianola and organized the first White Citizens' Council. Patterson then traveled around the state organizing new chapters and describing the Councils' objectives.

Later that year, Tom Brady, a judge from Brookhaven, gave a speech entitled "Black Monday." The White Citizens' Councils distributed it throughout the South. The title came from the label Congressman John Bell Williams gave to the day when the Supreme Court announced its ruling.

Black Monday explained segregationist ideology in detail. Brady severely criticized the Court's decision. He pledged that "we as Mississippians will not bow down to a court of nine old men whose hearts are as Black as their robes." He feared Whites and Blacks would marry each other if desegregation took place. He called for the White South to organize, saying, "We can die, if necessary, for our sacred principles."

Figure 14.2. Segregationist literature circulated in Mississippi. Courtesy of the Archives and Records Services Division, Mississippi Department of Archives and History.

THE WHITE CITIZENS' COUNCILS GROW

Patterson worked hard, and the Councils quickly spread across the Deep South. They were thus a Mississippi innovation, headquartered in the state, that was becoming a force throughout the region. By November 1954, leaders claimed chapters in 110 Mississippi towns and more than 25,000 members. Planters, bankers, lawyers, and businessmen joined. The goal was to build a solid front of more "respectable" Whites who would tolerate no attempts at integration at any level. The Councils wanted to be able to speak for all of White Mississippi.

WHITE CITIZENS' COUNCIL PRESSURE PAYS OFF

Their first act to save segregation was to destroy the NAACP petition movement to integrate schools in five Mississippi cities. In Yazoo City, Council leaders bought a full-page ad in the *Herald* advising readers to "look over carefully" the list of Black petition signers. The town's economic elites took action immediately. Many of the signers lost their jobs, were refused credit or supplies, and were eventually forced to leave town to look for work. Within two months, forty-seven of the original fifty-three who had signed the petition asked to have their names removed.

Similar pressure campaigns also overcame petition efforts in Natchez, Vicksburg, and Jackson. Council's leader William J. Simmons described what happened in Clarksdale:

> The good folks there had said, "We don't need a Citizens' Council, our n-----s are good n-----s, they don't want to integrate, if we organize a Citizens' Council it'll agitate 'em." But one bright morning they woke up with a school petition with 303 signers, including most of their "good ones." So they organized a Council. It's got 3,000 members now. The petition collapsed. They all started taking their names off. Really, about all the White people have to do is let 'em know they don't want to have all this stuff and that's about the end of it. Most of them got fired, I suppose.

By the end of summer 1955, the petition movement was dead. The council's pressure against the NAACP had been completely successful. The first attempt to crack the wall of segregation had ended in failure for Mississippi Blacks.

WHITE OPPOSITION TO THE COUNCILS

Some White Mississippians opposed the White Citizens' Councils movement. Hazel Brannon Smith, editor of the *Lexington Advertiser*, urged a progressive approach to race relations. Council leaders tried to silence her by starting a rival paper in Lexington with a segregationist editorial policy. Smith lashed out at their tactics in a 1959 editorial:

> Today we live in fear in Holmes County and in Mississippi. It hangs like a dark cloud over us, dominating every facet of public and private life. . . . None speaks freely without being misunderstood. Almost every man and woman is afraid to try to do anything to promote good will and harmony between the races.

When Hodding Carter II, editor of the *Greenville Delta Democrat-Times*, wrote an article on the Citizens' Councils titled "A Wave of Terror Threatens the South," the Mississippi House of Representatives voted to censure him for "lying about the state and the activities of the Councils, and for selling out the state for Yankee gold."

P. D. East, editor of the *Petal Paper*, compared the Councils to the Ku Klux Klan. He mocked the movement with "ads" such as the reprint shown in figure 14.3. But local Whites canceled their subscriptions and advertising, and his paper almost collapsed.

Still, only a few White Mississippians openly criticized this movement. By 1958, the Councils seemed to be in control of the White community in the state. Along

Figure. 14.3. *Petal Paper* ad.

with perhaps 80,000 paid members, the Councils had the support of thousands more. Until the end of Governor Ross Barnett's term of office in 1964, the Citizens' Councils dominated the decisions of state officials and drafted much of the state's most important legislation.

THE STATE GOVERNMENT AND SEGREGATION

In 1954 the legislature passed and voters approved an amendment to the state constitution. It empowered the legislature to abolish all public schools in the state. The legislature also submitted to the voters an amendment that required a citizen, to qualify to vote, be able to write in his own hand a "reasonable" interpretation of any section of the state constitution. It was openly intended to disqualify Black applicants with difficult questions about the constitution, while White applicants would get simple questions. In 1952, Mississippians had rejected a similar amendment, but this time it passed, 75,488 to 15,718.

The vote was a statewide demonstration of White reaction to the Supreme Court decision. Other Southern states began to follow suit. In 1954, Mississippi had come forward, as famed historian C. Vann Woodward put it, "in her historic role as leader of reaction in race policy, just as she had in 1875 to overthrow Reconstruction and in 1890 to disfranchise the Negro."

BLACK VOTING IS CUT

The chairman of the State Democratic Committee challenged the right of Blacks to vote in the Democratic primary. He argued that "Negroes might be national

Democrats but they are not Mississippi Democrats." For racist White Democrats, the party was akin to any private club that could police its own membership. He concluded by saying, "We don't intend to have Negroes voting in this primary, but we also intend to handle it in a sensible, orderly manner."

After this warning, few Black Mississippians tried to vote. At some of the polls where they did try, they were challenged and their ballots were not counted. Other Blacks were frightened from attempting to vote by intimidating behavior from the local Citizens' Council. The state's new voting requirements eliminated still more. Out of 22,000 reported registered Blacks in 1954, only an estimated 8,000 tried to vote the next year.

CONFESSIONS OF HATE: THE ARROGANCE BEHIND EMMETT TILL'S MURDER

In the tense aftermath of the *Brown v. Board of Education* decision and rising Black voter registration efforts, White opposition to racial equality escalated, leading to increased violence against African Americans, particularly in the South. The summer of 1955, just a year after the landmark ruling, brought a horrific event that would shock the nation and galvanize the civil rights movement: the murder of Emmett Till, a fourteen-year-old Black boy from Chicago visiting family in Mississippi.

The tragedy began when Till was accused of whistling at Carolyn Bryant, a White woman, in a local store. Days later, in the early hours of August 28, 1955, Roy Bryant (Carolyn's husband) and his half-brother J. W. Milam, along with other men, forcibly abducted Till from his great-uncle Mose Wright's home. They brutally beat and mutilated Till, gouging out one of his eyes and shooting him in the head before dumping his body in the Tallahatchie River.

When Till's body was recovered, the extent of the violence was horrifying. In a bold and courageous decision, his mother, Mamie Till, insisted on an open-casket funeral to expose the brutality of racial hatred. The sight of Till's disfigured body, along with photographs published in newspapers and magazines, shocked the nation and forced Americans to confront the grim reality of racism in the South. This gruesome display became a rallying cry for the civil rights movement, highlighting the urgent need for justice and equality.

The trial of Roy Bryant and J. W. Milam for Emmett Till's murder ended in their acquittal by an all-White jury, a stark illustration of the period's racial injustice. In a shocking turn of events, both men later admitted to the crime in a magazine interview, seemingly secure in the knowledge that the legal principle of double jeopardy protected them from further prosecution. This principle, which prohibits trying an individual twice for the same offense, meant that their confession, though damning, could not lead to legal consequences.

Figure 14.5. Mamie Till and mourners at her son's funeral. Collection of the Smithsonian National Museum of African American History and Culture, Gift of Lauren and Michael Lee.

This event became a powerful catalyst in the growing civil rights movement. It starkly illustrated the dangers faced by Black Americans in the segregated South and the urgent need for change. The widespread outrage over Till's murder helped galvanize support for the civil rights cause, bringing increased attention to racial injustice in America.

OPEN SEASON AGAINST BLACKS

During the same summer of the Till murder, another tragedy had unfolded that exemplified the dangers faced by civil rights activists. Reverend George Lee, a prominent NAACP leader in Belzoni, Mississippi, who tirelessly advocated for voting rights, was found dead in what authorities initially ruled an auto crash. However, the circumstances surrounding his death were far more sinister. Witnesses reported hearing gunshots before the crash, and medical examination revealed lead pellets in Reverend Lee's face. Despite this evidence, no one was ever brought to trial for his murder.

Later that year on November 25, Gus Courts, a Belzoni NAACP leader and friend of Lee, was shot by a White man while tending his grocery store. Courts blamed the local Citizens' Council for the attempted murder. Despite an FBI investigation, no one was ever brought to trial, and Courts was ultimately forced to flee the state. The next year in 1955, Lamar Smith had been shot to death at noon in front of a courthouse.

The pattern of violence and impunity that claimed the lives of Till, Smith, and Reverend Lee, and threatened Courts's life was not confined to a single summer or location. It persisted across the South, revealing a systemic disregard for Black lives and a failure of the justice system to protect civil rights activists.

Whites seemed increasingly emboldened in targeting and killing Blacks. In December 1955, Elmer Kimball, owner of a cotton gin, fatally shot Clinton Melton, a Black gas station attendant, reportedly over a dispute about the amount of gas Kimball had purchased while driving J. W. Milam's car—a detail that eerily connected this incident to the recent Till case.

As the decade progressed, the brutality continued unabated. In a chilling echo of earlier incidents, April 1959 saw another stark example of racial violence and judicial indifference. Mack Charles Parker, a Black man accused of assaulting a White woman, fell victim to mob "justice" in Poplarville, Mississippi. Parker was forcibly removed from his jail cell by a group of White men and lynched. Despite the FBI's involvement and the presentation of evidence to both state and federal grand juries in Mississippi, the case met the same fate as those of Lee and Courts—no indictments were issued.

In an article written in *The Reporter*, a local White man remarked, "There's open season on Negroes now. They've got no protection, and any White man who wants can go out and shoot one, and we'll let him go free."

Such violence gave Mississippi the reputation of being one of the most violent states in the country for Blacks. The national NAACP, for example, launched a campaign in 1955, noting "'M' is for Mississippi and Murder."

These attacks, left unchecked by the law, temporarily halted Black voter registration initiatives and compelled cautious approaches in challenging school districts following the *Brown* decision.

BROWN II

A year after its original decision, the Supreme Court issued a second unanimous opinion known as "Brown II." This implementation decision of the first case directed a "prompt and reasonable" start toward ending segregation in public schools. However, the Court did not insist on immediate desegregation. Instead, it ruled that local school districts could act to end segregation "with all deliberate speed." Around the South, leading Democratic politicians interpreted this phrase to mean that the region could stall desegregation for perhaps decades.

MISSISSIPPI'S ANTI-INTEGRATION LAWS, 1956

Rather than act "with all deliberate speed," the Mississippi Legislature, in 1956, passed a series of laws designed to make segregation even more secure. For example, it abolished compulsory school attendance. These laws were the legislature's response to Brown II. White Mississippi was increasing its resistance to desegregation. However, the legislature faced a problem: its laws could be challenged by Mississippians who believed them to be unconstitutional. If the courts upheld such challenges, then the laws would be thrown out. To prevent a challenge, the legislature passed a law prohibiting fundraising for the purpose of prosecuting lawsuits against the state.

In March 1956, Governor James P. Coleman signed an Interposition Resolution passed by the Mississippi legislature, condemning the US Supreme Court's *Brown v. Board of Education* decision for overstepping state powers. Interposition is the theory that states could resist federal laws or rulings they deemed unconstitutional.

THE STATE SOVEREIGNTY COMMISSION

In 1956, Mississippi established the State Sovereignty Commission through legislative action. This agency, created to maintain racial segregation, received strong backing from House Speaker Walter Sillers Jr., a committed segregationist leader. The Commission served as Mississippi's official agency to resist integration and civil rights efforts.

The commission also operated a public relations department to publicize to the nation the alleged benefits of Mississippi's segregated way of life. In 1960, the Sovereignty Commission began giving the Citizens' Councils $5,000 per month, even though the state constitution prohibited donations from a state agency to a private organization. Finally ceasing operations in 1973, thousands of the Sovereignty Commission's files are now available online via the state's Department of Archives and History.

EXIT THE 1950s

As the 1950s ended, Mississippi was still a segregated society. The first round of the struggle for civil rights had been won by the Citizens' Councils and its allies, the elected leadership of the state.

But the issues were far from settled. Other Southern states were beginning to desegregate their schools and public accommodations. The Supreme Court refused to back away from its decisions supporting desegregation. The main issue was well understood by all sides: Can states refuse to obey federal law? Would an extremist "states' rights" view of the Constitution and American federalism win the day? The specific question for Mississippi remained: How long could the state defy the courts? This question would be decided in the coming decade.

Recommended Readings

Devery S. Anderson, *Emmett Till: The Murder That Shocked the World and Propelled the Civil Rights Movement* (Jackson: University Press of Mississippi, 2015).

Erle Johnston, *Mississippi's Defiant Years 1953–1973* (Forrest, MS: Lake Harbor Publishers, 1990).

Yasuhiro Katagiri, *The Mississippi State Sovereignty Commission: Civil Rights and States' Rights* (Jackson: University Press of Mississippi, 2001).

Neil R. McMillen, *Dark Journey: Black Mississippians in the Age of Jim Crow* (Urbana: University of Illinois Press, 1989).

CHAPTER 15

LOCAL PEOPLE AND MISSISSIPPI'S MASSIVE RESISTANCE TO CHANGE

1960–1967

AFTER WORLD WAR II, CIVIL RIGHTS ACTIVISTS LED SUCCESSFUL VOTER REGistration drives for African Americans. In response, White officials pushed through a 1960 constitutional amendment adding a "good moral character" clause, giving registrars power to deny Black applicants. This marked the beginning of the most turbulent decade since Reconstruction. When Ross Barnett became governor in January 1960, few could have predicted how profoundly Mississippi would change in the years ahead.

Figure 15.1. Governor Ross Barnett. Courtesy of the Archives and Records Services Division, Mississippi Department of Archives and History.

The change from Governors White and Coleman to Barnett reflected a change in the ideology of many White Mississippians. During the 1950s, as other White Americans began to doubt segregation, they had increased their support for it. Barnett now took office committed to stopping racial integration at nearly any cost. Midway through his four-year term, however, the state was forced to give up its open resistance to integration. By the time Barnett handed over the governorship to Paul Johnson Jr., the civil rights movement had begun to force some of the changes that would continue throughout the 1960s.

The new civil rights leaders wanted to break the pattern of segregation itself. And like the civil rights pioneers of the 1950s, the new leaders risked jail, beatings, and even death.

Change was in the air all over the South. In Alabama and Georgia, Dr. Martin Luther King Jr. and others had challenged segregated seating patterns on buses, park benches, and other public accommodations.

In February 1960, Black college students in North Carolina began a wave of "sit-ins" in downtown businesses across the South. Now, late in April 1960, about forty-five Blacks conducted "wade-ins" when they walked onto the famous Gulf Coast beaches, trying to end their Whites-only status. These brave individuals waded into the waters and walked along the shoreline, asserting their right to enjoy the same recreational areas as their White counterparts. The peaceful protesters were met with violent resistance from White onlookers and local authorities. During the violent confrontations, some individuals hurled rocks at Black protesters, while others physically assaulted them using their fists, wooden sticks, and metal chains. Despite the presence of law enforcement officers at the scene, they remained passive observers, failing to intervene or make any arrests. Among those assaulted during this act of civil disobedience was Dr. Gilbert R. Mason Sr., a respected Black physician and community leader. Later that night, the violence spilled over into Biloxi itself, and eight Blacks and two Whites were shot in scattered incidents (none fatally).

The wave of direct-action protests that began with the North Carolina sit-ins in February 1960 soon spread across Mississippi. While brave protesters waded into the segregated waters of the Gulf Coast beaches, risking violent reprisals to claim their right to public spaces, another group of young activists was preparing to challenge segregation in one of Jackson's most symbolic institutions. The battle for civil rights would move from the shores to the Whites-only public library.

THE TOUGALOO NINE

On March 27, 1961, nine Tougaloo College students, members of the NAACP youth council, took decisive action against segregation by staging a peaceful sit-in at Jackson's Whites-only Municipal Library. Upon arrival, the staff questioned

Figure 15.2. Police threaten Tougaloo students with arrest during Mississippi's first sit-in at the Jackson Public Library in 1961. Library of Congress, Prints and Photographs Division, Visual Materials from the NAACP Records, LC-DIG-ds-10638.

their purpose, and when the students explained they were conducting research, they were directed to the "colored" library. Refusing to leave, the students took their seats. One student recalled being so nervous that she didn't realize when she was pretending to be reading, her book was upside down. After their refusal to comply, the police arrested all nine students.

Known as the "Tougaloo 9," they were held in custody for two days without legal representation, which sparked a peaceful protest vigil at Jackson State College. Organized by students Dorie and Joyce Ladner, along with NAACP's Medgar Evers, the protest led to the expulsion of Dorie and Joyce Ladner from Jackson State College. They eventually enrolled at Tougaloo College. This sit-in was Mississippi's first, and the different responses of the two schools highlighted a key reality: as a state-funded institution, Jackson State had to follow segregationist officials' demands, while private Tougaloo College had more freedom to support civil rights activism.

FIRST ROUND OF DESEGREGATION

In the 1920s, Black landowners in the community of Harmony, Mississippi, built a school with the help of a grant. This institution quickly gained a reputation for excellence, with one Black resident describing it as "one of the best schools in the state." However, this source of community pride and quality education was abruptly shuttered when the county decided to consolidate its Black schools.

The closure of their beloved school galvanized the Harmony community into action. Winson Hudson, who served as the president of the local NAACP chapter, joined forces with her sister Dovie to lead the charge. Together in 1962, they rallied other members of their community and formed alliances with NAACP chapters from the Gulf Coast and Jackson to file a desegregation lawsuit. Their legal battle proved to be a pivotal moment in Mississippi's history. In 1964, as a direct result of this lawsuit, the first schools in the state began the process of desegregation.

McCOMB WORKERS

Robert Parris Moses, a pivotal figure in the civil rights movement, emerged from an unlikely background to become a driving force for change in Mississippi. Born and raised in Harlem, Moses was a twenty-year-old with light brown skin and a few freckles near his nose. His journey from a mathematics teacher with a Harvard master's degree to a civil rights activist began with a transformative trip to Virginia, where he participated in some of the earliest sit-ins.

Inspired by these experiences, Moses began volunteering for the Southern Christian Leadership Conference (SCLC) in Atlanta. It was there where he encountered two influential figures: Ella Baker, a seasoned organizer in the movement, and Jane Stembridge, a White student working for the Student Nonviolent Coordinating Committee (SNCC). These connections would prove crucial in shaping Moses's future role in the civil rights struggle.

Persuaded to venture into Mississippi, Moses initially traveled to Clarksdale and Cleveland, where he met established civil rights workers Aaron Henry and Amzie Moore. These encounters further solidified his commitment to the cause. However, it was an invitation from the NAACP president in McComb, Curtis "C.C." Bryant, that would set the stage for Moses's most significant work for SNCC.

In July 1961, Bob Moses arrived in McComb as a SNCC staff member to establish a "Voter Education Project." His work was supported by a modest grant from the Taconic Foundation and received quiet backing from Attorney General Robert Kennedy's Department of Justice. For over a year, he had been laying the groundwork for this initiative, which aimed to secure equal rights for Black citizens as swiftly as possible. Moses's approach was grassroots and practical: he went door to door, persuading local families to provide room and board for ten student volunteers who would assist in the campaign.

This voter registration drive in McComb became a defining moment in the civil rights movement. Moses's work exemplified SNCC's commitment to empowering local communities and fostering grassroots activism. By bringing together outside volunteers with local residents, Moses created a powerful model for civil rights organizing that would be replicated across the South.

One of the volunteers was Bob Zellner, a young White man from Alabama. The son of an Alabama Methodist minister, Zellner attended Huntingdon College in Montgomery. In his senior year he was assigned to write a term paper on "The Racial Problem and Your Solution to It," and as part of his research he attended a federal trial of Dr. Martin Luther King Jr. and other civil rights leaders in Montgomery. Zellner was greatly moved by Dr. King and later joined SNCC.

His job was to work among young White Southerners, convincing them that segregation was wrong, but in McComb his greatest impact was probably on the Black community. As Moses wrote to him when they were confined to separate jail cells:

> Your presence has had an effect on the young Mississippians. They had never known a sympathetic White person before. The kids here had said, "We won't have anything to do with 'peckerwoods' [meaning White people]. But now since Bob Zellner demonstrated with us and was beaten, we believe that maybe there are some good White people after all."

EARLY BLACK-VOTER REGISTRATION: McCOMB

Like their predecessors during the First Reconstruction, the leaders of the Second Reconstruction considered the power of the ballot as the key to improving the lives of Black Mississippians. Volunteer workers, some from outside the state, began to organize voter-registration drives.

In a pivotal moment of the civil rights movement in Mississippi, three Black individuals, including fifteen-year-old Brenda Travis, were arrested for attempting to integrate the Greyhound bus station. This act of civil disobedience resulted in their arrest and subsequent jail sentences, highlighting the severe consequences faced by those challenging racial segregation in the state.

Upon their release, Travis and one of her fellow students attempted to return to school, expecting to resume their education. However, they were met with rejection from the principal, who denied them reentry. This denial of their right to education sparked immediate outrage among their peers.

In response to this injustice, the student body organized a walkout in solidarity with Travis and her fellow activist. It was described by a participant:

> The 115 students stopped in front of the city hall to begin praying. One by one . . . we were herded up the steps and into the city courthouse, and Bob Zellner, who was the only White participant, [was] attacked on the steps as he went up, and then a mob was outside, waiting, milling around, threatening. And inside, they brought the people down, the White people, the so-called good citizens of the town, one by one, to take a look at this Moses guy (in reference to Bob Moses). And they would come down and stand in front of the jail and say, "Where's Moses? Where's Moses?"

Figure 15.3. For months not one Black was registered in Hattiesburg. Courtesy of the Archives and Records Services Division, Mississippi Department of Archives and History.

The students were arrested. In the aftermath of these arrests, the police made the decision to release the majority of students under eighteen years of age. However, Brenda Travis, despite her young age, was singled out for harsher treatment. She was detained and received the most severe sentence among the protesters.

WHITES OPPOSE BLACK REGISTRATION

As Blacks began to register to vote, White resistance increased. Moses was arrested as he brought voter registration applicants to the courthouse at nearby Liberty. A few days later, again at Liberty, a White extremist violently hit him again and again with the butt end of a knife.

At about the same time, two eighteen-year-olds, Hollis Watkins and Curtis Hayes, staged a sit-in at the segregated Woolworth lunch counter in McComb. When the two were arrested, Blacks held a mass protest meeting.

On September 25, 1961, the civil rights movement in Mississippi suffered another devastating blow with the murder of Herbert Lee. Lee, a fifty-two-year-old farmer and logger from Amite County, had been actively involved in voter registration efforts, a cause that put him directly in the crosshairs of those determined to maintain White supremacy in the South. He was later remembered in a song of the Southern freedom movement:

> We have hung our heads and cried
> for all those like Lee who died,

Died for you and died for me,
died for the cause of equality.
We've been 'buked and we've been scorned,
We've been talked about, sure as you're born.
But we'll never turn back, no,
we'll never turn back,
Until we've all been freed and
we have equality.

The circumstances of Lee's murder were particularly chilling. E. H. Hurst, a White state legislator, shot him in broad daylight. Hurst claimed self-defense, alleging that Lee had threatened him with a tire iron. Bob Moses, in *Radical Equations: Civil Rights from Mississippi to the Algebra Project* (with Charlie Cobb), recalls a moment after Lee's funeral when Lee's wife approached Moses and Charles McDew, bitterly screaming, "You killed my husband! You killed my husband!"

Later, Louis Allen provided an account that differed from Hurst's, indicating that Lee had been unarmed. However, Allen was pressured to recant his statement. Eventually, with a troubled conscience, Allen testified that Lee was indeed unarmed. For his testimony, Allen himself was later gunned down in 1964.

THE FREEDOM RIDERS: DEFYING SEGREGATION AND FACING REPRESSION

In the spring of 1961, the Freedom Rides brought national attention to the civil rights struggle in the Deep South. Volunteers from the Student Nonviolent Coordinating Committee (SNCC) and Congress of Racial Equality (CORE) boarded integrated buses in Washington, DC, on May 4, traveling south to test the enforcement of *Morgan v. Virginia* (1946) and *Boynton v. Virginia* (1960), Supreme Court rulings that banned segregation in interstate travel facilities.

Their journey through Alabama was met with violent resistance. In Anniston, Birmingham, and Montgomery, White mobs attacked the riders, often with no intervention from local authorities. The brutality escalated to the point that Attorney General Robert F. Kennedy had to intervene. After a violent assault at the Montgomery bus terminal, Martin Luther King Jr. held a rally at First Baptist Church, where a White mob surrounded the building. In response, Kennedy sent federal marshals to protect the activists.

As the Freedom Riders approached Mississippi, President John F. Kennedy negotiated with Alabama and Mississippi's governors to prevent further violence. In exchange for protection from the highway patrol and the National Guard, Mississippi officials were given free rein to arrest the riders upon arrival. Once in Jackson, Mississippi, Freedom Riders were immediately arrested for attempting to use Whites-only facilities. Many chose imprisonment at Parchman State Farm over paying the $200 fine. Among them was Joan Trumpauer, a young White woman deeply committed to civil rights. She later participated in the Woolworth's sit-in in Jackson, facing violent opposition alongside other activists. Trumpauer also became the first White student to enroll at Tougaloo College, a historically Black institution.

The movement also saw the unjust imprisonment of Hezekiah Watkins, who, at thirteen years old, became the youngest person incarcerated at Parchman Farm during the civil rights movement. His case underscored the extreme measures used to suppress activists, as a child was thrown into a brutal adult prison after his friend pushed him into the Whites-only waiting room at the bus station.

Both Trumpauer and Watkins represented the diverse faces of the movement—young and old, Black and White—who risked their safety and freedom to challenge segregation. Their sacrifices, along with those of many others, shaped the civil rights struggle in Mississippi.

Though many activists imprisoned in Parchman Farm went on to play key roles in the movement, the next major civil rights battle in Mississippi would not be led by SNCC or CORE—but by one Black man against an all-White university.

JAMES MEREDITH AND OLE MISS

On January 26, 1961, James Meredith had applied for admission to the University of Mississippi. In his letter, Meredith, an Air Force veteran, let the registrar know that he was a student at what is now Jackson State University. Three times the registrar refused to answer his letters. Finally, he returned Meredith's room-reservation fee.

By now Meredith was convinced that he would have to force "Ole Miss" to admit him. After many legal battles and delays, the federal Fifth Circuit Court of Appeals ordered Ole Miss to admit Meredith. The court found that "from the moment the defendants [Ole Miss] discovered that Meredith was a Negro, they engaged in a carefully calculated campaign of delay, harassment, and masterly inactivity."

Opposition to Meredith

The idea that a Black man might enter Ole Miss aroused many White Mississippians. On a statewide telecast, Governor Barnett attempted to place his own authority as state governor between Mississippi citizens and the federal government. He demanded resistance, "We must either submit to the unlawful dictates of the federal government, or stand up like men and tell them 'Never.' . . . Every public official, including myself, should be prepared to make the choice tonight whether he is willing to go to jail, if necessary, to keep faith with the people who have placed their welfare in his hands."

The Ole Miss Riot

The situation at Ole Miss unfolded rapidly. On Sunday afternoon, September 30, 1962, the initial group of federal marshals arrived and positioned themselves at the Lyceum building. This drew the attention of a gathering crowd, which swelled in size as students came back from a football weekend in Jackson. Chants such as "Go to hell, JFK" filled the air. Few in the crowd realized that Meredith had been flown in from Memphis and was already in a dormitory room on the edge of the campus.

As evening set in, students started to toss gravel and lit cigarettes towards the marshals. Quickly, the situation escalated with the crowd hurling rocks, bottles, and pieces of pipe at the marshals. Vehicles nearby were flipped over, damaged, and set ablaze. Bullets started flying through the darkness.

Tragedy on Campus

At 8:00 p.m. the marshals fired tear gas to hold off the mob. By now, it was clear that Ole Miss students no longer dominated the crowd. Armed groups of outsiders, some of whom were die-hard segregationists from neighboring states, were firing rifles at the federal marshals. Before the night was over, a local jukebox repairman and a French newsman lay dead—both victims of shots from the crowd.

Figure 15.4. Burned-out vehicle on campus. Johnston (Erle E., Jr.) Papers, Special Collections, University Libraries, University of Southern Mississippi.

As dawn broke on Oxford, burned-out cars still smoldered. Smashed glass, rocks, and pipes lay everywhere. One hundred and sixty marshals were hurt, of whom twenty-eight had been shot. It had taken the use of National Guard troops, mostly native Mississippians, to halt the violence. Finally, President Kennedy sent in more than 31,000 federal troops.

EXPLAINING THE RIOT

Imagine having a friend in a distant country like Norway or Kenya. Write a letter explaining why the crowd at Ole Miss became so violent on that September night in 1962. Remember that your friend will probably know very little about race relations in Mississippi. You will need to mention many things from earlier chapters in this book.

The Limits of Defiance

The federal government sent troops to the University of Mississippi, but they avoided direct conflict with state forces. Governor Barnett's public speeches about defying federal authority and resisting integration played a role in inciting the riot. His inconsistent actions, unfulfilled promises, and submissive behavior during private conversations with President Kennedy and Attorney General Robert Kennedy also worsened the situation.

However, Barnett stopped short of ordering state police to completely block James Meredith's admission. This restraint was influenced by the lessons learned from the Civil War, which had firmly established that states couldn't openly challenge federal authority.

The crisis at Ole Miss, both the violent campus unrest and the legal battles, effectively marked the end of Mississippi's interposition doctrine, which the state had adopted in 1956 to resist federal desegregation orders. This doctrine had claimed that states could "interpose" themselves between their citizens and the federal government to prevent the enforcement of federal laws they deemed unconstitutional.

MEREDITH, OUTSIDE AGITATORS, AND THE RESURRECTION OF THE KLAN

James Meredith's famous statement, "We won the battle, but lost the war," referred to his successful admission to Ole Miss and the violent riots that followed. While

Meredith and the federal government ultimately prevailed, this defeat for segregationists had unintended consequences.

Evidence suggests that this loss, combined with the increasing presence of "outside agitators" (civil rights workers), led to a dramatic surge in Ku Klux Klan membership. Klan numbers in Mississippi exploded from fewer than 400 members in the summer of 1963 to approximately 7,000 by the end of 1964, coinciding with Freedom Summer.

This rapid growth in White supremacist organizations demonstrates how victories in the civil rights movement often sparked intense backlash, complicating the path toward racial equality in Mississippi and the broader South.

In the summer of 1963, near Greenwood, night riders ambushed a car carrying civil rights workers Jimmy Travis, Bob Moses, and Randolph Blackwell. The attackers unleashed a barrage of gunfire, with one shot striking Travis and lodging in his neck, critically wounding him. Moses and Blackwell emerged from the incident unscathed.

THE MOVEMENT IN THE DELTA

While the Meredith controversy unfolded, Black Mississippians continued their struggle for voting rights. SNCC concentrated its 1962 registration efforts in Greenwood, Leflore County, where two-thirds of residents were Black and most were impoverished. The county's wealth disparity was stark: thirty-six White families each earning over $25,000 annually collectively outearned the 3,600 poorest families. Healthcare access mirrored this inequality; 131 of 168 hospital beds were reserved for Whites. SNCC workers faced brutal opposition, including beatings, shootings, and arson. Despite this violence, they persevered, and the number of Black voting applicants steadily increased.

THE WHITTEN-SMITH CONGRESSIONAL CONTEST, 1962

While voter-registration attempts continued, an important election took place in North Mississippi. Because Mississippi had lost population compared with other states, it lost a seat in Congress. Congressional districts had to be redrawn.[1] Frank Smith, a White racial moderate and the Delta's United States representative for the previous twelve years, was paired against Congressman Jamie Whitten, a segregationist from the hills.

During the campaign, Smith was attacked for being a friend of President John F. Kennedy, allegedly favoring integration, supporting liberal trade programs with foreign nations, and "opposing the Mississippi way of life." Whitten won.

FOOD IS CUT OFF

Black voter registration efforts in Leflore County prompted a harsh response from local authorities. In October 1962, the County's Board of Supervisors halted distribution of federal surplus food, affecting 22,000 people, mostly Black. White leaders aimed to discourage voter registration by exerting economic pressure on the Black community.

This tactic backfired, ultimately aiding SNCC organizers. By bringing in food from out-of-state donors, SNCC workers connected with thousands of residents. As food deliveries increased, more people attempted to register at the courthouse.

Comedian Dick Gregory joined the relief effort, chartering a plane in Chicago and personally flying food supplies into Mississippi. Bob Moses and Charlie Cobb recount Gregory's defiant stance, quoting him as he challenged police: "We will march through your Dogs! And if you get some elephants we will march through them. And bring on your Tigers too."

YOUNG LEADERS AND LOCAL PEOPLE

In 1962, Congress of Racial Equality (CORE) organizer David Dennis arrived in Mississippi, seeing potential for change despite pervasive segregation. He focused on Madison County, where 29,000 African Americans owned 40 percent of the land but remained largely disfranchised, with only 200 registered voters and 100 active voters among the Black majority. Initially, Dennis and George Raymond were the sole CORE staff, later joined by Matt Suarez, Anne Moody, and Rudy Lombard, all in their early twenties.

CORE's success hinged on community support. Local leaders Annie Devine and C. O. Chinn were crucial to this effort. Despite police intimidation and White violence, they organized neighborhood canvassing, church meetings, and business boycotts. Their bravery and local connections helped CORE gain trust.

Chinn, a cafe owner, stood up to Canton's power structure, particularly Sheriff Bill Noble. He allowed CORE to use his cafe as an office, risking reprisal. Unlike many activists, Chinn was not committed to nonviolence and carried a gun for protection.

Annie Devine, a former teacher, became a prominent activist. In 1964, while running for Congress, she testified on the House floor in Washington, DC, demanding that Mississippi representatives be unseated due to Black voter suppression. Her compelling testimony provided crucial evidence of disfranchisement, later influencing the passage of the 1965 Voting Rights Act.

CELEBRITIES IN THE MOVEMENT

The civil rights movement in Mississippi saw significant contributions from various prominent figures from the entertainment industry. These individuals used their platforms and talents to support the struggle for racial equality and justice.

Dick Gregory, a comedian and civil rights activist, played a crucial role in Mississippi. He participated in protests in Greenwood, confronting police dogs during marches. Gregory also investigated the disappearance of civil rights workers James Chaney, Andrew Goodman, and Michael Schwerner in Philadelphia, Mississippi, offering a $25,000 reward that pressured the FBI to intensify their search efforts. Additionally, he provided food relief to impoverished Black communities in the Mississippi Delta.

Boston Celtics legend Bill Russell made his mark by opening the first integrated basketball camp in Mississippi following Medgar Evers's assassination. He actively participated in civil rights demonstrations and supported other initiatives, including the March on Washington.

In 1964, Harry Belafonte convinced Sidney Poitier to accompany him to deliver $70,000 in support of Mississippi Freedom Summer. The two entertainers packed the money into doctor bags and drove through the state to distribute the funds. During their journey, members of the Ku Klux Klan pursued them, repeatedly ramming their car, before their driver, Willie Blue, managed to escape.

Other influential singers including Aretha Franklin, James Brown, and gospel singer Mahalia Jackson provided musical support at rallies in Mississippi, inspiring and motivating civil rights activists. Her performances were essential in maintaining the morale of those involved in the movement. Nina Simone also contributed through her powerful music, writing and performing songs, like "Mississippi Goddam," which became anthems of the civil rights movement, expressing outrage over racial injustices in the state.

Folk singers were particularly active. In addition to Joan Baez, Pete Seeger frequently performed at civil rights events, including in Mississippi. Bob Dylan's "Only a Pawn in Their Game," about the murder of Medgar Evers in Mississippi, brought national attention to the state's racial struggles.

THE MOVEMENT BECOMES STATEWIDE

All over the state, civil rights activities were beginning. Small voter-registration drives were held in Laurel, Hattiesburg, Holly Springs, Vicksburg, Greenville, Cleveland, and Ruleville. Local groups and individuals took part; so did SNCC, CORE, and the NAACP. In addition to Moses, workers looked to Aaron Henry and Medgar Evers of the NAACP for coordination and leadership.

THE WOOLWORTH SIT-IN: A PIVOTAL MOMENT IN JACKSON'S CIVIL RIGHTS MOVEMENT

The movement's shift from rural communities to urban centers reached a dramatic turning point in Jackson. On May 28, 1963, three Tougaloo College students—Annie Moody, Memphis Norman, and Pearlena Lewis—took a brave stand against segregation by staging a sit-in at the Jackson Woolworth lunch counter. Their peaceful protest was immediately met with hostility as a waitress shut down the counter and turned off the lights.

The situation quickly escalated as a mob of approximately 300 White individuals surrounded the students. The protesters faced physical assault, with ketchup and mustard being poured over them. Memphis Norman endured a particularly brutal attack, being pulled from his seat, beaten unconscious, and subsequently arrested.

Despite the growing tension, two more Tougaloo students joined the protest. Joan Trumpauer, a White student, and Lois Chaffee sat alongside Annie Moody at the counter, demonstrating interracial solidarity. John Salter, a White professor at Tougaloo who had earlier dropped off the protesters, arrived after being alerted by a student monitor. His presence was misinterpreted by the mob, who mistakenly believed he was there to attack the protesters.

The violence continued to escalate. The sit-in participants were subjected to further assaults, including being spray-painted. Salter himself had pepper-laced water thrown into his eyes. As the situation worsened, George Raymond from the Congress of Racial Equality (CORE) and Dr. A. D. Beittel, Tougaloo College's president, joined the protesters at the counter in a show of support.

The chaos reached its peak when the angry mob began looting the store. Only then did law enforcement intervene, shutting down the establishment. The police escorted the protesters out, with Dr. Beittel requesting the protection of Captain J. L. Ray. The officer stayed with the group until they safely retrieved their car and returned to the Masonic temple.

Medgar Evers had wanted to join Salter at the sit-in, but Salter convinced him not to come. Salter knew that White people were targeting Evers, making it too dangerous for him to be there. This showed how risky it was for civil rights leaders like Evers to be involved in protests at that time.

Despite the death of Evers, civil rights workers persevered, continuing their efforts under the Council of Federated Organizations (COFO). COFO unified various groups under a single umbrella, which helped reduce some of the conflicts among them. A key dispute arose between young activists who wanted direct action protests and older members who preferred focusing on voter registration. Ella Baker helped bridge this generational divide by crafting a compromise between the two approaches, ultimately achieving both.

After several years of voter-registration drives, more than 70,000 Blacks had tried to register to vote. Less than 7,000 had been allowed to register. In the fall of 1963, to show that Blacks wanted to vote but were being kept from the polls, COFO organized a mock election referred to as the "Freedom Vote," where 60,000 Black citizens cast unofficial ballots for Aaron Henry for governor and Ed King for lieutenant governor—the first interracial ticket in Mississippi since Reconstruction. In the same unofficial election, civil rights activists Fannie Lou Hamer, Annie Devine, and Victoria Gray won overwhelming victories in their congressional races. Though unofficial, this symbolic election demonstrated Black Mississippians' determination to participate in the political process despite systematic disenfranchisement.

11:00, SUNDAY MORNINGS: THE MOST SEGREGATED HOUR OF THE WEEK

Facing financial constraints and mass arrests, Medgar Evers and Reverend Ed King shifted to smaller, targeted protests, confronting White Christians on the immorality of segregation. They organized church visits across Jackson to expose racial exclusion in places of worship.

On June 9, 1963, Black Tougaloo College students attended St. Peter's Catholic Church, while Baptist and Methodist churches turned others away. Two days later, Evers was assassinated in his driveway.

King continued the fight, leading students, faculty, and out-of-state ministers to Whites-only churches for ten months, resulting in over forty arrests.

Some White ministers took a stand. Dr. W. B. Selah resigned when his church refused Black worshippers, while twenty-eight others released a manifesto, *Born of Conviction*, condemning segregation and freedom of speech in the church. Many received threats and fled the state.

Ultimately, some of the White churches did change their closed-door policies to allow Blacks to worship. These protests exposed the deep racial divide within religious institutions, forcing White congregations to confront their role in upholding segregation.

MURDER IN JACKSON

In the months leading up to June 1963, Jackson, Mississippi's capital, was a powder keg of racial tension. Several key events and actions had contributed to this charged atmosphere. The Woolworth sit-in had taken place, bringing national attention to the city's segregation practices. Black residents were actively boycotting downtown businesses, pushing for two main demands: an end to job discrimination and the formation of a biracial committee to address racial issues. Numerous demonstrations had occurred throughout the city, resulting in hundreds of arrests.

Violence escalated across Mississippi. White supremacists fired shots into the home of Tougaloo College professor John Salter. On June 9, 1963, civil rights workers including Fannie Lou Hamer, Euvester Simpson, June Johnson, Annelle Palmer, Rose Marie Johnson, and Lawrence Guyot were arrested at a bus station while returning from a voter registration workshop in Charleston, South Carolina. They were then brutally beaten in the Winona jail. Meanwhile, Medgar Evers's home had been firebombed. Then came the night of June 12, 1963.

Figure 15.5. Medgar Evers.

That evening, Myrlie Evers let her children stay up past bedtime to wait for their father's return home from work. Earlier that evening, she had watched President John F. Kennedy's televised address denouncing racial injustice. Shortly after midnight, the sound of Medgar Evers' car pulling into the driveway broke the quiet of the night. He had been at a meeting with lawyers discussing civil rights matters. At the sight of their father's arrival, eleven-year-old Darrell and ten-year-old Rena exclaimed in unison, "There's Daddy!" Medgar Evers, carrying a stack of T-shirts that read "Jim Crow Must Go," was shot as he stepped out of his car. That fateful night, he had parked in the driveway and exited from the driver's side, a departure from his usual practice of using the passenger side for added safety. The abrupt gunshot echoed through the night air, its impact both terrifying and final. The lone gunman, Byron de la Beckwith, had a clear shot as he hid behind a set of bushes. Evers, a thirty-seven-year-old civil rights leader and World War II veteran, was dead. Shortly after Evers's death, a White instructor at Ole Miss wrote of him:

> Mississippi, after all, did produce Medgar Evers, a man who would not learn to be "practical" or "shrewd," would not learn to serve whimsical Time and brutal Circumstance, would not accept a definition of his "place" laid down by someone else (the kind of someone who would skulk in a thicket and shoot him in the back for disagreeing). Here was a man who knew precisely how much he was risking and why, and who had the courage and ultimate intelligence to do so; and I, witnessing his conduct . . . have felt myself grow.

After two trials, the murderer went unpunished. It took thirty-one years for Byron de la Beckwith to be convicted for the murder of Medgar Evers. His conviction was the result of Myrlie Evers's relentless pursuit of accountability for her husband's killer. With the help of investigative reporter Jerry Mitchell, she played a key role in uncovering new evidence that ultimately led to the conviction of Byron De La Beckwith.

DISMANTLING THE SANCTUARY: MISSISSIPPI'S CALCULATED ATTACK ON DR. BEITTEL AND TOUGALOO COLLEGE

Dr. A. D. Beittel, president of Tougaloo College, who routinely joined his students on the front lines of protest and activism, became a prime target of the Mississippi Sovereignty Commission due to his unwavering commitment to civil rights and his steadfast leadership of this vital stronghold of the movement.

As a private institution, Tougaloo operated beyond direct state control, providing a critical refuge for activists under Beittel's administration. This independence provoked intense hostility from state legislators, who, alongside Sovereignty Commission director Erle Johnston, sought to dismantle the college's influence and remove its progressive president.

On April 21, 1964, Johnston met with Tougaloo's Board of Trustees in New York, presenting documents branding President Beittel as an "agitator" rather than an educator. Just days later, on April 25, Beittel was dismissed from his position. Seizing the opportunity, Johnston then lobbied for legislation designed to undermine Tougaloo's accreditation—a measure that ultimately passed.

These efforts expose the lengths to which Mississippi's leadership went to suppress civil rights activism. The campaign against President Beittel and Tougaloo College underscores the state's systematic attempts to preserve segregation and stifle resistance, even as the institution remained a vital bastion for justice and equality.

MISSISSIPPI FREEDOM DEMOCRATIC PARTY

In April 1964, after the Freedom Vote, 200 activists and organizers gathered in Jackson for a pivotal meeting. This gathering resulted in the creation of the Mississippi Freedom Democratic Party (MFDP), an organization specifically formed to challenge the state's all-White Democratic Party.

Lawrence Guyot, a Mississippi native attending Tougaloo College and field secretary for the Student Nonviolent Coordinating Committee (SNCC), was appointed as the chair of this newly formed party. Guyot's leadership role underscored the youth-driven nature of the civil rights movement in Mississippi.

The MFDP quickly assumed a crucial role in the civil rights landscape of Mississippi. Perhaps most significantly, it served as the host organization for Freedom Summer, a major initiative that would bring national attention to the struggle for civil rights in the state. This strategic positioning of the MFDP as the backbone for Freedom Summer demonstrated the organization's commitment to direct action and its intent to shake up the political status quo in Mississippi.

THE FREEDOM SUMMER OF 1964

The 1964 Freedom Summer played an important part in changing the old system of segregation. About 1,000 volunteer workers—Black and White, northern and Southern, men and women, college-age and older—entered the state. Many of the students who joined conducted trainings at Western College for Women (now part of Miami University) in Oxford, Ohio. Their main aims were to help organize Black Mississippians for political action, to set up "freedom schools" for both young people and adults, and to bring national attention to conditions in Mississippi. According to the Freedom School's curriculum:

> We are going to talk about a lot of things: about Negro people and white people, about rich people and poor people, about the South and about the North, about you and what you think and feel and want.... And we're going to try to be honest with each other and say what we believe.... We'll also ask some questions and try to find some answers. The first thing is to look around, right here, and see how we live in Mississippi. (From Introduction to Unit I of the Citizenship Curriculum: *Comparison of Students' Realities with Others*)

The Freedom Schools were established under Charlie Cobb, with the assistance of Spelman College professor Staughton Lynd's guidance. These schools aimed to empower and educate through a comprehensive curriculum addressing academic skills, self-confidence, voter literacy, and political organization. The schools were closely tied to the Mississippi Freedom Democratic Party (MFDP); Edwin King, an MFDP candidate for lieutenant governor, likened the school to a political Parent-Teacher Association. This connection highlighted the dual role of Freedom Schools as both educational institutions and catalysts for political engagement and community organizing.

The Mississippi Summer Project of 1964, which encompassed the Freedom Schools, was directed by COFO and primarily staffed by SNCC and CORE volunteers, with additional support from the Mississippi NAACP and the Southern Christian Leadership Conference (SCLC). NAACP state leader Aaron Henry served as COFO president, while SNCC's Robert Moses, assisted by David

Figure 15.6. Freedom Schools taught voter education, community organization, and Black history. Wisconsin Historical Society, WHI-97888.

Dennis, directed the project. This collaborative effort aimed to create informed, confident, and politically active citizens capable of driving change in their communities, bridging the gap between education and grassroots political action.

In preparation for what he called an intrusion of "outside agitators," Jackson Mayor Allen Thompson militarized his police force with an armored riot-control vehicle that became known as "Thompson's Tank." The vehicle was designed to intimidate, covered in armor and metal bars, with searchlights, sirens, and machine guns mounted on its frame. Painted light-blue with white trim, it featured a water cannon designed to blast high-pressure streams at civil rights protesters, a brutal tactic commonly used to disperse peaceful demonstrations. While newspapers stoked fears of violence and the state legislature rushed through twenty laws targeting activists, Thompson issued his threat: "We're going to be ready for them . . . They won't have a chance." His tank became a symbol of the violent official resistance to civil rights activism in Jackson.

THE MURDERS OF SCHWERNER, CHANEY, AND GOODMAN

In the summer of 1964, the Ku Klux Klan intensified its presence in predominantly Black Mississippi counties, burning thirty-five Black churches. The Klan's influence extended to law enforcement, compromising investigations into their

Figure 15.7. FBI poster seeking missing civil rights workers Goodman, Chaney, and Schwerner.

crimes. The State Sovereignty Commission aided the Klan by providing information on civil rights workers.

On June 21, 1964, Michael Schwerner, James Chaney, and Andrew Goodman left Meridian to investigate church burnings in Neshoba County. Deputy Sheriff Cecil Price arrested them for alleged speeding and held them in jail, alerting local Klan members. After their release, Price followed and stopped them again outside town, handing them over to Klansmen led by Edgar Ray Killen.

Klansman James Wayne Roberts used his .38 caliber pistol to kill Schwerner and Goodman. James Jordan then shot Chaney multiple times. The Klansmen transported the victims' bodies to a dam site on Olen Burrage's property.

The bodies of Goodman, Chaney, and Schwerner remained undiscovered for forty-four days. When Mississippi refused to prosecute the perpetrators, the federal government stepped in. The Department of Justice charged eighteen men with civil rights violations. The Supreme Court, in *United States v. Price*, ruled that the men could be tried. Some were convicted, but Edgar Ray Killen escaped justice.

While the federal government responded forcefully to the murders, sending more than 150 agents to investigate, many Black activists noted a painful irony:

the nation seemed more outraged by this crime because two of the victims were White, while previous killings of Black citizens had failed to generate similar national attention or federal response.

Decades later, investigative reporter Jerry Mitchell's work led Mississippi to reopen the cold case, focusing on Killen. In 2005, Killen was finally convicted of manslaughter and sentenced to sixty years in prison, bringing a measure of closure to this long-standing injustice.

UNEXPECTED DISCOVERY

The intensive search for civil rights workers Goodman, Chaney, and Schwerner led to an unexpected and grim discovery. As authorities combed through local rivers and swamps, they uncovered the bodies of Charles Moore and Henry Dee in the Mississippi River. This finding highlighted the extent of racial violence in the state beyond the well-publicized case of the three missing activists.

The murders of Moore and Dee remained unsolved for decades, a stark reminder of the many unpunished crimes from the civil rights era. However, justice, though delayed, eventually came. In 2007, more than forty years after the killings, James Ford Seale, a known member of the Ku Klux Klan, was brought to trial for these murders. The court found Seale guilty, and he was sentenced to three life terms.

THE VIOLENCE SPREADS

Not only in Neshoba County did White Mississippians attack the Freedom Summer volunteers. In Hattiesburg, twenty young people attempting to integrate the By-Pass Inn were turned back at gunpoint, then picked up by police and beaten in jail. In Laurel, four civil rights workers were attacked by twenty-five pipe-carrying Whites while sitting in at a previously segregated drive-in. Police refused to help the injured workers, and instead arrested a nearby COFO volunteer.

White supremacist extremists bombed the Bovina Community Center, used for voter-registration classes, near Vicksburg; a Black grocery store in Soso; and Freedom Houses in Canton and McComb. The bombing in McComb injured two civil rights workers asleep inside. In Itta Bena, Greenwood, and other towns, sheriffs and deputies locked up civil rights workers and then denied any knowledge of their whereabouts. In Moss Point, White supremacists shot and seriously wounded seventeen-year-old Jessie Mae Stallworth at a voter-registration meeting. The federal government provided little protection for these and many other victims of racist violence.

Figure 15.8. A civil rights leader's house the morning it was firebombed. During the summer of 1964, Whites bombed thirty homes, burned thirty-seven Black churches, beat more than eighty civil rights workers, and made more than 1,000 arrests. Courtesy of the Archives and Records Services Division, Mississippi Department of Archives and History.

THE NATIONAL DEMOCRATIC CONVENTION, 1964

Against this backdrop of escalating terrorism, which by summer's end would include thirty bombed homes, thirty-seven burned churches, more than eighty beaten civil rights workers, and over a thousand arrests, the MFDP prepared to mount a bold challenge at the Democratic National Convention in Atlantic City. The stakes were immense—after more than seventy years of exclusion from Mississippi Democratic affairs, Black citizens were demanding their rightful place in the political process. Led by veterans of the blood-soaked Freedom Summer, the MFDP arrived at the convention with a clear mandate: the Credentials Committee must seat their biracial delegation instead of the state's all-White regulars.

The committee refused and suggested a compromise, which would have admitted only two MFDP members to the convention; meanwhile, the entire regular delegation would be seated. The MFDP rejected this token gesture. Instead, its supporters chose to dramatize their exclusion by holding a protest rally at the convention. Fannie Lou Hamer said, "We didn't come all the way up here for no two seats, 'cause all of us is tired."

The showdown at the national convention underscored the fierce battle for political representation and exposed the deep racial fractures within the Democratic Party. However, the fight for civil rights was not confined to the political arena alone. Activists recognized that economic leverage could be just as powerful as political pressure.

Hitting Them Where It Hurts: The Power of the Purse

Beyond the convention floor, the movement launched a series of economic resistance efforts during Freedom Summer. One successful strategy was the national boycott of products made in Mississippi, organized by the NAACP and Martin Luther King, Jr. This economic pressure had a significant impact on the state. According to one estimate, new plant construction in Mississippi dropped by 28 percent as many firms chose to relocate to disassociate themselves from the state. Within Mississippi, the Mississippi press reported that a group called the United Front distributed letters to 31,000 White residents in Jackson, informing them of the boycott. As a result, one in five stores was forced to close. This boycott strategy effectively hit the state's economy where it hurt, demonstrating the power of coordinated economic actions in driving social change.

In 1965, following the bombing of George Metcalfe's car and drawing from the lessons of Freedom Summer, Natchez residents launched a citywide boycott. Over 1,000 protesters took to the streets, demanding desegregated schools and equal employment opportunities. Their persistence paid off—city officials agreed to hire six Black police officers, desegregate all city-operated public facilities, and appoint a Black representative to the school board.

A year later, inspired by the success of the Natchez boycott, grassroots activists Nate Jones, Julia Jones, Rudy Shields, Charles Evers, and others led a bold campaign in Port Gibson. Organized through the local NAACP, they targeted discriminatory business practices, demanding fair treatment, equal job opportunities, and the desegregation of local establishments.

Local merchants, feeling the pressure, responded with a $3.5 million lawsuit against the NAACP, accusing the organization and its leaders of unlawfully disrupting their businesses. They initially secured a victory in the Mississippi appellate court, but the activists did not waver.

The legal battle became a defining moment in civil rights history. When the case, *Claiborne Hardware Co. v. NAACP*, reached the United States Supreme Court, the stakes were monumental—not just for the Port Gibson activists, but for the future of peaceful protest in America. In 1982, the Court delivered its verdict: the boycott was a constitutionally protected form of free speech under the First Amendment. The decision overturned the lower court rulings, safeguarding the right to organize for justice.

While organizations focused on building economic opportunities, the continuing threat of violence forced Black Mississippians to also consider self-defense. The establishment of health centers and cooperative businesses represented positive steps toward equality, but these gains had to be protected. As White resistance to civil rights progress turned violent, some African Americans concluded that nonviolent development had to be paired with armed protection of their communities and achievements.

"WE WILL SHOOT BACK"

The idea that African Americans in Mississippi passively accepted oppression is a myth. Many actively defended themselves, sometimes through armed resistance. C. O. Chinn carried firearms in Canton, despite the city's violent reputation. At an NAACP event, Charles Evers declared, "if a White man shoots a Negro in Mississippi, we will shoot back," signaling a shift toward armed self-defense.

In 1964, after Leake County schools were desegregated, White vigilantes bombed Black families' mailboxes. One night, Dovie Hudson's sons fired shotguns at a car suspected of planting explosives. The following year, a car bomb injured Natchez NAACP leader George Metcalf, leading to the formation of the Natchez Deacons of Defense, an armed group modeled after a similar Louisiana organization. Their presence at protests led local authorities to restrict firearm transport, limiting their mobility.

These events reflected the rising tensions that followed civil rights victories like school desegregation, the Civil Rights Act, and the Voting Rights Act. The Deacons of Defense represented a shift within the movement, embracing armed self-defense alongside traditional nonviolent activism. While some Black Mississippians took up arms to protect their communities, others fought in the courts to dismantle segregation. Both approaches underscored the urgent need to resist systemic racism, proving that the fight for civil rights took many forms.

BLACK LAWYERS IN THE 1960s

Trying to desegregate Mississippi's schools was extremely difficult because state leaders strongly refused to accept any form of integration. Progress could only be achieved through legal action, with parents required to sue on a district-by-district basis. This piecemeal approach necessitated extensive legal support.

The initial legal challenges against school segregation in Mississippi were spearheaded by four Black lawyers from the state: R. Jess Brown, Carsie Hall, Sidney Thorpe, and Jack H. Young. These local attorneys formed the frontline in the courtroom battles for educational equality. Their efforts were later bolstered by Marian Wright Edelman, who would go on to become a renowned civil rights activist and advocate for children's rights.

The scope and intensity of the legal fight expanded significantly during two crucial events: the James Meredith trial, which aimed to desegregate the University of Mississippi, and Freedom Summer, the 1964 voter registration campaign. These high-profile cases drew Black volunteer lawyers from across the country to Mississippi, amplifying the legal resources available to the civil rights movement.

Among the distinguished out-of-state attorneys who joined the cause were Constance Baker Motley, Robert Carter, and Derrick Bell. Each brought extensive experience in civil rights law, significantly strengthening the legal team. Their involvement not only provided crucial expertise but also underscored the national significance of Mississippi's civil rights struggle, transforming local courtrooms into battlegrounds for nationwide racial justice.

BLACK WOMEN LEADERS

While Black lawyers fought in Mississippi courtrooms, activists knew legal victories alone wouldn't be enough. The civil rights movement required a broad strategy—one that combined legal action, economic pressure, and grassroots organizing. Black women played a crucial role in bridging these efforts, using their businesses, homes, and leadership skills to turn legal gains into lasting community change.

Far from just supporting male leaders, Black women built their own powerful networks. Myrlie Evers worked alongside her husband, Medgar, before later becoming president of the NAACP. Constance Baker Motley broke barriers as one of the first Black women to argue civil rights cases in court. Meanwhile, women like Laura McGhee of Greenwood showed unflinching courage—when nightriders attacked her home, she fired back, and her farm became a refuge for activists.

Many women used their businesses as hubs for activism. Vera Mae Pigee's Clarksdale beauty shop served as a safe space for civil rights workers, while Claire Collins Harvey used her funeral home, insurance company, and cofounded State Mutual Savings and Loan to support Black economic independence.

A fierce advocate for grassroots organizing, Ella Baker shaped the movement through her belief in local leadership, famously stating, "Strong people don't need strong leaders." This philosophy inspired women like Mae Bertha Carter, a former sharecropper who became an activist when she and her husband enrolled their children in an all-White school in 1965. While raising thirteen children, she fought for voting rights and helped establish the Mississippi Freedom Democratic Party.

Black women also broke political barriers. Flonzie Brown Wright became the first Black woman elected to public office in Mississippi, overseeing voting rights as a Canton election commissioner. Unita Blackwell made history as the state's first Black woman mayor, leading Mayersville.

The work of these women and countless others fueled the civil rights movement, proving that real change happened at the local level. Their courage, strategy, and sacrifice reshaped Mississippi's fight for justice, leaving a legacy that continues to inspire today.

"SICK AND TIRED OF BEING SICK AND TIRED"

Unlike the traditional parties, the MFDP had women in leadership roles. In 1964, at the Democratic convention, Fannie Lou Hamer spoke before the television cameras. She had challenged Congressman Jamie Whitten for his House seat, claiming that since Blacks had not been allowed to vote, his election was a fraud. Now she told the story of her treatment in jail after she used the Winona bus station in 1963: "They carried me into a room and there were two Negro boys in this room. The state highway patrolman gave them a long, wide Blackjack and he told one of the boys, 'Take this . . . and if you don't use it on her, you know what I'll use on you.' . . . That man beat me till he give out. And I was trying to guard some of the licks with my hands and they just beat my hands till they turned blue." Hamer was no "outside agitator," no professional civil rights worker. Indeed, she had attended her first civil rights meeting only a year earlier. She was born in Montgomery County, the last of twenty children. When she was two, her parents moved to Sunflower County, where they sharecropped. Although her parents worked hard and at one time owned three mules and two cows, they could not escape Delta poverty. Hamer became convinced that things had to be made better.

She married Perry "Pap" Hamer in 1944 and lived quietly with her husband on a plantation near Ruleville. Then in 1962 the civil rights movement reached Ruleville. Hamer went with seventeen other Blacks to Indianola to try to register to vote. When she returned home, she found that the plantation owner had thrown the Hamers off his land. They were without a home or job.

They moved into Ruleville and she became an active SNCC worker. She was a founder of the Mississippi Freedom Democratic Party, and when the Freedom Summer was organized, she went to Ohio to work with the volunteers.

Realizing that poor people needed economic help as well as political participation, she organized the Freedom Farms Cooperative, a vegetable and livestock enterprise designed to raise the income and improve the diet of Sunflower County residents.

Her accomplishments garnered widespread recognition. She was invited to

Figure 15.9. Fannie Lou Hamer. Library of Congress, Prints and Photographs Division, LC-DIG-ds-07134.

speak at various colleges across the United States, and institutions like Tougaloo College and Shaw University awarded her honorary degrees. Despite this national acclaim, her primary dedication was to the communities of Ruleville and Sunflower County, where she chose to reside. A significant tribute to her was the celebration of Fannie Lou Hamer Day in 1970 at Ruleville Central High School. She died in 1977.

THE CADILLAC CROWD

During Freedom Summer, an unexpected group of allies emerged: Wednesdays in Mississippi, a network of middle- and upper-class Black and White women. Founded by Dorothy Height of the National Council of Negro Women and activist Polly Cowan, the group used their social status to discreetly support the civil rights movement.

Every Tuesday, these women flew into Mississippi, partnering with local leaders like Claire Collins Harvey, founder of Womanpower Unlimited. Dubbed the "Cadillac Group" for their elite backgrounds, they followed a two-day strategy. On Wednesdays, they visited freedom schools and civil rights hubs, gaining firsthand insight into activism. The next day, they attended tea gatherings, leveraging their influence to sway local decision-makers.

Local allies like Ruth Shirley hosted private meetings, bridging the gap between grassroots activists and the Black social elite. With backing from the National Council of Negro Women under Jessie Mosley, these gatherings facilitated strategy discussions and discreet collaboration.

Key members, including A. M. E. Logan of Jackson's NAACP and businesswoman Thelma Sanders, played crucial roles. They supported freedom riders, raised funds for medical aid, and guided women in securing federal grants when state officials blocked daycare funding.

Operating under the radar, the Cadillac Group used social influence, networking, and strategic fundraising to advance civil rights. Their work highlighted how quiet activism could be just as powerful as public protests, proving that the fight for justice relied on a range of approaches—some bold, others subtle, but all essential.

WHITE MASSIVE RESISTANCE TO CIVIL RIGHTS

The Mississippi Delta region, which has always had the largest population of Blacks in the state, historically constituted a single congressional district (District 2), beginning in 1882 and continuing through redistricting plans adopted in 1932, 1952, and 1962. This is illustrated by map 29.

In 1966, however, as is illustrated by map 30, the legislature redrew the lines of the district and divided the Delta region among three congressional districts, also known as cracking. This resulted in a majority-White voting-age population in

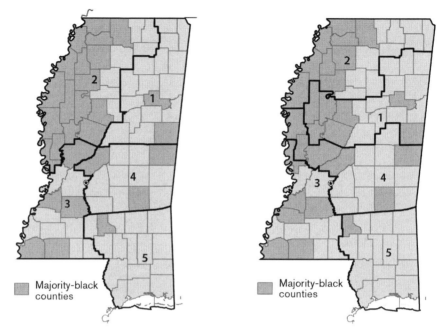

Map 29. Congressional District 2, 1962   Map 30. Gerrymandered District 2, 1966

all five districts. Such techniques prevented Blacks from electing the candidates of their choice.

In resisting efforts to diminish their electoral influence, Blacks in Mississippi employed a tactic known as the "challenge concept." This strategy, echoing the actions of the Mississippi Freedom Democratic Party at the Democratic National Convention, led to various groups coming together to legally confront the state's gerrymandering. This unified effort eventually resulted in a significant court case, *Connor v. Johnson*, which directly challenged the state's efforts to dilute Black voting power through redistricting.

WHITE VIEWS OF THE MOVEMENT

Many of the state's political, civic, and religious leaders told fellow Whites that the Freedom Summer volunteers were "communist-inspired agitators, immoral, filthy, frustrated beatniks." One state senator, less hostile to the movement, nevertheless said that COFO had created "a strong and bitter resentment on the part of the average White Mississippians against outside interference in the state's problems."

Whites realized that the violence and headlines were giving Mississippi a bad name throughout the nation. Some blamed this bad image on the civil rights

Map 31. Civil Rights Events, 1954–1967

workers. They felt that other states had just as many problems as Mississippi; it seemed unfair for the nation to single out Mississippi as the major trouble zone.

Some felt differently. Twenty-eight Methodist ministers spoke out against racial injustice. A few other leaders also took a stand. But too often they lost their positions in the church or community when they spoke out. One insurance man in McComb merely invited some civil rights workers to his home to talk with them; as a result, White supremacists destroyed his business, poisoned his dog, and forced his family to flee town.

Figure 15.10. Demonstrators march toward downtown Hattiesburg to protest the shooting of Lonnie Charles McGee by a patrolman in 1967. Courtesy of the Archives and Records Services Division, Mississippi Department of Archives and History.

BLACK VIEWS OF THE MOVEMENT

Initially, Black Mississippians, like Whites, chose not to associate with movement volunteers due to their (quite rational) fear of the repercussions. They knew what had happened to such pioneers as Lee and Courts, and they wanted to avoid trouble. In some towns it was difficult to find a family willing to let a volunteer sleep in their home. Younger Blacks, however, felt differently. High school and even elementary school students joined boycott movements, attended freedom schools, and volunteered for sit-ins.

At first, many Black people viewed the early volunteers, both Black and White, with awe due to their courageous efforts.

But as time went on, people realized that change would not come overnight. It also became clear that the residents of the community would have to take the lead in continuing the movement after the volunteers had left. And so, although it had seemed fine at first to welcome a White worker as one of the leaders for the local movement, gradually Blacks began to resent White leadership. They realized that the basic leadership of the Black community had to come from within that community.

RESULTS OF THE FREEDOM SUMMER

The summer of 1964 seemed like a modest success for civil rights workers in Mississippi. Freedom schools had low attendance, and Black voter registration remained under 6 percent. Yet, deeper changes were underway. Black and White activists worked together in unprecedented ways, reshaping Mississippi's social and political landscape.

The Mississippi Freedom Democratic Party (MFDP), despite its setback at the 1964 Democratic convention, gained momentum. It later challenged the seating of Mississippi's congressional delegation, arguing that Black voters had been systematically disfranchised and MFDP candidates unfairly excluded. Congressman William Fitts Ryan of New York backed their challenge, gaining the support of over sixty lawmakers.

Annie Devine, Fannie Lou Hamer, and Victoria Gray took their fight to Congress, becoming the first Black women to speak on the House floor. Though

Figure 15.10. The Delta Ministry helped establish some of the first Head Start programs in the state. Courtesy of the Archives and Records Services Division, Mississippi Department of Archives and History.

unsuccessful in their immediate goal, the MFDP's documentation of voter suppression provided crucial evidence that helped shape the 1965 Voting Rights Act.

The summer project also spurred lasting initiatives. Dr. Robert Smith and Dr. James Anderson mobilized medical care for activists, leading to the formation of the Medical Committee for Human Rights. This effort helped establish the Tufts-Delta Health Center, the first federally funded rural community health center in the US.

Economic justice efforts also grew. The Delta Ministry organized farmworker strikes and cooperative farms, while Mississippi residents launched cooperative grocery stores. The Poor People's Corporation supported local artisans, enabling them to sell clothing and woodcraft. Though the MFDP did not achieve immediate political victories, its legacy laid the groundwork for long-term change in Mississippi.

NATIONAL IMPACT OF THE FREEDOM SUMMER

The Freedom Summer of 1964 in Mississippi had far-reaching effects that extended well beyond the state's borders, influencing both national and global movements for social justice. The strategies and tactics developed during this intense period of activism in Mississippi became a blueprint for grassroots organizing and nonviolent resistance worldwide.

Freedom schools, offering alternative education centered on civil rights and African American history, became a model for similar initiatives worldwide. These schools inspired educational programs in other nations grappling with inequality and political oppression. Additionally, the voter registration strategies and community organizing methods developed in Mississippi were adopted and adapted by activists globally in their fight for democracy and human rights.

Moreover, the international media coverage of events in Mississippi, particularly the violence against civil rights workers, drew global attention to racial injustice in the United States. This scrutiny put pressure on the US government to respond to racial injustice, influencing foreign policy and America's image abroad during the Cold War era.

Among Freedom Summer's most profound and enduring impacts was its role in catalyzing the passage of two groundbreaking laws: the 1964 Civil Rights Act and the 1965 Voting Rights Act. These pivotal pieces of legislation marked significant milestones in the advancement of civil rights and voting equality across the United States. While initially aimed at addressing the systemic discrimination faced by Black Americans, the legacy of these laws has extended far beyond, serving to protect the rights of all citizens regardless of race, color, religion, sex, or national origin.

FOREVER CHANGED

Upon returning to their homes across the nation, Freedom Summer volunteers carried with them a profound new understanding of racial inequality and the power of grassroots activism. Their experiences in Mississippi proved to be a crucible, forging many into lifelong advocates for social justice. This newly awakened passion extended far beyond the initial scope of civil rights, inspiring involvement in diverse causes such as the antiwar movement, women's rights, and environmental activism.

Some, like the University of California, Berkeley's "free speech" activist Mario Savio, organized campus movements. Others, such as William Kunstler and Marian Wright Edelman, continued to lead legal fights. Joyce Ladner and Robert Coles turned to research and writing. James Forman and John Lewis remained active in Black organizations, Allard Lowenstein entered politics in New York, and David Dennis pursued a law degree and opened a law firm in Lafayette, Louisiana. He and Bob Moses later reunited in Mississippi and helped run the Algebra Project, which was designed to teach children math. The importance of their Mississippi experience, positive and negative, remains difficult to estimate; nor can the effects on the thousands of Black Mississippians who participated in meetings, went down to the courthouse, or attended freedom schools.

WHITE ATTITUDES BEGIN TO CHANGE

Gradually most White Mississippians began to tolerate the idea of reducing racial injustices. Even though they might still prefer segregation, they were not willing to sacrifice everything else to keep it. The first example of this new way of thinking took place at Mississippi State University in early spring of 1963. Mississippi State had won the right to represent the Southeastern Conference in the NCAA basketball tournament, but the team would meet teams with Black players in the tournament. For years there had been an "unwritten rule" that White schools would not participate under such conditions, but this time Mississippi State decided to play.

Meanwhile, in Jackson, Tougaloo faculty members and students contacted performers who were scheduled to give concerts in the capital city. They told the performers that the events were to be segregated and asked them not to perform under such conditions. Several performers agreed to withdraw, and White Jacksonians realized that they would have to be willing to integrate certain activities or lose the activities entirely.

After the conflict of the 1964 summer, many of the state's leaders realized that times had changed. During the summer of 1965, the legislature removed from the books all laws whose purpose had been to prevent Blacks from voting. The chairman of the House Committee on Registration and Elections spoke now for many Mississippians when he argued, "If you think, under color of law, this nation is going to let you discriminate, you're living in a world of fantasy."

The 1965 Voting Rights Act was instrumental in driving legislative changes. Following its enactment, federal voting registrars were dispatched to thirty-one counties across Mississippi. Their arrival prompted an immediate response, with long queues of Black applicants eager to register.

The impact was swift and significant. Prior to the act, only 6.7 percent of eligible Black Mississippians were registered to vote. This figure skyrocketed to approximately 59 percent by 1966. The trend continued, with Black voter registration reaching 76 percent by 1970.

Pressure from the business community also helped cause change. An Ohio industrialist refused to consider expansion of two Mississippi plants until the state "decides to become a part of the Union again." National chains such as Sears Roebuck and Company desegregated their staffs under pressure from both inside and outside the state. Business leaders realized that racial friction cost them money.

SOME WHITE MISSISSIPPIANS WORK FOR PROGRESS

Changes were also taking place within the churches and in the press. The Beacon of the First Baptist Church in Biloxi suggested: "Christians have not understood that to raise their voices against the evils of their state would be the finest thing they could do for her." Labor official Claude Ramsay of the state AFL-CIO worked against racial discrimination, and Mississippians reorganized the Council on Human Relations. Dan Orey Jr. was employed as the first Black field representative from Mississippi to work for the union's national headquarters in Washington, DC.

Some of the state's newspapers also began to change. The *Winona Times*, for example, confessed that the state "has been sadly lacking in the leadership department." The *Laurel Leader-Call* defended its acceptance of a COFO advertisement. Papers in Greenville, Lexington, Clarksdale, Batesville, Pascagoula, McComb, and Tupelo all argued for racial understanding.

While some White institutions were beginning to acknowledge Mississippi's need for change, as evidenced by shifting attitudes in churches, labor unions, and the press, activists were already pioneering a more radical transformation through education. The same period that saw the *Winona Times* confessing the state's leadership failures and religious leaders finding their moral voice against segregation also witnessed the emergence of a bold new vision for Mississippi's future—one that would begin with its youngest citizens.

EDUCATION AS LIBERATION: THE BIRTH OF HEAD START IN MISSISSIPPI

The Freedom Schools of 1964's Freedom Summer had demonstrated the transformative power of education in the fight for civil rights. Building on this foundation, Tom Levin collaborated with SNCC activists to address a critical gap in Mississippi's educational landscape: early childhood education for low-income families. The team's efforts secured federal funding from the Office of Economic Opportunity (OEO), leading to the creation of the Child Development Group of Mississippi (CDGM) at Mount Beulah in Edwards in 1965.

CDGM served multiple purposes: providing preschool education, offering health and nutrition services, and creating jobs for Black workers like Fannie Lou Hamer who had previously been limited to plantation labor. The program demonstrated how African Americans could work around White resistance to create meaningful change, particularly by partnering with sympathetic Whites and securing federal support.

Sadly, however, the Child Development Group of Mississippi (CDGM) encountered staunch opposition from Senators Eastland and Stennis, who mounted a concerted attack to terminate the program. CDGM made significant progress in enhancing early childhood education for Mississippi's low-income families. However, a combination of senatorial opposition, infiltration by sovereignty commission informants, and internal racial tensions led to the federal government's decision to withdraw funding. This unfortunate turn of events resulted in the program's premature closure in 1968.

While the loss of CDGM was a serious blow to Mississippi's educational system, the program's legacy lives on, as it paved the way for future initiatives such as Mississippi Action for Progress (MAP). Later, Friends of Children of Mississippi emerged as a successor organization to provide similar services and continues these efforts today.

CHANGES IN THE CIVIL RIGHTS MOVEMENT

Meanwhile, just as the civil rights movement appeared on the verge of success, it seemed to be falling apart. The new OEO programs, including Head Start, drew many local workers away from the movement. The federal government and northern students began to shift their attention from civil rights to the Vietnam War. A split had developed between the NAACP and the Mississippi Freedom Democrats, and leaders seemed uncertain as to what actions should be taken next. SNCC and CORE both experienced internal crises over both goals and strategies. Many of these problems came to the surface in the famed "Meredith March."

BLACK POWER

The courage of Black activists was exemplified by James Meredith during his "Walk Against Fear." In June 1966, Meredith set out alone on a 200-mile journey from Memphis to Jackson, Mississippi, aiming to encourage Black Mississippians to overcome their fear of White violence and exercise their civil rights, particularly voter registration. Emphasizing that it was a walk, not a march, he sought to mobilize Black communities through a different form of activism.

However, shortly after beginning his walk, Meredith was shot and wounded by a sniper, temporarily halting his journey. In his absence, leaders like Martin Luther King Jr. and Stokely Carmichael (Kwame Ture) continued what became the "March Against Fear." As the march gained momentum, it drew national attention and hundreds of participants, leading to increased voter registration and a renewed sense of empowerment among Black Mississippians.

The march brought together activists with differing ideologies. Some, like King, remained committed to nonviolent resistance, while others believed self-defense and direct confrontation were necessary. As the march reached Greenwood, tensions came to a head. Stokely Carmichael, recently jailed for erecting tents, returned to the march visibly frustrated. Inspired by Willie Ricks (Mukasa Dada), he took the stage and introduced a phrase that would reshape the movement: "Black Power."

Though Ricks had coined the slogan, Carmichael's delivery electrified the crowd. "Black Power" quickly spread beyond Greenwood, becoming a national rallying cry that championed racial pride, self-reliance, and political and

Figure 15.11. Meredith after shooting. Associated Press. © 1966.

economic empowerment. The moment marked a shift in the civil rights movement's rhetoric, signaling a more assertive stance on racial justice.

Days later, as the marchers reached Canton, they attempted to set up camp at a Black school but were met with violent resistance from authorities.

A reporter described the chaos: "The squads of highway patrolmen and county and city officers and conservation men began marching onto the east end of the field. Then it started coming, without warning, the psst-boom of exploding tear-gas canisters, some thrown, others fired at point-blank range into the scrambling bodies. No one can fight against gas. One good gulp and you have to run. I heard one call of protest ring above the nightmare, a curse at Whites. Then the troopers came, beating, kicking, striking out with rifle butts." That weekend, movement leaders debated the meaning of "Black Power" and the future direction of the struggle. On the final day, 20,000 marchers moved peacefully through Jackson to the State Capitol, where Meredith, now recovered, addressed the crowd. The march had ended, but it was clear—the movement had changed forever.

UNREST AT JACKSON STATE COLLEGE

The violent confrontation in Canton marked a turning point for the movement, not just in its embrace of Black Power ideology, but in exposing the continued willingness of authorities to use brutal force against peaceful protesters.

In May 1967, two nights of unrest were touched off when a policeman arrested Blacks riding in a car on Lynch Street in Jackson. Jackson State students had previously protested the fact that this main street passed through the middle of their campus. They claimed that White passers-by sped through the area throwing rocks at students.

During the turmoil, Benjamin Brown, a young Black man who had worked for the Delta Ministry, was shot and killed by police. Blacks organized a boycott of White businesses that refused to serve them in Jackson and presented a list of demands to city officials. Included in the demands were the hiring of Black firemen and policemen, lowering speed limits in certain Black neighborhoods, and installing an overhead walkway across Lynch Street to protect students from traffic.

BOMBINGS AND A NEW REACTION

The 1967 violence that claimed Benjamin Brown's life and sparked protests at Jackson State College was part of a broader racial conflict in Mississippi. While Black citizens organized boycotts and demanded safety improvements, White supremacists launched attacks to intimidate both Black activists and their White allies.

The Ku Klux Klan bombed Beth Israel Jewish Synagogue in Jackson and later targeted Rabbi Perry Nussbaum's home for his civil rights support. The attacks drew condemnation from state and city officials, and tensions escalated when a Jackson resident was arrested with 105 sticks of dynamite. These events underscored the deep divide between those pushing for progress and those resisting change.

Despite ongoing violence, legal authorities began taking action against White supremacist terrorism. In 1967, a Meridian grand jury indicted nineteen men for conspiring to kill James Chaney, Michael Schwerner, and Andrew Goodman. A White jury later convicted seven, including Neshoba County Deputy Sheriff Cecil Price and Klan leader Sam Bowers. Edgar Ray Killen walked free after a lone juror refused to convict a preacher.

In 1968, authorities arrested eleven men for the firebombing and murder of Vernon Dahmer, signaling a shift toward accountability. Investigative reporter Jerry Mitchell later helped reopen civil rights–era cold cases, leading to convictions decades later. In 1994, Byron De La Beckwith was convicted for Medgar Evers's 1963 assassination. In 1998, Sam Bowers was sentenced to life in prison for ordering Dahmer's murder. In 2005, Edgar Ray Killen was finally convicted for orchestrating the 1964 Freedom Summer murders.

TOKEN DESEGREGATION IN THE PUBLIC SCHOOLS

Change was also occurring, although very slowly, in the public-school systems. The first few Black students began attending White public schools in scattered towns around the state in 1964 and 1965. In many areas Whites intimidated

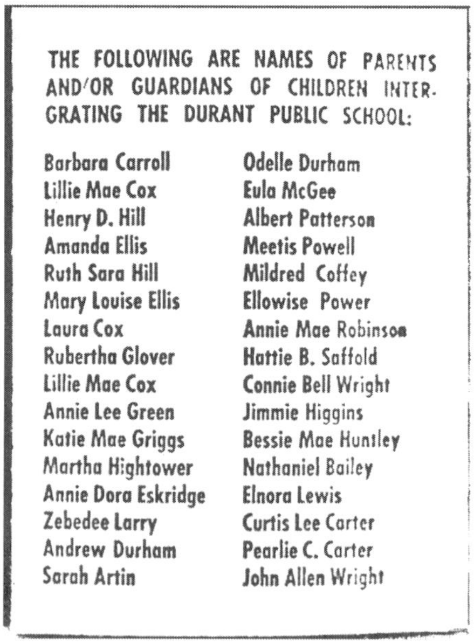

Figure 15.12. This notice appeared on telephone poles in Durant in the fall of 1965.

THE FOLLOWING ARE NAMES OF PARENTS AND/OR GUARDIANS OF CHILDREN INTERGRATING THE DURANT PUBLIC SCHOOL:

Barbara Carroll	Odelle Durham
Lillie Mae Cox	Eula McGee
Henry D. Hill	Albert Patterson
Amanda Ellis	Meetis Powell
Ruth Sara Hill	Mildred Coffey
Mary Louise Ellis	Ellowise Power
Laura Cox	Annie Mae Robinson
Rubertha Glover	Hattie B. Saffold
Lillie Mae Cox	Connie Bell Wright
Annie Lee Green	Jimmie Higgins
Katie Mae Griggs	Bessie Mae Huntley
Martha Hightower	Nathaniel Bailey
Annie Dora Eskridge	Elnora Lewis
Zebedee Larry	Curtis Lee Carter
Andrew Durham	Pearlie C. Carter
Sarah Artin	John Allen Wright

Black parents to get them to withdraw their children from the White schools. The worst violence came on the first morning of the fall term in 1966, when an angry mob of 400 Whites attacked 150 Black students attending Grenada's John Rundle High School.

In 1967, the United States Department of Justice filed legal suits to force various school districts throughout the state to desegregate all grades. Most districts, however, found ways of getting around the court orders. Desegregation was still little more than token by the end of the year.

BLACKS ACHIEVE POLITICAL REPRESENTATION

The 1967 elections marked a significant milestone in Mississippi politics. John Bell Williams, a well-known segregationist, was nominated for governor in the Democratic primary. However, following the November general election, he was joined in office by twenty-two newly elected Black officials. Among them was Robert Clark, who became the first Black member of the Mississippi legislature since Reconstruction. Clark, along with other Black candidates, ran as an independent and was a member of the Mississippi Freedom Democratic Party (MFDP). Unlike the NAACP, which worked within the confines of the Democratic Party and supported Democratic candidates, the MFDP operated independently.

The election of Black officials in Mississippi in 1967 paved the way for Charles Evers to be elected as the mayor of Fayette in 1969.

Mississippi had come a long way since the riot accompanying James Meredith's admission to the University of Mississippi. The conflict of the 1960s made possible the changes of the 1970s. Certainly there would be more conflict and change in the days ahead. But now there was also promise of a new and better future for all of Mississippi's citizens.

The political victories of the late '60s, though significant, threw into sharp relief the deep poverty that still plagued much of Black Mississippi. No place embodied this contrast between political progress and economic hardship more vividly than Marks, Mississippi.

MARKS, MISSISSIPPI, AND THE BIRTH OF THE MULE TRAIN

During the Meredith March Against Fear, participant Armstead Phipps suffered a fatal heart attack. Dr. Martin Luther King Jr. traveled to Marks, Mississippi, to deliver his eulogy, but what he saw there profoundly shaped his vision of economic justice.

Marks reflected the extreme poverty of the rural South—children went hungry because segregated schools denied them access to federal meal programs, and mechanized cotton picking had displaced thousands, forcing many to leave for Northern cities. Those who stayed lived in some of the worst conditions in the country.

Moved by what he witnessed, King embraced Marian Wright Edelman's idea for a Poor People's Campaign, aiming to fight for jobs and justice. He wanted it to begin in Marks, which Dr. Ralph Abernathy later described as "the end of the world."

Though King was assassinated before the campaign began, organizers pushed forward, launching the Mule Train—a powerful symbol of economic struggle. In May 1968, fifteen mule-drawn wagons left Marks, carrying poor Black and White Southerners to Washington, DC. The journey, slow and deliberate, drew national attention to poverty in the Deep South.

Upon arriving in June 1968, they joined thousands in creating "Resurrection City" on the National Mall, demanding jobs, unemployment insurance, fair wages, and education programs. The Mule Train became one of the last major civil rights campaigns of the 1960s, shifting the movement's focus toward economic justice and exposing the deep connection between race and poverty in America.

"SECOND RECONSTRUCTION"

Several writers have called the struggle for civil rights a "second Reconstruction." Reread the Reconstruction chapter and carefully compare the two eras. Do you agree? What were the similarities? Can you find major differences?

CAMPUS UPRISINGS: CIVIL RIGHTS AND TRAGEDY IN MISSISSIPPI, 1968–1970

The late 1960s and early 1970s were a turbulent time for higher education in Mississippi, marked by student protests, harsh repression, and violence. These events revealed the ongoing struggle for civil rights at the state's colleges and universities.

In 1968, civil rights activist Charles Evers led protests at Alcorn A&M College over the university president's opposition to civil rights demonstrations and low faculty wages. The response was brutal, with the National Guard intervening, leading to beatings and arrests.

In February 1970, Mississippi Valley State saw the largest mass arrest of students in US history, with nearly 900 detained and sent to Parchman Prison. Later that month, eighty-nine students at the University of Mississippi were

Figure 15.13. Alexander Hall. Associated Press. © 1970.

arrested for protesting the lack of Black faculty and an African American studies program. Eight of these students, known as the "Ole Miss 8," were expelled for their activism.

Tougaloo College became a sanctuary for these expelled students, providing a safe space for those committed to social justice. Its private funding allowed it to avoid state control, making it a vital institution for nurturing civil rights leaders.

The tension peaked with the Jackson State Tragedy on May 15, 1970. After racial tensions erupted on Lynch Street, the police confronted a group of students. What followed was a rapid escalation of violence—police opened fire on unarmed students, killing Phillip Lafayette Gibbs and James Earl Green, and injuring twelve others. This event underscored the extreme racial hostility and violence that activists faced.

The aftermath was grim: over 300 bullet holes riddled the dormitory, all from law enforcement weapons. Investigations followed, sparking protests, boycotts of White businesses, and marches at the governor's mansion. The President's Commission on Campus Unrest condemned the shootings as "an unreasonable, unjustified overreaction."

Despite this, the highway patrol and a Hinds County grand jury defended the officers. In 1972, an all-White jury dismissed a wrongful death lawsuit filed by attorney Constance Harvey-Slaughter on behalf of the victims' families. No officers were charged, leaving a deep sense of injustice.

These events underscored the risks Black students faced in their fight for equality. The violent crackdowns on Mississippi campuses became a pivotal moment in the civil rights movement, exposing racial injustice in higher education. The tragedy at Jackson State remains a powerful reminder of the ongoing struggle against racial inequality and police violence.

Note

1. These two stages are known as reapportionment and redistricting. Reapportionment happens every ten years and is based on a state's population.

Recommended Readings

Devery S. Anderson, *Emmett Till: The Murder That Shocked the World and Propelled the Civil Rights Movement*, Foreword by Julian Bond (Jackson: University Press of Mississippi, 2015).

Kenneth T. Andrews, *Freedom Is a Constant Struggle: The Mississippi Civil Rights Movement and Its Legacy* (Chicago: University of Chicago Press, 2004).

Charles C. Bolton, *The Hardest Deal of All: The Battle Over School Integration in Mississippi, 1870–1980* (Jackson: University Press of Mississippi, 2005).

Maegan Parker Brooks, *A Voice That Could Stir an Army: Fannie Lou Hamer and the Rhetoric of the Black Freedom Movement* (Jackson: University Press of Mississippi, 2014).

Maegan Parker Brooks and Davis W. Houck, eds., *The Speeches of Fannie Lou Hamer: To Tell It Like It Is* (Jackson: University Press of Mississippi, 2013).

Will D. Campbell, *Robert G. Clark's Journey to the House* (Jackson: University Press of Mississippi, 2003).

Nadine Cohodas, *The Band Played Dixie: Race and the Liberal Conscience at Ole Miss* (New York: Free Press, 1997).

Emilye Crosby, *A Little Taste of Freedom: The Black Freedom Struggle in Claiborne County, Mississippi* (Chapel Hill: University of North Carolina Press, 2005).

David J. Dennis Jr. and David J. Dennis Sr., *The Movement Made Us: A Father, a Son, and the Legacy of a Freedom Ride* (New York: Harper, 2022).

John Dittmer, *Local People: The Struggle for Civil Rights in Mississippi* (Urbana: University of Illinois Press, 1994).

John Dittmer, *The Good Doctors: The Medical Committee for Human Rights and the Struggle for Social Justice in Health Care* (New York: Bloomsbury Publishing USA, 2009)

Charles W. Eagles, *The Price of Defiance: James Meredith and the Integration of Ole Miss* (Chapel Hill: University of North Carolina Press, 2009).

Kate Ellis and Stephen Smith, "State of Siege: Mississippi Whites and the Civil Rights Movement," American RadioWorks, 1996. Available online: American RadioWorks—State of Siege.

Emma J. Folwell, *The War on Poverty in Mississippi: From Massive Resistance to New Conservatism* (Jackson: University Press of Mississippi, 2020).

Debbie Z. Harwell, *Wednesdays in Mississippi: Proper Ladies Working for Radical Change, Freedom Summer 1964* (Jackson: University Press of Mississippi, 2014).

Janet Sharp Hermann, *The Pursuit of a Dream* (Jackson: University Press of Mississippi, 1999).

Matt Herron, *Mississippi Eyes: The Story and Photography of the Southern Documentary Project*, Foreword by John Dittmer (Jackson: University Press of Mississippi, 2014.

Jeffery B. Howell, *Hazel Brannon Smith: The Female Crusading Scalawag* (Jackson: University Press of Mississippi, 2017).

Yasuhiro Katagiri, *The Mississippi State Sovereignty Commission: Civil Rights and States' Rights* (Jackson: University Press of Mississippi, 2001).

Hilliard Lackey, *Marks, Martin, and the Mule Train: Marks, Mississippi, Martin Luther King, Jr. and the Origin of the 1968 Poor People's Campaign Mule Train* (Xlibris, 2014).

Kate Clifford Larson, *Walk with Me: A Biography of Fannie Lou Hamer* (New York: Oxford University Press, 2021).

Jim Lucas, *A Past That Won't Rest: Images of the Civil Rights Movement in Mississippi*, edited by Jane Hearn (Jackson: University Press of Mississippi, 2018)

Carter Dalton Lyon, *Sanctuaries of Segregation: The Story of the Jackson Church Visit Campaign* (Jackson: University Press of Mississippi, 2017).

William McCord, *Mississippi: The Long, Hot Summer*, Introduction by Françoise N. Hamlin (Jackson: University Press of Mississippi, 2016).

James Meredith, *Three Years in Mississippi* (Jackson: University Press of Mississippi, 2019 [1966]).

Mississippi Department of Archives and History, *Telling Our Stories: Museum of Mississippi History and Mississippi Civil Rights Museum* (Jackson: University Press of Mississippi, 2017).

Anne Moody, *Coming of Age in Mississippi* (New York: Dell, 1992 [1968]).

Robert Moses and Charles E. Cobb, *Radical Equations: Civil Rights from Mississippi to the Algebra Project* (Boston: Beacon Press, 2001).

J. Todd Moye, Let the People Decide: Black Freedom and White Resistance Movements in Sunflower County, Mississippi, 1945–1986 (Chapel Hill: University of North Carolina Press, 2004).

Jere Nash and Andy Taggart, *Mississippi Politics: The Struggle for Power, 1976–2006* (Jackson: University Press of Mississippi, 2006).

M. J. O'Brien, *We Shall Not Be Moved: The Jackson Woolworth's Sit-In and the Movement It Inspired*, Foreword by Julian Bond (Jackson: University Press of Mississippi, 2013).

Ted Ownby, ed., *The Civil Rights Movement in Mississippi* (Jackson: University Press of Mississippi, 2013).

Charles M. Payne, *I've Got the Light of Freedom: The Organizing Tradition and the Mississippi Freedom Struggle* (Berkeley: University of California Press, 1995).

Crystal R. Sanders, *A Chance for Change: Head Start and Mississippi's Black Freedom Struggle* (Chapel Hill: University of North Carolina Press, 2016).

Carol Ruth Silver, *Freedom Rider Diary: Smuggled Notes from Parchman Prison*, Introduction by Raymond Arsenault, Photographs by Claude A. Liggins, Afterword by Cherie A. Gaines (Jackson: University Press of Mississippi, 2014).

James W. Silver, *Mississippi: The Closed Society* (Jackson: University Press of Mississippi, 2012 [1964]).

William Sturkey, *Hattiesburg: An American City in Black and White* (Cambridge, MA: Harvard University Press, 2019).

Akinyele Umoja. *We Will Shoot Back: Armed Resistance in the Mississippi Freedom Movement*. New York University Press, 2013.

Bruce Watson, *Freedom Summer: The Savage Season of 1964 That Made Mississippi Burn and Made America a Democracy* (New York: Penguin, 2010).

Vernon Weakley. Standing at the Edge of Madness, Fear No Evil (Ridgeland: ZWORLDNET Publishing (1999).

Clyde Woods, *Development Arrested: The Blues and Plantation Power in the Mississippi Delta* (New York: Verso Books, 2017).

C. Vann Woodward, *The Strange Career of Jim Crow*, third revised ed. (New York: Oxford University Press, 2002 [1974]).

CHAPTER 16

DESEGREGATION AND CULTURAL CHANGES

1970–1980

THERE WAS AN EXPLOSION OF CULTURAL CHANGE IN MISSISSIPPI DURING THE late 1960s and 1970s. The culture of Mississippi includes not only its art, music, and literature but also the ways Mississippians shook hands, talked, cooked, and interacted with one another.

During this era, Mississippi's alienation from the rest of the United States almost disappeared. Although racial discrimination continued, the system of segregation crumbled. One-party politics gave way, to be replaced briefly by three parties, and then by the more usual two.

TIMES OF CHANGE IN CULTURE

There have been periods when Mississippi's culture did not change, but remained constant. "Old South" Mississippi, the period from 1837 to 1860, may have been such a time, a period of development rather than of basic change. Relations between the races were about the same in 1860 as in 1837. The economy was based on cotton farming in 1837 and 1860.

Mississippi in 1950 was perhaps not very different from Mississippi in 1920. Cotton and sharecropping still dominated agriculture, and agriculture still dominated the state. Blacks were locked into segregated positions, just as they were in 1920. Even the number of people in the state was constant.

There have been times, however, when Mississippi's culture changed rapidly. The period during the Civil War and Reconstruction was one such time. White and Black people in 1873 did not act the same toward each other as they had in 1853. Farming arrangements were also quite different.

ERAS OF MISSISSIPPI HISTORY

Survey this book to decide where the main points of cultural change and the periods of little change might be located. Divide Mississippi's history into stable eras separated by times of rapid change. What label would you apply to each era?

What would you name the era we are now living in? Every age is "modern" to the people living in it, but what do you think historians in the year 2050 will call our present time period? Think about this question individually and then compare answers throughout your class.

BASIC CULTURAL CHANGE

As observers of history, our job is to learn about and understand times when culture changed a lot, because these changes are really important in how societies grow and change. Sure, knowing about things like governor's titles and who won battles is interesting, but it's not as important as understanding how people's ways of living and thinking change. We think that the early 1970s were a really important time for cultural changes in Mississippi, and to really get what was happening then, we need to look into something called reference groups.

Reference groups are basically the groups of people or communities that we feel a part of, and they help shape what we think, how we act, and what we believe in. By looking at the different reference groups in Mississippi during the early 1970s, we can better understand the cultural changes happening then and how these changes affected the way people in the state lived and thought about politics.

This way of studying history lets us do more than just list events; it helps us dig into the bigger cultural forces that have shaped Mississippi's history, how they still affect it today, and how they will in the future.

People are influenced by the people and culture around them. We all have an idea of what other people in our society are like, and we want to be like some and unlike others. A positive reference group is a group or type of people that you admire and want to be like, join, or be approved by. On the other hand, a negative reference group is a type of people that you don't want to be like, and you don't want to be associated with them.

For example, if you admire a talented musician and try to emulate their creativity and dedication, musicians become a positive reference group for you. Their artistry and work ethic inspire you to pursue your own passions. On the other hand, if you avoid behaving like a group known for making harmful choices, such as being dishonest or irresponsible, they would be a negative reference group for you. Their actions serve as a reminder of what you strive to avoid. Reference groups can be important in helping us understand who we are and who we want to be, as well as what kind of people we want to be associated with.

CULTURAL CHANGE IN THE EARLY 1970s

Before 1968, most White Mississippi teenagers held as their positive reference group older White Mississippians. High school students modeled themselves after college students, young adults, and their own parents. Black teenagers, similarly, looked up to older Black Mississippians.

By 1971, cultural shifts were underway, particularly among young Black Mississippians. The civil rights movement, Black Power movement, and protests in northern cities had exposed them to new ideas and ways of thinking. The assassination of Dr. Martin Luther King Jr. in 1968, while supporting a garbage workers' strike in Memphis, added to the unrest and sparked protests in both Memphis and small Mississippi towns. This led to a change in self-identification, with young Black Mississippians preferring to be called "Black" instead of "Negro." This shift was not just about terminology, but represented a new perspective on Blackness and a rejection of previous negative associations. Likewise, the death of George Floyd has inspired some people, both young and old, to support the Black Lives Matter platform.

Some Blacks later began to embrace the term "African American" in their self-description. A significant aspect of this change was the way it was driven by younger individuals, indicating that cultural changes from across the United States were influencing the younger generation.

Overall, the shift from "Negro" to "Black" to "African American," reflects deeper changes in the attitudes and identities of young Black Mississippians, influenced by broader social and political movements of the time.

The change among White youth was equally great. They were becoming more national than regional. Rock musicians in the North and in England wore old-fashioned glasses and let their hair grow long; suddenly, in the early 1970s, so did many young men and women in Mississippi. Today, young people, especially women and some men, are huge fans of global icons like Beyoncé and Taylor Swift, showing how music and pop culture continue to shape identities across generations. Beyoncé's devoted followers, known as the BeyHive, and Taylor Swift's loyal Swifties exemplify how fan communities form around artists, creating shared identities and cultural movements that transcend regional and generational boundaries. Students at Greenville High School in 1969 elected a Chinese Mississippian as president of the student body, something they would never have done two years earlier. After eighty years of choosing males, Millsaps College students elected a woman to head their student government in 1972, and again in 1979. Belhaven College, which would not allow Blacks even to attend events on campus until 1966, elected a Black woman to head its student body in 1979.

MISSISSIPPI AND THE NATION

Older Mississippians, too, were changing their reference groups. Beginning in about 1968, White adults gradually stopped resisting the changes coming in from beyond the state's borders. Owing to the civil rights movement, the state's economic development, and the greater movement of people into and out of Mississippi, two of the special aspects of the past culture of our state ended: segregation and the one-party system. Other differences between Mississippi and the rest of the nation decreased in the 1970s.

RACE RELATIONS

Race relations are a special aspect of culture in societies that have more than one race. In the 1970s, Mississippi still faced continued change in this area. In many industries, universities, and state agencies, only a token number of Black Mississippians held professional or executive jobs. New residential subdivisions were usually planned as either all-White or all-Black.

Some Blacks did not push for integration. The Detroit-based Republic of New Africa (RNA), for example, sent leaders to Jackson in 1970 to work toward achieving Black control of the state and eventual separation from the United States. But early morning gunfire in August 1971 erupted between the RNA and Jackson police, after the police stormed the house without identifying themselves. A patrolman died and most of the RNA staff landed in jail.

The civil rights movement had largely ignored northeast Mississippi in the 1960s. Perhaps as a result, this area had not experienced the positive changes that conflict can sometimes bring about, so it was the scene of strained race relations in the 1970s. In 1974, a fourteen-year-old boy from Byhalia was killed while in the custody of Marshall County law officers. Black citizens could not get a grand jury to investigate, so they boycotted local White businesses. Four years later, a similar charge of police brutality was made against two Tupelo policemen. Ku Klux Klansmen then opposed Black United League members in marches and demonstrations.

Nonetheless, massive improvements took place in race relations between 1967 and 1980. Although conflict forced these changes, the conflicts were no longer as violent as in the civil rights struggle. Demonstrations and boycotts were used as effective tools in Shelby, Port Gibson, and other towns. The most important site for conflict and conflict resolution in the 1970s was in the courtroom.

LEGAL CONFLICTS CAUSE CONTINUED CHANGE

After years of legal and administrative battles, WLBT-TV in Jackson was taken from the control of Lamar Life Insurance company, which had been accused of racist programming, and placed in the hands of a biracial firm. Owing to a 1971 court order, the Mississippi Highway Patrol finally began to hire Blacks as patrolmen. Similar lawsuits affected the Jackson Fire Department and several other state and local agencies. A suit forced the town of Shelby to pave streets in Black neighborhoods as well as in White areas. Using that case as a precedent, Black residents of Shelby persuaded that town to pass a bond issue to improve streets without a lawsuit.

Parchman State Farm operated in the 1960s much as it had for decades. Controlling the work and lives of prisoners were other prisoners with guns, called "trustees," with a small force of paid guards over them. The system could be extremely dangerous to prisoners who offended their trustees, and the penitentiary was finally declared "cruel and unusual punishment" by a federal judge. State officials were ordered to improve its facilities and end the trustee system.

In the Mississippi Code of 1972, the legislature systematically removed virtually all of the old "segregation laws."

The 1967 Supreme Court case *Loving v. Virginia* struck down laws banning interracial marriage, while *Obergefell v. Hodges* (2015) legalized same-sex marriage nationwide. In 1970, Rims Barber officiated the marriage of Berta Lison and Roger Mills, making them the first interracial couple to wed in Mississippi. Decades later, in 2015, Amber Hamilton and Annice Smith made history as the first same-sex couple to marry in the state.

The most sweeping legal change in race relations came in the area of school desegregation.

AT LAST: SCHOOL DESEGREGATION IN MISSISSIPPI

In the mid-1960s, school desegregation had been proceeding very slowly under "freedom of choice" court rulings and school district plans. "Freedom of choice" was supposed to be a step toward ending segregation.

Under "freedom of choice," the students were allowed to choose their own school. The courts hoped that for their convenience or other reasons, Whites would choose the schools closest to their homes, even if it had formerly been a Black school, and that Blacks would do the same. If this had happened, "freedom of choice" might have gradually led to effective school desegregation.

However, almost all districts maintained faculty segregation. Black schools still had all-Black or almost all-Black faculties; White schools were taught by White teachers. A few Black students chose to enter White schools, which took courage, since they left their teachers and friends behind. Some of these students faced silence or open hostility from their White classmates. Almost no White students chose Black schools.

In 1969, in *Alexander v. Holmes County Board of Education,* the Supreme Court declared that "freedom of choice" was not ending segregation and that therefore it was unconstitutional. The Court declared that it was time to end delays. Immediate action was required for school desegregation, particularly during the 1969–1970 academic year across many districts. For smaller districts that had no need for two separate high schools, the directive was to establish a single, integrated high school. In large towns, school lines were redrawn or schools were paired, so that a formerly Black school and a formerly White school shared the same students. Teachers were transferred so that schools could not be labeled "Black" or "White" by their faculties.

Throughout the state, school boards and parents had known for years that this day would come, but had somehow never prepared for it. Now, they hastened to adjust to the new changes. Three basic patterns emerged: cooperation, evasion, and withdrawal.

COOPERATION

Some administrators, school boards, and parents of both races tried to make the changes as smoothly as possible. Schools, classrooms, and faculties were desegregated without conflict. A few districts even desegregated without court orders; other districts waited for the court order but then tried sincerely to follow its instructions.

Figure 16.1. Cheerleaders for Greenville High School in 1973.

On the whole, the students themselves got along well. In several districts, students of different races united to vote for interracial student governments and homecoming courts. But in some schools, problems remained. Students regretted the closing of their former alma maters.

Yearbooks, dances, and clubs were canceled, usually not by students, who wanted them to continue, but because of pressure from parents or administrators. In some schools, Black students were not allowed to become cheerleaders, were not chosen for homecoming courts, or faced strict conduct rules not applied to their White classmates. Protesting such acts of discrimination, Black students walked out of schools in Yalobusha County, the Gulf Coast, Jackson, and elsewhere. As White and Black students began to communicate more honestly, these problems began to be solved.

EVASION

In other districts, White administrators, school boards, teachers, or parents attempted to make matters unpleasant for Black teachers, administrators, and children, usually in defiance of court orders. Black principals were placed under Whites; Whites were rarely put under Blacks. Some districts segregated their students by sex, which signaled to the Black community that Whites still feared interracial sex. Other districts agreed to integrate their schools, but then set up separate classrooms for White and Black students within each building.

Such practices did not last long. Most of these districts moved toward full cooperation, owing to legal pressure, protests from Black students, and White feelings in favor of progress and equality. A few of these districts moved toward the third response to the desegregation orders: White withdrawal.

WITHDRAWAL

In Indianola, Canton, Wilkinson County, and a number of other districts, all or most White parents withdrew their children from the public schools when classes were desegregated and placed them in private schools. In a way, this left the schools as segregated as ever, but with one important difference: they were now open to anyone without regard to race. No longer were all-White schools or nearly all-White schools maintained by taxes. Parents who wanted their children to be isolated from members of the other race now had to use their own money for that purpose.

CAUSES OF WITHDRAWAL

White parents who withdrew their children gave various reasons. Some claimed the public schools could no longer provide "quality education"; others said there was "too much confusion" because of the changes; and still others admitted openly that they did not want their children to attend school with students of a different race.

But the actual causes of their feelings and their actions were deeply embedded in the past. Therefore, in order to understand their actions, we must start far back in history. Before the Civil War, to justify their actions in a slave society, White people told themselves that their slaves were not really people at all, but inferior beings unable to care for themselves. The idea that Blacks were inferior lasted long after slavery ended, and was maintained by sharecropping, segregation, and political exclusion. Growing up under such a system, many White parents sincerely believed that Blacks were inferior; consequently, they did not want their children going to school with Black children.

The White Citizens' Councils built new schools for Whites in Jackson. Private "academies" sprang up in White churches throughout the state. Schools were even started overnight in gas stations and warehouses.

Figure 16.2. A 1972 Council School Foundation brochure. Courtesy of the Archives and Records Services Division, Mississippi Department of Archives and History.

As early as 1971, there were signs that total White withdrawal would not last long except in a few places. Two hundred White pupils reentered the Indianola public schools after one semester in private schools. The Citizens' Councils school system fell apart in 1977, although some Council schools kept going independently.

A DESEGREGATED SOCIETY

When the teachers' association met annually in Jackson, it automatically put large biracial groups into hotels and restaurants. Museums and college campuses were desegregated when high school field trips toured them.

School desegregation had an indirect impact on housing patterns, too. Whites who had resisted school desegregation for so long now felt less powerful than before. After all, the schools had desegregated anyway. So now when a Black family bought a home in a White neighborhood, White families either accepted it or moved out themselves. No longer did Whites feel they had the social power to force the Black family out.

When Black and White students or teachers went to fast food restaurants or movie theaters, owners realized they should hire Blacks as well as Whites. The Equal Employment Opportunity Commission opened an office for Mississippians who had not been hired because of their race or sex. Considerable employment discrimination lasted past 1980. But very few jobs were now listed as "all-White" or "men only."

"SECOND-GENERATION" DESEGREGATION ISSUES

The 1970s brought legal desegregation to Mississippi's schools, setting powerful changes in motion across society, yet the schools themselves struggled to achieve genuine integration. "Desegregation" means ending the laws and customs that separated the races in school. "Integration" in schools means establishing new policies so that all races participate equally.

For example, if a high school uses "Colonel Rebel" as its mascot and the Confederate flag as its symbol, then its Black students will likely be alienated. After all, the Confederacy was formed to keep their ancestors in slavery! Similarly, if a literature course includes short stories by Richard Wright but none by William Faulkner, then White students may feel the course is not intended for them.

Some Mississippi high schools sought to build a pluralist curriculum and activities that reflected the styles and interests of all their students. In this book, we aimed to present a pluralist history, capturing the hopes and motives of all major groups in Mississippi's past, with a strong focus on marginalized communities whose stories have often been overlooked.

WRITE THE HISTORY OF DESEGREGATION OF YOUR SCHOOL

Do your school and school district fit into any of the three patterns of school desegregation described above? Get newspaper clippings about your school's desegregation, or actual copies of the court rulings, if there were any. Analyze the present state of desegregation in your school. Finally, put all your facts together in a complete history of school desegregation in your school or district. See if you can analyze the role played by each group: Black parents, teachers, and students; White parents, teachers, and students; administrators; the courts; and the community.

PUBLIC EDUCATION GROWS STRONGER

In most public schools, meanwhile, the future looked better. In 1971–1972 the state spent almost twice as much per pupil as it had spent four years earlier. Some schools changed to individualized instruction: their students learned from packets, not books, so each could progress at a different rate. Other schools relied on educational television or on "open classrooms." The two teachers' associations, Black and White, merged. Black and White parents now worked together in PTSAs (Parent-Teacher-Student Associations).

FREEDOM TO READ

Perhaps because we succeeded, or perhaps because we did not, the first edition of *Mississippi, Conflict and Change* was not accepted by the Mississippi State Textbook Purchasing Board and its rating committee. In 1974, only two texts were available in state history: this one and *Your Mississippi* by John K. Bettersworth. *Your Mississippi* was revised from a text first published in 1961, before the desegregation era. It contained only two photographs of Black Mississippians and almost no treatment of the civil rights struggle.

The board and rating committee could have adopted both histories. In American history they chose five books. But they decided to select only *Your Mississippi* and refused to accept *Mississippi, Conflict and Change* as a text.

The authors, along with two school systems, parents, and teachers who wanted to use their book, took legal action against the rejection of the book. After years of delays, in 1980, the court ruled that the book had been rejected partly because it covered controversial topics such as desegregation and civil rights. The judge stated that students have a right to read controversial books, and the authors' rights were violated by the rejection.

This case, *Loewen v. Turnipseed*, is comparable to the landmark case of *Alexander v. Holmes*, which resulted in the rapid desegregation of schools in 1969. Both cases exemplify how legal challenges can drive change and address injustices, such as the violation of constitutional rights and the perpetuation of segregation in education.

Loewen v. Turnipseed not only affirmed the importance of academic freedom and the right to access diverse perspectives, but it also serves as a reminder of the ongoing struggle for equality and the critical role that the legal system plays in advancing social progress. This case adds to the legacy of legal battles that have helped shape a more just and inclusive society.

MISSISSIPPI CIVIL RIGHTS EDUCATION DILEMMA

Unlike the 1980s when this book was used, in 2006, Mississippi took steps to address a glaring omission in its schools: the lack of civil rights education being taught. Despite the state's central role in the civil rights movement, civil rights history had been largely absent from K-12 classrooms. The legislature passed § 37-13-195, creating the Mississippi Civil Rights Education Commission to provide teaching resources. However, the law had two crucial weaknesses: it made civil rights education voluntary rather than mandatory, and it gave the commission no power to enforce the teaching of this material. This meant that students' exposure to this vital history depended solely on individual teachers' decisions, creating an uneven educational landscape where some learned this crucial history while others did not.

A SOLUTION IN SEARCH OF A PROBLEM?

In 2022, Mississippi lawmakers passed a bill banning Critical Race Theory (CRT) in schools, even though this concept is usually taught in upper-level undergraduate, graduate, or law courses. CRT explores how racism has influenced laws and institutions, affecting areas like criminal justice, housing, education, and healthcare.

The law itself didn't mention CRT directly but instead banned teaching that any race, gender, or ethnicity is superior or inferior. Supporters claimed it would prevent schools from pushing racial ideas onto students, but there was no proof that CRT was actually being taught in Mississippi's K-12 schools. This led Senator John Horhn to call it "a solution without a problem." The bill's wording was nearly identical to a law passed in Texas, suggesting both states followed the same political playbook.

Efforts to control what students could learn didn't stop with race. That same year, Ridgeland Mayor Gene McGee tried to block $110,000 in funding from the

Madison County Library System unless they removed LGBTQ+ books. Although this wasn't an official book ban, the move sparked public outrage, and funding was restored in April 2022—a win for intellectual freedom and against censorship.

THE NEW SEGREGATION: MISSISSIPPI'S EDUCATIONAL DIVIDE

In 2024, Mississippi's schools remain divided by race and income. In Clarksdale, Lee Academy is 92 percent White, while Clarksdale High is 92 percent Black, reflecting statewide patterns—private schools are mostly White, with only 19 percent students of color. Public school are 47 percent Black and 42 percent White.

These divides impact educational achievement. Eighteen percent of Black Mississippians lack a high school diploma, compared to 10 percent of White residents. College graduation rates also differ, with 29 percent of White residents earning degrees compared to 18 percent of Black residents. In Jackson, White families have moved to suburbs like Madison and Ridgeland, leaving public schools over 90 percent Black, while some private schools in the area remain as much as 95 percent White.

Madison County highlights this divide—while the county is 54 percent White and 38 percent Black, Canton High is 99.7 percent Black, and Madison Central is 61 percent White. In 2016, the federal government forced the Cleveland School District to merge segregated schools. Mississippi's 2024 funding plan now provides $6,695 per student, with extra support for those in need.

Segregation also happens in subtle ways. In Brookhaven, a "parental request" policy lets families pick teachers, leading to racially divided classrooms. Though schools are legally integrated, Mississippi's education system still reflects deep racial and economic gaps, keeping true equality out of reach.

Recommended Readings

Natalie G. Adams and James H. Adams, *Just Trying to Have School: The Struggle for Desegregation in Mississippi* (Jackson: University Press of Mississippi, 2018).

Charles C. Bolton, *The Hardest Deal of All: The Battle over School Integration in Mississippi, 1870–1980* (Jackson: University Press of Mississippi, 2005).

Nancy K. Bristow, *Steeped in the Blood of Racism: Black Power, Law and Order, and the 1970 Shootings at Jackson State College* (New York: Oxford University Press, 2020).

Teena F. Horn et al., eds., *Lines Were Drawn: Remembering Court-Ordered Integration at a Mississippi High School* (Jackson: University Press of Mississippi, 2016).

Amy Lemco, *Wading In: Desegregation on the Mississippi Gulf Coast* (Jackson: University Press of Mississippi, 2023).

John A. Peoples, *To Survive and Thrive: The Quest for a True University* (Jackson, MS: Town Square Books, 1995).

David G. Sansing, *Making Haste Slowly: The Troubled History of Higher Education in Mississippi* (Jackson: University Press of Mississippi, 2008).

Frederick M. Wirt, *We Ain't What We Was: Civil Rights in the New South* (Durham, NC: Duke University Press, 1997).

CHAPTER 17

BARRIERS AND BREAKTHROUGHS

Mississippi's Political Evolution through Reform and Resistance

DURING THE 1960S AND 1970S, THERE WAS A CHANGE IN THE TONE AND ISSUES candidates campaigned on. What most changed the way candidates spoke on many of these issues was the existence of half a million potential new voters. In 1971, the Twenty-sixth Amendment lowered the voting age to eighteen, adding about 130,000 potential new young voters in Mississippi. More importantly, the Voting Rights Act and changes in state law in 1965 allowed Black Mississippians to vote in significant numbers for the first time since Reconstruction. Results were dramatic. In 1960 only 5.2 percent of the Black voting-age population was registered; ten years later, following the passage of the Voting Rights Act and impressive voter-registration drives, the proportion had jumped to 67.5 percent.

POLITICAL POWER EMERGES

This surge in voter registration fundamentally altered Mississippi's political landscape. Backed by this newfound voting power, Black political leaders had by the late 1960s become key players in state elections. Many school boards included Black members. By 1980, seventeen small towns had Black mayors.

RESISTANCE AND LEGAL CHALLENGE

Yet this growing wave of Black political power met determined opposition. White legislators, desperate to maintain their White supremacy, fought back by redrawing district lines to weaken Black voting strength and block Black candidates from winning office. They also changed the structure of the election system by creating districts that included more than one seat/official. This was another way of diluting the Black vote. Black citizens refused to let their rights be stripped away. The Mississippi Freedom Democratic Party (MFDP) and Peggy Jean Connor responded by taking their fight to the federal courts, launching a landmark challenge to the state's discriminatory voting system in *Connor v. Johnson*.

NEW VICTORY IN THE STATE LEGISLATURE

After a fourteen-year long legal struggle, justice was finally served in 1979 when the US Supreme Court delivered its groundbreaking ruling in *Connor v. Finch*, dismantling Mississippi's discriminatory voting structure. The case, which originated as *Connor v. Johnson*, targeted the state's manipulative multimember district system, a mechanism that had systematically diluted Black voting power. The Court's decision abolished this system and mandated the creation of single-member districts, a pivotal change that empowered Black communities to elect representatives who genuinely reflected their voices and interests.

The impact was both immediate and transformative. The Mississippi Legislature, once dominated by a system designed to suppress Black political influence, saw a remarkable shift: seventeen Black representatives and senators took their seats, a significant increase from the mere four who had served under the earlier framework. While seventeen out of 174 seats may appear modest in a state where Black residents made up nearly forty percent of the population, this marked a profound and hard-won advancement from the stark underrepresentation that had persisted before the ruling. The decision not only reshaped the political landscape, it also symbolized a critical step toward greater equity and representation in Mississippi.

TRANSFORMATION OF LOCAL GOVERNMENT

Just as the *Connor* victory reshaped the state legislature, federal courts stepped in to dismantle unfair voting practices in cities and counties across Mississippi. The landmark case *Allen v. State Board of Elections* provided the guidelines for how the Voting Rights Act could be enforced, leading many jurisdictions to eliminate at-large elections, which had been used to weaken the Black vote. The first successful challenge to at-large municipal elections came with *Stewart v. Waller*.

The impact of the *Allen* decision extended to county-level elections as well. In *Kirksey v. Board of Supervisors of Hinds County*, a federal court ordered Hinds County, the state's most populous, to change its electoral system. The message

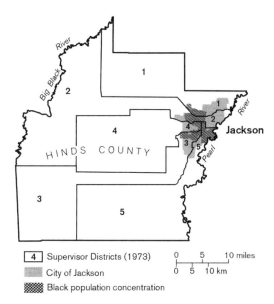

Map 32. Hinds County Board of Supervisors Districts Challenged by Black Voters

was clear: the old system of at-large elections—where everyone voted for all the seats—had to go. Under that system, White voters could outnumber Black voters and elect an all-White government, even in areas with large Black populations.

Now, counties had to redraw their districts into smaller, fairer pieces, like rearranging a puzzle. The results were immediate. In Hinds County, Black voters finally gained a real voice in local government, electing two of the five county supervisors in 1979—something that would have been unthinkable just a few years earlier. These court cases marked a turning point, ensuring fair representation for Black Mississippians.

Municipal and county redistricting and legislative reapportionment (the process of reallocating legislative seats based on population changes) meant that politics now became a process wherein disputes could be discussed and decided by voters from every segment of society. No longer was one social group fully shut out.

DESCRIPTIVE AND SUBSTANTIVE REPRESENTATION

Political representation comes in two important forms. Descriptive representation means voters see people who look like them in office—for example, leaders who share their race or gender. But there's also substantive representation, which gets to the heart of what elected officials do. It asks a simple but crucial question: once in power, do these leaders fight for what their voters really need?

CHAPTER 17.

A QUIET REVOLUTION

The landmark legal battles in Mississippi's courts reshaped the state's political landscape. It led to Mississippi possessing the highest number of Black elected officials in the nation. These court victories, anchored in the Voting Rights Act, became a blueprint for challenging discriminatory voting practices across the South. Mississippi's cases established crucial precedents for dismantling racist electoral strategies. This success stemmed from the dedicated work of a remarkable team: civil rights attorneys like Frank Parker, Carroll Rhodes, Robert McDuff, and Ellis Turnage, alongside expert witnesses and map drawers, including Henry Kirksey, Hollis Watkins, Derrick Johnson, and James Loewen, and testimony from A. B. Britton. Together, they meticulously crafted legal strategies to create majority-Black districts, finally giving African American communities the power to elect representatives who would truly serve their interests.

Armed with their earlier victories, civil rights lawyers returned to federal court to challenge Mississippi's congressional district boundaries. Once again, they prevailed against the White power structure, by creating a majority Black districts that would allow Black people to elect the candidate of their choice. The result was historic: Mike Espy won election as Mississippi's first Black congressman since Reconstruction. His achievements reached new heights when he became Secretary of Agriculture, though his tenure was cut short by false ethics charges—accusations a jury would later thoroughly reject. Building on Espy's legacy, Bennie Thompson succeeded him in representing this majority-Black district, despite minimal White support. Thompson's influence grew nationally

Figure 17.1. Mike Espy.   Figure 17.2. Bennie Thompson.

Figure 17.3. Reuben Anderson. Johnston (Erle E., Jr.) Papers, Special Collections, University Libraries, University of Southern Mississippi.

as he chaired the powerful House Homeland Security Committee and later led the Select Committee investigating the January 6th attack on the Capitol.

The state's highest court also saw a historic breakthrough. In 1985, Governor Bill Allain shattered another racial barrier by appointing Reuben Anderson as the first Black justice on the Mississippi Supreme Court. Anderson's election victory the following year told a remarkable story of changing times. Unlike most Black candidates who faced unified White opposition, Anderson earned crucial endorsements from prominent White leaders. Perhaps most telling was his defeat of Richard Barrett, an avowed White supremacist—a clear signal that Mississippi voters were turning their backs on the state's segregationist past. This wasn't just an election; it was a milestone marking Mississippi's slow but steady march toward racial progress.

In the federal judiciary, Henry Wingate broke ground as Mississippi's first African American federal judge when appointed to the US District Court in 1985. Carlton Reeves later joined the federal bench as another African American US district judge. Following Reuben Anderson's retirement from the Mississippi Supreme Court, Fred Banks was appointed to fill his remaining term. Subsequently, James E. Graves Jr. was appointed to the state's highest court. Graves later achieved a significant milestone when he was appointed to the United States Court of Appeals for the Fifth Circuit in New Orleans, becoming the highest-ranking Black judge from Mississippi to serve in the federal judiciary. These appointments further showed the increasing representation of Black judges in Mississippi's legal system and their growing influence in both state and federal courts. In 1997, Harvey Johnson made history by becoming the first Black mayor of Jackson, the state capital.

The electoral successes of Black politicians in Mississippi might suggest improved race relations. However, these candidates have primarily succeeded due to court-ordered majority-Black districts or by winning in majority-Black cities. As of 2025, no Black candidate had been elected to a statewide office since Reconstruction.

The absence of Black statewide officeholders is not solely a racial issue but also a partisan one. Black candidates overwhelmingly run as Democrats due to the party's position on issues related to the economic challenges and social inequities faced by their communities. This partisan alignment creates a significant hurdle for Black candidates in statewide races, as they struggle to capture the votes of conservative Whites who predominantly support Republicans. However, this alignment also affects White Democrats, with only one White Democrat being elected to any statewide office in recent years. As of 2025, there was not one Democrat at the state level.

Trent Lott's analysis provides insight into the political dynamics of Mississippi: "If they subscribe to the national Democratic Party's principles, they are clearly going to alienate the overwhelming majority of the White people in Mississippi. . . . So, if they go with the typical national Democrat base, they wind up with Blacks and labor and your more liberal, social-oriented Democrats, White people. Put those groups together and they are a minority in Mississippi."

History shows that Mississippi can make meaningful progress when its citizens unite across racial lines. After Black legislators secured more seats in the state legislature and formed alliances with White Democrats, they began to experience not only descriptive representation but also substantive representation—gaining tangible influence over policies and decisions. This era of cooperation highlighted Mississippi's potential for advancement when people come together to overcome racial divisions.

However, similar to the patterns seen during Reconstruction, this progress has proven most durable when Black lawmakers are part of the majority party. The shifts that followed the 1979 elections serve as a compelling illustration of this dynamic, underscoring the importance of inclusive political structures in sustaining meaningful change.

THE POWER OF BIRACIAL COALITIONS IN MISSISSIPPI

Even as Black lawmakers secured more seats in the legislature, gaining real influence remained a challenge. Research shows they are far more likely than their White colleagues to introduce bills focused on critical issues in Black communities, such as healthcare, welfare, and education. However, passing these bills is another hurdle.

As a minority in the legislature, to achieve substantive change, they needed to collaborate with White lawmakers. One of the most notable examples of this cooperation came in 1982 when Robert Clark, a pioneering Black legislator, teamed up with Governor William Winter, a White Democrat, to pass the Education Reform Act of 1982. This landmark bill expanded early childhood education, increased teacher salaries, and improved schools, marking a major turning point in Mississippi's political history.

This wasn't just about Governor Winter and Robert Clark; however, a broad coalition—including progressive Black and White legislators, the media, and Winter's young aides, known as the "Boys of Spring"—rallied behind the bill. However, not all compromises held. Some broke down along racial lines, exposing deep divides within the legislature. So, Black people had to make some concessions. One key issue was Head Start, a program that had proven to be tremendously beneficial for Black children by providing early childhood education, nutrition, and healthcare. Many White legislators, however, were unwilling to support its expansion, viewing it as a federal overreach that disproportionately benefited Black communities. As a result, while the Education Reform Act expanded early education, it did not fully integrate Head Start into the state's long-term education strategy.

Another dividing issue was taxation. To fund education reform, new taxes were proposed, but Black legislators feared these increases would disproportionately burden Black families, who were already struggling under economic inequality. Despite their concerns, the tax hikes remained, reinforcing a system where Black Mississippians bore a heavier financial burden while wealthier, predominantly White communities faced fewer hardships.

Despite not getting everything they bargained for, education reform was a success. The success of this collaboration, however, didn't stop with education reform. A new wave of biracial political partnerships emerged, leading to the formation of "House 26," a group of young, progressive White and Black legislators determined to push forward more policy changes. Their rise sparked a confrontation with Speaker of the House Buddie Newman, who had long controlled the legislature. Despite being sidelined with weak committee assignments, as punishment from the Speaker, House 26 members fought back, and their persistence helped erode Newman's grip on power. Eventually, he retired—a major shift in Mississippi politics.

The momentum carried beyond legislation. Winter, with the support of the Black Caucus, successfully led the effort to remove the racist Theodore Bilbo statue from the Capitol. More than just a symbolic victory, it showed that when Black and White leaders worked together, they could dismantle long-standing power structures and bring real change.

THE FIGHT FOR BLACK LEGISLATIVE POWER

The Education Reform Bill provides us with a clear case of coalition building. However, when the electorate voted for a conservative Republican governor, there was a shift from not only racial politics, but to partisan politics. Previously, the legislature and the governor were all Democrats.

A key example of this power struggle emerged when Republican Governor Kirk Fordice nominated four White men, all with ties to Mississippi's historically White universities, to the state's College Board. Black legislators opposed the move, but they had an influential ally to challenge it—Hillman Frazier, a Black Senator who chaired the Senate Judiciary Committee. Frazier formed a subcommittee to push for more Black nominees, and when the full committee—consisting of five Black Democrats, five White Republicans, and three White Democrats—voted, two White Democrats joined Black Democrats in rejecting Fordice's picks. This forced the governor to submit a more diverse slate, which included one Black man, one White woman, and two White men.

The examples discussed so far show how Black legislators skillfully navigated the political system and rapidly gained influence. However, as the political environment evolved, advancing substantive legislation became increasingly challenging, forcing Black lawmakers to adopt more creative and strategic approaches. Despite their growing representation, the emergence of a Republican-dominated legislature created significant obstacles to passing meaningful policy reforms. To tackle some of Mississippi's most urgent issues, they had to forge broader coalitions and mobilize the wider community. Among the most formidable challenges they confronted was the effort to change the state flag—a symbol deeply tied to the state's history and identity.

THE REMOVAL OF A DIVISIVE SYMBOL

One of the most significant political battles in the state's history was the fight to change its controversial flag. For 126 years, a simple piece of cloth ignited fierce debate. Adopted in 1894, the flag prominently displayed the Confederate battle emblem—an image that had long been embraced by White supremacists and the Ku Klux Klan. To many White Mississippians, it was a badge of "heritage." But for Black citizens, it was a constant reminder of slavery, segregation, oppression and hate. The fight over its future wasn't just about history; it was about identity, power, and the soul of Mississippi itself.

Black leaders fought back with courage and creativity. State Senator Henry Kirksey called it—the Confederate "Slavery" Flag. When White supremacists threatened violence, Dr. Ollye Shirley, Jackson's Black school board president, stood firm: remove the Confederate flag from the majority-White school, she

Figure 17.4. 1894 Mississippi state flag.

warned administrators, or watch her "snatch it down." NAACP members Delores Orey and Ineva Mae Pittman launched their clever strategy, bombarding a local mall with calls in different voices making it appear that a large number of people were calling. They continued this daily, until the flag came down. In the halls of power, Senators Dr. Aaron Henry and Senator Kirksey fought through courts and introduced bill after bill demanding change.

In 1993, the NAACP's lawsuit revealed an unexpected twist: Mississippi technically had no official flag—the 1894 design had been accidentally abolished in 1906. This revelation set the stage for a statewide referendum to officially adopt a state flag. On April 17, 2001, Mississippi held a public vote to decide between retaining the 1894 design or adopting a new flag. The 2001 referendum that followed exposed the state's deep racial divide: 64 percent voted to keep the old design, closely matching the state's racial demographics. Governor Ronnie Musgrove paid a political price for standing against the old flag. His support for change contributed to his defeat in the next election. While other issues factored into his loss, his stance on the flag undoubtedly turned many voters against him.

By 2020, the ground shifted beneath the old flag. The killings of George Floyd, Breonna Taylor, and other unarmed Black Americans ignited the largest protests since the 1960s. A new generation of activists like Maisie Brown and Taylor Turnage led the charge to change the flag, joined by an unlikely ally—Republican House Speaker Philip Gunn. After seeing photos of the Charleston church shooter with Confederate flags, Gunn's view of the symbol changed forever. Gunn said, "We must understand that this flag is a point of offense that needs to be removed. We are all created in the image of God, and we should all be treated

Figure 17.5. New state flag.

equally. We need to look at the potential of what Mississippi can be. For the sake of our children and grandchildren, we need to change the flag." His leadership helped break decades of resistance. Following Gunn's announcement, the push to replace the state flag gained momentum from a diverse coalition, including business leaders, clergy members, coaches, athletes, and educators, reflecting a growing consensus that Mississippi needed a new state symbol. Indeed, Kylan Hill, Mississippi State University football player, tweeted, "Either change the flag or I won't be representing this State anymore & I meant that. I'm tired." Such activism put pressure on the state legislators.

Through a series of strategic moves, the legislature worked together to push the legislation forward. In July 2020, the old flag was finally removed. Governor Tate Reeves signed its retirement to the Museum of Mississippi History, and a commission created a new design that 73 percent of voters approved. On January 11, 2021, Mississippi officially adopted its new flag—choosing unity over division and looking toward the future rather than the past.

UNINTENDED CONSEQUENCES?

The surge of Black elected officials in Mississippi changed the state's political scene—but not without controversy. Some argue that the push for majority-Black districts, designed to increase Black representation, came with unintended consequences. Political scientist Marvin Overby pointed out that while these court-ordered districts secured more seats for Black lawmakers, they also played into the hands of White conservatives. By packing Black voters into a handful of supermajority districts, the surrounding areas became overwhelmingly White and solidly Republican. Before redistricting, Black voters and White Democrats had shared influence in key districts, giving them a fighting chance in elections. However, once those districts disappeared, racial polarization in voting only deepened. By 2024, Mississippi's Democratic Party was almost entirely Black, while Republicans were nearly all White—except for one Black individual.

Not everyone sees this as a loss. Some argue that in a state as racially divided as Mississippi, the best way to ensure Black political power was to maximize Black-majority districts, even if it meant sacrificing "influence districts." NAACP National President Derrick Johnson pointed to the reality of racial segregation, explaining that drawing true influence districts was nearly impossible. Representative Ed Blackmon, a key player in the redistricting process, dismissed concerns that Democrats had lost ground, insisting that party labels were irrelevant when it came to race in Mississippi. "I don't know if it's true elsewhere, but it's not true here . . . because we don't know the difference between a Republican and a Democrat, conservative or a liberal, when it comes to issues that really matter to Black folk," Blackmon argued. He added, "If it's purely a Black issue, you can bet that, save for a few, whether they call themselves moderate, whether they call themselves Democrat or Republican, it comes down to a Black-White issue and that's unfortunate." Attorney Carroll Rhodes, a long-time voting rights lawyer, echoed those sentiments, arguing that Mississippi's racial divide in politics left little room for so-called influence districts. "There's no such thing as an influence district . . . Whites will vote together. There are only a few White Democrats who will crossover and vote with Black people. This is indicative in the Jim Hood and Brandon Presley (two White candidates) gubernatorial races."

VOTING RIGHTS AT THE CROSSROADS

In 2013, a seismic shift rocked America's voting rights landscape. The Supreme Court gutted a cornerstone of the 1965 Voting Rights Act, freeing states like Mississippi from federal oversight of their election rules. States with long histories of racial discrimination no longer needed Washington's permission to change how their citizens voted.

Mississippi wasted no time. The state quickly rolled out new voting restrictions, including a strict voter ID law. While defenders claimed these rules prevented fraud, the reality hit harder in Black and low-income communities. When driver's license offices—the primary source for obtaining IDs—moved to far-flung locations, many citizens without cars found themselves facing a simple but devastating choice: finding transportation to get an ID or losing their vote.

The state then launched another strategy: a voter purge system. Skip voting for two consecutive election cycles, and your name could vanish from the rolls unless you respond to a notification and vote in future elections. Even with a four-year grace period to reclaim voting rights, the damage was clear. Eligible voters, often unaware they'd been purged, found themselves stripped of their fundamental right to participate in democracy.

These modern barriers tell a familiar story in Mississippi's struggle for true democracy. While the state had made tremendous strides since the 1960s, new obstacles kept appearing—sophisticated replacements for the crude tools of the past.

ECHOES OF JIM CROW

The hard-won victories of Black Mississippians today mirror an earlier era of promise—Reconstruction. But just as the 1890 state constitution crushed that period's hopes, modern progress faces its own shadow: a carefully crafted system of voter suppression that endures.

In 1890, Mississippi's White leaders designed a deceptively simple weapon against Black voting rights. Their tool? A felon disenfranchisement law that never mentioned race but struck with surgical precision at Black communities. The crimes they chose to trigger voting bans revealed their true intent: burglary, theft, and bigamy would strip citizens of their voting rights. Yet murder and lynching—crimes Whites routinely committed against Black citizens—were conspicuously absent from the list. These weren't random choices. The selected crimes targeted the economic hardships forced upon formerly enslaved people, who often faced theft charges while struggling against systematic poverty. Even bigamy made their list—a cruel twist given that slavery had legally banned Black marriages, creating complex family relationships that White lawmakers could now criminalize. The law's bias was clear: Whites could terrorize and kill Black citizens without losing their vote, while Black citizens could lose their rights for simply trying to survive.

Today, this seemingly colorblind law remains. Though Black citizens make up nearly 40 percent of Mississippi's population, they represent 61 percent of those stripped of voting rights through the criminal justice system. Once lost, these rights rarely return. The numbers are staggering: between 2000 and 2015, only 335 people out of 166,494 who completed their sentences managed to regain their voting rights—a mere 0.2 percent. A federal district court recognized this injustice and struck down Mississippi's lifetime disenfranchisement law in *Hopkins v. Watson*. But the victory was short-lived—the 5th Circuit Court of Appeals reinstated the law, dismissing claims it violates the Eighth Amendment. It's a stark reminder that sometimes the most effective discrimination never needs to mention race at all—its results speak loudly enough.

THE ONGOING STRUGGLE FOR EQUITY: FROM VOTING RIGHTS TO EDUCATIONAL JUSTICE

While Blacks have been unable to get a favorable outcome with respect to felon disenfranchisement, they continue to use the court system as an alternative to the legislative process. In the battle for education equity, for example, Black Mississippians often found the legislature's doors closed, forcing them to seek justice through the courts. This approach led to one of the state's most significant legal challenges—the 1975 *Ayers v. Fordice* lawsuit. Attorney Isaiah Madison filed the case for Jake Ayers Sr., whose child attended Jackson State University, claiming the state systematically underfunded historically Black universities while generously supporting predominantly White institutions.

When Madison left Mississippi, attorneys Alvin Chambliss, Bob Pressman, and later Armand Derfner kept the fight alive through a legal marathon that spanned nearly three decades. Their persistence finally secured a $503 million settlement to fund new academic programs, facilities, and endowments at state-supported historically Black universities. Ironically, the settlement required these schools to increase their non-Black enrollment to at least ten percent within three years.

This inequality has deep historical roots in the Morrill Acts of 1862 and 1890, which established land-grant colleges nationwide. Mississippi designated Alcorn University (now Alcorn State University and a historically Black school) in 1871 and what is now Mississippi State University (in 1878) under this system, but equality existed only on paper. Alcorn State University was promised initially 60 percent of Mississippi's land-grant funds and $50,000 annually for ten years—promises were quickly broken. By 1875, funding dropped to $15,000, then to $5,500 in 1876.

Fast forward to 2024 and the pattern remains. A Department of Education report revealed that Alcorn had been denied over $257 million in agricultural funding that went to Mississippi State instead. The stark contrast in educational opportunities and resources between these institutions is vividly illustrated by a statement from an Alcorn student who noted that their agricultural curriculum focused on harvesting small-scale, family-farm vegetables like greens, peas, and okra. In contrast, students at Mississippi State University were being trained to cultivate large-scale, commercially lucrative crops such as cotton, corn, and soybeans.

The magnitude of this funding imbalance prompted federal intervention, with both the US Secretary of Education and the Secretary of Agriculture appealing directly to Mississippi's governor for immediate action.

WOMEN IN MISSISSIPPI POLITICS: BARRIERS AND PROGRESS

Mississippi's political landscape has long been dominated by men, with women facing significant barriers to entry. Today, women make up just 17 percent of the state legislature, reflecting slow progress despite a century of political engagement.

Women's political participation began to shift after gaining the right to vote in 1920.

Nellie Nugent Somerville, a leader in the suffrage movement, was elected to the Mississippi House in 1923, and Belle Kearney was elected to the Mississippi Senate in 1924. After World War II, women began securing statewide offices, with Nellah Massey Bailey becoming the first woman elected to a statewide position in 1947. Evelyn Gandy followed, serving as state treasurer and later as lieutenant governor, though her 1979 gubernatorial bid was unsuccessful.

When it comes to the low level of women elected officials, the issue is not that women keep losing elections—it's that too few are running. Unlike neighboring Louisiana, where women's political organizations have actively recruited female candidates, Mississippi has lacked a strong support network for women in politics.

Figure 17.6. Men in Vicksburg poke fun at women's suffrage. When was this photo taken? From the photo collection of the Old Court House Museum, Vicksburg, MS.

Figure 17.7. Evelyn Gandy. Courtesy of the Archives and Records Services Division, Mississippi Department of Archives and History.

Women gained visibility in other areas by the 1970s, entering fields such as law enforcement and the judiciary. However, Mississippi's resistance to gender equality was clear in its refusal to ratify the Equal Rights Amendment (ERA). By 1980, it remained one of fifteen states that had not ratified the ERA—and the only state where the amendment never made it past committee. Ironically, legislator Betty Jane Long, serving from 1956 to 1984, played a key role in blocking it, arguing it was "broad enough to create problems not envisioned by the proponents."

Mississippi's political gender gap reflects a broader struggle for equality. While women are still underrepresented in elected positions and high-ranking party leadership, they have wielded considerable influence behind the scenes. Some of the most effective lobbyists at the Mississippi Capitol are women, proving that power isn't always tied to elected office.

Efforts to challenge this male-dominated landscape have gained traction. Organizations like Women for Progress are working to support and encourage women, particularly Black women, to run for office. Yet, the reasons behind Mississippi's low female representation remain debated. Is it tradition? A lack of support networks? A reluctance to run? Whatever the cause, one thing is clear: until more women step forward, the state's political power structure will remain overwhelmingly male.

An analysis of the percentage of legislators by race and gender presented in Figure 17.8 reveals significant racial and gender disparities in legislative representation. Black women legislators are severely underrepresented, with their numbers amounting to merely one-third of their Black male counterparts. This

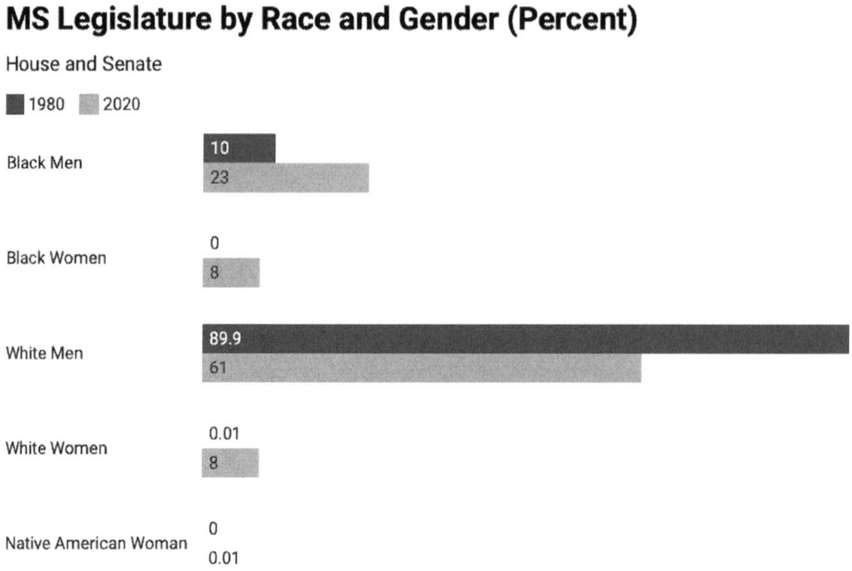

MS Legislature by Race and Gender (Percent)

House and Senate

■ 1980   ▨ 2020

Group	1980	2020
Black Men	10	23
Black Women	0	8
White Men	89.9	61
White Women	0.01	8
Native American Woman	0	0.01

Figure 17.8. Mississippi Legislature by Race and Gender

disparity is even more pronounced among White legislators, however, where men outnumber women by an astonishing factor of nearly eight to one.

The most dramatic change is the substantial decrease in White male representation, contrasted by a significant increase in Black male representation. This shift can be attributed to the historical overrepresentation of White males in the legislature. However, they are still overrepresented.

A notable milestone for women's representation occurred in 2018 when Governor Phil Bryant appointed Cindy Hyde-Smith to the US Senate, following Thad Cochran's health-related resignation. This appointment made Hyde-Smith the first woman to hold this office. She later won reelection for a full term in 2020. However, her campaign took a troubling turn when she remarked during a speech that "if [someone] invited me to a public hanging, I'd be on the front row." The comment drew intense criticism, especially given Mississippi's dark history of having the most lynchings in the nation during the late 1800s and early 1900s.

THE INTERSECTION OF RACE AND GENDER AND THE STRUGGLE FOR SUBSTANTIVE REPRESENTATION

Black women in Mississippi's state legislature have been some of the most progressive voices, championing policies that address racial, gender, and economic inequality. They have led efforts in education, healthcare, and labor rights, ensuring marginalized communities are not left behind. Yet, despite their impact, their numbers are still disproportionately low.

Black women in politics face a unique struggle, confronting both racial and gender discrimination. They are often excluded by men because of their gender and overlooked by White women because of their race. In 1985, Alyce Griffin Clarke made history as the first Black woman elected to the Mississippi state legislature, yet she was still treated as an outsider. She recalled how a newly elected White female legislator was immediately given a key to the women's restroom on the House floor—an unspoken privilege Clarke was never offered. Instead, she had to walk upstairs to the second floor to use a restroom, a quiet but clear reminder of the barriers she still faced in a space where she belonged.

Beyond representation, Black women lawmakers often struggle to pass legislation due to their progressive stance. Many of the policies advocate extending social programs, increasing wages, and strengthening civil rights protections—face resistance from more conservative legislators, making it difficult to turn their proposals into law.

One example highlights this challenge. At the Mississippi powerlifting state championship, a Black student was forced to remove beads from her hair before competing, reigniting demands for laws against hair discrimination. In response, Representative Zakiya Summers, and her colleagues, introduced the CROWN Act (Creating a Respectful and Open World for Natural Hair) to ensure individuals could not be penalized for wearing their natural hair. Despite its straightforward purpose, the bill did not pass, illustrating the ongoing resistance Black women lawmakers face in their fight for equality.

Figure 17.9. Alyce Griffin Clarke

Although Black women are underrepresented in the legislature, there is a notable instance of them wielding significant influence. This occurred during the 2008 election for Speaker of the House. The incumbent Speaker faced strong opposition from a staunch conservative, sparking concerns among Black lawmakers that their progressive agenda would be blocked. In a pivotal moment, Representative Linda Coleman, a Black woman who had initially backed the conservative candidate, switched her vote to break a tie, ultimately casting the deciding vote in favor of the Speaker. Though an isolated incident, it highlights the potential for even small acts of influence to shape pivotal outcomes.

Recommended Readings

Frank R. Parker, *Black Votes Count: Political Empowerment in Mississippi after 1965* (Chapel Hill: University of North Carolina Press, 1990).

CHAPTER 18

THE GREAT DIVIDE

Mississippi's Journey from Democrats to Republicans

THE END OF ONE-PARTY POLITICS: MISSISSIPPI'S BIG CHANGE

FOR NEARLY A CENTURY, MISSISSIPPI OPERATED AS A ONE-PARTY STATE, WITH the Democratic Party maintaining almost complete control over its political landscape. In other words, only candidates from one political party won elections. From around 1876 onward, Democratic candidates often ran unopposed, and the party's dominance was deeply intertwined with the state's resistance to civil rights advancements. When national Democratic leaders began advocating for reforms like anti-lynching laws, many Mississippi Democrats pushed back fiercely. In 1948, this resistance reached a boiling point when Mississippi Democrats staged a walkout at the Democratic National Convention and threw their support behind the States' Rights Democratic Party, commonly known as the "Dixiecrats." This White supremacist faction nominated Strom Thurmond for president, with Mississippi Governor Fielding Wright as his running mate, signaling the state's staunch opposition to civil rights progress.

The 1960s brought even more dramatic changes. In 1964, the Mississippi Freedom Democratic Party (MFDP) challenged the all-White Democratic Party for excluding Black members. Although the MFDP did not succeed in replacing the regular delegation, their efforts marked a turning point. By the 1968 and 1972 Democratic conventions, interracial delegations from Mississippi were seated under the banner of the Loyalist Democratic Party, a stark contrast to the 1964 convention, which had upheld segregationist politics by recognizing the all-White Regular Democrats.

However, these shifts within the Democratic Party alienated many White Democrats, who began to abandon the party in droves. In 1964, Republican Barry Goldwater capitalized on this discontent by campaigning on "states' rights"—a term historically linked to resistance against federal intervention in matters like slavery and segregation. Goldwater explicitly targeted White voters, stating, "We're not going to get the Negro vote as a bloc in 1964, so we ought to go hunting where the ducks are." His strategy paid off, as he won an overwhelming 87 percent of the vote in Mississippi.

The 1968 election showed just how divided Mississippi's political environment had become. Many White Democrats backed George Wallace, the segregationist former governor of Alabama, who ran as an independent. Meanwhile, the official Democratic candidate mostly got votes from the Loyalist faction, a biracial group. These results made it clear that conservative politics and the legacy of segregation still had a strong hold on the state.

In 1967, all six candidates running for the Democratic nomination for governor spoke to the White Citizens' Councils and openly supported segregation. But by 1971, things were starting to change. Four of those candidates no longer publicly supported segregation, and the two who still did receive very few votes. It seemed that many White voters, especially those with children in desegregated schools, no longer believed segregation was the "best way of life." By 1975 and 1979, none of the major candidates for governor were willing to publicly support segregation anymore.

By the 1970s, Mississippi's political scene was shifting in a big way. The state began moving away from being a Democratic stronghold and toward a more competitive two-party system where Republicans began to win some offices. This shift occurred primarily for two reasons: a significant number of established Democratic politicians began defecting to the Republican Party, while a growing wave of new politicians chose to launch their careers as Republicans. This marked the start of a new era in Mississippi politics, one where the old one-party dominance was fading, and political competition was on the rise.

The days of unchallenged Democratic control were over, and the state entered a period of significant political realignment.

COUNTING THE DAYS: THE SHIFT IN MISSISSIPPI POLITICS

The momentum from the 1964 and 1968 bolting of the White Democrats continued into 1972, when President Richard Nixon secured nearly 80 percent of Mississippi's vote—his highest margin in any state. That same year, Republicans began to make significant gains in local and state offices, solidifying their position as a formidable political force rather than a marginal presence.

During this period, Mississippi's political landscape was divided into three primary factions:

1. Regular Democrats, the traditional powerholders who were gradually losing their influence.
2. Loyalist Democrats, a biracial coalition gaining traction in select counties.
3. Republicans, the emerging contenders, are rapidly expanding their base.

Faced with declining support, the Regular and Loyalist Democrats attempted to unite in a bid to preserve their relevance. They merged into a single Democratic Party and selected two cochairs to represent their combined interests: Aaron Henry, a prominent Black civil rights leader, and Tom Riddell, a White politician who had previously opposed the Loyalists.

While they did come together to support Jimmy Carter's bid for the presidency in 1976, the tide was turning. The Republican Party's momentum was undeniable, and Mississippi's political future was poised for a profound shift. The era of Democratic dominance was coming to an end, marking the beginning of a new chapter in the state's political history.

DEMOCRATS HOLD THE GOVERNOR'S MANSION

Republicans did not nominate a candidate for governor in 1971, partly because Charles Evers, the Black mayor of Fayette and a prominent civil rights activist, ran as an independent. Here, race trumped political party, as Whites did not take any risks of splitting the White vote. It also may have been the case that the Republicans could not recruit a competitive candidate. They lined up behind Regular Democrat William Waller. Running as the first African American for governor since Reconstruction, Evers's campaign received national attention, but Waller captured 77 percent of the votes.

In 1975, Batesville attorney Cliff Finch was elected governor after a populist campaign against then–Lieutenant Governor William Winter, who had gone into the race as the frontrunner. Winter, who had previously aligned himself as a Jim Eastland and John Stennis Democrat supporting segregation, did not invoke that stance during this election. Finch positioned himself as a friend of the working man. Although never charged or convicted of any crime, he spent much of his administration fending off state investigations into allegations of mismanagement and corruption.

The 1979 governor's race featured a significant milestone in Mississippi politics when Evelyn Gandy, who had made history four years earlier as the state's first female lieutenant governor, launched a strong campaign for governor. While Gandy initially led in the Democratic primary against former Lieutenant Governor William Winter, she ultimately lost to him in the runoff election. Winter then defeated Republican challenger Gil Carmichael in the general election. Winter, with his experience in the state legislature during the 1950s and 1960s, had skillfully navigated racial issues, maintaining Black voter support.

CHAPTER 18.

THE REPUBLICAN COMEBACK: MISSISSIPPI'S POLITICAL REALIGNMENT

In the mid-twentieth century, Wirt Yerger played an important role in revitalizing the Republican Party. Appointed as the state's first modern Republican chairman in 1956, he was a key figure behind the election of Republican Prentiss Walker to the US House of Representatives in 1964.

The 1972 US House of Representatives race signaled a pivotal change in the state's political dynamics. Thad Cochran, running as a Republican, faced off against Ellis Bodron, an experienced Democratic state legislator. The race took an unexpected turn when Charles Evers, embroiled in personal disagreements with Bodron, threw his support behind Ernest McBride, a Black candidate running as an independent.

McBride's candidacy resonated strongly with Black voters, who constituted a significant electoral force in Mississippi's Fourth district. This overwhelming support from Black voters effectively split the vote that likely would have gone to the Democratic candidate. As a result, Cochran emerged victorious.

In the same election cycle, fellow Republican Trent Lott secured a House seat. These dual Republican victories were not isolated incidents but rather indicative of a broader shift. They signaled the beginning of a trend where Republicans were increasingly finding success in Mississippi's federal elections. Cochran's political ascent continued in 1978 when he won the Senate seat vacated by longtime Senator James Eastland.

Despite these Republican gains in national politics, Democrats maintained control at the state level. Winter, for example, was elected governor. While Winter had gained solid support from the Black electorate, one of his first major decisions as governor proved controversial. Since 1976, the state's Democratic Party had traditionally used a biracial leadership model with both White and Black cochairs. Winter, worried about increasing White support for Republicans, proposed a single party chair and recommended a White individual. Black political leaders, however, were not supportive of this decision, one that would later prove costly for the Democrats.

The controversy surrounding Winter's approach revealed the fragility of the biracial Democratic coalition, which ultimately proved short-lived. This vulnerability was starkly exposed during the 1978 Senate race after Senator Eastland's retirement. The election laid bare the enduring racial and ideological divides within Mississippi's electorate, underscoring the challenges of maintaining unity in a deeply polarized political environment.

Charles Evers, entered the race as an independent candidate. Evers's campaign drew significant support from former Loyalist Democrats, particularly Black voters. This development effectively split the Democratic vote, creating an opportunity for the Republican candidate.

Taking advantage of this division, Republican Thad Cochran secured a decisive victory over the White Democratic candidate. Cochran's election was historically significant, as he became Mississippi's first Republican senator since Reconstruction. Notably, the last Republican to hold a Senate seat from Mississippi was Blanche K. Bruce, an African American who served from 1875 to 1881.

Cochran's victory was a turning point in Mississippi's political history. It showed how the Republican Party was gaining strength in the state, while the Democratic Party struggled to keep its diverse coalition together across racial lines. This election was a sign of things to come, as the GOP (Grand Ole Party/Republicans) began to rise as the dominant force in Mississippi politics.

The years between 1964 and 1978 were a time of major change in Mississippi. The Republican Party was on the rise, the Democratic Party was dealing with internal divisions, and racial and regional issues were shaping how people voted. While the 1976 presidential election showed that Democrats could still attract support from both Black and White voters, the 1978 Senate race revealed the deep tensions and splits within the party. This period set the stage for a gradual but steady shift of White voters toward the Republican Party, a trend that would define Mississippi's politics for decades to come.

The political scene got even more complicated during a 1980 congressional election. Republican incumbent Jon Hinson was caught up in a scandal involving alleged homosexual activities in Washington, DC. While this might have helped the Democrats win, an independent candidate named Leslie McLemore drew enough Black voters away from the Democratic candidate to allow Hinson to win reelection with just 39 percent of the vote. This election, along with the fallout from Governor Winter's controversial leadership proposal, showed that Black voters were willing to break from the Democratic Party to pursue their own political interests.

These events marked a broader shift in Mississippi's politics, as the state moved from Democratic to Republican control, especially at the national level. They also highlighted the complicated relationship between race, party loyalty, and voter behavior in Mississippi.

White Mississippi voters, like White voters across the country, became dissatisfied with Carter's presidency. They found Ronald Reagan's conservative message more appealing. Reagan's campaign strategy focused on winning over not just urban and suburban voters but also rural communities, helping him gain strong support in Mississippi and beyond.

ECHOES OF THE PAST: REAGAN'S SPEECH AND THE RISE OF THE GOP IN THE SOUTH

In 1980, Ronald Reagan's presidential campaign made a strategic stop at the Neshoba County Fair in Philadelphia, Mississippi, on August 3. While the fair was a popular spot for political speeches, the location carried heavy historical significance. It was in Neshoba County that three civil rights workers—James Chaney, Andrew Goodman, and Michael Schwerner—were murdered in 1964 during the Freedom Summer movement.

At this symbolic location, Reagan pulled a page out of Barry Goldwater's book and used the phrase "states' rights" in his speech—a term that had long been tied to opposition against federal civil rights laws and racial integration. For many, this phrase was a coded way of appealing to White voters who resisted federal intervention in state matters, especially on issues of race.

Reagan's decision to speak in Neshoba County and his use of this loaded language were seen as a deliberate move to win over White conservative voters in the South. This approach was part of what political experts call the "Southern Strategy," which used carefully chosen language and locations to attract White voters without explicitly using racist rhetoric. To no surprise, Reagan carried the state, solidifying the Republican Party's growing influence in Mississippi.

Reagan's presidency, along with Thad Cochran's earlier Senate victory, marked a major shift in Mississippi's politics. Cochran, who had been elected to the Senate in 1978, became a key figure in this transformation. While he was a conservative, Cochran was viewed as more moderate than many of his Republican colleagues. He gained a reputation for "bringing home the bacon," a phrase referencing his skill in securing federal funding for Mississippi. This included critical support for Hurricane Katrina recovery efforts, military installations, and Historically Black Colleges and Universities (HBCUs). Cochran also played a key role in funding the Jackson Medical Mall, a once-dilapidated shopping mall located in the heart of the majority Black capital. This facility was transformed into a crucial healthcare center, providing essential services to a large segment of poor patients.

These efforts helped Cochran win some support from Black voters during his 2014 reelection campaign—a rare achievement for a Republican in Mississippi. While this crossover support was limited to that election, it proved crucial in his narrow victory over Tea Party challenger Chris McDaniel. Some Black voters may have seen McDaniel's rhetoric, including his stance on keeping the state flag and other conservative views, as a threat.

Meanwhile, Trent Lott, another Mississippi Republican, had been elected to the Senate and was steadily climbing the ranks of its leadership. Lott became minority whip and later majority leader, the most powerful position in the US Senate. However, his career faced a major setback in 2002 when he made controversial remarks about the late Strom Thurmond, a noted segregationist and former Dixiecrat presidential candidate. Lott stated, "When Strom Thurmond ran for president, we voted for him. We're proud of it. And if the rest of the country had followed our lead, we wouldn't have had all these problems over all these years, either." These comments were widely interpreted as endorsing Thurmond's segregationist views, sparking accusations of racism and significant backlash. Lott ultimately resigned his leadership position, but his career remained a reminder of the complicated racial history that continued to shape Mississippi's politics.

While Cochran and Lott's careers highlighted the evolving dynamics of Mississippi's political landscape, another twist came in November 2007. Just one year after being reelected, Lott unexpectedly announced his resignation from the Senate. Around the same time, a federal grand jury indicted Richard "Dickie" Scruggs, a high-profile lawyer and Lott's brother-in-law, on charges of attempted bribery. In one case, Scruggs was accused of receiving privileged information to help him win an asbestos lawsuit that earned him millions in legal fees. In exchange, the indictment alleged, Scruggs had promised to help secure a federal judgeship for the person who provided the information. This scandal added another layer of complexity to Mississippi's political story, showing how personal connections and legal controversies could intersect with the state's broader political narrative.

THE DOMINO EFFECT: REPUBLICAN NATIONAL VICTORIES AND STATE-LEVEL CHANGES

Republicans continued to make significant progress in Mississippi politics. In 1991, Kirk Fordice made history by becoming the first Republican elected as governor since Reconstruction. Thanks to a 1987 amendment to the state

Figure 18.1. Kirk Fordice.

Figure 18.2. Haley Barbour. Photo by Gage Skidmore, licensed under CC BY-SA 3.0. https://creativecommons.org/licenses/by-sa/3.0/deed.en.

constitution, he was also the first governor in over a century to serve two consecutive four-year terms. Fordice ran on a strongly conservative platform, focusing on "family values," opposition to affirmative action, and a deep connection to conservative Christian ideals. His stance on issues like abortion earned him strong support from Christian voters. At the same time, Democratic incumbent Ray Mabus struggled to gain traction, partly because he failed to pass an education package—a key part of his platform. This combination of factors helped Fordice secure a victory, marking a major shift in Mississippi's political direction.

Fordice's victory came during a time when more and more Democratic politicians were switching to the Republican Party. This trend gained even more momentum in 2003 when Haley Barbour, a former chairman of the Republican National Committee, won the race for governor. Barbour's election solidified Republican dominance in Mississippi, but his leadership would soon face one of the state's greatest challenges: recovering from the devastation of Hurricane Katrina in 2005.

When Hurricane Katrina devastated Mississippi, Barbour leveraged his political expertise and connections to secure substantial federal funding for the state's recovery efforts. He worked closely with President George W. Bush's administration, Senator Thad Cochran, and other members of Congress to bring much-needed resources to the state. This effort is widely seen as one of the biggest achievements of his time as governor, helping to rebuild communities that had been torn apart by the hurricane. Barbour's ability to navigate the complex world of Washington, DC, and deliver for Mississippi earned him widespread praise.

Meanwhile, Republicans continued to strengthen their hold on the state. By 2011, they had gained control of both the state House and Senate for the first time

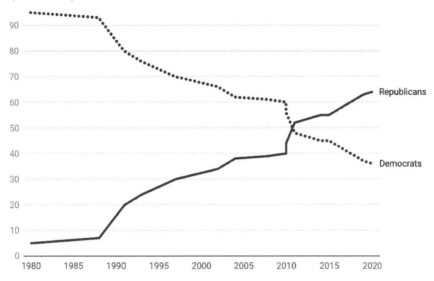

Figure 18.3. 1 percent House party.

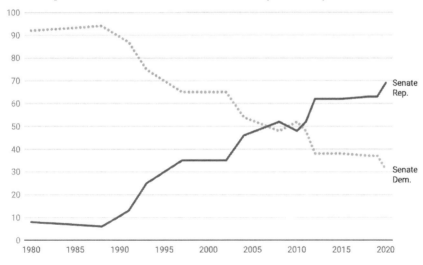

Figure 18.4. 2 percent Senate party.

in over a century. Legislative changes in the state's House and Senate are illustrated in Figures 18.3 and 18.4. This marked the beginning of Mississippi becoming a one-party state again—but this time, with Republicans in charge. With control of both the executive and legislative branches, the state experienced what political experts call *realignment*, a major shift in its political identity.

By 2025, Mississippi's legislature was deeply divided along racial lines. In the House of Representatives, only 3 percent of Democrats were White, and in the state Senate, White Democrats made up just 4 percent of their party. On the Republican side, nearly every lawmaker was White, with only one exception. This clear divide highlighted the growing racial polarization in the state's politics, showing how race and party loyalty were increasingly shaping Mississippi's future.

NARROWING THE GAP: MISSISSIPPI'S FUTURE POLITICAL LANDSCAPE

While Republicans dominate Mississippi's national elections—as seen in Trump's commanding 61-38 percent victory over Harris in 2024—the story at the state level has become far more dramatic. Gone are the days of predictable Republican landslides. The 2020 Senate race showed the first signs of change when Hyde-Smith faced a strong challenge from Espy, who garnered 46 percent of the vote. In the governor's races, Tate Reeves barely secured victory in 2019 with 52 percent of the vote to Jim Hood's 47 percent. The 2023 race proved even tighter, with Reeves clinging to a slim 50.9 percent win over Brandon Presley's 47.7 percent, while Independent Gwendolyn Gray captured 1.4 percent. That razor-thin margin of 26,619 votes signals a shifting political landscape where Democrats, though still underdogs in this Republican stronghold, are mounting increasingly competitive challenges for state offices.

In sum, Mississippi's political landscape has undergone a dramatic shift, evolving from a one-party Democratic state to a one-party Republican state. This transformation has been deeply influenced by cultural issues like race and religion, with the Republican Party gaining dominance as the Democratic Party has become increasingly associated with Black voters. Today, the political divide in Mississippi largely falls along racial lines: the majority of Black voters align with the Democratic Party, while the majority of White voters support the Republican Party. This dynamic has created a system where, at least at the state and federal levels, Whites consistently win and Blacks consistently lose, resulting in a pattern of permanent winners and permanent losers.

Despite these challenges, Democrats may have a glimmer of hope based on the last few statewide elections, which have shown signs of growing competitiveness. These developments suggest that the state's political future may not be as firmly entrenched as it once seemed.

For now, though, the state's political system remains a stark reflection of its racial divides, with power concentrated in the hands of the Republican Party and Black voters struggling to achieve proportional influence.

Recommended Readings

Lee Annis. *Big Jim Eastland: The Godfather of Mississippi*. Jackson: University Press of Mississippi, 2016

Haley Barbour with Jere Nash. *America's Great Storm: Leading through Hurricane Katrina*. Jackson: University Press of Mississippi, 2015

Charles C. Bolton *William F. Winter and the New Mississippi: A Biography*. Jackson: University Press of Mississippi, 2013

Westley F. Busbee, Jr., *Mississippi A History* 2nd Edition. (Oxford: Wiley Blackwell Press, 2015)

Will D. Campbell and Richard C. Godfrey. *Robert G. Clark's Journey to the House: A Black Politician's Story*. Jackson: University Press of Mississippi, 2003

Joseph Crespino, *In Search of Another Country: Mississippi and the Conservative Counterrevolution* (Princeton: Princeton University Press, 2007)

Charles W Eagles. *Civil Rights, Culture Wars: The Fight Over a Mississippi Textbook*. Chapel Hill: University of North Carolina Press, 2017

Alexander P. Lamis, ed., *Southern Politics in the 1990s* (Baton Rouge: Louisiana State University Press, 1999)

Trent Lott. *Herding Cats: A Life in Politics*. New York: HarperCollins, 2005

Marable, Manning. *Race, Reform, and Rebellion: The Second Reconstruction and Beyond in Black America, 1945-2006*. 3rd ed. Jackson: University Press of Mississippi, 2007

Minor, Bill. *Eyes on Mississippi: A Fifty-Year Chronicle of Change*. Jackson: J Prichard Morris Books, 2001

Dennis J. Mitchell, *Mississippi: A New History* (Jackson: University Press of Mississippi, 2014)

William Mounger. *Amidst the Fray: My Life in Politics, Business, and the Military*. Jackson: University Press of Mississippi, 2016

Jere Nash and Andy Taggart. *Mississippi Politics: The Struggle for Power, 1976-2006* (Jackson: University Press of Mississippi, 2006)

Melany Neilson. *Even Mississippi*. Tuscaloosa: University of Alabama Press, 1989

Frank R. Parker, *Black Votes Count: Political Empowerment in Mississippi after 1965* (Chapel Hill: University of North Carolina Press, 1990).

Joseph B. Parker (editor) *Politics in Mississippi*, second edition (Salem: Shefield Publishing Company, 2005)

Brian A. Pugh. *Chaos and Compromise: The Evolution of the Budgeting Process* (Jackson: University Press of Mississippi, 2020)

William L. Waller. *Straight Ahead: The Memoirs of a Mississippi Governor*. Brandon, MS: Quail Ridge Press, 2007

Wirt A. Yerger, III. *A Courageous Cause: A Personal Story of Modern Republicanism's Birth from 1956 to 1966*. Jackson, MS: Pediment Publishing, 2010

CHAPTER 19

FROM COTTON TO CASINOS

Mississippi's Economic Shifts Through History

BOOM TO BUST: THE FALL OF KING COTTON

DURING WORLD WAR I, COTTON FARMING WAS BOOMING IN MISSISSIPPI. PRICES soared, and farmers hoped to make a dollar per pound in 1919. But as soon as the war ended, everything crashed.

Cotton prices dropped fast—falling from 38.5 cents per pound to just 9.8 cents in one year. By 1931, the price had sunk to just 6.16 cents per pound, leaving farmers struggling to make a living. At the same time, cotton production dropped sharply, from over a million bales to just 604,000 by 1923.

For farming families, times were tough. In 1923, even a "good year" meant a family working 10 acres of cotton made just $302—before paying for seeds, fertilizer, or extra help. That wasn't nearly enough to survive, and as the 1920s rolled into the 1930s, things only got worse. By the time the Great Depression hit, many Mississippi farmers had already lost everything.

THE NEW MISSISSIPPI

The post–World War II era marked a period of profound transformation for Mississippi. By 1980, cotton—once the backbone of Mississippi's economy and way of life—had lost its crown. The agricultural world shifted dramatically as farmers embraced mechanization, moving away from manual labor and diversifying into a variety of crops and livestock.

This shift triggered the great migration from rural areas. Thousands of Mississippians migrated to growing industrial centers within the state or sought employment opportunities beyond its borders. The magnitude of this change was so significant that it could aptly be termed an "economic revolution."

CHANGES IN AGRICULTURE

After World War II, Mississippi farming changed in big ways. Farmers faced tough problems: worn-out soil, boll weevils eating their cotton, low cotton prices, and new government rules. They couldn't rely on cotton anymore, so they started growing different crops like soybeans, corn, wheat, and rice. Many also began raising cattle, hogs, and chickens. Except for the Delta region, most parts of Mississippi stopped being cotton country and became ranching country instead.

Mississippi farmers also found new ways to sell their products. Instead of just selling locally, they started sending their goods across the country. One success story was Adams Egg Farms in Edwards. This farm grew so big it became the world's largest egg producer at one point, showing that Mississippi farmers could compete with anyone in the world.

Moore's Circle M Ranch in Senatobia specialized in breeding and supplying purebred cattle, establishing a global reputation and contributing to the improvement of cattle herds worldwide. The ranch's success highlighted Mississippi's expertise in livestock breeding and its influence on international agricultural practices.

This agricultural revolution was driven by several factors, with labor shortages being a primary spark. The labor crisis began during World War II, as wartime demands drew workers to urban centers in the Midwest and Pacific regions. This trend continued after the war, with agricultural workers attracted to other regions and cities both within and outside the South. Higher wages and better access to public services in urban areas fueled this migration, reshaping Mississippi's farming practices and rural demographics.

FARM MECHANIZATION

Dating back to 1945, farmers used more and more machines to plant and harvest their crops and care for their livestock. The first tractors had been brought into the state during the 1920s. Following World War II, Mississippi farmers began to buy them in large numbers. By 1950, there were five times as many tractors in the state as in 1940.

In the early 1950s, farmers introduced the mechanical cotton picker. The early machines were not very effective, but later machines could pick twenty times the amount one laborer could pick in one day. In the mid-1960s, the job of "chopping" cotton was tackled through the use of chemical weed killers, sprayed from tractors or airplanes.

With the end of chopping and picking on the cotton farms, sharecropping was dead. Plantation owners replaced man and mule power with much more efficient machine power. The displaced sharecroppers and small farmers had to move to cities in and outside the state to find work.

At the same time, telephones and electricity were transforming Mississippi's rural life. Before World War II, many farms had been relatively isolated and enjoyed few modern conveniences. But after the war the picture changed. From 1945 to 1950, the Tennessee Valley Authority, the Mississippi Power and Light Company, the Mississippi Power Company, and the Rural Electrification Administration nearly tripled the number of farms with electricity. This meant better living standards, including the adoption of refrigerators, freezers, and washing machines. It also meant the introduction of radio and television, which connected farm families to urban America.

EASTLAND'S DOUBLE STANDARD: OPPOSING AID WHILE PROFITING FROM SUBSIDIES

Senator James Eastland, opposed programs like Head Start, food stamps, Medicare, and anti-poverty initiatives that would have helped poor Mississippians, especially African Americans. Yet, he skillfully manipulated farm subsidies for personal gain. By 1969, his $3 million fortune included nearly $170,000 in federal subsidies just for limiting cotton production—part of the $6.8 million paid to Sunflower County farmers in 1968. When Congress capped subsidy payments at $55,000, he divided his plantation among family members to continue receiving massive payouts.

As Eastland found ways to keep government money flowing to his plantation, Fannie Lou Hamer launched a bold experiment to help poor farmers escape such dependency. She had a vision: Black farmers working their own land, free from White control. In 1969, she turned this dream into reality with the Freedom Farm Cooperative, using money from Wisconsin supporters to buy forty acres in the Delta. Farmers would work together and live off what they grew. She even started creative projects like a pig-sharing program to help families get started. But when the money dried up, so did this brave experiment in independence.

The huge disparity between Eastland's operation and small Black-owned farms revealed how federal agricultural policies primarily benefited wealthy landowners who could navigate the system. While Eastland used his position to circumvent restrictions he helped create as a senator, smaller farms lacking political connections and financial resources struggled to survive.

DECLINE OF THE FAMILY FARM

Between 1950 and 1974, Mississippi's agricultural sector underwent a dramatic shift. United States Department of Agriculture data show that the number of farms plummeted from 251,383 to 53,620. Despite this decrease, farm income from crops, livestock, and government subsidies nearly doubled, with large-scale operations reaping most of the benefits. The trend continued, with farm numbers further declining to 42,150 by 1997 and 31,290 in 2022.

Farm sizes grew substantially during this period. In 1945, the average farm was seventy-four acres, but by 1987, this had increased to 315 acres, indicating widespread consolidation of agricultural land.

This agricultural transformation had a disproportionate impact on Black farmers. In 1964, Mississippi had 37,715 Black farmers and 109,145 White farmers. By 2022, these numbers had dramatically decreased to 4,312 Black farmers and 26,771 White farmers. The steeper decline in Black-owned farms can be partially attributed to historical discrimination, including practices such as the USDA's denial of loans to Black farmers.

BLACK FARMERS FIGHT BACK

After being shortchanged by the government, Black farmers sought justice through a national class-action lawsuit (*Pigford v. Glickman*) in response to decades of discrimination. While the suit resulted in a significant settlement, individual farmers received an average of only $50,000—a sum far below the value of their land losses. Recognizing the inadequacy of this compensation, further efforts to address the injustice continued. As a result, in 2024, a new initiative emerged using COVID-19 Stimulus Package funds. This program aimed to provide additional aid to 23,000 Black farmers in Alabama and Mississippi, with payments ranging from $10,000 to $500,000 based on the extent of discrimination faced. This more recent attempt at restitution seeks to more adequately address the historical and ongoing economic impact of discriminatory practices on Black farmers in the region.

Despite these challenges to Black farmers, agriculture as a whole continued to thrive in Mississippi, though in new and different forms.

BEYOND KING COTTON:
MISSISSIPPI'S DIVERSE AGRICULTURAL EMPIRE

While the number of farms has declined, agriculture remains Mississippi's economic powerhouse, generating $8.24 billion annually and employing 17.4 percent of the state's workforce as of 2024. The state's agricultural landscape is surprisingly diverse: chickens, not cotton, now rule the roost, with poultry bringing in over $3.1 billion. The waters are just as productive—Mississippi leads the nation in farm-raised catfish sales at $230.7 million, while its coastal waters yield everything from shrimp to red snapper.

The legendary Delta soil still proves its worth. In 2018, 824 cotton farms produced 1.48 million bales worth $623 million, while corn brought in $351 million and cattle added another $305 million. Drive through the Pine Belt, and you'll see the state's other green giant—a forestry industry that in 2010 produced 900 million board feet of logs and 5 million cords of pulpwood, putting $403,000 in local landowners' pockets.

Even Christmas trees tell a story of adaptation. From a 1985 peak of 450 farms producing 330,000 trees, the industry has shifted to 170 choose-and-cut farms serving local markets. Perhaps most remarkable is Vardaman, the "Sweet Potato Capital of the World." Named for a White supremacist governor, the town has transformed into a multicultural success story where Hispanic (32.7 percent), Black (26 percent), and White (39.4 percent) residents work together in its thriving sweet potato industry—a living example of how Mississippi's agricultural communities can grow beyond their troubled past.

DELTA WATERS: MISSISSIPPI'S CATFISH INDUSTRY

As Mississippi agriculture diversified, catfish farming emerged as a major industry, especially in the Delta region. By 2024, the state led the nation in catfish production, with 34,100 acres of ponds converted from former farmland. Belzoni, which calls itself the 'Catfish Capital of the World,' became the center of processing operations, with companies like Freshwater Farms leading the way. Other major processors, including Delta Pride, America's Catch, Simmons Catfish, and Heartland Catfish, established significant operations throughout the region. However, rising feed costs, competition from foreign imports, and flat fish prices put pressure on the industry, causing a decline in pond acreage.

FROM RICE FIELDS TO CATFISH PONDS

Ed Scott Jr. expanded on his father's legacy in Sunflower County, Mississippi, where Ed Scott Sr. had amassed 1,900 acres as one of the state's first rice farmers in the 1940s. As markets for traditional crops like cotton and soybeans declined, Scott Jr. turned to catfish farming, becoming the first African American to own and operate a catfish farm. Facing declining markets for traditional crops like cotton and soybeans, Scott Jr. transitioned to catfish farming. Despite discriminatory loan denials from the Farmers Home Administration, he eventually secured financing and established the Leflore-Bolivar Catfish Processing Plant and Scott's Fresh Catfish, becoming the only African American catfish processor in the industry.

Despite initial success, Scott faced coordinated opposition from larger processors and continued discrimination in federal lending. When financial pressures forced him out of farming, he pivoted to processing, then to a successful catering business that earned him national recognition. After losing his land to foreclosure, Scott joined the *Pigford v. Glickman* class action lawsuit against the USDA for discriminatory lending practices. The successful settlement enabled him to reclaim 900 acres of his family's land.

THE LABOR MOVEMENT IN MISSISSIPPI

As Mississippi's economy grew, its workers struggled for fair treatment. Labor unions—organizations where workers unite to demand better pay, safer conditions, and benefits like healthcare—faced major obstacles in Mississippi. The state's "right-to-work" laws weakened these unions, allowing companies to offer lower wages and fewer benefits. Some businesses even moved to Mississippi specifically to avoid unions.

Labor organizing came late to Mississippi. The Knights of Labor arrived in 1883, welcoming all workers regardless of race or skill, but faded by 1904. The American Federation of Labor took its place nationally but found little success in the South. Even when the Mississippi Federation of Labor formed in 1918, it excluded unskilled and Black workers.

The biggest union battles happened in transportation and timber. Railroad workers struck in McComb in 1911, facing violence and martial law before losing to Illinois Central Railroad. Lumber workers also tried to organize, but mill owners cleverly pitted Black and White workers against each other. The turpentine industry was especially harsh—some workers were held under armed guard.

After World War II, unions briefly gained strength when the Congress of Industrial Organizations (CIO) reached 50,000 members by 1950. But Mississippi's push for industrialization, which relied on low wages to attract factories, weakened union power. Though unions and civil rights leaders attempted to work together, this alliance never gained enough strength to protect Mississippi's workers.

Figure 19.1. The Gulfcoast Pulpwood Association won a 1971 strike at Masonite Corporation in Laurel. Ken Lawrence collection, Eberly Family Special Collections Library, University Libraries, Pennsylvania State University.

MISSISSIPPI'S CONTINUED ECONOMIC PROBLEMS

In 1975, the median family household income was $14,268 for Whites and $8,779 for Blacks. One-third of the families in the state had incomes below $6,000. There were not enough jobs, particularly high-paying jobs, to meet the needs of Mississippi's population.

Many of the industries that came to Mississippi were in low-paying fields such as lumber, clothing, and paper. Therefore, the average wage paid to Mississippi's industrial workers was much lower than the national average. The state needed more high-skilled, high-wage jobs, and was not attracting them quickly enough.

Low levels of education were a key reason. An uneducated worker was usually able to find only a low-paying, unskilled job. In 1970, Mississippi was the only state in the nation without a compulsory school-attendance law. Decades of an economy reliant on low-wage farmworkers and of a consistent refusal not to invest in the education of its citizens meant that, even in 1970, 40 percent of the state's adults had less than a ninth-grade education.

INDUSTRY COMES TO MISSISSIPPI

As far back as the Great Depression, state leaders realized that Mississippi must develop more manufacturing jobs to raise incomes. The Balance Agriculture with Industry (BAWI) program encouraged towns all over the state to finance industrial construction through bonds. In a short time, BAWI plants accounted for one-quarter of Mississippi's total industrial payroll.

The Ingalls Shipbuilding Corporation at Pascagoula became the most significant success of this early program. During World War II, Ingalls constructed all-welded ships for the nation's merchant marine. Afterward, Ingalls built luxury liners, cargo ships, and atomic submarines. By the late 1950s, it had become the state's largest single manufacturer.

In 1944, the legislature passed a stronger BAWI act with five-year tax exemptions to attract new industries. The Mississippi Agricultural and Industrial (A&I) Board was created to run the program. The A&I Board's main job was to conduct research and distribute publicity so that positive facts about Mississippi could be used to encourage out-of-state firms to invest in Mississippi and expand the state's economy.

In the 1970s, probably the most important state agency working to improve the economy was the Research and Development (R&D) Center, located in Jackson. R&D staff members developed studies of possible markets, labor supplies, natural resources, and transportation. They encouraged industries to come to Mississippi and help existing businesses expand.

Figure 19.2. This Litton shipyard used a then-new assembly-line technique of shipbuilding. Courtesy of the Archives and Records Services Division, Mississippi Department of Archives and History.

MILITARY-INDUSTRIAL JOBS

One result of the R&D work was the $130,000,000 "Shipyard of the Future" at Pascagoula. The state-financed project was leased to Litton Ship Systems.

The National Aeronautics and Space Administration (NASA) opened its Mississippi Test Facility (MTF) in 1966. Located in Hancock County, the MTF tested the huge Saturn V engines for America's moon rockets. In 1970, it was converted into an Earth Resources Laboratory to work on problems of ecology.

At Vicksburg, the Army Corps of Engineers ran a Waterways Experiment Station. Engineers built models of the Mississippi River and other rivers and harbors throughout the world. They could then study in miniature the problems of erosion, pollution, and flooding. In the 1970s, the station also tested helicopter landing pads and other military hardware.

The jobs created by military and space spending proved to be a double-edged sword. The Ingalls shipyard experienced recurring cycles of employment fluctuation over several decades, as various Naval contract decisions made in Washington affected the workforce. These periodic shifts between hiring booms and layoffs created economic instability in local communities. Despite these challenges, some facilities demonstrated remarkable resilience. The NASA Stennis Space Center, for instance, weathered the uncertainties of government funding and in 2021 marked its nineteenth year of continuous operation in Mississippi.

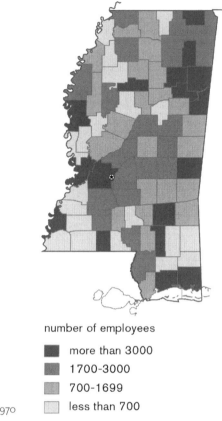

Map 33. Manufacturing, 1970

number of employees
- more than 3000
- 1700-3000
- 700-1699
- less than 700

INDUSTRY AND SOCIETY

Mississippi's economic development is closely intertwined with its social and cultural progress. The state's industrial growth has often been shaped by factors such as race relations, education, and cultural development. In the early 1970s, this relationship was particularly evident in Jackson, where, for example, the decision of a major corporation to locate a manufacturing plant in the area was influenced by concerns about the impact of school integration on the local community.

At the time, the Allis-Chalmers Corporation was considering placing a large manufacturing plant in Jackson. However, the company's managers were worried that White residents might choose to abandon the public schools as desegregation took place, potentially leading to social and educational disruptions that could impact the local workforce and business environment. This highlights the complex interplay between economic development, social progress, and cultural factors in Mississippi's history.

The economic growth of Jackson, which was driven in part by the decision of companies like Allis Chalmers to locate near the city, underscores the importance of investing in public education and infrastructure to attract businesses and support long-term economic development.

From the Gulf Coast to the Tennessee line, Mississippians were developing new industries and agencies to supply new jobs. Baxter Laboratories in Cleveland, a maker of drugs and hospital products, was one example. The Herschede Hall Clock Company in Starkville was another, but it closed in the 1980s. Insurance companies were a major source of employment in the 1970s, but by 2024 only the Farm Bureau remained.

THE CHANGING FACE OF MISSISSIPPI INDUSTRY 1980–2024

Mississippi has undergone significant economic changes since 1980. NASA, Ingalls Shipyard, and Chevron remained strong contributors to the workforce and economy. Relativity Space is a company aiming to be the first to launch a 3D-printed rocket into orbit. The company located operations at Stennis Space Center in Hancock County Mississippi in 2018. This $282 million expansion was projected to create 630 new full-time jobs with an average salary of $87,470. Ingalls is one of the largest manufacturing employers in the state, employing over 10,000 people.

Mississippi is recognized for its furniture manufacturing industry, especially in the northern region. Tupelo, Mississippi, is often referred to as the "Furniture Capital of the World" due to its hosting one of the largest furniture markets in the United States. However, according to the Bureau of Labor Statistics, manufacturing jobs in general have declined, dropping from 25 percent in 1990 to around 12 percent by 2024. Meanwhile, the service economy has experienced significant growth. Today, the largest employment sectors in the state include government, K–12 education, restaurants and food services, health care, and agriculture. Poultry processing facilities operated by major corporations like Tyson and Sanderson Farms have long been a significant presence in Mississippi's economic landscape.

Other companies include Howard Industries, which specializes in electrical products such as transformers and employs roughly 5,343 people. Peavey Electronics is highly known for its guitar amplifiers and has roughly 2,400 employees. International Paper Company, one of the leading companies in paper products, has a high presence across the state.

ECONOMIC DIVERSIFICATION AND GROWTH

While agriculture has remained central to the state's economy, Mississippi has made significant strides in technology. Cities like Jackson saw an influx of tech startups and information technology (IT) firms. Companies like C Spire in Ridgeland emerged as key players, offering tech solutions on a national scale. This technological growth was accompanied by a commitment to renewable energy, with solar farms being established in places like Tunica County during the 2010s and wind energy projects appearing along the Gulf Coast.

CORPORATE SCANDAL AND ECONOMIC CRISIS

Mississippi's economy rode a roller coaster in the early 2000s. The good news came when car makers moved in—Nissan built a plant in Canton and Toyota in Blue Springs. However, trouble hit in 2002 when Clinton-based WorldCom crashed after its CEO Bernard Ebbers was caught hiding $11 billion in fake assets, landing him in prison.

The 2008 financial crisis hit Mississippi hard. The state lost 38,000 jobs, with factories taking the biggest hit. Help came through President Obama's American Recovery and Reinvestment Act (ARRA), which sent $2.8 billion to Mississippi—including $479 million for schools and $779 million for Medicaid.

The Mississippi Development Authority (MDA) worked to bring new business to the state through tax breaks and other incentives. Their efforts paid off: Continental Tires and Milwaukee Tools opened new facilities. Then came even bigger investments: Amazon Web Services committed $10 billion to Madison County for 1,000 tech jobs, Aluminum Dynamics announced a $2.5 billion project, and a new $1.9 billion battery plant promised 2,000 high-paying jobs making parts for electric cars.

Not everything was smooth sailing—when Nissan workers tried to form a union in 2017, the company fought back hard. But Mississippi's growing Port of Gulfport helped create more diverse jobs by expanding trade with Central America, showing how the state's economy keeps finding new ways forward.

GROWTH AND GAPS: MISSISSIPPI'S ECONOMIC DIVIDE

Mississippi hit a record in 2024: unemployment dropped to just 2.8 percent. But this good news came with a catch—the state still had the nation's lowest average salaries and only about half of working-age people had jobs. Why? Many residents lack advanced education, the state has limited money for programs, and a high prison population struggles to find work due to their records.

The state is trying to fix these problems through community colleges and better infrastructure. In 2024, lawmakers gave Madison County money to improve roads, water, and sewer systems to support Amazon Web Services' $10 billion investment in two new data centers.

But this growth isn't reaching everyone. While mostly White suburbs like Madison, Ridgeland, and Flowood attract new businesses, Jackson—the state capital with an 80 percent Black population—has seen little of this prosperity. The city still has some industry, like the Eaton Aerospace plant, but struggles to grow. Now Jackson is in court fighting to keep control of its Medgar Evers International Airport, along with valuable nearby land for development.

INDUSTRY AND ECONOMIC DEVELOPMENT

Mississippi's economy has evolved significantly through targeted industrial development across different regions of the state. Strategic investment in infrastructure, workforce development, and business incentives has helped attract diverse industries, from distribution centers to advanced manufacturing. Yet this growth has been uneven, with some areas prospering while others face persistent economic challenges.

DISTRIBUTION CENTERS

The Mississippi Official and Statistical Register Blue Book highlights the state's success in attracting various industries between 2012 and 2016, including distribution centers, automotive, alternative energy, aviation, and aerospace facilities.

Olive Branch emerged as a key location for distribution centers, starting with the FedEx Ground facility. The city also became home to several healthcare-related distribution centers, including those of McKesson Corporation (the world's largest pharmaceutical company), Cardinal Health, and Anda Distribution. Amazon has established a distribution center in Olive Branch, while Hamilton Beach relocated its distribution operations from Memphis to the same area. Southaven has also seen growth in the distribution sector, with significant investments from Kimberly-Clark and WPG Americas, totaling $2 million and $1.5 million, respectively.

AEROSPACE INDUSTRY

Tupelo and Columbus are emerging as key hubs for innovation and manufacturing. Tupelo is home to General Atomics while Columbus has Aurora Flight Sciences, now a Boeing company. Companies in these areas benefit from a strategic location and access to robust transportation networks, including the Golden Triangle Regional Airport.

In the aerospace industry, Columbus attracted three major facilities to its GTR Global Industrial Aerospace Park. These include Stark Aerospace (a subsidiary of Israel's IAI North America), which manufactures tactical unmanned aerial systems used in US military operations, as well as Aurora Flight Sciences and

American Eurocopter. Mississippi's largest employer in this area is Northrop Grumman. Batesville has GE Aviation, which manufactures advanced composite components for jet engines and aircraft systems. It is the largest producer of jet engines for commercial and military aircraft.

ENERGY SECTOR DEVELOPMENTS

Pascagoula has made significant strides in the oil and gas industry. The city invested $1.4 billion in an oil facility capable of producing 25,000 barrels daily. Additionally, Gulf LNG Energy established a $1.1 billion liquefied natural gas storage facility. Natural gas storage extends to salt domes utilized by D'Lo Gas Storage of Louisiana.

Mississippi has also embraced renewable energy solutions. The Mississippi Technology Alliance reports that the state hosts over fifty biomass-related projects, thirty-two solar initiatives, and eighty-two energy efficiency endeavors.

In the solar energy sector, Hattiesburg attracted Stion, a San Jose–based company, manufacturing solar panels. Stion is projected to create 1,000 jobs and anticipates annual profits of $500 million. Similarly, Twin Creeks Technology opened a solar panel manufacturing facility in Senatobia, further bolstering the state's green energy portfolio.

LEGALIZED GAMBLING

In 2023, the World Population Review ranked Mississippi as the most conservative state in the country, with half of its respondents identifying as conservative. This political leaning is characterized by support for small government and a commitment to preserving traditional Christian conceptions of morality.

Mississippi's approach to gambling illustrates the state's ability to adapt its conservative stance when faced with economic opportunities. In the 1950s, illegal gambling in bars and supper clubs was shut down following a government investigation. However, in 1987, a creative attempt to circumvent state laws emerged with the "Europa Star" offering "cruises to nowhere" for gambling in federal waters, though this was short-lived due to legal issues.

A turning point came with the Mississippi Gaming Control Act, which legalized dockside casinos along the Mississippi River and Gulf Coast. This decision, seemingly at odds with traditional conservative values, proved economically significant. The first Gulf Coast casinos opened in 1992, quickly becoming a lucrative industry. By the 2003 fiscal year, Mississippi collected over $329 million in gaming revenues, with local governments receiving an additional $109 million. By 2020, the state's annual gaming revenue had reached approximately $1.8 billion.

In the aftermath of Hurricane Katrina, the legislature further adapted by allowing casinos to be built on land, aiming to stimulate coastal economic recovery. This decision, while controversial, demonstrated Mississippi's willingness to prioritize economic benefits over strict adherence to conservative ideologies.

After Mississippi legalized dockside casinos in 1990, the Mississippi Band of Choctaw Indians was able to open a casino on their tribal land near Philadelphia.

TUNICA COUNTY'S ECONOMIC TRANSFORMATION: CASINO IMPACT AND PERSISTENT CHALLENGES

The transformation of Tunica County—a predominantly Black Delta region historically dependent on enslaved labor—offers insights into the impact and limitations of targeted economic development. The arrival of casinos dramatically reduced unemployment from 13 percent in 1990 to less than 4 percent in 2024, while poverty rates fell from 56.8 percent to 31.4 percent over the same period.

The casino industry's influence is further reflected in food stamp usage, which dropped from 53.8 percent in 1991 to 24.2 percent by 1997, though it later rose to 33 percent by 2024 as the number of casinos decreased from nine to four. This pattern challenges assumptions about government assistance dependency in Black communities, demonstrating that when meaningful employment opportunities arise, people eagerly pursue them.

However, despite these improvements, Tunica's still-high poverty rate reveals the challenges of overcoming deeply rooted economic disparities through single-industry development, highlighting the need for more diverse and sustainable economic strategies in historically marginalized communities.

THE LOTTERY

During the middle 1800s, Mississippi granted contracts to private organizations to run a statewide lottery. When Mississippi rewrote its constitution following the end of the Civil War, the state prohibited gambling and the lottery. The state was sued. However, in 1879, in *Stone v. Mississippi*, the US Supreme Court upheld the state's provision. The Court's decision was based on the principle that a state's police powers extend to moral issues, including gambling and lotteries.

A significant change came in 2018 when the state legalized a state lottery, though this development came with its own complexities. The path to lottery legislation was long. Former governor Ray Mabus had first proposed it during his 1988–1992 administration, but the idea failed to gain support. The eventual passage in 2018 largely resulted from Representative Alyce G. Clarke's persistent efforts, as she introduced lottery legislation repeatedly despite numerous defeats.

While this marked a notable shift in Mississippi's revenue generation approach, the lottery's implementation raised important equity concerns, as such programs typically place a disproportionate financial burden on lower-income residents who are more likely to participate.

This legislation stipulated that up to $80 million from the lottery proceeds would be allocated to the State Highway Fund. Any funds exceeding this $80 million threshold were designated for Mississippi's Education Enhancement Fund. Additionally, the state legalized sports betting, further expanding its gambling industry.

TOURISM

Mississippi's tourism has become a vital economic force, built on the state's rich history, culture, and natural beauty. The state features interconnected thematic trails, notably the Mississippi Blues Trail and Freedom Trail, which guide visitors through significant musical and civil rights sites through informative markers at historical locations.

The Museum of Mississippi History and the Mississippi Civil Rights Museum —ranked as the nation's fourth best museum by USA Today—anchor Jackson's cultural offerings. Across the state, visitors can explore the B. B. King Museum, Grammy Museum Mississippi, Black Prairie Blues Museum, the Back in the Day Museum in the Baptist Town community in Greenwood, Museum of the Mississippi Delta, Mississippi Agriculture and Forestry Museum, Old Capitol, Mississippi Sports Hall of Fame, Natchez Museum of African-American History and Culture, and the Frank Gehry-designed Ohr-O'Keefe Museum in Biloxi. Jackson also features the Smith Robertson Museum and Cultural Center, Children's Museum, Museum of Natural Science, Museum of Muslim Cultures, and the Jackson Planetarium. Vicksburg National Military Park preserves a crucial Civil War battlefield, while Meridian's MAX (Mississippi Arts + Entertainment Experience) combines live performances with a hall of fame celebrating state culture.

Jackson State University hosts two significant cultural institutions: the COFO Civil Rights Education Center and the Margaret Walker Alexander Center, both dedicated to preserving Mississippi's civil rights history and cultural heritage.

CELEBRATING MISSISSIPPI: A STATE OF FESTIVALS

Mississippi's festivals showcase the state's rich culture in many ways. The historic Neshoba County Fair doubles as a major political stage during election seasons.

The state celebrates its diverse heritage through events like the Choctaw Indian Festival and the Mississippi Book Festival. Music festivals dominate the calendar, especially those honoring the blues: Clarksdale's Red's Old Timers Blues Festival, the Juke Joint Festival, Greenville's Delta Blues and Heritage Festival, and the B. B. King Homecoming in Indianola. Beyond blues, there's the Tupelo Elvis Festival and Madison's Township Jazz Festival.

Food takes center stage at many celebrations: the Mississippi State Fair draws crowds statewide, while Belzoni's World Catfish Festival celebrates its title as "Catfish Capital of the World." Other food festivals include the Blueberry Jubilee, Slugburger Festival, Jxn Food and Wine Festival, Gulf Coast Beer, Bacon and BBQ Festival, and the Delta Hot Tamale Festival.

The Canton Flea Market, held twice yearly, attracts thousands seeking arts, crafts, and antiques, while events like the Double Decker Arts Festival in Oxford and the Farish Street Festival in Jackson blend music, food, and local culture.

Recommended Readings

Sharon D. Wright Austin, *The Transformation of Plantation Politics: Black Politics, Concentrated Poverty, and Social Capital in the Mississippi Delta* (Albany: State University of New York Press, 2006).

Mary D. Coleman, *Land, Promise, and Peril* (New York: Cambridge University Press, 2023).

Gerard Helferich, *High Cotton: Four Seasons in Mississippi Delta* (Jackson: University Press of Mississippi, 2017).

Joseph B. Parker, *Politics in Mississippi*, 2nd ed. (Salem, MS: Sheffield Publishing Company, 2001).

Brian A. Pugh, *Chaos and Compromise* (Jackson: University Press of Mississippi, 2020).

Julian Rankin, *Catfish Dream: Ed Scott's Fight for His Family Farm and Racial Justice in the Mississippi Delta* (Athens: University of Georgia Press, 2018).

Clyde Woods, *Development Arrested: The Blues and Plantation Power in the Mississippi Delta* (New York: Verso Books, 2017).

Gavin Wright, *Sharing the Prize: The Economics of the Civil Rights Revolution in the American South* (Cambridge, MA: Harvard University Press, 2013).

CHAPTER 20

CELEBRATING ACHIEVEMENTS IN FOLKLORE, ART, MUSIC, LITERATURE, JOURNALISM, AND SPORTS

DUE TO THE STATE'S POLITICAL AND ECONOMIC DEVELOPMENT AFTER SLAVERY, most Mississippians were poor during the first four decades of the twentieth century. Public schools were scarce; industry was even scarcer. Tuberculosis and other diseases struck down men and women in their prime. Mothers died in childbirth because good health care was both limited and hard to access, especially for African Americans excluded from the state's few hospitals. But even though their situation often seemed hopeless, the people did not give up.

From dire conditions, Mississippians managed to create a strong tradition of folklore, music, and literature. Some told stories, others wrote novels, showing the bravery and misery, the happiness and the hope, of those around them. Even a sharecropper without money was able to find musical instruments and compose songs—songs that did not cause the singer to forget his poverty, but helped him live through it. Mississippi's tradition of creativity in folklore, music, and literature shows what William Faulkner meant when he said in his Nobel Prize speech, "I believe that man will not merely endure; he will prevail."

FOLKLORE

Folklore includes beliefs, myths, riddles, recipes, ways of making things, folk songs, tales, and superstitions. One of the great collectors of Mississippi folklore, Arthur P. Hudson, once gave a series of lectures entitled "Folklore Keeps the

Past Alive." He asserts that folk songs, folktales, and other items of folklore are formed by history. They show the influence of the past. Thus, folklore is one of the past's gifts to the present.

Among the folklore traditions passed down from generation to generation are family recipes. Historically, a young girl did not use cookbooks; she learned how to cook from her mother or grandmother. And her recipes, which she kept in her head, were passed on to her children. Often, these recipes were different from the detailed measures and directions found in cookbooks.

Beaten Biscuits

The following recipe has been served for many years in Mississippi homes. There are two versions here: the first provides a recipe as handed down over the years, while the second is a modern version.

Original version
Mix: 1 quart of flour, lard the size of a hen's egg, and one dessert spoonful of salt. Make into a fairly stiff dough with as much sweet milk as needed. Beat with a mallet for half an hour. Roll sections of the dough in your hand to shape. Stick with a fork and bake in a hot oven. (At least one Mississippi home had a backyard tree stump that was used only for beating the biscuit dough!)

Version in 1970
Mix: 4 cups flour, ¼ cup lard, and 1 teaspoon of salt. Add 1½ cups of milk, beating slowly with electric mixer until dough is moderately stiff. Put it through a meat grinder twelve times. Roll out to ½-inch thickness on wax paper. Cut with a biscuit cutter. Place biscuits, just touching, on ungreased cookie sheet. Pierce each biscuit with a fork and bake at 350° for 30 minutes.

Version in 2024
Baking biscuits from scratch is no longer necessary in today's world, as people can easily make them from a can or buy them from a fast-food restaurant.

Church Singing

Singing is also part of folklore. Sacred Harp singing was named after an early hymnbook and still survives in northeast Mississippi. Other traditions of religious music are also important in Mississippi. Especially in rural areas, congregations met for all-day singing events. In other churches, hymns were an important part of Sunday morning services. William Alexander Percy, a son of a prominent planter and Greenville poet, was raised in this tradition of hymn singing. Later he wrote lyrics for the hymn "The Fisherman of Galilee," which was sung in many Protestant churches throughout the world.

CHAPTER 20.

CHURCH SINGING IN YOUR COMMUNITY

Visit two or three different kinds of churches in your area, and notice the different ways they sing hymns. If you can, visit a rural church and an urban church.

SPIRITUALS

The roots of Black religious music in Mississippi can be traced back to the era of slavery, when enslaved Blacks brought their own religious songs and musical traditions to America. However, the experience of slavery led to the development of new forms of religious music, such as spirituals, that drew on both African and American influences.

Spirituals emerged as a distinct form of religious expression among enslaved Blacks in the American South, combining elements of African musical traditions with the hardships and struggles of life under slavery. These songs served as a source of comfort and hope, and their enduring popularity has made them an important part of the broader American musical tradition. The evolution of Black religious music in Mississippi reflects the complex interplay between African and American cultural influences, and its significance extends far beyond the era of slavery.

According to writer Anthony Heilbut: "During the Great Awakening that spread from New England to Kentucky, millions of pioneers shouted, danced, barked, and jerked. Enslaved Blacks attended these services and were profoundly influenced. They combined the revival hymns of eighteenth-century England with an African song style and created our greatest national music." Spirituals spoke of Jesus and Heaven, and they related the hope of a better life to the hopeless conditions of the singers under slavery. Spirituals such as "Wade in the Water" contained encoded messages instructing runaway slaves on how to avoid capture, and in some instances they even served as a form of resistance to slavery. "Sometimes I Feel Like a Motherless Child," for example, came from Mississippi, and its words expressed enslaved Blacks' feeling that their family had been broken up by slavery and that nobody really cared for them.

GOSPEL MUSIC

After Emancipation, the tradition of religious music among Black Mississippians did not die out. By the 1920s and 1930s, what is now called gospel music had developed. Like spirituals, gospel music reflects the hard times of the people who sing it and tells of their hope for a better future.

CELEBRATING FOLKLORE, ART, MUSIC, LITERATURE, JOURNALISM, AND SPORTS 365

Figure 20.1. The steeple of First Presbyterian Church in Port Gibson is a Mississippi landmark. Photographs in the Ben May Charitable Trust Collection of Mississippi Photographs in the Carol M. Highsmith Archive, Library of Congress, Prints and Photographs Division, LC-DIG-highsm-46910.

There is also a strong tradition of gospel singing in White churches in Mississippi. By now, the origins of gospel songs are so mixed that it is hard to tell where "Black" influence begins and "White" enters in. "Amazing Grace," sung by both White and Black groups, is by an Englishman, John Newton. "There'll Be Peace in the Valley for Me," a favorite of White groups, is by the Black gospel singer T. A. Dorsey, who also wrote the famous hymn "Precious Lord, Take My Hand."

The Southern gospel genre was significantly shaped by several influential groups and artists from Mississippi. The Blackwood Brothers, a distinguished gospel group from Choctaw County, were known for their soulful renditions of gospel classics and tight harmonies, setting a high standard in the genre. This tradition was carried forward by the Five Blind Boys of Mississippi, another influential group based in Piney Woods. As the twentieth century progressed, Jackson became the birthplace of a new wave of gospel music with the emergence of the Mississippi Mass Choir. Under the leadership of Frank Williams of the Williams Brothers, the choir became one of the most influential gospel groups of the 1980s and 1990s, earning three Grammy Awards. Among individual artists, James Blackwood stood out. As a member of the renowned Blackwood Brothers quartet, he is regarded as one of southern gospel's finest tenors. The influence on southern gospel was not limited to these artists; groups such as the Jackson Southernaires also made significant contributions to the genre.

Gospel music's influence extended across multiple genres, with Willie Mae Ford serving as one of the genre's earliest and most influential pioneers. Following in this rich tradition, the Staple Singers emerged as transformative artists. Led by Roebuck "Pop" Staples and his daughter Mavis, the family group began their musical journey in gospel's sacred traditions. Over time, their distinctive sound evolved to embrace soul, R&B, blues, funk, and pop, while maintaining the spiritual depth of their gospel roots, demonstrating how gospel's influence continued to shape American popular music. Annie Mae McDowell sang gospel and was accompanied by her husband, the great blues artist Fred McDowell.

WORK SONGS

While religious singing was certainly an important part of the musical tradition in Mississippi, it was not the only form of music-making that took place in the state. The tradition of work songs, which originated in West Africa and was brought to Mississippi by enslaved Blacks, also played a significant role in the state's musical heritage.

These work songs, which were sung by groups of laborers as they worked on tasks such as building levees or straightening railroad tracks, typically involved a call-and-response pattern between the foreman and the workers. The songs

Figure 20.2. John A. Lomax preserved many examples of Mississippi folk songs. Library of Congress, Prints and Photographs Division, LC-USZ6-2229.

served not only as a means of entertainment and social cohesion but also as a way to coordinate the workers' movements and increase their productivity.

The work song tradition continued well into the twentieth century, and its impact on the state's musical heritage can still be felt in contemporary genres such as blues, gospel, and country music. Pioneering folklorist John A. Lomax recorded a version of this work song from a crew that was lining track:

> LEADER: If I could I surely would. Stand on the rock where Moses stood.
> CHORUS: Ho, boys, can't ya' line 'em?
> Ho, boys, can't ya' line 'em?
> Ho, boys, can't ya' line 'em?
> See Eloise go lining track!
> LEADER: Old Moses stood on the Red Sea shore; Smote the water with a two-by-four
> CHORUS: Ho, boys, can't ya' line 'em? (etc.)

PRISON SONGS

Parchman State Farm, the sprawling cotton plantation that is the site of Mississippi's state penitentiary, has been the scene and the source of many prison work songs and blues. The song "Midnight Special" is well known throughout America in both blues and rock music:

Figure 20.3. Early morning work at Parchman. Special Collections, University of Mississippi Libraries.

Here comes your woman, a pardon in her hand,
Gonna say to the warden, "I want my man."
Let the Midnight Special shine her light on me.
Oh let the Midnight Special shine her everlovin' light on me!

The song is about Parchman. In earlier years, visiting day for families and friends at Parchman was the fifth Sunday of the month. Since most months have only four Sundays, visiting day came only two or three times each year. On each visiting day, the Yazoo and Mississippi Valley (which became the Illinois Central and then the Canadian National) would run a special train, the "Midnight Special," which left Jackson at midnight and arrived at the penitentiary near dawn. Prisoners at Parchman created the myth that if a prisoner, working in the fields at dawn, was caught in the glare of the Special's headlight, he would be the next man/woman up for parole.

MINSTREL SHOWS

In the early twentieth century, particularly around World War I, minstrel shows became a significant part of Mississippi's musical landscape. These traveling troupes, often moving from town to town by bus or private train, performed a diverse repertoire including jazz, ragtime, blues, and even classical music.

The minstrel show format, however, was deeply problematic. White performers often performed in "blackface," a racist practice of darkening their skin to portray caricatured Black characters. This perpetuated harmful stereotypes and appropriated Black culture for White entertainment.

One of the most notable minstrel groups, the Rabbit Foot Minstrels, was based in Port Gibson from 1918 to 1950. This troupe featured several performers who would go on to become influential figures in American music, including Rufus Thomas, Ma Rainey, Ida Cox, and Louis Jordan.

Despite their popularity, minstrel shows began to decline as other forms of entertainment emerged. The rise of television in the 1950s largely contributed to their demise, with the last few shows touring Mississippi until around 1959.

MISSISSIPPI BLUES

The blues emerged from the harsh realities of post-Reconstruction Mississippi, where sharecropping trapped many Black families in cycles of debt and poverty. The Dockery plantation, often hailed as the blues' birthplace, played a crucial role in this musical evolution.

Charlie Patton, a key figure in Delta blues, honed his craft under Henry Sloan's mentorship. Patton's 1929 recording "Pony Blues" exemplified his innovative style, blending raw emotion with sophisticated guitar techniques. His influence rippled through the genre, directly shaping Howlin' Wolf's (Chester Arthur Burnett) powerful vocals and stage presence. While not Patton's direct student, Robert Johnson absorbed and reimagined his approach through recordings and live performances, contributing to Johnson's own legendary status.

H. C. Speir, a talent scout based in Jackson, Mississippi, played a pivotal role in bringing Delta blues to a wider audience. His recordings of artists like Charlie Patton, Eddie "Son" House, and Robert Johnson helped preserve and popularize this emerging musical form.

Blues themes reflected daily life, incorporating work songs, prison experiences, and personal struggles. W. C. Handy's "Yellow Dog Blues" and other songs about travel gained popularity. In the 1920s and 1930s, record companies began recording Mississippi blues singers, leading to national fame for some.

Patton's impact, along with other Mississippi blues artists, fundamentally shaped the sound of Delta blues and American music, becoming, as Jim O'Neil of *Living Blues* magazine stated, "the single most important root source of modern popular music."

"BIG BILL"

William Lee Conley Broonzy was born in Scott, Mississippi, on June 26, 1893, into a family with twenty other children. He farmed in Mississippi and Arkansas, and then served in the Army in World War I. After the war, he found the South's segregation unbearable. Later, he wrote a famous song about it:

> If you're White, you're all right.
> If you're brown, stick around.
> But if you're Black, get back! Get back! Get back!

He went north to Chicago in 1920. At first he worked as a redcap with the railroads. But he worked continuously on his music, and by the age of thirty-four his first recording was released by Paramount Records. After more years of hard work, his records began to sell and he performed in nightclubs and concert halls.

After World War II, however, he seemed to be forgotten. For a while he worked as a janitor at Iowa State College. But then new audiences discovered his records and he played to sold-out crowds in Paris and London on a world tour.

In the summer of 1958, he released what would become his final recording, *The Big Bill Broonzy Story*, which covers five records of singing, playing, and talking. The morning after the last recording session, he was operated on for lung cancer. And on the morning of August 14, as an ambulance rushed him back to the hospital, he died.

Figure 20.4. Big Bill Broonzy

But his life was not a tragedy. He left behind a golden treasure of friendships and recordings. As he wrote of himself in his autobiography: "When you write about me, please don't say that I'm a musician or a guitar player—just write Big Bill was a well-known blues singer and player and has recorded 200 blues songs from 1925 up till 1952; he was liked by all the blues singers; some would even get a little jealous sometimes, but Bill would buy a bottle of whiskey and they would all start laughing and playing again. . . ."

THE DIVERSITY OF THE BLUES

Mississippi's blues legacy is woven by an extraordinary array of talented artists, reflecting both Delta and hill country styles. The state has produced some of the most influential figures in blues history, including Robert Johnson, John Lee Hooker, B. B. King, Muddy Waters, Howlin' Wolf, and many others, each contributing significantly to shaping the genre and influencing generations of artists. Robert Johnson, born in Hazlehurst in 1911, stands as a towering figure in blues lore, his life shrouded in mystery and legend. B. B. King rose from humble Mississippi beginnings to become a global ambassador for the blues, his distinctive style inspiring countless musicians across various genres.

Mississippi's cultural influence extends beyond natives to include adopted sons and daughters who became part of the state's artistic "diaspora." Blues and R&B legend Bobby Rush, for example, exemplifies this pattern—though born in Louisiana, he made Mississippi his home and has performed well into his nineties, making him the oldest active blues artist as of 2025.

Women have also played a crucial role in shaping the blues landscape, with figures like Bessie Smith, Zora Young, Mississippi Matilda (Matilda Witherspoon) Mamie "Galore" Davis, Koko Taylor, Lucille Spann, Denise LaSalle, and Memphis Minnie leaving indelible marks on the genre.

The state's blues scene also includes unique styles, such as the fife and drum blues championed by Otha Turner and his Rising Star Fife and Drum Band, blending African rhythms with American blues. Other notable Mississippi blues figures include Fred McDowell, Little Milton (James Milton Campbell Jr.), Robert Petway, Hayes McMullan, Big Jack Johnson, Nehemiah "Skip James" Curtis James, R. L. Boyce, R. L. Burnside, Jimmy Reed, Otis Spann, Willie Dixon, David "Honeyboy" Edwards, and Magic Slim (Morris Holt), while Grammy winner James Cotton, recognized on the Mississippi Blues Trail and inducted into the Rhythm and Blues Music Hall of Fame, further highlight the state's significant contributions to blues music. This rich diversity of artists and styles underscores Mississippi's enduring importance in the world of blues, showcasing a legacy that continues to influence and inspire musicians worldwide.

BESSIE SMITH: THE BLUES EMPRESS WHO DEFIED JIM CROW

Bessie Smith was another artist who was not born in Mississippi, but was a part of the Mississippi diaspora. She transformed American music and broke racial barriers in the 1920s with her powerful voice and emotional depth. Her 1923 recording of "Downhearted Blues" sold 780,000 copies in six months, launching her to national fame. The success of her record sales and touring allowed her to command up to $2,000 per week, making her one of the highest-paid Black entertainers of her era. Between 1923 and 1931, she recorded over 160 songs for Columbia Records, her powerful voice and emotional depth crossing racial and social boundaries.

Smith challenged Jim Crow conventions, managing her own finances and touring in her custom-built railroad car. She famously confronted the Ku Klux Klan when they attempted to disrupt her show, embodying artistic and personal courage in an era of intense racial oppression.

Her death on Highway 61 near Clarksdale, Mississippi, in 1937, generated controversy that persists to this day. While initial reports, including John Hammond's account in *Down Beat* magazine, claimed her arm had been severed in a car accident and she was denied treatment at a Whites-only hospital, biographer Chris Albertson's research conclusively showed she was taken directly to G. T. Thomas Afro-American Hospital, where she received care but died from severe injuries sustained in the crash. Though the hospital rejection story proved inaccurate, its widespread acceptance reflected the very real healthcare discrimination African Americans routinely faced during the Jim Crow era. Smith's legacy endures as a testament to both artistic triumph and the complex realities of race in America.

THE DELTA BLUES GO NORTH

When Black Mississippians moved north after World Wars I and II, they took the blues with them. Writer Robert V. Weinstein described the result: "As the Black man changed his lifestyle, moving from the fields to the towns and finally to the big cities, his music also changed." Electric instruments came in, and the bass guitar was added. Larger groups often replaced the solo performer.

The northward migration of blues musicians included several notable figures. Big Bill Broonzy was among the first to make the journey to Chicago. He was soon joined by Sonny Boy Williamson (Rice Miller), who introduced his distinctive harmonica style to the city. Charlie Musselwhite, a rare White performer on the blues circuit, also arrived with his harmonica.

Muddy Waters, whose birth name was McKinley Morganfield, emerged as a pivotal figure among blues musicians who made the journey to Chicago. While living on the Stovall plantation in Coahoma County, he first mastered the harmonica but changed course after hearing "Son" House play, switching to guitar. During this time, he learned from fellow Stovall resident Henry "Son" Thomas. Upon reaching Chicago, Waters found a mentor in Broonzy, who helped launch his career by connecting him with Sylvio's, a prominent South Side venue.

Another significant blues musician who made the move to Chicago was Howlin' Wolf (Chester Burnett). In 1952, he joined Chess Records, where his career rapidly took off. His distinctive, forceful vocals and authentic Delta blues approach made him stand out among Chicago's many blues performers. Working with Willie Dixon's songwriting talents, he created enduring blues standards like "Smokestack Lightnin'" and "Spoonful."

Although Chicago became the new hub of the blues, its roots—and the birthplace of many legendary performers—remained in Mississippi. Before making their way to Chicago, many of these musicians honed their craft at venues such as those in "the Gold Coast, Cross the River." This area served as a thriving center for live music for decades, continuing its influence well into the 1960s.

KING OF THE BLUES

Born Riley B. King, B. B. King was born in Itta Bena, Mississippi, in 1925. His unique voice, combined with the melodies from his guitar named "Lucille," made him a musical icon. The story behind "Lucille" began in Arkansas during the 1950s. Two men fighting during one of his shows accidentally caused a fire by knocking over a kerosene heater. King courageously dashed back into the flames to rescue his guitar. He later found out the men's altercation was over a woman named Lucille. In her memory, and as a lesson about the dangers of foolish actions, he named his guitar "Lucille." Throughout his illustrious career, King's

Figure 20.5. B. B. King. Photo by Tom Beetz, licensed under CC BY 2.0, https://creativecommons.org/licenses/by/2.0/.

powerful songs like "The Thrill Is Gone" and "Every Day I Have the Blues" earned him numerous accolades, including fifteen Grammy awards.

BLUES TODAY

Mississippi's blues legacy continues to thrive through a new generation of artists who honor tradition while pushing the genre forward. Jesse Robinson, a veteran bluesman, exemplifies this enduring spirit. Once a fixture at the historic Subway Lounge in Jackson, along with King Edward Antoine (Edward (Antoine), Robinson's career spans decades and bridges the gap between classic and contemporary blues. In the small town of Bentonia, James "Duck" Holmes serves as both musician and guardian of the region's distinctive blues tradition. From behind the counter of the Blue Front Café—one of Mississippi's last authentic juke joints—Holmes not only performs the unique Bentonia-style blues but preserves a vital piece of musical history. The Blue Front stands as a living museum where the raw, haunting sounds of yesterday meet the energy of today's blues scene. Meanwhile, in Duck Hill, Little Willie Farmer carries forward the pure, unvarnished sound of traditional blues. His performances serve as a masterclass in authenticity, demonstrating how the genre's foundational elements remain powerful and relevant in the modern era.

The state's modern blues landscape is rich with talented performers who each bring their unique flair to the genre. Castro Coleman, better known by his stage name "Mr. Sipp," has earned the moniker "The Mississippi Blues Child" for his energetic performances that infuse traditional blues with a youthful vitality. His dynamic stage presence and virtuosic guitar playing have garnered him national attention and helped introduce the blues to younger audiences.

Carrying on a family legacy, Cedric Burnside continues the Hill Country blues tradition pioneered by his grandfather, the legendary R. L. Burnside. Cedric's music maintains the hypnotic, rhythmic style characteristic of North Mississippi blues while incorporating contemporary elements, earning him multiple Grammy nominations.

Artists like Eddie Cotton, Jr., Grady Champion, and Jarekus Singleton represent the evolving face of Mississippi blues. Champion, a harmonica virtuoso and skilled vocalist, blends traditional Delta blues with elements of soul and modern R&B. Singleton, on the other hand, brings a fresh perspective to the blues, incorporating influences from his background in rap and jazz to create a sound that's both innovative and deeply rooted in blues tradition.

Zac Harmon was nominated for a Grammy, and the Homemade Jamz Blues Band from Tupelo brings a young feel to blues. Christone "Kingfish" Ingram from Clarksdale is known for his guitar and singing. The Delta bluesman, James "Super Chikan" Johnson, is celebrated for his vibrant homemade guitars and his mastery of the diddley bow, a traditional one-string instrument with deep roots in the Mississippi Delta blues tradition, originating from West Africa. Additionally, Sir Charles Jones and T. K. Soul are modern "southern soul" blues singers. Eden Brent is a female artist whose music is often referred to as "Little Boogaloo" because of her energetic boogie woogie style.

This modern blues scene stands on the shoulders of a deeply rooted tradition. Historically, the heart of blues culture beat in juke joints—informal, often improvised clubs that served as crucial social hubs for African American communities, particularly in the rural South. These establishments, frequented by sharecroppers and laborers seeking respite after grueling workdays, provided more than just entertainment. They offered a safe space for cultural expression, social bonding, and the development of a distinctive musical style. Juke joints played an indispensable role in nurturing and spreading blues music. In these intimate, often crowded spaces, musicians honed their craft, exchanged ideas, and forged the raw, emotive sound that would come to define the genre. The direct connection between performers and their audience in these venues helped shape the call-and-response patterns and improvisational nature characteristic of the blues.

Though no longer open, several historic juke joints remain notable for the cultural legacy they represent. Among them is the Subway Lounge in Jackson, which by the mid-1990s had become a rare, integrated gathering spot, and Po Monkeys in Merigold, celebrated for its unique character and enduring place in juke joint history. Today, the tradition lives on in venues like Club Ebony in Indianola, the

Blue Front Café in Belzoni, and Morgan Freeman's Ground Zero in Clarksdale. Jackson's Hal and Mal's carries on the blues tradition with its Blue Monday open mic nights, while Red's in Clarksdale and Jackson's Queen of Hearts and Dick's Place remain essential stops on the Mississippi blues circuit.

Today's Mississippi blues artists, while often performing on more formal stages, carry forward the spirit of those juke joint pioneers. They maintain the genre's capacity for storytelling, emotional expression, and social commentary, adapting these elements to resonate with contemporary audiences. This continuity demonstrates the enduring power of the blues to evolve while remaining true to its roots, reflecting the ongoing narrative of the communities from which it springs.

SOUL AND RHYTHM AND BLUES

As blues migrated north to Chicago, it evolved from solo performances into band music, helping create rhythm and blues (R&B). From this musical foundation emerged soul pioneers like Clarksdale's Sam Cooke, who transformed his gospel background into pop stardom. The Red Tops lived segregation's stark reality—their music moved White audiences to dance, but when thirteen-year-old Andy Hardwick joined the band, he learned that Black musicians who created this joy still couldn't sit among those they entertained.

Mississippi's musical influence continued to grow. Whynot's David Ruffin powered the Temptations' classics like "My Girl," while Mary Wilson helped shape the Supremes. Jackson produced Dorothy Moore's soulful "Misty Blue" and sparked a funk revolution with bands like Sho-Nuff and Freedom. The state's rhythm and soul legacy extends through an array of artists like Natchez's Alexander O'Neal and McComb natives Brandy and Ray J Norwood. Mississippi's impressive roster also includes Chi-Lites founder Robert "Squirrel" Lester, Al Goodman of Ray, Goodman & Brown, McKinley Mitchell, Bobby V, Thelma Houston, Spinners founder G. C. Cameron, Jimmy Ruffin, Ike Turner, Rufus Thomas, the Chambers Brothers, Motown Funk Brothers member Eddie "Bongo" Brown, Michael Henderson, Margie Joseph, Jerry "The Iceman" Butler, Fern Kinney, former Supremes lead Velma Jean Terrell, Al Wilson, and Danny Pearson.

COUNTRY MUSIC

Country music, a vocal tradition that gained popularity particularly among White Mississippians, emerged in the wake of the blues. Both genres drew significant inspiration from sacred music. Early string bands, featuring banjos, guitars, and fiddles, often included both Black and White musicians, reflecting the genre's diverse roots.

The Mississippi Sheiks, a prominent multi-racial string band, left an indelible mark on the development of country music. Another influential group was the Leake County Revelers, who helped define the early sound of the genre.

The advent of radio in the 1920s and 1930s played a crucial role in expanding country music's audience. This new medium propelled the career of Jimmie Rodgers, now revered as the "Father of Country Music." Rodgers became the genre's first major recording star, helping to establish country music's commercial viability and cultural significance.

"My Time Ain't Long"

James "Jimmie" Rodgers was born in Meridian on September 8, 1897. He grew up around the freight yards where railroad men worked. At fourteen he got a job carrying water for the work gangs, and the Black workers taught him how to play the banjo and guitar and sing work songs and blues.

He kept his job on the railroad until Christmas 1923, when he found himself unemployed and penniless in New Orleans. He traveled by boxcar to Meridian, only to discover that his youngest daughter had passed away. The following year, he was diagnosed with tuberculosis, making railroad work untenable. He then performed in Tennessee as part of a minstrel show in blackface. Following that, he hosted a local radio show in North Carolina. Eventually, he achieved his major breakthrough.

Figure 20.6. This memorial in Meridian stands near the thing Jimmie Rodgers loved most—a steam locomotive. Courtesy of the Archives and Records Services Division, Mississippi Department of Archives and History.

Ralph Peer, a scout for Victor Records, had set up auditions in Bristol, Tennessee. Rodgers went to see him in 1927, and Peer liked what he heard. Gradually Jimmie's records started to sell, and during the Depression they reached millions of people. In her biography of Jimmie, his wife Carrie explained why: "The poverty-stricken, gripped by sickness and troubles almost more than they could endure, knew that here was a fellow who understood, who had 'been there.' Far, lonely cabins on Western plains, on the high ranges, knew that this boy knew them, too."

In 1933, he traveled to New York for a final recording session. He was so weak that Victor provided him a cot in the studio, and there he rested between numbers. Two days later, he died in his hotel room. His widow and many friends went to the station in Meridian to meet his funeral train. This is how she described the scene: "Then—like a part of the night itself, a low mellow train whistle. Not the usual whoo-whoo-oo, but a whistle that was not a whistle. A long continuous moaning that grew in volume as the train crept toward me along the silver rails." The train crew had remembered how Jimmie Rodgers loved train whistles.

He has not been forgotten. He was the first person to be honored in the Country Music Hall of Fame. His records are still popular all over the world. And his mixture of cowboy music and blues styles has lived on to influence folk singers and bluesmen as well as country music itself.

Another early country-music star was Rod Brasfield from Monroe County. Two of the best-known country singers, Charley Pride and Conway Twitty, were born within a few miles of each other in the Delta. Jimmy Buffett, while considered a country singer, blended elements of country, folk, and rock.

Tammy Wynette, born in Tremont, became an icon of the genre with her emotional delivery and hits like "Stand by Your Man." Faith Hill, hailing from Ridgeland, rose to stardom in the 1990s and 2000s with crossover hits such as "Breathe" and "This Kiss." Both artists have garnered numerous accolades, including multiple Grammy awards, cementing Mississippi's place in country music history.

The state's country legacy also includes Bobbie Gentry, a native of Greenwood, whose mysterious narrative song "Ode to Billie Joe" became a cultural phenomenon in 1967. Representing a more contemporary sound, Shelly Fairchild emerged in the mid-2000s, blending country with Southern rock influences.

Carl Jackson won Grammy Awards for his contributions to country and bluegrass music. Marty Stuart toured with Johnny Cash. Paul Overstreet, along with Jackson native LeAnn Rimes, made a mark in country music, with Rimes winning the Best Female Country Vocal.

Mississippi's country music scene continues to evolve and diversify. A notable recent addition is the African American trio Chapel Hart, composed of sisters Danica and Devynn Hart, along with their cousin Trea Swindle. Their emergence underscores the genre's expanding inclusivity and Mississippi's ongoing role in shaping the country music landscape.

Themes of Country Music

Like the blues, country music tells of the troubles and hopes of the people who sing and listen to it. Rodgers sang of poverty, of trains and "moving on," and of tuberculosis and other troubles. The audiences for country music and for blues are almost completely different—one mostly White, the other mostly Black—but the themes and elements of the musical traditions are very similar. Rodgers and Broonzy both knew this. Broonzy once wrote: "Of course, we know it ain't just Negroes that play and sing the blues, because there's some hillbillies and cowboys that sing the blues, too. They sing it their way, and we sing it our way, and we know and love our way, and they know and love their way."

ROCK AND ROLL

Rock and roll, a genre with roots deeply embedded in Mississippi's musical soil, emerged from a fusion of various musical styles. Like the blues before it, rock and roll's evolution can be traced back to the rich musical traditions of the state.

One notable influence on the genre's development was the musical duo of the Graves brothers: "Blind" Roosevelt Graves and Uaroy Graves. These versatile Mississippi musicians were known for their unique ability to blend gospel and blues in their performances. Their contribution to American music history is significant, with music historian Gayle Dean Wardlow proposing that their 1929 recording "Crazy About My Baby" could be considered one of the earliest examples of rock and roll.

This claim highlights the crucial role that Mississippi musicians played in laying the groundwork for rock and roll. The Graves brothers' innovative fusion of styles exemplifies how the genre evolved from a diverse musical landscape, drawing elements from gospel, blues, and other forms of American roots music.

Ike Turner, a Mississippi native, was another pivotal figure in rock and roll's evolution. Though later known for his turbulent musical and personal relationship with Tina Turner, Ike's early career significantly shaped the genre. Trained by the legendary Pinetop Perkins, Turner led several bands and produced the 1951 recording "Rocket 88," often cited as one of the first rock and roll records. Though credited to Jackie Brenston and his Delta Cats, it was actually Turner's Kings of Rhythm performing, with Turner and James Cotton writing the song. His innovative approach to rhythm and blues laid crucial groundwork for the emerging rock and roll sound.

The mid-1950s saw a flurry of early rock and roll recordings. In 1954, Joe Almond and the Hillbilly Rockers recorded "Gonna Roll and Rock" and "Rock Me" in Jackson's Trumpet studio. Bo Diddley (Ellas McDaniel) recorded his self-titled track "Bo Diddley" in 1955, while Warren Smith released "Rock and

Figure 20.7. Elvis Presley was born in this house in Tupelo. Photographs in the Carol M. Highsmith Archive, Library of Congress, Prints and Photographs Division, LC-DIG-highsm-15161.

Roll Ruby" in 1956. These recordings showcased the genre's evolution from its roots in country, gospel, and rhythm and blues, with early rock and roll forms like rockabilly emerging from this fusion.

Elvis Presley and Jerry Lee Lewis stand as two of rock and roll's most iconic figures, both deeply influenced by the South's rich musical heritage, particularly Mississippi's. Born in Tupelo, Mississippi in 1935, Elvis Presley began as a country singer but was heavily influenced by Black gospel, blues, and rhythm and blues. In the late 1950s, he became a key figure in popularizing rock and roll. His first Victor record, "Heartbreak Hotel," sold over 1.5 million copies, and along with his famous television appearances, helped pave the way for the 1960s popular music revolution. Other hits like "Hound Dog" further cemented his status as the "King of Rock and Roll." Continuing the tradition of genre-blending in Mississippi's music scene, Cedric Burnside represents a more contemporary example of this practice. While primarily categorized as a blues artist, Burnside's music often incorporates distinct rock elements, demonstrating the ongoing fluidity between blues and rock in Mississippi's musical landscape. His approach not only pays homage to the state's rich blues heritage but also showcases how modern artists continue to evolve and expand upon traditional forms.

Mississippi's musical influence extends well beyond its traditional blues and rock roots, contributing significantly to more contemporary genres as well. Hayley Williams, born in Meridian, gained international recognition as the lead vocalist of the alternative rock band Paramore. Her powerful vocals and songwriting have made her a prominent figure in the rock scene since the mid-2000s.

The rock band Three Doors Down, formed in 1996, hails from the small town of Escatawpa. Founded by four local musicians, the group achieved mainstream success with their post-grunge sound, demonstrating Mississippi's continued relevance in modern rock music.

In the realm of pop music, Lance Bass, a native of Clinton, rose to fame as a member of the hugely popular boy band NSYNC. While NSYNC's music was primarily associated with the pop genre, Bass's Mississippi roots highlight the state's diverse musical output.

HIP HOP

Though less recognized for its hip-hop contributions, Mississippi has produced several influential figures. Charlie Braxton, a hip-hop historian, has chronicled this history in a comprehensive article in the *Jackson Advocate*. Early Mississippi hip hop acts include Ice Cold Rappers, whose 1988 LP *Claiming the Fame* was released on the New York–based label Next Plateau. They were the first Mississippi hip hop act to sign with a major label.

David Banner, known off-stage as Lavell Crump, is one of the state's best-known hip hop artists. He joined forces with Kamikaze, or Brad Franklin, to create the duo Crooked Lettaz in 1996. Two years later, the duo released their debut album, *Grey Skies*, on Penalty Records. The group disbanded in 2000, and Banner went solo. His standout solo project, *Mississippi: The Album*, reached number one on the *Billboard* Top R&B and Hip-Hop charts.

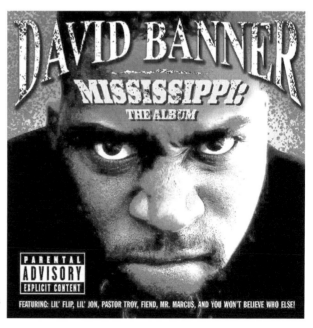

Figure 20.8. David Banner's *Mississippi: The Album*.

As the millennium dawned, Maurice Mosley and Myreon Howard stepped into the limelight, going by the moniker Reese and Bigalow. A setback came their way when their track "Never Scared," which originally featured Bonecrusher and Killer Mike, was revamped to add famed rapper T. I. but exclude them. This rendition achieved a spot in the top ten on the *Billboard* Hot R&B and Rap Charts, boosting Bonecrusher's album to gold status. The state's hip-hop legacy is far from stagnant, with artists like Big K. R. I. T. and Dear Silas making waves. Dear Silas's track "I Ain't Stressin' Today" especially gained traction when actress Lupita Nyong'o used it in a promotional campaign for the film *Black Panther: Wakanda Forever*, propelling the song to go viral on the popular social media app TikTok. Additionally, Mississippi's rich hip-hop history also boasts names like Afroman, Rick Ross, and Nate Dogg.

LOCAL RECORD LABELS

Mississippi's rich musical legacy, particularly its influence on global popular music, can be attributed in part to local record labels: Trumpet Records and Malaco Records. Trumpet was founded in 1951 in Jackson by Lillian McMurry, who was one of the few women executives in the male-dominated music industry. The label was successful in recording artists from the Mississippi Delta like Sonny Boy Williamson and Elmore James.

Also, based in Jackson, Malaco Records was founded by Tommy Couch, Mitchell Malouf, and Wolf Stephenson and is an independent label that has been producing and distributing pivotal blues, soul, and gospel tracks since 1967. Some of the label's standout artists include Dorothy Moore, known for her 1976 hit "Misty Blue"; King Floyd, renowned for his 1970 hit "Groove Me"; Jean Knight, known for "Mr. Big Stuff"; and Johnnie Taylor, often referred to as "The Philosopher of Soul." Beyond promoting individual artists, Malaco Records has played a vital role in preserving African American musical heritage. Contemporary hip-hop artists like Drake and Kanye West have drawn inspiration from this legacy, sampling songs from the label in their own work.

JAZZ

Jazz evolved from diverse musical traditions, including the rhythmically complex syncopations of minstrel bands. In its early stages, jazz shared many similarities with the blues, while also drawing influence from string band music. The Mississippi Sheiks, for instance, recorded "The Jazz Fiddler," highlighting this crossover.

Mississippi produced numerous influential jazz artists. Saxophonist Lester "Prez" Young, who performed with Count Basie's band and Billie Holiday, helped

Figure 20.9. Cassandra Wilson. Photo by Professor Bop, licensed under CC BY 2.0, https://creativecommons.org/licenses/by/2.0/.

shape the genre's sound. The Swinging Rays of Rhythm, an interracial all-female swing band, gained popularity during this era. Teddy Edwards, after relocating to California, became a key figure in the development of bebop. Milt "The Judge" Hinton established himself as a renowned bassist with Cab Calloway's orchestra.

Contemporary jazz vocalist Cassandra Wilson, a Mississippi native, has achieved worldwide acclaim. Her innovative approach incorporates elements of country, folk, and pop into jazz. Wilson's albums, including the Grammy-winning *New Moon Daughter* (1996) and *Loverly* (2008), showcase her versatility. She has collaborated with diverse artists like Wynton Marsalis and Elvis Costello. Her discography includes critically acclaimed works such as "Blue Light 'Til Dawn," "Traveling Miles," "Belly of the Sun," and "Coming Forth by Day."

Mississippi's rich jazz legacy extends to many other notable artists, including Mose Allison, Alvin Fielder, Dick Griffin, Freddie Waits, Olu Dara, Mulgrew Miller, Gerald Wilson, Hank Jones, Ishmael Wadada Leo Smith, Mose Binson, Michael Henderson, Eddie Edwards, Dexter Gordon, Benny Goodman, Tom Waits, Ezra Brown, and Red Holt. Each of these musicians has contributed to the evolving tapestry of jazz, reinforcing Mississippi's significant role in the genre's history.

THE RHYTHM CLUB FIRE: NATCHEZ'S DARKEST NIGHT

On April 23, 1940, Natchez's Black community turned out in their finest clothes to see a big city band play in their small town. Walter Barnes and His Royal Creolians, a celebrated jazz and swing band, drew a crowd that packed the Rhythm Club far beyond its capacity, with over 300 people squeezed inside. As the music filled the overcrowded venue, tragedy struck when a fire broke out. The band continued playing, hoping to prevent panic while the fire was extinguished. But with only one exit and sealed windows, more than 200 people lost their lives in what became one of the deadliest nightclub fires in American history.

CLASSICAL MUSIC

From Natchez to the stages of Europe, from plantation to palace, Elizabeth Taylor Greenfield, known as "The Black Swan," became the first African American classical concert singer to gain international acclaim, performing operatic works across America and for Queen Victoria in 1854.

Decades later, another Mississippi native, soprano Leontyne Price, achieved global renown and made history by opening the Metropolitan Opera's first season at Lincoln Center. She shared the Met stage with fellow Meridian natives John Alexander and Gail Robinson.

Following in Price's footsteps, Carroll Freeman, another notable figure in classical music, has received prestigious accolades such as the National Opera Institute Awards, presented by Beverly Sills and Hal Prince. His exceptional work

Figure 20.10. Leontyne Price with Robert Merrill at the groundbreaking ceremony for the new Metropolitan Opera House. Library of Congress, Prints and Photographs Division, LC-DIG-ds-10680.

as a stage director was recognized in 2010 when he was named "Stage Director of the Year" by *Classical Singer* magazine.

In addition to her individual achievements, Maryann Kyle has made significant contributions to the field of music education. Her students have achieved top placements at state and regional Metropolitan Opera National Council auditions and have won numerous awards including the Sullivan Award, Savannah VOICE Festival Opera Idol, Washington International Competition, Palmai Tenser/Mobile Opera Competition, and the John Alexander Vocal Competition (Mississippi Opera).

Mildred Sterling's contributions to classical music have been recognized by the National Junior Classical League, which created an award in her honor in 1997. The Mildred Sterling Award stands as a testament to her enduring influence on classical music.

More contemporary singers include Edwin Jhamal Davis, operatic bass from Utica; James Martin, operatic baritone from Camden; and Tiffany Townsend, operatic soprano from Jackson.

Two leading composers of classical music were from Mississippi. William Grant Still, born in Woodville, studied with Edgard Varèse in his youth. Still then turned to his Afro-American heritage for inspiration, and composed many symphonies and chamber works. Milton Babbitt grew up in Jackson. Among his works, many of which were composed directly onto magnetic tape, are *Philomel* and *Composition for Synthesizer*.

The Jackson Symphony Orchestra has performed music by the world's great composers dating back to 1943. It was joined by orchestras in Greenville, the Gulf Coast, Meridian, and Starkville, and by orchestras at several state universities. By 2020, Greenville had lost its orchestra but Tupelo had gained one.

During the 1980s, the Mississippi Opera Association presented at least two operas each season. Opera South was composed of performers from Jackson State, Tougaloo, and Utica colleges, with professional soloists who staged full-scale productions. The University of Mississippi, the University of Southern Mississippi, Mississippi College, Tougaloo, and Delta State hold opera workshops. The Mississippi Opera provides educational events and concerts.

There have been a number of composers and conductors who have been selected to the Mississippi Music Hall of Fame. They include John Alexander (opera), Dee Barton (classical composer), Lehman Engell (Broadway conductor), Elizabeth Taylor Greenfield (concert vocalist), Samuel Jones (classical composer and conductor), Willard Palmer (classical pianist), William Grant Still (classical composer), and Walter Turnbull (opera).

FOLKTALES

Historical events are often remembered years later in the form of folksongs and folktales. One of America's best-known songs, "Casey Jones," describes an event that took place in Mississippi in 1900. On an April evening, Casey Jones raced his train out of Memphis and headed for Canton. He was filling in for the regular engineer, and the train left Memphis an hour and a half behind schedule. Casey had made up an hour of the time when he noticed a stalled train on the tracks ahead. He braked and threw the train into reverse; at 70 miles per hour he could not halt his train. Casey Jones was killed near Vaughan, Mississippi, but his name lives on in song.

A more recent example of history turned into song is this description of the civil rights movement in Greenwood, sung to the tune of "Hard Travelin'":

> I've been walkin' the streets of Greenwood
> I thought you knowed.
> I've been walkin' the streets of Greenwood way
> down the road.
> Guns a-blastin,' bullets a-flyin,'
> Poor Jimmy Travis almost dyin':
> He's been havin' some hard travelin,' Lord.

In addition to singing, much of folklore includes storytelling. When people gathered at the country store or went on hunting trips or sat around the table at night after dinner, they told stories.

Folk traditions in Mississippi are unusually rich. They are filled with wisdom and humor. This folklore is available to Mississippi writers and singers, and it may help explain why Mississippi has produced some of the greatest works in American literature.

William Faulkner

Four of the greatest Mississippi writers include William Faulkner, Richard Wright, Eudora Welty, and Tennessee Williams. Most of Faulkner's novels and short stories take place in North Mississippi, where he lived. He wrote of the American Indians who first lived there, the White people, rich and poor, who pushed them out, and the Black people who worked for the Whites.

In "The Bear," one of his finest short stories, the influence of hunting tales on this man who loved Mississippi folklore is clear. "The Bear" also stresses two of Faulkner's major themes: man's sins against nature, and the sins of Whites against Blacks. But above all, Faulkner wrote of humanity's possibilities of overcoming its own errors. For this achievement, he received the 1950 Nobel Prize for Literature.

Figure 20.11. Faulkner's words are scattered throughout this book. This bust of him is by Leon Koury of Greenville. Special Collections, University of Mississippi Libraries.

Richard Wright

Richard Wright, born in 1908 on a plantation near Natchez, overcame a challenging childhood to become one of the most important American writers of the mid-twentieth century. After his father's departure and his mother's illness, Wright moved between relatives before settling in Jackson, where he began his high school education in 1921.

Seeking opportunities beyond the segregated South, Wright later moved to Chicago as part of the Great Migration. This move profoundly shaped his writing, offering new perspectives on urban African American life. Eventually, Wright expatriated to Paris, where he spent his final years until his death in 1960.

Wright's literary legacy is anchored by two groundbreaking works. His autobiography, *Black Boy*, published in 1945, offers a searing account of his youth in the Jim Crow South, vividly portraying the harsh realities of poverty and racism. His novel *Native Son*, released in 1940, tells the story of Bigger Thomas, a young Black man in Chicago's South Side. Through Bigger's tragic tale, Wright explores the psychological effects of systemic racism and oppression on African Americans in urban settings.

These works are characterized by their unflinching portrayal of racial injustice and their critique of American society. Wright's writing style blends naturalism with elements of existentialism, creating a unique voice that captures the complexities of the African American experience. He was among the first Black writers to achieve both critical acclaim and commercial success, paving the way for future generations of African American authors. In 2009, he was honored with a US postage stamp.

"Many Ways of Seeing a Place"

Eudora Welty was born in 1909 in Jackson, her home until her death in 2001. She attended Mississippi University for Women and the University of Wisconsin. Then she did something very rare for young women of the day: she entered the Columbia University School of Business in New York City.

When she graduated in 1931, the Depression was in full force. She returned to Mississippi, where, as she put it, she was "among the many who found their first full-time jobs with the Works Progress Administration." As publicity agent for the WPA, she visited all eighty-two of the state's counties, taking photographs and talking with people.

Her love and knowledge of Mississippi grew, and she began to write novels and short stories about Mississippians and their history. In "First Love," for example, a young deaf-mute meets Aaron Burr in Natchez in 1807. "A Still Moment" tells of an encounter between the artist John J. Audubon, a minister, and a Natchez Trace outlaw in the midst of a Mississippi forest. Her novella *The Robber Bridegroom* features Indians, frontiersmen, and bandits along the Natchez Trace.

Welty wrote about isolation and loneliness in "A Worn Path" and about the never-ending talk in small-town life in "Why I Live at the P.O." and *The Ponder Heart*. "Where Is the Voice Coming From?" and "The Demonstrators" concern racial strife in Mississippi in the 1960s.

Her novels and short stories covered all sections of the state. There were stories of river towns, like "The Wide Net," and of the truck farms in the southern Loess Hills, such as "The Whistle." Her last novel, *Losing Battles*, takes place in the hill country of Northeast Mississippi in the 1930s; *Delta Wedding* and her short story "The Hitch-Hikers" are set in the Delta.

Figure 20.12. Eudora Welty. Courtesy of the Archives and Records Services Division, Mississippi Department of Archives and History.

She made a conscious decision to stay and write about Mississippi. "Writers must always write best of what they know," she said, "and sometimes they do it by staying where they know it." Yet she did not feel that writing of one place—Mississippi—limited her. "There must surely be as many ways of seeing a place as there are pairs of eyes to see it."

Although the situations she described were local, her themes of suffering and humor and triumph were not. That is why her books were translated and read around the world. It is also why in 1973 she received the Pulitzer Prize for Fiction.

Tennessee Williams

Tennessee Williams, from Columbus, Mississippi, was once called America's greatest living playwright. Many of his plays were set in small Mississippi towns; others took place in Europe or Mexico. He received a Pulitzer Prize in 1948 for *A Streetcar Named Desire* and again in 1955 for *Cat on a Hot Tin Roof*.

Margaret Walker Alexander

Margaret Walker Alexander made lasting contributions to literature and Black history. Her 1966 novel *Jubilee*, based on her great-grandmother's life, was among the first to depict the Civil War and Reconstruction from a Black woman's perspective. Her 1942 poetry collection, *For My People*, won the Yale Series of Younger Poets Award, making her the first Black woman to receive the honor. One of her last contributions is her 1988 book, *Richard Wright, Daemonic Genius: A Portrait of the Man, a Critical Look at His Work*.

In 1968, she founded the Institute for the Study of Black History at Jackson State University, now the Margaret Walker Center. It became a key research institution, collecting oral histories and preserving Black life in Mississippi.

MISSISSIPPI LITERATURE AND THE PAST

Perhaps because of the state's folklore tradition, most Mississippi writers have located their work in a definite place and time. Usually, the place is Mississippi. And in most novels and short stories by Mississippi authors, history is important. The effects of the past linger on, and they affect the present and future lives of the characters.

The following paragraph ends the novel *So Red the Rose* by Stark Young. In it, a Civil War battle is remembered. The past can be felt so intensely that it has almost replaced the present: "Agnes only glanced at the child, seeing what was in his face, and stirred by it more than she knew. At the same moment memory was stronger he returned to her thoughts. She was at Shiloh; but now she heard nothing, only the silence; then, inside her body, she heard her heart beating. Edward was among them somewhere but the others too were hers. She stood there looking out across the darkness and the field where the dead lay; as if they were all sleeping." Mississippi's literary heritage helped shape American humor writing while spanning multiple genres. When A. B. Longstreet became University of Mississippi's chancellor in 1848, he brought with him his influential *Georgia Scenes*, which established a pattern of anecdotal wit that flourished in subsequent works. Joseph G. Baldwin's *Flush Times of Alabama and Mississippi*, Joseph B. Cobb's *Mississippi Scenes*, Henry Clay Lewis's *The Swamp Doctor's Adventures in the Southwest*, and T. W. Caskey's *Seven Years in Dixie* all followed this tradition, blending historical observation with social commentary through humor.

William Faulkner, a native son, masterfully captured the state's essence, people, and sociopolitical challenges in his works. Other notable writers like Richard Wright, Stark Young, Will D. Campbell, Shelby Foote, Walker Percy, Barry Hannah, Larry Brown, Willie Morris, and Eudora Welty have also explored Mississippi's complex issues, particularly race relations, in their writings. Anne Moody, an activist during the 1960s, documented her story in *Coming of Age in Mississippi*. It won the Brotherhood Award from the National Council of Christians and Jews, the Best Book of the Year Award from the National Library Association, and the International PEN/Faulkner Award. Tennessee Williams often set his plays in his home state, while John Grisham, an Oxford lawyer-turned-novelist, has gained worldwide fame with his legal thrillers, many of which are set in Mississippi and have been adapted into successful films. William Attaway wrote during the Harlem Renaissance. He is known for his novels *Let Me Breathe Thunder* and *Blood on the Forge* to capture segregation and the migration of Blacks from the South. Ellen Douglas's *A Family's Affair* won the Houghton Mifflin Award and was listed as one of the five best novels in 1961 by the *New York Times*.

The state continues to produce literary talent. Recent years have seen the emergence of award-winning authors such as Jesmyn Ward, Nikki Finney, Angie Thomas, and Kiese Laymon. Laymon's memoir *Heavy* garnered several accolades, including the Andrew Carnegie Medal for Excellence in Nonfiction. Both Laymon and Ward received the prestigious MacArthur Foundation "genius grant," with Ward also claiming two National Book Awards. Kathryn Stockett's novel *The Help* won multiple honors, including the Goodreads Choice Award and the *Christian Science Monitor* best book award. Poet Natasha Trethewey's work earned her a Pulitzer Prize. Historians, Winthrop Jordan and David Sansing, have made great contributions in areas such as race relations. Other contemporary writers include Willie Morris, Richard Ford, Barry Hannah, Frederick Barthelme, Olympia Vernon, Jack Butler, Tom Franklin, and Cynthia Shearer.

Jerry Washington Ward Jr. and Catherine Pierce have also made significant contributions to literature. Ward Jr. is recognized for his work as a poet, essayist, literary critic, and Richard Wright scholar. Pierce served as Mississippi's poet laureate in 2023, further cementing the state's ongoing literary prominence.

In their creations, as in the composition of bluesmen and country singers, Mississippi folklore and history have been made immortal.

Some of Mississippi's most notable writers often show up at the Mississippi Book Festival. This event has emerged as a premier literary event in the South, drawing a constellation of distinguished authors to Jackson. Since its inception in 2015, this annual celebration of the written word has quickly become a literary landmark, attracting thousands of book lovers from across the nation. Often referred to as the "literary lawn party," the festival takes place on the picturesque grounds of the Mississippi State Capitol.

EXCELLENCE IN JOURNALISM

Three early champions won Pulitzers for fighting racial injustice: Hodding Carter II (Greenville *Delta Democrat-Times*, 1946); Ira Harkey (Pascagoula *Chronicle*, 1963); and Hazel Brannon Smith (Lexington *Advertiser*, 1964). Bill Minor, the "conscience of Mississippi journalism," fearlessly covered civil rights struggles for seven decades, including the Emmett Till trial and Ole Miss integration.

A wave of Mississippi journalists transformed national media: Turner Catledge rose from the *Tunica Times* to executive editor at the *New York Times*, while Craig Claiborne revolutionized food writing there. Lerone Bennett became *Ebony*'s senior editor and wrote *Before the Mayflower*. Mark Ethridge led the Fair Employment Practices Committee, Willie Morris became *Harper's* youngest editor, Norman Bradley edited the *Chattanooga Times*, William Raspberry won a Pulitzer for commentary, and Charles Overby led the *Clarion-Ledger* during its Pulitzer-winning years. Sid Salter's political columns reached across the state through the *Scott County Times* and *Clarion-Ledger*. Emily Wagster Pettus was a longtime reporter for the Associated Press covering Mississippi politics.

Jerry Mitchell's investigations have solved civil rights–era murders, while Donna Ladd and Kimberly Griffin carry on the tradition with the digital Mississippi Free Press. Anna Wolfe's investigative work at *Mississippi Today* has garnered national acclaim, while Dr. Ivory Phillips, Rick Cleveland, and Roscoe Nance made their marks in news and sports journalism.

The *Clarion-Ledger*, founded in 1837, shifted from its segregationist stance under the Hederman brothers (Thomas and Robert) to later investigate civil rights cases. Today's media landscape includes new voices through the *Magnolia Tribune* (formerly *Y'all Politics*) and *Super Talk* radio.

THE BLACK PRESS

The Black press has been crucial in representing the Black perspective. The first Black newspaper in Mississippi, *The Colored Citizen*, was established in 1867. During segregation, numerous Black newspapers emerged. The *Delta Leader* was edited by Reverend H. H. Humes of Greenville. The paper was owned by the Associated Negro Press. Thus, it covered both local and national issues. Humes followed the philosophy of Booker T. Washington and thus wrote more conservative columns. The same can be said of the *Southern Advocate* and *Mississippi Enterprise*. While the *Jackson Advocate* under Percy Greene's editorship covered civil rights issues, his stance was compromised by payments from the Mississippi State Sovereignty Commission. This financial relationship led Greene to take moderate positions on segregation, effectively diluting his paper's coverage of civil rights struggles. Reverend J. W. Jones, who owned New Albany's *Community Citizen*, was similarly paid to maintain moderate positions, though his views were even more conservative than Greene's. In 1961, Medgar Evers and an interracial team launched the *Mississippi Free Press*, a weekly newspaper covering the Freedom Movement and African American community news. Between 1961 and 1967, the paper had three editors: Henry J. Kirksey, Paul E. Brooks, and Charles Butt. In 1964, Ollye Shirley and Dilla E. Irwin helped start the *Vicksburg Citizens' Appeal*. Other notable papers during the 1960s include the *Mound Bayou Weekly*, the *Saint Augustine's Messenger*, and the *Meridian Memo Digest*. Two other publications of note are the *Jackson Advocate* and the *Mississippi Link*. Following the death of Percey Green, Charles Tisdale and Deborah LeSure helped to revive the *Jackson Advocate*. It remains in circulation as of 2025. The *Mississippi Link* was one of the first Black newspapers to establish an online presence.

Several Mississippi-born journalists have made their mark on the national stage as news anchors. Randall Pinkston, a native of the state, served as a White House correspondent before becoming a well-known figure in broadcast journalism. Robin Roberts, another Mississippian, has achieved prominence as a cohost on ABC's popular morning show, *Good Morning America*. Likewise, DeMarco Morgan, also hailing from Mississippi, has joined Roberts as a cohost on the same program, further highlighting the state's contributions to the field of journalism.

EDUCATIONAL TELEVISION

A major development in culture and education in Mississippi began in 1966 when the legislature established the Mississippi Authority for Educational Television. ETV provides instructional programs for in-school use. Many special subjects that would be beyond the means of local schools reached students throughout the state. In a bold departure from Mississippi's racial conservatism, ETV's

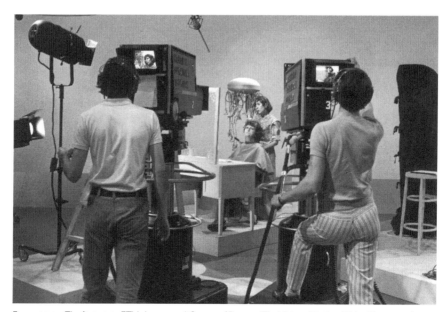

Figure 20.13. The first state ETV show was *A Season of Dreams: The Vision of Eudora Welty*. Courtesy of Mississippi Authority for Educational Television/Mississippi Public Broadcasting.

programming showed something rarely seen in the state: Black and White children learning and playing together. This multicultural approach to education through television offered viewers a vision of racial harmony that stood in stark contrast to the segregated reality of daily life.

Besides classroom work, Mississippi ETV provided programs from national public television into homes and schools. Mississippi ETV also produced its own programs. In ETV's first full year of production, these shows won the famed Peabody Award for "enhancing the educational system of Mississippi through innovative use of television."

THEATER

The Jackson Little Theatre was the state's oldest stage organization still in existence in 1970 having performing plays in 1925. In 1965, it gave birth to a more professional company, New Stage, still in existence today.

Beyond Jackson, by this time twenty-two community theater groups operated throughout the state. Among them is the Meridian Little Theatre. It opened its doors in 1932 and continues to host shows.

In the early 1960s, the Free Southern Theater was founded at Tougaloo College. The performers then toured the state, playing in churches, community centers, and even vacant lots. Their performances were free, and many Mississippians who had never been to a play were able to see *In White America*, *Waiting for Godot*,

Figure 20.14. New Stage Theater in Jackson is housed where the Jackson Little Theater once stood. Courtesy of New Stage Theater.

and other important dramas. The Free Southern Theater then moved to New Orleans; several of its members then became active in experimental New York theater companies; one directed part of the television drama *Roots*.

Lehman Engel of Jackson also moved to New York, where he conducted and directed several Broadway musicals. Frederick O'Neal, originally from Brooksville, helped establish the American Negro Theatre in New York before World War II. In 1968, Mart Crowley's play, *The Boys in the Band*, was successful on Broadway and as a movie.

During the 1970s, among the state's most famous actors were James Earl Jones and Stella Stevens. Jones, born in Tate County, starred in many movies including *The Great White Hope* and *Claudine*. Stevens, from Yazoo City, was in many motion pictures. As the years progressed, Morgan Freeman emerged as another major talent from Mississippi. His impressive filmography includes acclaimed performances in *Driving Miss Daisy* and *The Shawshank Redemption*, among many others. Other Mississippians making film and television careers include Aunjanue Ellis-Taylor, M. C. Gainey, Anthony Herrera, Roscoe Ates (known for his "western" character "Soapy Jones"), Mary Ann Mobley, Dana Andrews, Lacey Chabert, Eric Roberts, Fred Armisen, Gerald McRaney, Diane Ladd, Mary Alice, Tonea Stewart, Beah Richards, and Sela Ward. Oprah Winfrey's impact extends far beyond her iconic role as host of *The Oprah Winfrey Show*, as she built a media empire while pioneering new forms of television journalism.

Other notable figures in the entertainment industry include Jim Henson, the creator of the beloved Muppets, was born in Leland, Mississippi. In the culinary world, Cat Cora, a native of Jackson, made history as the first female Iron Chef on the popular television show *Iron Chef America*. Another Mississippi chef, Nick Wallace, has garnered national attention through his appearances on various cooking competition shows. Wallace has showcased his skills on programs such as *Cutthroat Kitchen*, *Chopped*, and *Fire Masters*, even winning the 2017 season of *Chopped*.

COMEDIANS

Mississippi has produced numerous comedians who have left their mark on the national stage, blending Southern charm with sharp wit. Jerry Clower, born in Liberty, became famous for his folksy humor and colorful stories of rural Southern life, often featuring characters from the fictional Amite County. Tig Notaro, hailing from Jackson, has gained acclaim for her deadpan delivery and deeply personal comedy, tackling topics like her battle with cancer with honesty and humor. Rod Brasfield, born in Smithville, was a Grand Ole Opry star known for his self-deprecating humor and rural character portrayals.

Recent comedians from Mississippi have been making notable strides in the comedy scene, bringing their unique Southern humor and perspectives to a broader audience. One standout is Rita Brent, a Jackson native, whose career has blossomed from local radio DJ to nationally recognized stand-up comedian and writer. Brent's sharp wit and relatable humor about Southern life and Black culture have garnered her spots on major platforms like HBO and Comedy Central. Jeremiah (JJ) Williamson has also made a significant impact on the comedy scene with his unique style and his performances across the country.

INTERNATIONAL BALLET COMPETITION

The Mississippi International Ballet Competition, also known as the USA International Ballet Competition (USAIBC), is a prestigious event held every four years in Jackson, Mississippi. Established in 1979, it is one of the oldest and most respected ballet competitions in the world, joining the ranks of similar contests in Varna, Bulgaria, and Moscow, Russia. The competition attracts talented young dancers from across the globe, providing them with a platform to showcase their skills and potentially launch international careers.

THE VISUAL ARTS

The stories told in Mississippi's music and writings really help define the state's unique culture. And the visual arts in Mississippi add even more to this mix. Mississippi has always had a strong tradition of art and creativity.

Painting and Sculpture

During the early 1900s, African Americans were frequent subjects in Mississippi art. Leon Koury, a Syrian sculptor from Greenville, gained recognition for his portrait busts of Black subjects. Similarly, artist John McCrady often focused on Black themes in his work, as seen in his painting *Swing Low, Sweet Chariot*, which depicts African American spiritual beliefs about death and ascension.

In 1948, the Allison Art Colony was established at a resort near Canton. However, after a fire destroyed the resort in 1963, it relocated to Stafford Springs and was renamed the Mississippi Art Workshop. Throughout Mississippi, various workshops and college art departments have been in operation. Most colleges in the state have art galleries that showcase works by their students and local artists.

The Mississippi Art Association used to offer art classes for both children and adults. They organized art exhibitions in communities across the state,

Figure 20.15. Theora Hamblett of Oxford was known for her "primitive" style. Used by permission of the University of Mississippi Museum and Historic Houses.

had a slide library of art pieces for lending, and accumulated a collection of original art. The first art museum in Mississippi was the Lauren Rogers Library and Museum of Art in Laurel. Other notable art venues include the Mississippi Museum of Art in Jackson, the Mary Buie Museum in Oxford, the Ohr-O'Keefe Museum of Art in Biloxi, the Walter Anderson Museum of Art in Ocean Springs, the GumTree Museum of Art in Tupelo, and the Kate Freeman Memorial Art Gallery in Holly Springs.

Mississippi nurtured a diverse array of artists, each leaving their unique imprint on the art scene. Among them is John James Audubon, known for his nineteenth-century paintings. The state's rich history has given rise to artists such as Richmond Barthé, the first Black sculptor in the National Academy of Arts and Letters, whose works have been exhibited at the Metropolitan Museum in New York and throughout the United States.

Artists and teachers Karl and Mildred Wolfe, along with Marie Hull, significantly contributed to Mississippi's art scene. Other notable artists include Walter Anderson, known for his Shearwater Pottery and paintings, and George Ohr, often described as the "Mad Potter of Biloxi," whose innovative pottery designs were ahead of their time.

Contemporary artists such as Sandy McNeal, Elijah Watson, Sophia Lee, Charlie Buckley, Rory Doyle, George Wardlaw, Amy Giust, Betty Press, Jerrod Partridge, Fletcher Cox, and Lauren Stennis continue to enrich Mississippi's artistic landscape with their unique styles and themes.

African American artists such as Henry Jackson Lewis and Sam Gilliam have made significant contributions to the national art scene. Mississippi's Native American artists such as Harold "Doc" Comby and Jeffrey A. Gibson have also left an indelible mark on the art scene.

Artists such as Eudora Welty have made significant contributions to Mississippi's rich artistic heritage. Welty's photographs, which captured the essence of Mississippi during the Great Depression, offered a visual narrative that beautifully complemented her literary works. Similarly, Kate Freeman Clark's artistic prowess was recognized during her time in New York, where she studied under the renowned William Merritt Chase.

OTHER ARTS IN THE STATE

Architecture, ceramics, photography, basketry, leather craft, woodworking, and many other arts are developing in Mississippi.

Quilting, crafted by enslaved Blacks, served as another form of visual art expression. Notable quilters include Sarah Mary Taylor, Gwendolyn A. Magee, and Hystercine Rankin.

THE MISSISSIPPI ARTS FESTIVAL

All the arts in Mississippi came together every spring at the Mississippi Arts Festival, a weeklong event held in Jackson. The activities at the festival took in practically all areas of creative work: painting, sculpture, and photography; choral music, folk singing, jazz, blues, and rock; opera, ballet, marching bands, and the Jackson Symphony Orchestra; children's theater, puppet shows, and theater productions from around the state; folklore and crafts; and concerts by nationally famous guest stars. After the first statewide festival in 1965, journalist Jere Real wrote: "Last summer, the mood of the state was tense; Mississippians because of the racial situation, viewed the future with concern. Today, racial affairs are no longer the number one topic of conversation; one hears less reference to the 'Mississippi Way of Life.' It is a subtle change, but, nonetheless, it is there. There were Negroes in the Festival audiences, and no one seemed to notice. The main concern seems to be the new prosperity, the image of the New South. And the unfamiliar sounds emerging from last week's Arts Festival were the sounds of a new Mississippi." The state has come a long way from the days when it was too poor and too rural even to see and hear opera or television or drama. Now the state produces its own TV shows, arts festivals, and symphony concerts. The First International Ballet competition ever held in America was held in Jackson in June 1979. The new Mississippi economy has helped to make it all possible; Mississippi's creative energy has brought it about. The arts have a bright future in Mississippi.

Figure 20.16. The Mississippi Museum of Art in Jackson. Photographs in the Ben May Charitable Trust Collection of Mississippi Photographs in the Carol M. Highsmith Archive, Library of Congress, Prints and Photographs Division, LC-DIG-highsm-6996.

SPORTS

Many great athletes were born in Mississippi or have strong Mississippi connections. Archie Manning and his son Eli played quarterback for the University of Mississippi's football team. Archie was inducted into the College Football Hall of Fame in 1989. Eli led Ole Miss to several bowl wins and later played for the New York Giants, winning two Super Bowls. Running back Walter Payton, a native of Columbia, played for Jackson State University and won a Super Bowl with the Chicago Bears in 1986. When he retired in 1987, he held the record for the most yards gained by any runner in professional football history. The National Football League (NFL) inducted him into the Hall of Fame in 1993 and honored his legacy in 1999 by naming its Man of the Year Award after him. Regarded by many as the greatest wide receiver in NFL history, Jerry Rice grew up in Crawford and played for Mississippi Valley State University and several teams in the NFL. Rice holds thirty-six NFL records—more than any other player—and boasts three Super Bowl rings and a Super Bowl Most Valuable Player award. Another standout receiver was Hall of Famer Lance Allworth, who played high school football at Brookhaven High. Other NFL greats from Mississippi include Hall of Famers Jackie Slater, Robert Brazile, and Lem Barney from Jackson State University, and Deacon Jones from Mississippi Valley State. Others include Deuce McAllister (University of Mississippi); Willie and Gloster Richards (Jackson State University); L. C. Greenwood (Canton); Steve McNair (Alcorn State University); and Brett Favre (University of Southern Mississippi). Current Dallas Cowboys quarterback Dak Prescott attended Mississippi State University and won the NFL's Walter Payton Man of the Year Award in 2022.

Basketball greats include Lusia Harris (Delta State University), the first woman drafted by an NBA team; Latoya Thomas (Mississippi State University); Victoria Vivians (Mississippi State University); Peggie Gillom (University of Mississippi); Quinndary Weatherspoon (Mississippi State University); Monta Ellis (Jackson); Maurice "Mo" Williams (Jackson); Chris Jackson, later known as Mahmoud Abdul Rauf (Gulfport); Chet Walker (Bradley University); Larry Smith (Alcorn State University); Purvis Short (Jackson State University), Al Jefferson (Monticello), and Antonio McDyess (Quitman).

Baseball players include Jame Thomas "Cool Papa" Bell (Starkville); Dave Parker (Calhoun City); Ellis Burks (Vicksburg); Dennis "Oil Can" Boyd (Jackson State University); Curtis Ford (Jackson State University); George Scott (Greenville); David "Boo" Ferris (Shaw); and Curt Ford (Jackson). In 2021, Mississippi State won baseball's College World Series. They were followed by the University of Mississippi in 2022.

Track stars include Calvin Smith (University of Alabama); Tori Bowie (University of Southern Mississippi); Brittany Reese (University of Mississippi); Ralph Boston (Tennessee State University); and Larry Myricks (Mississippi College).

Recommended Readings

Patti Black and Robin C. Dietrick, eds., *The Mississippi Story* (Jackson: Mississippi Museum of Art, 2007).

Charlie Braxton, "Hip-Hop: Voice of a Generation," *Jackson Advocate*, October 26, 1993.

Margo Cooper, *Deep Inside the Blues: Photographs and Interviews* (Jackson: University Press of Mississippi, 2023).

Robert Gordon and Bruce Nemerov, Editors, *Lost Delta Found: Rediscovering the Fisk University-Library of Congress Coahoma Study, 1941-1942* (Nashville: Vanderbilt University Press, 2005)

Peter Guralnick, Robert Santelli, Holly George-Warren, and Christopher John Farley, editors. *Martin Scorsese Presents The Blues* (Amistad, 2003).

Birney Imes, *Juke Joint: Photographs*, introduction by Richard Ford (Jackson: University Press of Mississippi, 2012).

Stephen A. King, *I'm Feeling the Blues Right Now: Blues Tourism and the Mississippi Delta* (Jackson: University Press of Mississippi, 2011).

Mississippi Department of Archives and History, *Telling Our Stories* (Jackson: University Press of Mississippi, 2017).

Mississippi Department of Archives and History, *All Shook Up* (Jackson: Mississippi Department of Archives and History, 1995).

Robert Palmer, *Deep Blues* (New York: Penguin Books, 1981).

Julius E. Thompson. *The Black Press in Mississippi, 1865–1985* (Gainesville: University Press of Florida, 1993).

Annette Trefzer, Jay Watson, and James G. Thomas, Jr., eds., *Faulkner, Welty, Wright: A Mississippi Confluence* (Jackson: University Press of Mississippi, 2024).

CHAPTER 21

MISSISSIPPI AT THE CROSSROADS

Moving in Two Directions at Once

CHAPTERS 1 THROUGH 20 HAVE TOLD THE STORY OF MISSISSIPPI FROM PREHIStory to the year 2024. Although most history texts stop at some point in the recent past, history itself does not stop. The state's future will be influenced by similar factors that have influenced its past development.

As we reflect on Mississippi's historical development, we are uniquely positioned to consider its potential future. This chapter will explore recent events and trends in the state, projecting these developments forward to envision possible trajectories for Mississippi. It's important to recognize that the state stands at a critical point, with the potential to progress or regress, and that these movements may not be uniform across its population.

In the last edition of this book, the authors offered a few predictions regarding the future of Mississippi. While some of those predictions came to fruition, others missed the mark. In this chapter, we will revisit some of those predictions while also looking into Mississippi's future. Our analysis will focus on four key areas: population trends, migration patterns, overall quality of life, and poverty. These interconnected factors will shape Mississippi's future in significant ways.

Throughout this exploration, we'll keep in mind that progress may be uneven. While some segments of Mississippi's population may experience advancements, others may encounter setbacks simultaneously. This nuanced approach will assist us in constructing a more precise representation of the multiple possible futures that the state may encounter.

HOW TO ANALYZE THE FUTURE

As you read this chapter, remember that you are already living the future we are writing about. For this reason, we challenge you to use the events that have taken place since this book was written to try to disprove us or to predict the future more accurately than we could.

While anticipating the future involves more than just imagining technological advances, understanding historical patterns of human movement and cultural change can provide valuable insights into what lies ahead. Looking at Mississippi's rich history of migration illustrates how population shifts have long shaped societies and will likely continue to do so.

MIGRANTS TO MISSISSIPPI

Mississippi has experienced significant in-migration throughout its history. A complex interplay of various cultural groups and populations has shaped the state's demographic composition. The history of immigration dates back to the Indigenous Native American inhabitants and was subsequently influenced by the arrival of European colonists and forcibly transported enslaved individuals from West African regions. The arrival of these diverse populations has greatly contributed to the cultural diversity of Mississippi.

During the antebellum period, Mississippi experienced a significant wave of immigration, including an influx of Jewish merchants from Russia, Poland, and Western Europe. Germans made up the largest group of foreign-born immigrants, while many Jewish settlers sought refuge from oppression in the Austro-Hungarian Empire. In 1840, the state's first organized Jewish congregation, B'nai Israel, was established, marking a key moment in the growth of Mississippi's diverse cultural and religious landscape.

Irish immigrants began arriving in Mississippi during the 1840s and 1850s, working primarily as manual laborers on railroads and levees. Their presence contributed to a notable rise in the Catholic population.

These immigrants played a significant role in the state's economic development, primarily by establishing commercial enterprises. Their cultural impact was also evident in the religious sphere, as Jews founded synagogues in several urban centers across Mississippi, including Clarksdale, Cleveland, Greenville, Meridian, and the state capital, Jackson. This influx further diversified the state's socio-cultural landscape and contributed to its economic growth.

Mississippi also became home to immigrants from Lebanon and Syria, who primarily settled in river towns and built lives in retail trade, with some achieving prominent civic roles, including a mayorship in Natchez. The arrival of Chinese migrants in the Delta in the 1870s marked another significant chapter in the state's

Figure 21.1. Beth Israel Congregation in Jackson dates back to before the Civil War. Courtesy of Beth Israel Congregation.

history. Chinese immigrants, initially recruited as railroad workers and sharecroppers following the abolition of slavery, soon abandoned plantation labor. Instead, they established themselves as entrepreneurs, primarily opening grocery stores throughout the Delta region that served both Black and White communities.

They often purchased merchandise from White suppliers and sold it to Black customers, carving out a unique role in the segregated economy. By the 1970s, Mississippi had developed a relatively sizable Chinese American community, with John Wing of Jonestown making history as the first Chinese mayor in the United States.

Italian immigrants arrived in the Mississippi Delta in the early 1900s to work as sharecroppers, helping to fill the region's labor shortage. Starting at Sunnyside Plantation in eastern Arkansas along the Mississippi River, these immigrants gradually established themselves in Mississippi communities, where many eventually prospered as merchants and farmers. The Gulf Coast once hosted Yugoslav American communities, while Greek Americans were scattered throughout the state. In the early 1940s, a group of Mennonites from Alabama migrated to Monroe County, Mississippi. This move was primarily motivated by their desire to educate their children according to their religious beliefs, free from state interference.

Mississippi's agricultural industry has long attracted Mexican and Mexican American workers, initially drawn to the state for seasonal employment opportunities. Over time, some of these workers chose to settle permanently, enriching Mississippi's cultural diversity. Today, Latinos represent the third-largest demographic group in the state, comprising about three percent of the population,

Figure 21.2. A Chinese-owned grocery store in Leland. Library of Congress, Prints & Photographs Division, Farm Security Administration/Office of War Information Black-and-White Negatives, LC-USF34-052450-D.

though this figure does not account for undocumented residents. Before Immigration and Customs Enforcement (ICE) workplace raids became prevalent, many Latino workers also found industrial jobs, particularly in the poultry processing industry, further integrating into Mississippi's economic and social fabric.

Additionally, the Vietnamese began arriving around 1975. Drawn to the state by opportunities in the fishing and shrimping industries, many found work through Richard Gollott, owner of the Golden Gulf Seafood processing factory.

Some immigrant groups often faced discrimination. An Italian planter near Shaw remarked, "We were treated as a minority group all the way through." For a period, Italians and Mexicans were excluded from White schools. In Delta towns like Greenville and Cleveland, Chinese American students attended separate, unequal schools alongside the existing segregated White and Black school systems. The US Supreme Court reinforced this racial categorization in the 1927 *Gong Lum v. Rice* case, which classified Chinese Mississippians as "colored," barring them from White public schools.

POPULATION SHIFTS

The demographic landscape of Mississippi is currently undergoing a significant transformation, which has prompted apprehension among policymakers and experts. Dr. John J. Greene, an economics professor at Mississippi State University, identifies a concerning trend in the state's population dynamics. In

2010, Mississippi was still experiencing natural growth, with 40,000 births outnumbering 30,000 deaths. However, by 2022, the state reached a critical tipping point—births and deaths hovered around 35,000, a phenomenon known as a natural decrease. This shift is akin to watching the state's population renewal engine sputter and stall.

While its Southern neighbors experienced population growth between 2010 and 2020, Mississippi charted a different course, recording a slight population decline of 0.2 percent. This downward trend wasn't uniform across the state as a striking sixty-four out of eighty-two counties saw their population numbers dwindle. The uneven distribution of this decline paints a picture of a state facing varied demographic challenges in different regions.

These shifts are more than just statistics—they're sounding alarm bells for Mississippi's future. The population slide threatens the state's economic vitality and social fabric, potentially unraveling longstanding communities and altering the cultural landscape. Moreover, it puts Mississippi's political influence at risk, potentially diminishing its voice on the national stage. As the state grapples with these changes, the need for innovative solutions to attract and retain residents becomes increasingly urgent, making Mississippi's demographic story one of the most compelling in the modern American South.

Remember when Mississippi had a louder voice in Congress? In 2000, the state lost one of its five congressional seats, leaving it with four representatives to champion its causes in Washington. Now, as residents continue to pack their bags or the population fails to replenish itself, Mississippi finds itself in a precarious position. Arguably, if this trend continues, the state could be looking at another round of musical chairs in the US House of Representatives—and this time, Mississippi might be left without a seat when the music stops.

The potential loss of another congressional seat isn't just about bragging privileges. It would mean a quieter voice for Mississippi in national debates, less leverage in committee assignments, and potentially, less federal attention and resources. It's a reminder that in the world of politics, sometimes numbers really do speak louder than words.

Looking to the future, Mississippi's low wages may potentially attract companies seeking to lower their labor costs. This scenario poses significant concerns regarding the ethical implications of companies exploiting economic hardships for their own financial gain, as well as the potential impact on local workers and communities. However, despite the concerns, it highlights the need for balanced economic development that promotes sustainable growth, good jobs, and shared prosperity for all residents of Mississippi.

Furthermore, it is important to evaluate whether Mississippi can attract businesses that are not only seeking lower labor costs but also potential employers for its university graduates, particularly those with qualifications in fields such as engineering and computer science. This could be a strategic move to curb the "brain drain" phenomenon, in which graduates leave to pursue career opportunities in other states.

Brain Drain

In the last edition of this book, the authors questioned if Mississippi might see "reverse migration," where young people leave but return later in life. Unfortunately, as reported by the State Auditor's office, current trends point toward persisting youth out-migration without return.

The departure of ambitious youth seeking opportunities elsewhere stunts Mississippi's advancement. It deprives the state of the skilled labor force needed to attract modern industries and jobs. Although some young individuals maintain connections to their hometowns, a small number of them return to Mississippi to reside and work permanently after completing their higher education.

To combat brain drain, Mississippi must invest in education, infrastructure, and quality of life. Mentorship programs, higher wages, tech hubs, and support for entrepreneurship can help retain and attract young talent. The State Auditor's report highlights that graduates from the University of Mississippi and Mississippi State University, both of which receive a higher allocation of state funding, exhibit a greater propensity to relocate outside of the state. Conversely, graduates from Historically Black Universities, which receive less funding, tend to stay. This suggests a need to reassess higher education funding to retain skilled graduates better and maximize economic contributions to the state. Without such interventions, brain drain will continue to impede Mississippi's progress. Therefore, prioritizing youth opportunities is crucial for the state's future prosperity.

REVERSE MIGRATION?

In the 1970s, many young adults left Mississippi, taking their ideas and talents to cities and suburbs in other states. Most "Sun Belt" states, from Florida to Arizona, experienced rapid population growth during this time. In this book's previous edition, the authors questioned whether Mississippi, like other Southern states, could attract some of those who had departed during the 1960s and 1970s. There are instances where Black individuals and or their descendants who migrated to cities like Chicago during the Great Migration are now returning to Mississippi. Additionally, Oxford, which has been designated as a Certified Retirement City, has been appealing to retirees.

DeSoto County has experienced a significant population shift as former Memphis residents migrate back to Mississippi. This movement pattern illustrates development scholar Albert O. Hirschman's framework of how people respond to deteriorating conditions: they either "exit" by relocating, "voice" their concerns by advocating for change, or demonstrate "loyalty" by remaining in place despite challenges. The migration from Memphis to DeSoto County represents the "exit" response in Hirschman's model, as residents choose relocation as their solution to urban challenges.

Many individuals appear to exercise the "exit" option in the context of Memphis and its surrounding areas. However, their choice is nuanced; while they may have physically relocated to DeSoto County in Mississippi, they often maintain employment ties to Memphis. This suggests a preference for residing in a less densely urban environment while retaining access to the economic opportunities of a larger metropolitan area.

Population Gains and Losses

Mississippi's population trends from 2010 to 2020 reveal a stark contrast between urban and rural decline and suburban growth. According to Table 20.1, smaller counties experienced the most severe population losses, with Benton and Tunica counties leading the decline. While population loss in rural counties followed expected patterns, Hinds County's significant decrease was particularly noteworthy. As home to Jackson, Mississippi's capital city, Hinds County's population decline reflected the broader challenges facing the state's major urban center.

However, some areas thrived during this period. Lamar County led the state with a 15 percent population increase, closely followed by DeSoto and Madison counties at over 14 percent growth. Harrison and Rankin counties also showed robust growth at around 11 percent. These growing counties shared a common characteristic: proximity to urban centers, suggesting residents sought a balance between suburban living and urban amenities.

In northern Mississippi, DeSoto County emerged as a suburban haven for Memphis residents. Southaven's population grew from 16,071 in 1980 to 17,949 in 1990, exemplifying the broader growth trend in DeSoto County. The county experienced its most dramatic growth between 1995 and 2000, when 12,920 people moved from Shelby County, Tennessee. Though this migration has slowed considerably—with only 3,997 new residents from Shelby County by 2020—DeSoto County continues to benefit from its proximity to Memphis, illustrating the ongoing evolution of Mississippi's suburban communities.

This patchwork of growth and decline paints a picture of a state in transition, with suburban areas near major cities thriving while many rural communities struggle to retain their residents. Mississippi's population story is one of contrast, highlighting the complex demographic challenges facing the Magnolia State.

This demographic shift presents complex challenges for urban planners and policymakers. The pattern of urban-to-suburban migration has reshaped the region's landscape, requiring careful analysis of the factors driving this change and its implications for larger cities like Jackson and its surrounding communities.

Table 20.1. Top 5 Population Loss/Gain for Selected Mississippi Counties, 2010–2020

	County	Total	Rate
Top 5 Gain			
	Lamar County	8,564	15.39%
	DeSoto County	24,062	14.92%
	Madison County	13,942	14.64%
	Harrison County	21,516	11.50%
	Rankin County	15,414	10.88%
Top 5 Loss			
	Benton County	-1,083	-12.41%
	Tunica County	-996	-9.24%
	Marshall County	-3,392	-9.13%
	Hinds County	-17,543	-7.15%
	Perry County	-739	-6.03%

Source: US Population Data, Census 2010, 2020.

MIGRATION WITHIN THE STATE

In the swinging sixties, Mississippi saw a mass exodus from the countryside. Folks were packing up their rural lives, making pit stops in small towns, and then beelining it to the bright lights of big cities—in Mississippi, elsewhere in the South, or even up North and out West. It was like a statewide "follow the leader" game to urban centers.

By the late seventies and early eighties, however, the tide had turned. A 1979 report from Mississippi State's Social Science Research Center spotted a trend that was flipping the script nationwide. Suddenly, cities were experiencing rapid population losses while rural areas and small towns were becoming increasingly attractive to new residents. Between 1970 and 1974, the South's countryside was particularly captivating, with nonmetropolitan regions expanding at a rate exceeding that of any other region. It was as if someone had pressed the "reverse" button on the great urban migration.

Fast forward to 1990, and some of Mississippi's once-sleepy rural areas were transforming into boomtowns. Take Olive Branch, for instance. This former rural outpost's population increased nearly sevenfold by 2020, as evidenced by Table 20.2. Not to be outdone, Madison tripled its headcount in the same period. It was like these towns had stumbled upon a secret formula for rapid growth.

Table 20.2. City Changes in Population from 1990–2020			
City	1990	2020	Difference
Jackson	196,637	153,701	-42,936
Southaven	17,949	54,648	36,699
Hattiesburg	41,882	48,730	6,848
Biloxi	46,419	49,144	2,725
Gulfport	40,775	72,926	32,151
Source: US Population Data, Census: 1990, 2020.			

The data paints a clear picture: people were fleeing the urban areas of Jackson and Memphis for greener pastures. The allure of wide-open spaces and smaller communities seemed too strong to resist. This great reshuffling has reshaped Mississippi's demographic landscape, turning former farmland into bustling suburbs and leaving city planners scratching their heads. It's a reminder that in the world of demographics, today's ghost town could be tomorrow's boomtown—and vice versa!

Also according to Table 20.2, Jackson, the capital city of Mississippi, has been experiencing a significant population decline that warrants attention from urban planners and policymakers. It is undergoing substantial out-migration, with many residents relocating to neighboring suburban areas, particularly Madison and Ridgeland. This pattern of urban-to-suburban migration has been reshaping the region's demographic landscape since the 1980s.

Initially, this migration trend was predominantly observed among the White population, a phenomenon often referred to in urban studies as "White flight." However, the out-migration has become increasingly diverse in recent years, encompassing individuals from a variety of racial and ethnic backgrounds, such as African Americans and other minority groups.

The shifting population patterns around Jackson reveal a city in transformation. As residents move between urban and suburban areas, they reshape not just neighborhoods but the very identity of Mississippi's capital region. This demographic dance between city and suburb creates ripple effects through schools, businesses, and community life, challenging leaders to reimagine the future of greater Jackson.

The numbers tell a stark story. In 1980, the US Census revealed that Jackson was riding high with a population of 202,895. But by 1990, the city had already lost its footing, slipping to 196,637 residents—a 3 percent tumble that was just the beginning of a larger trend.

By 2020, the trend had shifted dramatically. Over three decades, from 1990 to 2020, Jackson saw a significant population decline, with 49,580 residents leaving the city, as shown in table 20.2. That's akin to losing a small city's worth of residents!

Table 20.3. Increase in Former Rural Populations from 1990–2020			
City	1990	2020	Difference
Olive Branch	8,813	46,419	37,606
Madison	8,996	27,987	18,991
Horn Lake	13,508	26,736	13,228
Ridgeland	12,908	24,340	11,432
Source: US Population Data, Census: 1990, 2020.			

Meanwhile, as is pointed out in Table 20.3, Madison and Ridgeland have been playing the role of welcome wagons, their populations swelling as Jackson's shrinks.

This urban-to-suburban shuffle isn't just about changing addresses. It's a story of shifting preferences, evolving economic landscapes, and the complex interplay of factors that make people choose one community over another. Jackson's loss has been its suburbs' gain, turning once-quiet bedroom communities into bustling centers.

AN URBAN MISSISSIPPI?

In the previous edition of this book, we discussed Mississippi's urbanization trends. Our forecasts suggested population declines in certain rural areas, with potential population growth in the Gulf Coast region, the Jackson metropolitan area, northeastern Mississippi, the Memphis suburban areas, and various small urban clusters throughout the state. Upon review, the outcomes have varied. As evidenced by Table 20.2, most of our predictions have proven accurate, except for Jackson. The coastal regions have experienced population growth, as have the areas surrounding Memphis.

The potential for gentrification in Jackson, Mississippi's capital, has been a topic of discussion, though concrete evidence of this phenomenon remains elusive. Gentrification typically involves more affluent residents in historically lower-income urban areas, often resulting in neighborhood changes that can displace longtime residents.

Jackson's context is unique due to its significant population decline and relatively low housing costs. These factors have led to speculation about the city's vulnerability to gentrification. Some observers suggest that investors might be enticed to purchase and renovate properties in Jackson, given the low entry costs and potential for appreciation.

If such a trend were to materialize, it could potentially revitalize certain city areas, improving infrastructure and attracting new businesses. However, this scenario also raises concerns about the possible displacement of current lower-income residents who might find themselves priced out of their neighborhoods.

CHAPTER 21.

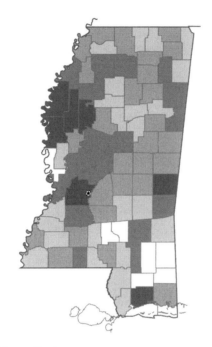

Map 34. Population, 1940

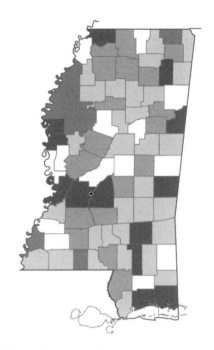

Map 35. Population, 1980

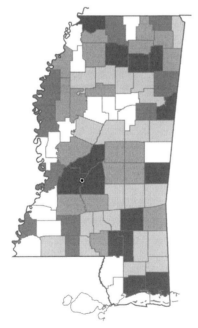

■	more than 50,000	68K
▓	30,000-50,000	47K
▒	20,000-30,000	30K
░	10,000-20,000	15K
□	less than 10,000	0K

Population Legend for maps 27-29
(shared by 1940, 1980, 2020 maps)

Map 36. Population, 2020

While Jackson's possibility of gentrification remains a point of discussion, there is little evidence that widespread gentrification is taking place or imminent. The city continues to grapple with various urban challenges, and any future redevelopment efforts will likely need to balance urban renewal goals with existing residents' needs and rights.

CAUSES OF IN-MIGRATION

The patterns of migration from rural areas to small towns, from towns to cities, and subsequently from cities to suburbs are driven by a complex interplay of factors. While economic considerations often serve as the primary motivator, a broader set of variables frequently influence the decision to relocate.

One of the most salient factors is the pursuit of improved economic opportunities. Urban centers typically offer a more diverse job market with potentially higher compensation, attracting individuals from less economically robust areas.

However, the availability and quality of services also play a crucial role in migration decisions. Individuals often seek locations that can provide enhanced living conditions and superior educational institutions for their families. These factors can be particularly influential for those with school-age children or those planning for future family expansion.

It's worth noting that this migration pattern is not unidirectional. While many Mississippians may be drawn to urban areas for their economic and service advantages, others prefer the distinctive characteristics of small-town or rural life. This countervailing trend suggests that factors beyond pure economic calculus, such as community ties, lifestyle preferences, and cultural affinities, also significantly influence residential choices.

The dynamics of migration in Mississippi are more complex than simple job availability. Some individuals prepare for migration long before actively seeking employment, acquiring skills for positions that are scarce in rural areas.

Moreover, not everyone has the ability or desire to relocate. Some Mississippi residents face constraints that prevent them from moving, resulting in long commutes to work. This situation highlights the intricate relationship between job location, population distribution, and individual circumstances in shaping migration patterns within the state.

CITIES "DRAW" PEOPLE

The primary reason for the migration of jobs and people to cities is the perception that cities offer a higher quality of life. This belief is based on cities providing a wider range of economic, social, and cultural experiences and possibilities.

Figure 21.3. A mural in downtown Jackson. Photo by Alexandra Melnick.

People relocate in search of better lives and the ability to fulfill their individual interests and aspirations.

Cities attract people due to their complexity and diversity, offering a variety of occupations and cultural experiences, from various cuisines to different movie options, diverse religious institutions, and cultural groups. This richness and variety allow people to pursue their unique interests and find fulfillment in their personal and professional lives.

In contrast, rural areas often cannot provide the same diversity and opportunity, leading many residents to leave.

QUALITY OF LIFE

In Mississippi, two crucial measures of quality of life are fundamental necessities: access to clean water and healthcare. The state's health challenges are deeply intertwined with poverty, exacerbated by recent medical facility closures that have widened disparities, often along racial lines. The water crisis in Jackson in the early 2020s epitomizes these issues, drawing parallels to Flint, Michigan. Decades of neglect have led to aging infrastructure plagued by lead contamination and frequent service disruptions.

The crisis highlighted long-standing problems: aging pipes, staffing shortages, billing issues, and a shrinking tax base (due to White and Black flight) had contributed to repeated system failures, including during a 2021 winter storm that left residents without water for weeks. The Environmental Protection Agency had previously warned the city about violations of the Safe Drinking Water Act, including high levels of lead and bacterial contamination.

Figure 21.4. Mississippi National Guard distributes bottled water to Jackson residents in 2022. US Army National Guard photo by Staff Sgt. Connie Jones. Licensed under CC BY 2.0, https://creativecommons.org/licenses/by/2.0/.

During the 2022 legislative session, a proposed $4 million bond for Jackson's water and sewer improvements failed to pass. Tensions between Jackson's leadership and state officials have intensified over perceived inadequate state support. Governor Reeves defended withholding aid, stating, "It's important that the City of Jackson start collecting their water bill payments before they start going and asking everyone else to pony up more money."

The discourse surrounding the issue has taken on racial undertones. For instance, when discussing the city's water infrastructure, Lieutenant Governor Delbert Hosemann, referencing Jackson's last White mayor, asked a reporter, "You remember during Kane Ditto's administration? He did repair work on water and sewer. So, what happened since then?" This statement is particularly charged, given that Jackson has not had a White mayor since Ditto. In response, Mayor Chokwe Antar Lumumba denounced what he termed "plantation politics" and described the state's actions as "a colonial power taking over our city."

In the face of state inaction, the federal government invested over $800 million in funding. However, this amount was short of the estimated $2 billion required for a comprehensive overhaul of Jackson's water system.

POLITICAL DETERMINANTS OF HEALTH

As of 2024, Mississippi faces significant healthcare challenges, with the state recording the nation's lowest life expectancy at seventy-two years. Racial disparities are stark: White residents average about seventy-three years, while Black residents have the lowest life expectancy at sixty-seven years. These figures reflect broader issues, including the closure of rural hospitals, forcing patients to travel long distances for care. Rural residents, often grappling with higher poverty rates, face additional barriers to accessing affordable healthcare.

Census data highlights racial disparities in insurance coverage: 68 percent of White residents have private insurance, compared to 46 percent of Black residents. Meanwhile, 47 percent of Black residents rely on public insurance, versus 35 percent of White residents. About 14 percent of Black and 12 percent of White residents lack insurance altogether, underscoring widespread access issues.

The debate over Medicaid expansion, introduced by the 2010 Affordable Care Act, remains central to Mississippi's healthcare discourse. Proponents argue it would cover over 300,000 low-income residents, bring federal funds, and save rural hospitals. Opponents cite concerns about long-term costs and expanding government programs. Despite similar Republican-led states adopting expansion, Mississippi remains one of the few holdouts, leaving vulnerable populations—like the elderly, disabled, and low-income families—without critical access to healthcare, including mental health and substance abuse treatment.

Food, Hospital, and Pharmacy Deserts

Health is influenced by genetics, lifestyle, environment, and diet. In Mississippi, many impoverished communities lack access to healthy food options due to "food deserts." The World Health Organization describes the poverty-health relationship as a "vicious cycle." Mississippi ranks at or near the bottom in almost all poverty and health-related categories nationally, with disparities along racial and economic lines. A 2015 report by the Mississippi Department of Health showed that those without a high school diploma and annually earning less than $15,000 had the worst health outcomes, particularly among minorities.

In 2023, the Commonwealth Fund ranked Mississippi as the unhealthiest state based on factors including reproductive and women's health, racial health equity, and overall health system performance. The state struggles with high rates of preterm birth, infant mortality, and deaths from breast and cervical cancer.

These issues are exacerbated by food deserts, hospital deserts, and pharmacy deserts, particularly in communities with high Black populations, such as the Delta and parts of Jackson. These "deserts" limit access to nutritious food, healthcare facilities, and necessary medications, contributing significantly to the state's health and economic disparities.

Deserts to Oasis: Urban Health Revival

To address current health disparities, Mississippi could draw inspiration from past innovations, such as the 1970s comprehensive health centers that served underserved communities. Pioneered by Drs. Aaron Shirley, James Anderson, and Robert Smith, these efforts laid the groundwork for a more equitable healthcare system. Dr. Shirley, a MacArthur "genius" grant recipient, led the transformation of a neglected shopping mall into the Jackson Medical Mall in 1995, creating a national model for community-based healthcare. The project improved healthcare access, stimulated local economic growth, and addressed food and pharmacy deserts. By revisiting these successes, Mississippi can develop new strategies to tackle ongoing health challenges in underserved areas.

COVID-19: A Deadly Pandemic

In early 2020, a global pandemic reached the United States and elsewhere across the world. COVID-19, also known as the Coronavirus, caused various health outcomes, from mild respiratory symptoms to death. The 2022 State Scorecard on State Health System Performance ranked Mississippi 51st out of the 50 states plus the District of Columbia on access to quality health care, health disparities, and health outcomes during the Coronavirus pandemic.

From 2020 to 2022, the Mississippi State Department of Health reported over 900,000 coronavirus cases and 14,155 deaths. Although African Americans comprised 38 percent of the state's population, they represented 54 percent of the COVID-19 cases.

THE VESTIGES OF SLAVERY, JIM CROW SEGREGATION, AND ECONOMIC DISPARITIES

During slavery, Mississippi's economy thrived as the "king of cotton," fueled by enslaved labor and fertile Delta soil. After emancipation, the state's economy collapsed, leaving it one of the poorest in the nation. Today, 19.1 percent of Mississippians live in poverty, with 67 percent of its 82 counties classified as having "persistent poverty"—where rates have exceeded 20 percent for thirty years. Over half of residents in these counties are people of color, with 30 percent of Black residents living below the poverty line compared to 12 percent of Whites.

Poverty rates remain strikingly high in regions with a history of high slavery concentrations. For instance, in the Mississippi Delta, Black poverty rates reach 46 percent in Washington County and 42 percent in Coahoma County. These statistics underscore the lasting economic legacy of slavery on Black communities. This connection is further emphasized by the lack of significant economic

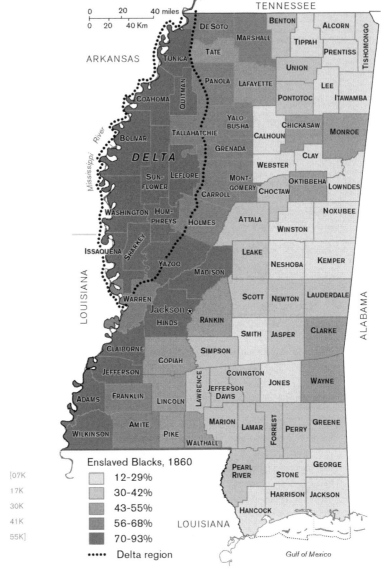

Map 37. Mississippi Slavery, 1860

development in areas where slavery was once widespread. Ironically, the largest employer in the region is the Mississippi State Penitentiary, which incarcerates a disproportionate number of Black individuals, highlighting the deep-rooted systemic inequities that continue to shape the economic and social landscape of the region.

Mississippi's population is uniquely binary, with over 90 percent identifying as Black or White. This divide is starkest among children: 45 percent of Black children live in poverty, compared to 14 percent of White children. This racial poverty gap fuels cascading issues, including strained public services, a weak

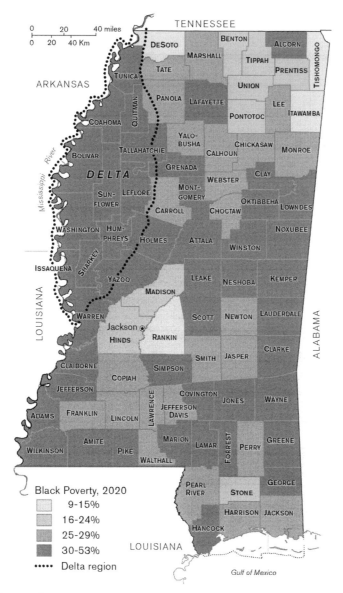

Map 38. Mississippi Poverty, 2020

tax base, and underfunded healthcare and education systems. The state's largest welfare scandal, involving $77 to $94 million misused from the TANF program, further hindered efforts to support those in need.

The Mississippi Delta, once a cotton powerhouse built on slave labor, now struggles with poverty and limited economic opportunities. Maps 37 and 38 show a clear link between areas with high historical enslavement and current poverty rates, underscoring slavery's lasting economic impact. Until Mississippi addresses these disparities, its growth and progress will remain stunted, leaving its most vulnerable residents—especially Black children—trapped in cycles of poverty.

EDUCATION

Mississippi's education system has made remarkable progress in recent years, overcoming historical challenges through strategic initiatives. The 2013 Literacy-Based Promotion Act, or "Third-Grade Gate," has been pivotal in boosting reading proficiency, making Mississippi a national leader in fourth-grade reading improvements. According to the 2024 National Assessment of Educational Progress (NAEP), the state ranked first in fourth-grade academic gains, with reading scores averaging 219—above the national average of 214. Record-high graduation rates further highlight the state's commitment to student success, driven by targeted interventions and support programs.

Career and technical education programs have also bridged the gap between education and industry, equipping students with skills for high-demand jobs and contributing to economic growth. School turnaround initiatives have improved performance in struggling schools by focusing on leadership, teacher quality, and community engagement.

However, challenges remain. Teacher shortages, particularly in rural areas, are worsened by low salaries and a lack of advanced qualifications among educators. High poverty rates limit access to essential resources, and racial disparities persist, with Black and Hispanic students often attending underfunded schools. For example, 89 percent of schools with failing grades are in districts where 90 percent or more of students are Black. Chronic underfunding of the Mississippi Adequate Education Program (MAEP) and limited early childhood education access have further widened achievement gaps.

In 2024, the legislature replaced MAEP with the Mississippi Student Funding Formula, aiming to allocate resources based on district-level enrollment and attendance. Rural schools face additional hurdles, including limited technology, fewer extracurricular options, and difficulties recruiting qualified teachers. The digital divide, particularly the lack of broadband access in rural areas, remains a barrier, though the state is investing $162 million to expand broadband to 27,000 residents across nineteen counties.

While Mississippi has made significant strides, addressing teacher shortages, funding inequities, and technological gaps is essential to ensure all students have access to quality education and opportunities for success.

A MODERATE MISSISSIPPI?

According to the Gallup Poll, Mississippi has consistently ranked as the most conservative state in the nation. Conservatism can take many forms, from supporting school prayer and opposing taxes to being unsupportive of same sex marriages, among other beliefs. However, in recent years, Mississippi has taken notable steps that signal a shift away from its traditionally conservative stance. In 2020, the state made a significant cultural change by retiring its old state flag, which featured Confederate imagery, and adopting a new design. This move reflects a growing recognition of the need to move beyond divisive symbols and embrace a more inclusive and unified identity for the state.

That same year, Mississippi legalized medical marijuana, a move that diverged from the state's typically conservative approach to drug policy. This decision aligns with a growing national trend toward recognizing the potential medical benefits of cannabis.

Additionally, Mississippi eliminated a racially discriminatory law that was originally designed to dilute the Black vote. This action addressed a long-standing issue of electoral fairness and represented a step toward dismantling systemic racial barriers.

The state has also embraced renewable energy by adopting wind power as a means of electricity production. This shift toward cleaner energy sources demonstrates a willingness to adapt to changing environmental and economic realities despite traditionally conservative attitudes toward energy policy.

These changes collectively suggest that Mississippi is undergoing a period of transformation, balancing its conservative heritage with more progressive policies in response to evolving social, economic, and environmental needs.

MISSISSIPPI: STANDING AT THE CROSSROADS

Mississippi has made significant strides in recent years, showing signs of progress and hope. The state removed the Confederate emblem from its flag, a powerful step toward a more inclusive future. It also opened the Two Mississippi Museums—the Museum of Mississippi History and the Mississippi Civil Rights Museum—which honor the state's complex past and the struggles and triumphs of its people. Additionally, the Mississippi Department of Archives and History launched a repatriation project, returning hundreds of Native American remains to the Chickasaw Nation, acknowledging and respecting Indigenous heritage.

Politically, Mississippi sent its first woman, Cindy Hyde-Smith, to the US Senate and continues to lead the nation in the number of Black elected officials. Education has seen improvements, and the state's rich cultural heritage, from blues music to celebrated authors like Margaret Walker Alexander, Richard Wright, William Faulkner, and Eudora Welty, remains a source of pride. Recent athletic achievements, like national championships in college football and baseball, have also brought positive attention to the state.

Economically, Mississippi is working to attract new industries and foster innovation. Investments in projects like the Thad Cochran Mississippi Center for Innovation and Technology and the AI Innovation Hub show the state's commitment to growth and technological advancement.

Efforts toward racial reconciliation have also been notable, with biracial commissions established to address historical traumas, such as the murders of Emmett Till and civil rights workers Andrew Goodman, James Chaney, and Michael Schwerner. These commissions have helped communities heal and move forward, with tangible results like the election of Philadelphia's first Black mayor and the creation of memorials honoring Till's legacy.

Yet, beneath these signs of progress lies a deeper tension that continues to shape Mississippi's identity. The state remains at a crossroads, grappling with its past while striving to build a more equitable future. This tension is evident in the way Mississippi honors both Martin Luther King Jr. Day and Robert E. Lee Day or observes Confederate Heritage Month alongside efforts to celebrate civil rights achievements. The vague law on critical race theory raises concerns about sanitizing history, which can distort the truth and erase important lessons about race. Governor Tate Reeves defended it, claiming the state does not need children "indoctrinated" by teachers, but limiting honest discussions of history risks ignoring its complexities and lasting impacts. Even with more Black elected officials than any other state, almost all of them are elected in majority-Black districts, as White voters in majority-White areas rarely support Black candidates. This divide was also visible when the state opened the Two Mississippi Museums; the invitation of then-President Donald Trump sparked protests, with some Black leaders choosing not to attend.

Mississippi's ambivalence toward its history is further reflected in its choices for National Statuary Hall in the US Capitol, where each state selects two notable figures to represent it. Mississippi's choices—Confederate president Jefferson Davis and J. Z. George—highlight a lingering attachment to its Confederate past. Similarly, buildings at historically Black Mississippi Valley State University still bear the names of segregationists like Walter Sillers Jr. and Fielding L. Wright. These symbols stand in stark contrast to the progress made during the civil rights movement, underscoring the state's ongoing struggle to reconcile its history with its future.

The most pressing issue facing Mississippi is the future of its youth, particularly the high poverty rate among Black children, with 45 percent living in poverty, according to the Annie E. Casey Foundation. This widespread poverty increases reliance on state and federal aid, weakens the tax base, and jeopardizes healthcare and education quality, undermining the state's economic vitality. Compounding these challenges, Mississippi faced its largest welfare scandal, with $77 to $94 million in funds meant for needy families misappropriated, further deepening the struggles of its most vulnerable populations.

Mississippi's reputation has been further tarnished by a series of troubling incidents, including law enforcement misconduct that has necessitated federal intervention. One such case involved the Rankin County "Goon Squad," where officers tortured two Black men, drawing national outrage. During legal proceedings, Rankin County Sheriff Bryan Bailey's testimony revealed a disturbing link to past practices when he admitted to receiving training from former state trooper Lloyd "Goon" Jones, who had been implicated in serious misconduct. Jones was notably involved in the fatal shooting of Benjamin Brown during a 1967 protest near Jackson State University, underscoring a troubling legacy of systemic abuse and injustice.

While isolated, racially motivated incidents involving younger generations have also drawn national attention. A group of White teenagers attacked James Craig Anderson, a Black man who was walking in Jackson, beating him and running him over with a truck while shouting racist slurs. White students also placed a noose around the neck of the James Meredith statue at the University of Mississippi, desecrating a memorial to the school's first Black student. Though these acts do not represent most young Mississippians, they have sparked important conversations about racial tensions and the need for change.

Mississippi's future depends on its ability to build on recent progress while honestly confronting these challenges. The state has the potential to become a model for positive change by addressing systemic inequalities and leveraging its diverse population and resources. However, failing to tackle these issues risks perpetuating historical patterns of marginalization and could lead to a continued loss of talent and resources. Mississippi stands at a crossroads, with the choice to fully embrace a more inclusive and equitable future or remain tethered to the divisions of its past. The path it chooses will shape its identity for generations to come.

Recommended Readings

Paul V. Canonici, *The Delta Italians Volume II* (Madison, MS: Cedar Grove Publishing, 2013).

James W. Loewen, *The Mississippi Chinese: Between Black and White* (Cambridge: Harvard University Press, 1971)

James W. Loewen, *Lies Across America: What Our Historical Sites Get Wrong* (New York: The New Press 2019 (1999)

INDEX

Aberdeen, 18, 76, 161, 167–68, 169
abolition, 94, 106–7, 108–9, 113, 134, 146–47, 402
absentee landlords, 97, 220
Ackia, Battle of, 39
actors, 393
Adams, John, 76–77
Afroman, 381
Agricultural Adjustment Administration (AAA), 236
agricultural high schools, 210, 222, 224, 226
agriculture, xxiii, xxiv, 20, 21, 26, 29–30, 65, 66–67, 75–76, 105, 159, 163, 176, 195, 210, 236–37, 304, 320, 329, 347–50, 355–56; and freedmen, 135–36, 143–45; and Native Americans, xxiii, 29–30, 36, 66; plantation, 3, 75, 119; and Whitecaps, 208. *See also* cotton
Alabama Black Belt, 18
Alcorn, James L., 116, 155–56, 157–58, 160, 162, 169, 177, 184, 194
Alcorn State University, 159, 244, 249, 300, 329, 398
Alexander, John, 383
Alexander, Margaret Walker, 388, 419
Alexander v. Holmes, 309
Alford, Bessie C., 233
Algebra Project, 267, 293
Allain, Bill, 321
Allen v. State Board of Education, 318
Allison, Mose, 381
Allison Art Colony, 395
Allworth, Lance, 398
American Federation of Labor, 356
American Library Association, xvii
American Negro Theatre, 393
American Recovery and Reinvestment Act, 356
American Revolutionary War, 39–40, 71, 73, 106
American Social History Project, xix
Ames, Adelbert, 155, 157, 162–63, 165–66, 167, 170–71, 172, 195
Amite County, 133, 266, 394
Anderson, James, 415
Anderson, James Craig, 420
Anderson, Phyliss, 56
Anderson, Reuben, 321
Andrews, Dana, 393
archaeology, xvii, 24, 27
Armisen, Fred, 393
art: xxn2, 28, 305, 360, 361, 362, 395–97. *See also* folklore; literature; music; pottery; sculpturers
Association of Southern Women for the Prevention of Lynching, 233
Ates, Roscoe, 393
Atoka Agreement, 54
Attaway, William, 389
Ayers v. Fordice, 329

Babbitt, Milton, 384
Bailey, Bryan, 420
Baker, Ella, 264, 274, 285
Balance Agriculture with Industry (BAWI) Program, 17, 238, 352
banks, 88, 92, 108, 207, 208, 215, 235
Banks, Fred, 321
Bankston, 130
Banner, David, 38
Barbour, Haley, 342
Barnett, James, 45

Barnett, Ross, 4, 255, 261–62, 268, 270
Barney, Lem, 398
Barrett, Richard, 321
Barthelme, Frederick, 389
Barton, Dee, 384
Bass, Lance, 380
Bates, Glady Noel, 242
Baton Rouge, Louisiana, 76, 80
battles. *See individual names*
"Bear, The," (Faulker), 385
Beittel, A. D., 274, 277
Belafonte, Harry, 273
Belhaven College, 180, 360
Bell, John, 114
Beth Israel Jewish Synagogue, 292, 402
Bettersworth, John K., xiv, xv, xvi, xvii, xviii, xix, xxn5, xxn7, 171, 172, 313
Beyoncé, 306
Big K. R. I. T., 381
Bilbo, Theodore G., 211–13, 223, 234–35, 239, 241, 323; senate investigations of, 235
Biloxi (city), 63, 129, 239, 262, 294, 360, 396, 408
Biloxi (tribe), 28, 63
bird, Mississippi state, xxiii
Black America (Nearing), xviii
Black Boy (Wright), 386
Black Codes, 68, 149–51, 170
Black Lives Matter, xix, 306
Black Monday, 252
Black Panther: Wakanda Forever, 381
Black Power, 296, 306
Black Prairie, 18–19, 360
Black Warrior River, 41
Blackmon, Ed, 327
Blackwell, Unita, 285
Blackwood Brothers, 365–66
Blood on the Forge (Attaway), 389
Blue Front Café, 373, 375
boll weevil, 16, 210, 220–21, 347
Bonecrusher, 381
Boston, Ralph, 398
"Bourbons," 176, 182, 193
Bowen, Keith, 188
Bowers, Sam, 298
Bowie, Tori, 398
boycotts, 190, 272, 275–76, 283, 290, 297, 301, 307
Boyd, Dennis "Oil Can," 398

Boynton v. Virginia, 267
Boys in the Band, The (Crowley), 393
Brady, Tom, 252
"brain drain," 7, 405
Brandon, Gerard, 84, 89, 105
Brasfield, Rod, 394
Braxton, Charlie, xi, 380
Brazile, Robert, 398
Breckinridge, John C., 114
Brent, Rita, 394
Brewer, Earl, 210
Brice's Crossroads, Battle of, 128–29
Broonzy, William Lee Conley, 369–70, 372
Brown, Albert Gallatin, 91, 108, 110, 118, 157
Brown, Benjamin, 297, 421
Brown, Ezra, 382
Brown, James, 273
Brown, John, 94, 110, 113, 169
Brown, Larry, 389
Brown, Maisie, 325
Brown, R. Jess, 242, 284
Brown v. Board of Education, 242–43, 247–48, 249–52, 256; Brown II, 258–59
Bruce, Blanche K., 160, 184, 339
Bryant, Phil, 332
Buchanan, James, 87–88
Buffett, Jimmy, 377
Bureau of Indian Affairs, 54–55, 57
Burkitt, Frank, 202
Burks, Ellis, 398
Burnside, Cedric, 374, 379
Burnside, R. L., 371, 374
Burr, Aaron, 80
Bush, George W., 342
Butler, Jack, 389

Cadillac Group, 287
Calhoun, S. S., 195
Camp McCain, 239
Camp Shelby, 232, 239
Campbell, Will D., 389
Campbell College, 180
campus uprisings, 269–70, 293, 297, 300–302, 306
Canton, 16–17, 124, 272, 285, 310, 315, 356, 385; and art, 361, 395; racial violence in, 241, 272, 281, 284, 297
Cardozo, Thomas W., 170
Carmichael, Gil, 337

Carmichael, Stokely (Kwame Ture), 296–97
carpetbaggers, 151–53, 193–94
Carroll County Massacre, 167
Carter, Hodding, II, 254, 390
Carter, Jimmy, 337, 339
Carter, Mae Bertha, 285
Carter, Robert, 284
Cat on a Hot Tin Roof (Williams), 388
Chabert, Lacey, 393
Chaffee, Lois, 274
Champion's Hill, 124
Chapel Hart, 377
chefs, 394
Cheney, James Earl, 420
Cherokee (tribe), 47, 57
Chess Records, 372
Chicago Tribune, 150
Chickasaw (tribe), xxiii, 28–30, 32–45, 47–48, 52–53, 60–61, 67–68, 71–72, 78, 80–81, 82, 87, 103, 202; removal to Oklahoma, 53, 54; repatriation of remains, 57, 419
child labor regulations, 207, 210, 216, 221
Chinn, C. O., 272, 284
Choctaw (tribe), xxiii, 28–30, 32–33, 34, 37–60, 69, 71–72, 78, 80–81, 82, 87, 88, 559, 361; as farmers, 29–30; and the French, 38; removal, 48–49, 52, 54
Choctaw County, 130, 241, 365
churches, 46, 107, 161, 200, 294, 311, 363, 365, 392; burning of, 208, 279, 282; segregation in, 184, 191
civil disobedience, 262, 265
civil rights, x, xvii, xxiii, 107, 134, 140, 148–51, 156, 158, 162, 173, 189, 190–91, 202, 209, 233, 241–42, 244, 283; advancements in, 333, 335, 420; and journalism, 385, 390–91
Civil Rights Act of 1866, 149
Civil Rights Act of 1870, 158
Civil Rights Act of 1875, 173; as unconstitutional, 189–90
Civil Rights Act of 1964, 284, 292
civil rights activists, 258, 261, 262, 264, 265, 271, 273, 275, 276, 279–80, 281–82, 284, 285, 286, 289, 291, 300–301
Civil Rights Culture Wars: The Fight Over a Mississippi Textbook (Eagles), xix
civil rights movement, xxiv, 3, 55, 249, 256–60, 261–68, 271–79, 280–302, 307, 313, 314; and attorneys, 320; celebrities and, 273

Civil War, xiii–xiv, 10, 13, 14, 16, 20, 37–53, 54, 88, 93, 94, 98–99, 131, 132, 139–40, 141, 144, 151, 176, 180, 186, 189, 193, 311; myths of, 7, 203
Claiborne, Craig, 390
Claiborne, Ferdinand L., 80–81
Claiborne, William C. C., 77
Claiborne Hardware Co. v. NAACP, 283
Clark, Charles, 132–33, 140–41
Clark, Daniel, 91–92
Clark, George Rogers, 39, 40
Clark, Kate Freeman, 396
Clark, Robert, 299, 323
Clarke, Alyce Griffin, 333–34, 359–60
Clarksdale, xvi, 226, 252, 254, 264, 285, 294, 315, 361, 371, 374, 375, 401
Clarion-Ledger, 240
Clinton, 17, 90, 100, 124, 165, 166, 167, 224, 356, 380
Clower, Jerry, 394
Coahoma Community College, 226, 244
Cobb, Charlie, 272, 278
Cochran, Thad, 332, 338–39, 340–41, 342, 419
Colbert, James, 39
Colbert, Levi, 45, 53
Coldwell, Charles, 167
Coleman, Castrol "Mr. Sipp," 373–74
Coleman, James P., 249, 259
Coleman, Linda, 334
Coles, Robert, xiv–xv
College Football Hall of Fame, 398
colonialism, 35, 38–39, 65, 67–70, 77, 153, 413
Colored Advisory Commission, 230
Columbus (city), xxiv, 132, 165, 169, 180, 357, 388
Columbus, Christopher, 24, 59–60, 90
comedians, 394
Coming of Age in Mississippi (Moody), 389
Committee on Elective Franchise, Apportionment, and Elections, 195
community colleges, 224, 226, 244, 356
Compromise of 1850, 109, 110, 112, 118
Confederacy, xxiii, 37, 53, 90, 117–20, 129–31, 134–35, 137, 140, 142, 149–50, 151, 154–55, 173, 186, 190, 312; memorials, 203
Confederate Congress, 129, 130, 135
Confederate Heritage Month, 420
Confederate States of America. *See* Confederacy

Congress of Racial Equality (CORE), 267, 272, 274
Connor, Peggy Jean, 318
Connor v. Johnson, 288, 318
Conscription Act, 130
conservatism, 418–19
Constitution of the Confederate States of America, 117
convict leasing, 180–81, 194, 207
Cooke, Sam, 375
Cora, Cat, 394
Corinth, 120–22, 135, 141
Cortés, Hernán, 59–60
cotton, 214, 215, 220; gins, 91–92, 258
Cotton, James, 372, 378
Council of Federated Organizations, 274
"courthouse gangs," 202
Courts, Gus, 257–58
COVID-19, 415
Cox, Minnie, 205
Crawford, Carolyn, 56
Creek War, 80–81
Critical Race Theory (CRT), 314, 420
Crooked Lettaz, 381
Crosby, Sheriff Peter, 163–64
Crowley, Mart, 393
CROWN Act, 333
C Spire, 355–56
cultural change, 304–5

Dara, Olu, 382
Davis, Alexander K., 170
Davis, Ben, 135–37
Davis, Edwin Jhamal, 384
Davis, Jefferson, 109, 110, 111, 117–19, 135, 157, 177, 196, 204, 420
Davis, Joseph, 137, 199
de Bienville, Jean Baptiste Le Moyne, 38–39, 63–64, 67–68
de la Beckwith, Byron, 276–77, 298
de Soto, Hernando, 59–60, 61, 128
Dear Silas, 381
Debo, Angie, 52
Debra, Charles, 249
Dee, Henry, 281
Delta and Pine Land Company (DP&L), 220
Democratic Party, 87, 88, 108, 111–12, 114, 160, 164–65, 167, 169, 170, 171, 172, 176–77, 178, 180, 182, 183, 193, 195, 202–3, 204, 205, 232, 233, 238, 240, 241–42, 255–56, 258, 277, 282, 285, 286, 299, 322, 335–37; realignment of, 338–40, 344
Democratic White Men's Party of Mississippi, 154
Democratic National Convention of 1964, 282
Dennis, David, 272
Dent, Louis, 155
desegregation, 246, 263–64, 298–99. *See also* education: race and
Devine, Annie, 272, 275, 291
d'Iberville, Pierre LeMoyne, 63–64
Diddley, Bo, 378
disenfranchisement, 189, 198, 201, 275, 328; felony, 328–29
Douglas, Ellen, 389
Douglas, Frederick, 146, 186
Douglas, Stephen, 112
Down by the Riverside (Wright), 230
Dred Scott, 112
Dunbar, William, 75, 76, 104
Dupree, Jack, 166–67

East, P. D., 254
East Mississippi Insane Hospital, 79
Eastland, James O., 2, 3–4, 239, 251, 295, 337–38, 348
Eaton, Clemont, 104
Eaton, John, 135
economy. *See* industry
Edelman, Marian Wright, 284, 293, 300
education, xvi, xxiv, 90–91, 154, 180, 210, 222–24, 417–18; antebellum, 90; civil rights history in, 314–15; and "equalization" program, 242; and "freedom of choice," 308–9; and Head Start, 295, 323; limits to, 176, 205, 214, 222–23, 352; Native American, 53, 56; progress in, 18, 103, 264; public, 91, 153, 158–59, 180, 250, 294, 313, 354, 356, 222–23, 352; race and, 90–91, 139, 149, 190–91, 205, 206–7, 208, 209, 218, 224–25, 242, 243, 246–47, 249–50, 263, 284, 311, 314, 315, 322, 329; school consolidation, 263. *See also* community colleges; "separate but equal"
Education Reform Act of 1982, 323
Edwards, Eddie, 382
Edwards, Teddy, 382
Eisenhower, Dwight D., 232, 233

Election of 1867, 151, 152
Election of 1868, 152
Election of 1869, 155
Election of 1903, 205
Election of 1911, 211–12
Elizabeth Female Academy, 90
Ellicot, Andrew, 75, 76
Ellis, Monta, 398
Ellis-Taylor, Aunjanue, 393
Emancipation Proclamation, 133, 142
Engell, Lehman, 384
Environmental Protection Agency, 410
Equal Opportunity Commission, 312
Equal Rights Amendment (ERA), 331
equalization, 242–43, 251–52
Espy, Mike, 320, 344
Evers, Charles, xxn2, 283, 284, 299–300, 337, 338
Evers, Medgar, 249, 263, 273–74, 275–76, 298, 391
Evers, Myrlie, 276, 285
Exodus of 1879, 185. *See also* Great Migration

Facts of Reconstruction, The (Lynch), 173
Fairchild, Shelly, 377
Family's Affair, A (Douglas), 389
Farm Security Administration, 238
Farmers' Alliance, 182
farming, 14, 15–16, 22, 42, 44, 54, 91, 135, 205, 215–16, 237, 304, 346–47
Faulkner, William, 385, 419
Favre, Brett, 398
FBI, 258, 273
Federalist Party, 77
Ferris, David "Boo," 398
Fielder, Alvin, 382
Fifteenth Amendment, 112, 140, 155, 156, 193, 197, 205
Finch, Cliff, 337
Finney, Nikki, 389
"Fire-Eaters," 109, 110, 111, 115–17, 132
Five Blind Boys of Mississippi, 365
flag, Mississippi state, 324, 325–26, 419
floods, 13, 16, 48, 179, 214, 230–31, 251, 353
Florida, 190, 405; early settlement of, 39, 60, 62, 69, 71–74, 80
flower, Mississippi state, 324
Floyd, George, xxn5, 306, 325
folktales, 385; recipes as, 363

Foote, Henry, 100–101, 111–12
Foote, Shelby, 389
For My People (Alexander), 388
Ford, Curtis, 398
Ford, Willie Mae, 366
Fordice, Kirk, 324, 341–42
Forman, James, 393
Forrest, Nathan Bedford, 122, 128
Fort Maurepas, 63
Fort Mims, 41, 80–81
Fort Pillow, 128
Fort Rosalie, 37–38, 64, 68, 72
Fort Sumner, 119
Fourteenth Amendment, xvii, 140, 149, 150–51, 189–90, 225, 247–48
Franklin, Aretha, 273
Franklin, Tom, 389
Franklin Academy, 90
Frazier, Hillman, 224
free Blacks, xvi, 49, 67, 94, 101–2, 106, 140–41, 149. *See also* abolition
Free Southern Theater, 392–93
Freedman's Bureau, 143–44, 145, 150
Freedmen, 135, 141, 155, 173
Freedom Riders, 267–68, 287
freedom schools, 278–79, 287, 290, 291–92, 293, 295
Freedom Summer, x, 271, 278, 291, 295
Freedom Vote, 275, 277
Freeman, Carroll, 383–84
Freeman, Morgan, 393
French and Indian War, 69
frontier conditions, 13, 82–89, 91–93, 103, 186, 387
Fugitive Slave Act of 1850, 108
fusion (in politics), 182, 194

Gainey, M. C., 393
Gandy, Evelyn, 330–31, 337
Garrison, William Lloyd, 106
gentrification, 409, 411
Gentry, Bobbie, 377
George, J. Z., 169
George, James Z., 195–96
gerrymandering, 183, 288
Gettysburg, Battle of, 123
Gillom, Peggie, 398
Gilmer, Elizabeth Meriwether, 20
Goodman, Andrew, 420

Goodman, Benny, 382
Gordon, Dexter, 382
Grand Ole Opry, 394
Grange, The, 182
Grant, Ulysses S., 120
Graves, "Blind" Roosevelt and Uaroy, 378
Graves, James E., Jr., 321
Gray, Gwendolyn, 344
Gray, Victoria, 275, 291
Great Depression, 18, 232, 235–36, 346, 352, 396
Great Flood of 1927, 227–31
Great Migration, 219, 405
Green, Benjamin T., 199
Greenback Party, 182
Greene, John J., 403
Greene County, 130
Greenfield, Elizabeth Taylor, 383
Greenville Delta, 254
Greenwood, 50, 51, 129, 271, 273, 281, 296, 360, 385
Greenwood, L. C., 398
Gregory, Dick, 272
Grenada, 16, 122, 167, 237
Grierson, Benjamin H., 123
Griffin, Dick, 382
Grisham, John, 389
Gulf Coast, 13, 22–23, 36, 40, 63, 80, 119, 131, 220–21, 262, 264, 310, 355–56, 358, 361, 384, 402, 409
Gulf of Mexico, 13, 22, 27, 60, 61
GumTree Museum of Art, 396
Gunn, Phillip, 325–26
Guyot, Lawrence, 276, 277

Hall, Carsie, 284
Hamer, Fannie Lou, 275, 276, 282, 286–87, 291, 295, 348
Hannah, Barry, 389
Harlan, John Marshall, 190, 191
Harpers Ferry, 94, 111, 113
Harris, Lusia, 398
Harrison, Pat, 238–39
Harvey, Claire Collins, 285, 287
Hattiesburg, 21, 210, 232, 247, 266, 273, 281, 290, 358, 408
Hayes, Curtis, 266
Hayes, Rutherford, 169, 173
healthcare, 226, 248, 271, 314, 322–23, 332, 340, 351, 357, 371, 412, 417, 420; and closing of rural hospitals, 414; and declining life expectancy, 414; deserts, 414–15
Heavy (Laymon), 389
Help, The (Stockett), 389
Hemingway, William L., 178
Henderson, Michael, 382
Henry, Aaron, 325
Henson, Jim, 393
Herrera, Anthony, 393
Hill, Faith, 377
Hinds, Thomas, 45
Hinds Community College, 224, 226
Hinton, Milt "The Judge," 382
History of the Old South, A (Eaton), 104
Holbrook, A. M., 201
Holiday, Billie, 186, 381
Holmes, James "Duck," 373
Holmes Junior College, 226
Holt, Red, 382
Hood, Jim, 327, 344
Hooker, John Lee, 370
Hosemann, Delbert, 410
House, Eddie "Son," 26, 323
Howard, Perry, 233
Howard, T. R. M., 248
Howlin' Wolf, 369, 370, 372
Hudson, Winson, 264
Humphreys, Benjamin, 148, 150, 154
Hurricane Katrina, 340, 342, 359
Hurst, E. H., 267
Hutchinson, Anthony, 77
Hyde-Smith, Cindy, 419

Ice Cold Rappers, 380
immigration, xxiv, 163, 401, 403. *See also* migration
Immigration and Customs Enforcement (ICE), xxiv, 403
impeachment, 170–71
Indian Child Welfare Act, 56
Indian Healthcare Improvement Act, 56
Indian Removal Act, 48
Indian Self-Determination and Education Assistance Act, 56
industry: Aluminum Dynamics, 356; Amazon, 356, 357; automobile, 16, 17, 356; catfish, 349–50; cattle, 16, 18, 20, 128, 347, 350; failure to grow, 222; gambling, 15, 22,

358–60; lumber, 207, 214, 220; oil and gas, 22, 358; and race relations, 354; shipbuilding, 239, 353; solar, 22, 356, 358; space, 355, 357–58; tourism, 360–61; woodworking, 214
Ingalls Shipbuilding Company, 239
Institute for the Study of Black History (Margaret Walker Center), 388
integration, 159, 242, 246, 249, 253, 259, 262, 270, 271, 284, 307, 312, 340, 354, 390. *See also* education: and race
Iron Chef America, 394

Jackson, 16, 20, 50, 81, 86–87, 95, 100, 123–24, 127, 131, 132, 140, 141, 153, 163–64, 170, 183, 194, 210, 242, 253, 254, 262–63, 264, 267–68, 269, 274–75, 279, 283, 292, 296, 297–98, 308, 311, 312, 315, 324, 352, 354, 355–56, 360, 361; population decline of, 408; water crisis in, 410–11
Jackson, Andrew, xxiii, 41, 42, 47–48, 50, 81, 86, 88–89, 92, 110, 115
Jackson, Chris (Mahmoud Abdul Rauf), 398
Jackson, Mahalia, 273
Jackson Little Theater, 392
Jackson Medical Mall, 415
Jackson Prairie, 20
Jackson State University, 180, 224, 297–98, 301–2, 329, 360, 384, 388, 398, 421
Jackson Symphony Orchestra, 384, 398
Jefferson, Al, 398
Jefferson, Thomas, 44–45, 77–78
Jefferson College, 90, 91
Jim Crow, 137, 189–91, 205, 208, 224–25, 233, 248, 276, 328, 371–72, 386, 415–20
John Rundle High School, 299
Johnson, Andrew, 137–38, 139, 144
Johnson, Derrick, 327
Johnson, Harvey, 321
Johnson, Paul, 223–34
Johnson, Paul B., Jr., 212, 223
Johnson, Robert, 369–70
Johnson, William, 101
Johnston, Albert Sidney, 120
Johnston, Amos R., 146
Johnston, Erle, 249
Johnston, Oscar, 237
Joliet, Louis, 61
Jones, Cornelius, 200–201
Jones, Deacon, 398
Jones, Hank, 382
Jones, James Earl, 393
Jones, Samuel, 384
Jones County, "The Free State of Jones," 131
Jordan, Winthrop, 389
Journal of Mississippi History, xix
journalism, 131, 201, 362, 390–92
Jubilee (Alexander), 388
juke joints, 373, 374
junior colleges. *See* community colleges

Kamikaze, 381
Kansas-Nebraska Act, 112
Kate Freeman Memorial Art Gallery, 396
Kearney, Belle, 330
Keesler Air Force Base, 239
Kennard, Clyde, 249–50
Kennedy, John F., 267, 270, 271, 276
Kennedy, Robert F., 264, 267, 270
Key, V. O., 218
Killen, Edgar Ray, 280–81, 298
Killer Mike, 381
King, Clemon, 249
King, Martin Luther, Jr., 262, 265, 267, 283, 296, 299, 306, 420
Kingsbury, Cyrus, 43
Kirksey v. Board of Supervisor, 318–19
Knight, Newt, 131
Koury, Leon, 395
Ku Klux Klan, xiv, 128, 160–61, 162, 165–66, 169, 254, 271, 273, 279, 281, 298, 307, 324, 371
Kunstler, Williams, 293
Kyle, Maryann, 384

labor unions, 178, 294, 351
Ladd, Diane, 393
Ladner, Joyce, 263, 293
Lafayette County, 113, 133
Lamar, Lucius Quintus Cincinnatus, 116, 178
Landau, Saul, 60
Laurel, 21, 273, 281, 294, 396
Lauren Rogers Library and Museum of Art, 396
Law, John, 65
Laymon, Kiese, 389
Lee, George, 257
Lee, Herbert, 266

Lee, Robert E., 120, 420
Leflore, Greenwood, 50–51
Let Me Breathe Thunder (Attaway), 389
levees, 13, 41, 158, 179, 184, 227–28, 366, 401
Lewis, Jerry Lee, 379
Lewis, John, 293
Lewis, Pearlena, 274
Lexington, 113, 167, 254, 294
Liberator, 106
Liddell, James, 167
Lincoln, Abraham, 87–88, 94, 113–14, 115, 119, 130, 133, 134, 135, 139
Literacy-Based Promotion Act, 418
literature, 385–90
Livingston Conspiracy, 106
Lomax, John, 367
Long, Betty Jane, 331
Lord, Walter, 141
Lott, Trent, 322, 338, 340–41
lottery, 359
Louisiana Purchase, 76, 108
Louisville, New Orleans, and Texas Railroad Company v. Mississippi, 190
Love, Betsy, 103
Loving v. Virginia, 308
Lowry, Robert, 177
Loyalist Democratic Party, 335
Lumumba, Chokwe Antar, 413
Lynch, John Roy, 172–73
Lynch Street, 297, 301
lynching, xi, xvii–xviii, xix, 186–89, 202, 205, 208, 233, 235, 237, 239, 328, 332, 335

Mabus, Ray, 359
Macon, 129, 132, 165, 170
Madison, Isaiah, 329
Madison, James, 83
Madison County, 101, 106, 272, 315, 356, 407
Manifest Destiny, 108
Manning, Archie, 398
Manning, Eli, 398
marijuana, legalization, 419
Marks, 299–300
Marquette, Pierre, 61
martial law, 152, 171, 351
Martin, James, 384
Martin Luther King Jr. Day, 420
Mary Alice, 393
Mary Buie Museum, 396

Mason, Gilbert R., Sr., 262
Massacre at Wounded Knee, 198
McAllister, Deuce, 398
McBride, Ernest, 338
McCrady, John, 395
McDaniel, Chris, 340
McDyess, Antonio, 398
McGhee, Laura, 385
McLemore, Leslie, 339
McNair, Steve, 398
McRaney, Gerald, 393
Meredith, James, 270–71; and University of Mississippi, 268–69
Meridian, 17, 20, 127, 132, 170, 179, 224, 280, 298, 360, 376, 377, 379, 383, 384, 401; and riot, 161–62
Meridian Little Theater, 392
Metcalf, George, 284
migration: to Mississippi, 401–3; reverse, 405–6; within state, 407–8, 411–12
migration, Black, 6, 141, 219, 226, 241, 372, 386, 389, 405. *See also* Great Migration
Miller, Mulgrew, 382
Millsaps College, xvi, 180, 306
minstrel shows, 189, 368, 376, 381
missionaries, 31, 37, 38, 42–43, 48
Mississippi, meaning of, xxiii
Mississippi Adequate Education Program (MAEP), 418
Mississippi Art Association, 395–96
Mississippi Art Workshop, 395
Mississippi Arts Festival, 397
Mississippi Authority for Educational Television, 391–92
Mississippi Band of Choctaw Indians, 55
Mississippi Blues Trail, 360, 371
Mississippi Civil Rights Education Commission, 314
Mississippi Civil Rights Museum, 360, 419
Mississippi Code of 1972, 308
Mississippi College, 90, 91, 103, 383
Mississippi Colonization Society, 102
Mississippi Constitution of 1868, 152
Mississippi Constitution of 1869, 155
Mississippi Constitution of 1890, 181, 194, 197, 198
Mississippi Council of Negro Leadership, 248, 252

Mississippi Department of Archives and History, xviii, 10, 57, 259, 419
Mississippi Department of Corrections, 181
Mississippi Department of Health, 414, 415
Mississippi Gaming Control Act, 358
Mississippi Industrial Institute and College, 180
Mississippi International Ballet Competition, 394
Mississippi legislature, xiv, 14, 48, 76, 84, 86, 88–89, 90, 91, 103, 105, 106, 110, 113, 115, 132, 140, 148, 149–50, 153, 154, 155, 156–58, 16–, 163, 170, 178, 180, 182, 184, 190, 194–95, 204, 206–7, 210, 222, 234, 255, 259, 279, 287, 292, 299, 308, 314, 318, 322–24, 326, 329, 330, 332–33, 334, 336, 344, 352, 359, 391–92, 418
Mississippi Mass Choir, 365
Mississippi Museum of Art, 396
Mississippi Music Hall of Fame, 384
Mississippi Opera Association, 384
"Mississippi Plan," 167–70, 197, 233
Mississippi River, 15, 28, 29, 38, 39, 40, 43, 61, 63, 69, 72, 73, 74–75, 76, 77, 78, 79, 80, 82, 119, 120, 122, 128, 135, 179, 183, 184, 199, 227, 281, 353, 358, 402
Mississippi Sheiks, 381
Mississippi State Mental Hospital, 249
Mississippi State Textbook Purchasing Board, x, xvi
Mississippi State University, xv, 180, 195, 248, 293, 326, 329, 398, 403, 405
Mississippi Student Funding Formula, 418
Mississippi Summer Project, 278
Mississippi Teacher's Association, 243
Mississippi territory, 41, 44–45, 72, 75–78, 81, 82, 83, 84; Georgia claims to, 79–80
Mississippi Valley State University, 244, 398, 420
Mississippi: A History (Bettersworth), 171
Mississippi: Yesterday & Today (Bettersworth), xiv
Missouri Compromise, 108, 112
Mitchell, Jerry, 277, 281, 298, 390
Mobley, Mary Ann, 393
Montgomery, Benjamin, 135
Montgomery, Isaiah T., 195
Moody, Anne, 389
Moore, Charles, 281

Morgan, A. T., 152
Morgan v. Virginia, 267
Morrill Acts, 159, 329
Morris, Willie, 389
Moses, Robert Parris, 264
Motley, Constance Baker, 284, 285
Mound Bayou, 199–200
Mule Train, 299–300
Murphy, Harry S., 249
Museum of Mississippi History, 326, 360, 419
museums, 312, 326, 360, 373, 396, 419, 420
Musgrove, Ronnie, 325
music: as activism, 266–67, 273; Blues, 261, 360, 366–67, 368–76, 377, 378, 379, 381, 390, 397, 419; church singing, 363–64; classical, 383–84; country, 375–76; folksongs, 362–63; gospel, 365–66; hip hop, 380–81; jazz, 381–82; and local record labels, 38; and slavery, 100, 133–34; spirituals, 364
Myricks, Larry, 398
myths: Native American, 29, 30, 43; of "Lost Cause," 137–38, 203; of "negro domination," 193, 203; at Parchman, 362; passivity to oppression, 284; of Reconstruction, 7–8, 171, 172, 173; of "separate but equal," 224–25; White Southern womanhood, 102

NASA, 353–55
Nash, Jere, xi, 137, 169
Natchez (city), 15–16, 73, 74, 76, 82, 83, 84, 85, 87, 88, 91, 95, 101, 113, 133, 141, 171, 172, 220, 241, 252, 283, 284, 382, 386, 387, 401. *See also* Rhythm Club Fire
Natchez (tribe), 28–29, 30–35, 37–38, 39, 61, 64, 68, 69–70, 72–73
Natchez Trace, 36, 78–79, 83, 84, 387
Nate Dogg, 381
National Assessment of Educational Progress (NAEP), 418
National Association for the Advancement of Colored People (NAACP), 186, 233, 247, 249, 250, 252, 253, 254, 257, 258, 262–64, 273–74, 278, 283–84, 285, 287, 295, 299, 325, 327
National Guard, 76, 230, 267, 270, 300, 413
National Negro Business League, 209
National Union of Republican Party, 155
Native Americans, 37–38; and Christian missionaries, 42–43; and European influence,

36; before European contact, 24–25; forced assimilation, 55; Grave Protection and Repatriation Act, 57; interracial marriage, 42; land cession, 44–45, 49–50, 87; and Mississippi resentment, 44–45; religion, 30–31, 32; relocation of, 43–45; as slave owners, 36–37. See also specific names
Native Son (Wright), 386
Nearing, Scott, xviii
Negro Fellowship League, 202
Neshoba County, 280–81, 298, 340, 360
Neshoba County Fair, 340, 360
"Never Scared," 381
New Deal, 19, 232, 235–37, 239
New Orleans, Battle of, 81
New Orleans, Louisiana, xxiii, 37, 38, 39, 41, 67, 69, 73, 75, 78, 81, 85, 126, 190, 321, 376, 393
New Stage, 392
Newman, Buddie, 323
1984 (Orwell), 10
Nixon, Richard, 336
Noble, Bill, 272
Noel, Edmund F., 210
Normal School, 159
Northrop Grumman, 358
Notaro, Tig, 394
NSYNC, 380
Nusbaum, Perry, 298
Nyong'o, Lupita, 381

Obama, Barack, 356
Obergefell v. Hodges, 308
Office of Economic Opportunity, 55
Ofos (tribe), 28
Ohio River, 39
Ohr-O'Keefe Museum of Art, 396
Ole Miss. *See* University of Mississippi
Ole Miss Riot, 270
oligarchy, 176–77, 202
Olmsted, Frederick Law, 95
O'Neal, Frederick, 393
Opera South, 384
Ord, E. O. C., 151
Orey, Dan, Jr., 294
Orwell, George, 10
Osband, E. D., 140
"outside agitators," 270–71, 279
Overby, Martin, 236

Palmer, Willard, 384
Panic of 1873, 164
Parchman, 181, 207, 268, 301–2, 308, 367–68
Parker, Dave, 398
Pascagoula (tribe), 28
Patterson, Robert, 252–54
Patton, Charlie, 369
Payne Field, 232
Payton, Walter, 398
Pearl River Community College, 226
Peavey Electronics, 355
Peer, Ralph, 377
Pemberton, John C., 123–24, 126
Pensacola, Battle of, 81
People's Party, 162–63
Percy, LeRoy, 210–11
Percy, Walker, 389
Petal Paper, 254
Pettus, John, 113
Pierce, Catherine, 389–90
Pigee, Vera Mae, 285
Pigford v. Glickman, 349, 351
Pizarro, Francisco, 59
plantations, 3, 13–14, 15, 48, 51, 67, 68, 76, 82, 87, 88, 93, 94–95, 99, 100–101, 103, 107, 113, 130, 133, 135, 141, 143, 172, 181, 184, 207, 214–15, 220, 237, 286, 295, 348, 368, 372, 402; Davis Bend, 135–37, 199; economy of, 92; life on, 97, 99, 103, 216; White women on, 102, 132
Plessy v. Ferguson, 190, 191
Poindexter, George, 80
Poindexter Code, 84
Poitier, Sidney, 273
politics, 8, 14–15, 22, 111, 133–34, 178, 191, 213, 235–41, 335–41, 344, 390, 404, 413; Black representation in, 299, 319, 324, 327; Black women in, 332–34; boycott by Whites, 152, 165; controlled by planters, 82–83, 95; cultural changes and, 305; "demagogue," 234, 235; European, 35; Native American, 35, 42, 47; one party system, 202, 307; Republican comeback in, 338; restricting Blacks from, 183, 194, 197, 202, 204, 232; two party system, 336; White women in, 330–32
Polk, James K., 87, 108–9
poll tax, 196, 197–98, 200, 235, 239
Poor People's Campaign, 300

popular sovereignty, 112, 114, 153
population, xxiii–xxiv, 6, 417–18; decline, 402–3, 404–5, 406–7, 408–9, 410; gains, 406–7, 409, 410
Populist party, 202–3
Port Gibson, 102, 124, 167, 194, 282, 307, 368
Port Hudson, 122, 126
Porter, David D., 122
Potter, George, 146
pottery, 24, 26, 28, 396
poverty, ix, 40, 56, 176, 185, 196, 198, 200, 215, 218, 286, 299, 300, 328, 348, 359, 368, 378, 386, 400, 412, 414, 415–17, 418, 420
Pratt, Richard Henry, 55
Prentiss, S., 105
Prescott, Dak, 398
Presley, Brandon, 327, 344
Presley, Elvis, 379
Price, Cecil, 280, 298
Price, Leontyne, 383
Pride, Charlie, 377
Progressive Voters League, 241
Prohibition, 194, 212
Pushmataha, 40–41, 45, 46–47

Quitman, John A., 109

race relations, xix, 134, 146, 149, 193–213, 233, 252, 254, 270, 307–8, 322, 354, 389
Rankin County, 407; and "Goon Squad," 420
Raymond, 124, 142
Raymond, George, 272, 274
Reagan, Ronald, 339–40; at Neshoba County Fair, 340
Reconstruction, xiii–xiv, xvii, 4, 53, 144, 147, 149, 150–168, 169–70, 171–73; Black male suffrage during, 139, 146, 151–52; Black men holding office during, 149, 150–51, 156, 160; changes to Mississippi legislature during, 156–57; Congress control over, 151; failure of, 173; and "ironclad oath," 151, 155; myths, 7–8, 171; political, 130, 133; rebuilding infrastructure during, 158; White Southerners react to, 151
Reconstruction Acts of 1867, 139
Red Cross, 228–30
Red River, 46–47
Reese, Brittany, 398
Reeves, Carlton, 321

Reeves, Tate, 326, 344, 413, 420
Reid, Whitelaw, 143
Republic of New Africa, 307
"Resurrection City," 300
Revels, Hiram Rhodes, 157
Revolutionary War, 73
Rhodes, Carroll, 320, 327
Rhythm Club Fire, 382–83
Rice, Jerry, 398
Richards, Beah, 393
Richards, Gloster, 398
Richards, Willie, 398
Ridgeland, 409
Rimes, LeAnn, 377
Robert E. Lee Day, 420
Roberts, Eric, 393
Roberts, James Wayne, 280
Robinson, Gail, 383
Robinson, Jesse, 373
Rogers, Jimmie, 376–77
Roosevelt, Franklin Delano, 232, 236, 239
Roosevelt, Theodore, 200, 205
Ross, Rick, 381
Ross v. Vernet, 102
Rush, Bobby, 370
Russell, Bill, 273

Safe Drinking Water Act, 410
sales tax, 236
Salter, John, 274, 276
Sanderson Farms, 355
Sansing, David, 389
Sargent, Winthrop, 76, 77
"scalawags," 151–52
Schwerner, Chaney, and Goodman, 279–86, 420
Schwerner, Michael, 420
Scott, Anne Firor, 102
Scott, Ed, 350
Scott, George, 398
Scruggs, Richard, 341
sculpturers, 395
Seale, James Ford, 281
secession, 115–17, 137–38; opposition to, 116, 129–31
Second Creek, x, 113
Second Reconstruction, 194, 265, 300
sectionalism, 82, 88–89, 107, 108. *See also* civil rights movement; slavery; voting

segregation, xiv, 3–4, 16, 159, 189–91, 219, 225, 233, 242–44, 246–55, 259, 262–63, 265, 267–68, 272, 274–75, 277, 278, 284, 293–94, 304, 308, 309, 311, 315, 321, 324, 327, 335–37, 340–41, 369, 375, 389, 390, 415. *See also* desegregation; Jim Crow
"separate but equal," 224, 225, 242, 247–48. *See also* Jim Crow; segregation
Sesame Street, 6
Seven Years' War, 69. *See also* French and Indian War
sharecropping, 214–16, 217–19, 220, 223
Sharkey, William L., 147–48, 150
Shaw University, 159
Shearer, Cynthia, 389
Shelby, 308
Sherman Anti-Trust Act of 1890, 195
Shiloh, Battle of, 120–21, 129, 388
Ship Island, 119
Shirley, Aaron, 415
Shirley, Ruth, 287
Short, Purvis, 398
Sillers, Walter, Jr., 250
Simone, Nina, 273
Sipuel v. Board of Regents of the University of Oklahoma, 244
"sit-ins," 262, 264, 290
Slater, Jackie, 398
slavery, xiv, xvii, 3–4, 83, 87–88, 92, 94–95, 104–5, 106–12, 118, 130, 133, 134–35, 137–38, 140–42, 143, 145–46, 148–50, 152, 171–72, 177, 180–81, 189, 191, 198, 214, 217, 219, 230, 311, 312, 324, 364, 402, 415–17; causes of, 68, 75, 82; end of, xiii, 133, 145–46, 147; and French, 67; and Protestantism, 107
Smith, Bessie, 370, 371
Smith, Calvin, 398
Smith, Hazel Brannon, 254
Smith, Ishmael Wadada Leo, 382
Smith, Larry, 398
Smith, Orma, xvi, xvii
Smith, Robert, 415
Smith v. Allwright, 240
So Red the Rose (Young), 388–89
Somerville, Nellie Nugent, 330
South Carolina, 39, 88–89, 114, 115, 119, 144, 242, 276
"South Solid," 176
Southern Regional Education Compact, 244

Southern Strategy, 340
sports, 398
St. Catherine's Greek, 37
Starkville, 180, 355, 384
State Board of Health, 179
statehood, 82, 83
states' rights, 129, 137–38, 239, 260; movement, 108, 110–11; party, 242, 335
Stennis, John C., 239
Sterling, Mildred, 384
Stevens, Stella, 393
Stewart, Tonea, 393
Still, William Grant, 384
Stockett, Kathryn, 389
Stone, John M., 170, 177
Stowe, Harriet Beecher, 112
"Strange Fruit," 186
Streetcar Named Desire, A (Williams), 388
Stuart, Marty, 377
Student Nonviolent Coordinating Committee (SNCC), 264
Subway Lounge, 373, 374
Sullens, Fred, 236, 237
Swift, Taylor, 306
Swinging Rays of Rhythm, 382

Tariff of 1932, 88
Tecumseh, 40–41
Tennessee Valley Authority, 18, 348
Texas v. White, 151
Thad Cochran Mississippi Center for Innovation and Technology and the AI Innovation Hub, 419–20
Thirteenth Amendment, 140, 146, 149, 156, 180
Thomas, Angie, 389
Thomas, James "Cool Papa" Bell, 398
Thomas, Latoya, 398
Thompson, Allen, 279
Thompson, Bennie, 320
Thorpe, Sidney, 284
Three Doors Down, 380
Thurmond, Strom, 242, 335, 340–41
Till, Emmett, x, 256, 390, 420
Tombigbee River, 18, 40, 73, 80, 82
Tougaloo College, 159
"Tougaloo Nine," 262–63
tourism, 360–61
Townsend, Tiffany, 384

transportation, 85–86, 88; and automobile, 226
Travis, Brenda, 265–66
Treaty of Dancing Rabbit Creek, 49
Treaty of Doak's Stand, 49
Treaty of 1763, 73
Treaty of Fort Adams, 44
Treaty of Mount Dexter, 45
Treaty of Paris 1783, 73
Treaty of Pontotoc, 52–53
Treaty of San Lorenzo, 75
tree, Mississippi state, xxiii
Trethewey, Natasha, 389
Truman, Harry, 98, 241, 242
Trump, Donald, 420
Trumpauer, Joan, 267
Tunica (tribe), 28
Tunica County, 356, 359, 406
Tupelo, 294, 307, 355, 357, 361, 374, 379, 384, 396
Turnbull, Walter, 384
Turner, Ike, 375, 378
Turner, Otha, 371
Turner, Tina, 378
Turnipseed, John, xvii
"twenty negro law," 131
Twenty-Sixth Amendment, 317
Twitty, Conway, 377
Two Mississippi Museums, 419, 420

Uncle Tom's Cabin (Stowe), 112
United Southeastern Tribes, 57
United States Supreme Court, 47, 178, 189, 197, 240, 246, 247, 283
United States v. Price, 280
University of Mississippi, xix, xxiv, 4, 90, 159, 177, 249, 268, 270, 284, 299, 300–301, 384, 389, 395, 398, 405, 421. *See also* Meredith, James
University of Mississippi Medical Center, xxiv
University of Southern Mississippi, 210

Vardaman, James K., 181, 205–7; defunding Black schools, 206–7
Vernon, Olympia, 389
Vicksburg, 15, 16, 52, 79, 111, 113, 123, 124, 127, 128, 129, 134, 135, 140, 146, 154, 163–64, 165, 170, 233, 252, 254, 273, 305, 353, 360, 391; siege of, 125–26

Vicksburg, Battle of, 115, 121–23, 124–26, 127–28, 129, 134
Vicksburg Daily Times, 152
Vicksburg National Military Park, 360
Vicksburg Riot, 163–64
violence, racial, 165–66, 167, 169, 170–71, 186, 208, 218, 256, 258, 262, 267, 270, 281, 288, 292, 298, 300–302; against Black schools, 159; against Black voters, 183, 184, 188, 233, 235, 246, 271, 272, 296; frontier, 82, 84; plantation, 97, 106, 113, 141; as political weapon, 161–62, 165, 171, 172, 178, 188, 195, 202; toward freed people, 150. *See also* lynching; voting
Vivians, Victoria, 398
voting: and Black militias, 163, 166; and Black registration, 241, 255–56, 264, 266–67, 419; and "fusion," 182, 194; "good moral character" clause, 261; legal battles and, 320; and reapportionment, 195, 302n1, 319; and redistricting, 287–88, 319, 327; and restrictions, 196–98, 200, 327, 348; and super majorities, 327; and suppression, 163, 165, 167–68, 173, 178–79; violence during, 183, 235, 241; voter ID, 327; voter purge, 327–28. *See also* disenfranchisement; violence: racial
Voting Rights Act of 1965, 272, 284, 291–92, 294, 317, 318, 320, 327

"wade-ins," 262
Waits, Freddie, 382
Waits, Tom, 382
Walker, Chet, 398
Walker, David, 106
Walker, Robert, 86–87
Wallace, George, 336, 394
Wallace, Nick, 394
Waller, William, 337
Walter Anderson Museum of Art, 396
War of 1812, 41, 43, 46–47, 80, 84
Ward, Jerry Washington, Jr., 389–90
Ward, Jesmyn, 389
Ward, Sela, 393
Ward, William Colonel, 45
Washington, Booker T., 200
Waters, Muddy, 370, 372
Watkins, Hezekiah, 267
Watkins, Hollis, 266

Weatherspoon, Quinndary, 398
welfare scandal, 420
Wells, Ida B., 201, 202; and *The Red Record*, 202
Welty, Eudora, 387–88, 419
West, Cato, 77
West Point, 232
White, Hugh, 223, 238
White Citizens' Councils, 246. *See also* Ku Klux Klan
"white flight," 408
White supremacy, xiv, xv, 8, 49, 113, 137, 149, 160, 161, 165, 176, 183, 186, 188, 195, 198, 203, 210, 235, 251, 266, 317. *See also* lynching; violence
Whitney, Eli, 91–92
Wilkinson, James, 74–75
Williams, Haley, 379
Williams, John Bell, 299
Williams, John Sharp, 210
Williams, Maurice "Mo," 398
Williams, Tennessee, 385
Williams v. Mississippi, 201
Williamson, Jeremiah (JJ), 394
Wilson, Cassandra, 382
Wilson, Gerald, 382
Wilson, T. B., 241
Winfrey, Oprah, 393
Wingate, Henry, 321
Winter, William, 323–24, 337–39
WLBT-TV, 308
women: as Black leaders, 285–87, 291, 331–34; in Blues, 370; education of White, 90, 180; enslaved, 97, 133; as executives, 381; Native American, 35–36, 42; rights of White, 201, 223, 330–31; suffrage for White, 103, 232; White activists, 201–2, 233; White, and lynching, 186, 188–89, 205
Woolworth Sit-In, 274
Works Progress Administration (WPA), 222
World War I, 232–33
World War II, 239
Wounded Knee, Battle of, 198
Wright, Fielding, 241
Wright, Flonzie Brown, 285
Wright, Richard, 386, 419
writers. *See* literature; journalism
Wynette, Tammy, 377

Yazoo City, 16, 102, 129, 134, 163, 165, 170, 183, 252, 253, 393
Yazoo River, 122
Yerger, Wirt, 338
York, Emmett, 57
Young, Jack, 284
Young, Lester "Prez," 381
Young, Stark, 388, 389

Zellner, Bob, 264–65

ABOUT THE EDITORS

James W. Loewen (1942–2021) was author of *Lies My Teacher Told Me: Everything Your American History Textbook Got Wrong*; *Lies Across America: What Our Historic Sites Get Wrong*; *Teaching What Really Happened: How to Avoid the Tyranny of Textbooks and Get Students Excited About Doing History*; *Sundown Towns: A Hidden Dimension of American Racism*; and coeditor of *The Confederate and Neo-Confederate Reader: The Great Truth about the Lost Cause*, published by University Press of Mississippi. He was professor emeritus at the University of Vermont.

Byron D'Andra Orey is professor of political science at Jackson State University, and his research focuses on race and politics. He has served as the president of the Southern Political Science Association.

Charles Sallis (1934–2024) was professor emeritus of history at Millsaps College, where he taught from 1968 to 2000.

Printed in the United States
by Baker & Taylor Publisher Services